D0198898

INSIGHT GUIDES

BRAZIL

Discovery CHANNEL

APA PUBLICATIONS
Part of the Langenscheidt Publishing Group

INSIGHT GUIDE
BRAZIL

About This Book

Editorial
Project Editor
Jane Ladle
Managing Editor
Huw Hennessy
Editorial Director
Brian Bell

Distribution
UK & Ireland
GeoCenter International Ltd
The Viables Centre , Harrow Way,
Basingstoke, Hants RG22 4BJ
Fax: (44) 1256 817988

United States
Langenscheidt Publishers, Inc.
36–36 33rd Street, 4th Floor
Long Island City, New York 11106
Fax: (1) 718 784 0640

Australia
Universal Publishers
1 Waterloo Road
Macquarie Park, NSW 2113
Fax: (61) 2 9888 9074

New Zealand
Hema Maps New Zealand Ltd (HNZ)
Unit D, 24 Ra ORA Drive
East Tamaki, Auckland
Fax: (64) 9 273 6479

Worldwide
Apa Publications GmbH & Co.
Verlag KG (Singapore branch)
38 Joo Koon Road, Singapore 628990
Tel: (65) 6865 1600. Fax: (65) 6861 6438

Printing
Insight Print Services (Pte) Ltd
38 Joo Koon Road, Singapore 628990
Tel: (65) 6865 1600. Fax: (65) 6861 6438

First Edition 1988
Fifth Edition 1999
Updated 2004; Reprinted 2006

CONTACTING THE EDITORS
We would appreciate it if readers would alert us to errors or outdated information by writing to:
Insight Guides, P.O. Box 7910,
London SE1 1WE, England.
Fax: (44) 20 7403 0290.
insight@apaguide.co.uk

www.insightguides.com
In North America:
www.insighttravelguides.com

The first Insight Guide pioneered the use of creative full-colour photography in travel guides in 1970. Since then, we have expanded our range to cater for our readers' need, not only for reliable and practical information about their chosen destination, but also for a real understanding of the history, culture, people, and workings of that destination. Now, when the internet can supply us with inexhaustible (but not always reliable) facts, our books marry text and pictures to provide those much more elusive qualities: knowledge and discernment. To achieve this, they rely heavily on the combined authority of locally based writers and photographers.

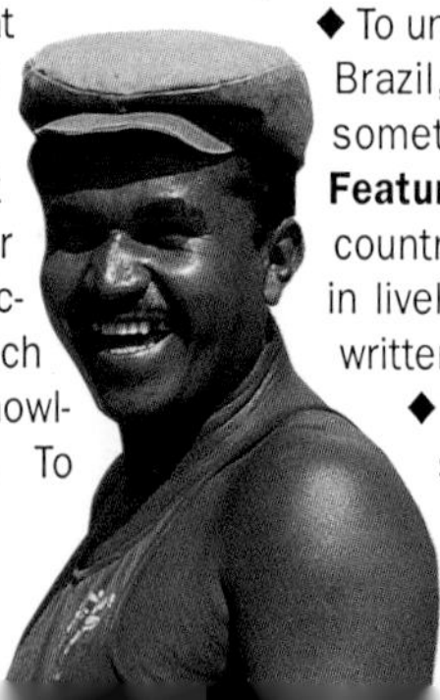

How to use this book

The book is carefully structured to convey an understanding of Brazil and to guide the readers through its sights and activities:

◆ To understand contemporary Brazil, you need to know something of its past. The **Features** section covers the country's history and culture in lively, authoritative essays written by specialists.

◆ The main **Places** section provides full

Fisherman on a tributary of the São Francisco River, Pernambuco.

details of all the sights in Brazil worth seeing. Chief places of interest are cross-referenced with specially drawn, full-color maps.

◆ The **Travel Tips** listing section offers a handy source of reference for information on transport, hotels, restaurants, culture, language tips, and much more.

◆ **Photographs** are chosen not only to illustrate the Brazilian landscape and the beauty of its cities, nature reserves and beaches, but also to convey its cultural diversity.

The contributors

Guidebook editor **Jane Ladle** supervised this edition. The original editor, and contributor of historical chapters and those on Rio and the south, was **Edwin Taylor** of the USA, resident of Brazil, who has written extensively about his adoptive country.

Fellow US citizen **Tom Murphy**'s contributions included the chapters on race, Carnival and the rest of the southeast. **Richard House** handled the Amazon and the west. He jointly authored the northeast chapters with **Elizabeth Herrington**, and also wrote about the mixed fortunes of Brazil's Amerindians. Other contributors were: British journalist **Moyra Ashford** (music and art); novelist and Brazilian art expert **Sol Biderman**, who also wrote on that subject; a senior official at the Canadian embassy in Brasília, **Michael Small** (Brasília); and Rio resident **Steve Yolen** (soccer).

Revisions to historical chapters and new short features were supplied by British expert on all things Brazilian, **Patrick Cunningham**. Contributors to the Places and Travel Tips sections include **Daniela Hart**, and **Ricardo Buckup**. BBC journalist **Sue Branford** pricks our consciences with the features on wealth disparity, the Amerindians, and *favelas* (shanty towns). Ecology lecturer **Richard Ladle** wrote about the disappearing rainforest.

This version was updated by **Jane Egginton** and edited by **Alyse Dar**. Egginton also revised the Brazilian TV and Rio *favelas* features, and wrote the Body Beautiful chapter. **Sylvia Suddes** and **Paula Soper** helped with text editing, **Isabel McLean** compiled the index, and picture research was carried out by **Hilary Genin** and **Monica Allende**.

Map Legend

- International Boundary
- State Boundary
- National Park/Reserve
- Ferry Route
- Metro
- Airport: International/ Regional
- Bus Station
- Parking
- Tourist Information
- Post Office
- Church / Ruins
- Monastery
- Mosque
- Synagogue
- Castle / Ruins
- Archeological Site
- Cave
- Statue/Monument
- Place of Interest

The main places of interest in the Places section are coordinated by number with a full-color map (e.g. ❶), and a symbol at the top of every right-hand page tells you where to find the map.

INSIGHT GUIDE
BRAZIL

CONTENTS

Maps

Introduction

History

Features

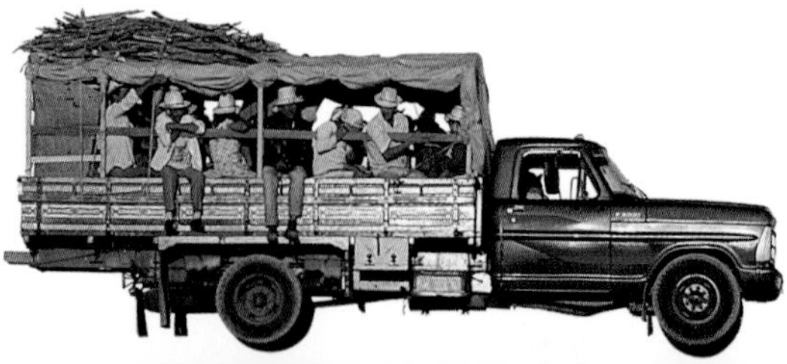

Colonial fountain in Tiradentes, Minas Gerais

Insight on....

Information panels

Travel Tips

♦Full Travel Tips index is on page 331

Places

LAND WITHOUT FRONTIERS

Brazil is the mythical "land without frontiers," with limitless potential and a perpetually optimistic population

Since its colonization by the Portuguese in the 16th century, Brazil has held a constant fascination for foreigners. First it was gold, then rubber and coffee and, more recently, the exotic sights and sounds of the nation. No less captivated are the Brazilians. Genuinely in love with their nation, they, like foreign visitors, have always been slightly dazed by the size of their country. The sensation is that hidden in some far corner of this great nation may be an immense treasure just waiting to be discovered. The problem is knowing which corner.

Since the 16th century, Brazilians and foreigners alike have been looking for and, in the process, gradually occupying the enormous empty spaces of this continent-sized country. They have populated them with some 175 million souls, composing one of the world's most heterogeneous populations. Brazilians are black, brown, white, yellow and all the shades in between. They live amidst modern splendor in sprawling cities and in squalid deprivation in rural backwaters. They work in high-tech industries with one foot in the millennium and push wooden plows behind laboring beasts. Within the confines of the same Brazil live indians in near Stone-Age conditions, feudal peasants and lords, pioneers hacking out jungle settlements and yuppie princes and princesses.

And all of this is constantly in motion. Perhaps nowhere on earth is the process of development as tangible as in Brazil. The dynamism of the country is its greatest achievement. Even in the midst of a period of stagnation, Brazilians have continued to get on with the process of nation building. The once-impregnable Amazon rainforest is being opened up quickly – many say too quickly – and is the last great frontier of a nation that is still not entirely explored.

The contradictions of Brazil are united by a common language, Portuguese; a common religion, Catholicism (more than 90 percent of Brazilians are Roman Catholic); and a common dream, that sometime, somehow, Brazil will be a great nation. A concomitant of this dream, though, is a common frustration with the stop–start pace of Brazil's path towards greatness. Nevertheless, despite often enormous social and economic difficulties, Brazilians are a remarkably happy people: it is even said that hope is a national profession. Spontaneous, enthusiastic and high-spirited, they tend typically to live in the moment. Cautious, long-range planning types go mad when faced with the Brazilian "charge the ramparts" style of living. For Brazilians, however, nothing could be more natural. In the land of Carnival, seize the moment. After all, at any moment, you may just find treasure. ❑

PRECEDING PAGES: Amazon River country; scalloped shore and islands along the Costa Verde; Congresso Nacional buildings in Brasília; New Year's in Rio.
LEFT: pause for reflection.

FROM SANDY BEACHES TO AMAZON JUNGLE

Brazil occupies such a large landmass, and is so diverse topographically, socially, and economically, that it is hard to consider it as a single entity

Brazil is the smallest big country in the world. Although it is the fifth largest nation on the planet, four times the size of Mexico and more than twice that of India, the Brazil where most Brazilians live, work and play forms only a small fraction of the country's total landmass of 8,509,711 sq. km (3,285,618 sq. miles). One in four people crowd into five metropolitan areas in the southern part of the country.

Together, the southern and southeastern states contain more than 60 percent of Brazil's population yet account for only 16 percent of the country's geographic area. In effect, over 100 million Brazilians live in an area slightly smaller than Alaska, while another 72 million populate an area the size of the continental United States minus Texas. What Brazil has is space – enormous regions of vast, empty space.

A regional structure

For administrative purposes, Brazil's 26 states and one federal district are divided into five regions; north, northeast, center-west, southeast and south. The two largest regions are also its least populated. The north, home to the mighty Amazon basin rainforest, occupies 42 percent of Brazil, a country large enough to accommodate all of Western Europe. Yet its population is smaller than that of New York.

Located just south of the Amazon is the center-west, dominated by a vast elevated plateau, and covering 22 percent of Brazil's territory. The population here has doubled since the 1970s and now represents 15 percent of the country as a whole. These two great landmasses, which together are larger than most of the world's nations, are both the promise and challenge of Brazil's future.

The north's living enigma

The legendary Amazon is one of the planet's last unsolved mysteries. The world's largest river basin, it contains not only one fifth of all the freshwater on earth, but also the planet's greatest rainforest, a teeming biological storehouse whose true potential remains largely unknown and untapped.

Despite the encroaching devastation along the forest's frontiers, it is still possible to fly for hours over the Amazon and see no break in the carpet of greenery except for the sinuous curves of the region's rivers. On boat journeys, the wall of vegetation at the river's edge rolls by for days on end, broken only by the occasional wooden hut.

These huts, however, are clues to a fact that has been largely ignored both by Brazil's development planners and by many of the ecologists who campaign to protect the forest as the "lungs of the world": the Amazon is no empty wilderness. Aside from the remnants of the populous Amerindian nations who once ruled

LEFT: beach solitude in Salvador, Bahia.
RIGHT: lush Amazon vegetation.

the jungle, an estimated three million people live scattered over this huge area, eeking out a living as their forefathers have for generations. Collectively known as *caboclos*, these true Amazonians are rubber-tappers, Brazil nut gatherers, fishermen and subsistence farmers.

More recently, waves of cattle ranchers, land speculators and small farmers have been encouraged to move into the area by government incentives, the promise of free land and the scent of quick profits. Cattle barons and land speculators have carved up swathes of virgin forest, employing unscrupulous methods and gangs of gunmen to intimidate anyone who dares stand in their way. The main victims of this land invasion, along with the trees, plants, and wildlife, are the forest people, both *caboclos* and Amerindians, many of whom have been driven off the land into shanty towns on the margins of the cities.

Yet there is hope for the future. Substantial investment is being poured into the education of settlers, teaching them appropriate forms of agriculture and encouraging small businesses to adopt sustainable extractive techniques. These programs demonstrate that the forest has more value for everyone if it is left standing than if it is cut down. As a result, settlers

are gradually being enabled to stay on the land they initially occupy, instead of being forced to move on to new areas because the fertility of that first piece of land declines after only a few years due to their excessive cropping.

The wealth of the Amazon is not restricted to its huge land area. Below the surface lie untold riches. In the Serra dos Carajás, 879 km (546 miles) southwest of Belém, there is enough iron ore to keep the entire world supplied for 500 years, while elsewhere gold, tin, rare metals and oil have been found. Carefully exploited, these valuable commodities are capable of bringing development to the region without the need to destroy the forest.

THE FIRST ECO-MARTYR

Chico Mendes, a rubber-tapper from the state of Acre, led the forest people of the Amazon in the first grassroots organization to defend the forest and its people's way of life. He and his followers peacefully resisted the bulldozers in what were known as *empates*, or standoffs. The cattle barons had him murdered in 1988 – the centenary of the abolition of slavery in Brazil.

Pressure from the world's media forced the government to act, creating "Extractive Reserves" where forest people could pursue a life closer to that of their forebears. But, although Mendes' legacy lives on, the rainforest is still disappearing at an alarming rate.

The center-west

In Brazil's other great void, the center-west, the pace of development has slowed after a quick burst in the 1970s. The planned capital of Brasília was placed in the central plateau so that it would act as a magnet for settlers and integrate this region with the coastal areas. But while Brasília has matured into a city with a population of more than 2.1 million, it has failed to spawn the growth hoped for by its planners.

In terms of its geography, the center-west offers none of the natural barriers of the Amazon. An elevated plateau at 1,000 meters (3,300 feet) above sea level, the *Planalto Central* is divided up into two kinds of areas – forest and woodland savanna known as *cerrado*.

Made up of stunted trees and grasslands, the *cerrado* appears to be a scrubland with little value. Experience has shown, however, that once cleared, the *cerrado* land is extremely fertile. Farmers from southern Brazil have turned areas of the *cerrado* into sprawling farms and ranches, including the world's largest soybean farm. Roads and bridges have been built, corn and cotton production improved, and an increasing number of qualified people have moved into the area. The grasslands of the southern part of the region have also been adapted to pasture and some of Brazil's largest cattle herds now graze there.

The northeast

Brazil's third-largest region, the northeast, occupying 18 percent of the country, is the nation's poorest. Although sugar plantations made it the original economic and political center during the colonial period, the northeast has not kept pace with the development that has occurred in the southern and southeastern states. Unlike the north and center-west, the northeast is neither isolated nor underpopulated. Its fatal flaw has been its climate.

The region is divided into four zones: its northernmost state, Maranhão, combines characteristics of the northeast and the Amazon; along the coast from the state of Rio Grande do Norte to Bahia runs a narrow 100–200-km (60–120-mile) wide strip of fertile land known as the *zona da mata*; just west of this strip begins a transition zone of semi-fertile land called the *agreste*; the final zone occupies the bulk of the interior of the northeast's states, a dry, arid region known as the *sertão*.

It is the *sertão* that has given Brazil its most devastating poverty. It is an area of periodic

LEFT: Amazon ferries docked at Manaus.
ABOVE: the frothing red waters of the Iguaçu Falls.

drought, of parched earth, of temporary rivers that swell to flood stage in times of rain, of a thorny scrub called *caatinga;* and it is an area of widespread human suffering.

One drought ended in 1984 after five years. Another – a result of El Niño in 1998 – caused massive destruction, while in 2000, one of the worst droughts in over 70 years struck the region, propelling millions of the *sertão's* residents to the urban centers of the southeast, mainly to São Paulo and Rio de Janeiro.

Sparkling beaches

The irony of the northeast is that just a few hours from the despair of the *sertão* is the beautiful coastal zone where white sand beaches sparkle beneath the tropical sun. It is here that Brazil's famed coastal beaches begin, and from here they stretch the length of the country from Maranhão to the southernmost state of Rio Grande do Sul. Altogether, Brazil's coastline encompasses 7,700 km (4,600 miles) – the longest continuous coastline in the world.

Having been blessed with adequate rainfall, the northeast coast is the site of the bulk of the region's agricultural production, which is concentrated in sugar and cocoa, and home to a constantly increasing percentage of the region's population. Lacking investment capital, the economy of the northeast has remained dominated by farming, with a few isolated pockets of industry. Tourism, however, may yet prove to be the northeast's real saviour.

Running along the southern edge of the northeast is the São Francisco River, the second of Brazil's main river systems. Beginning in the central plateau, the river flows east for over 3,000 km (1,865 miles), reaching into the northeast at its southernmost state of Bahia and providing a link between the northeast and central Brazil. In addition, the São Francisco has provided a reliable source of water for the interior through which it passes, creating a narrow belt of productive farmland for a region that has never been able to feed itself.

The southeast

At the other end of the development scale from the northeast is the southeast region, which comprises only 11 percent of the national territory but which is home to Brazil's three largest

LEFT: Ouro Preto, colonial gem of Minas Gerais.

cities, São Paulo, Rio de Janeiro and Belo Horizonte, and 45 percent of the country's population. The region is divided between a narrow coastal zone and an elevated plateau, with a coastal mountain region (the escarpment) beginning in Bahia and running the length of the coast south to Rio Grande do Sul.

The dense tropical foliage of the *mata atlântica* has wrapped the coastal mountains in a rich, deep cloak of green. But the very development that has brought prosperity to the southeast is threatening the survival of this tropical vegetation. In many parts of the state of São Paulo, the forest has been destroyed by

pollutants in the air, a by-product of the state's industrial park, the largest in Latin America. The best preserved example of Brazil's coastal tropical forest is found in the southern state of Paraná.

With the exception of the coastal cities of Rio and Santos (two of Brazil's busiest ports) the south-east's main population centers are on the plateau at an average altitude of 700 meters (2,300 ft). This area of rolling hills and temperate climate, where there is a clear distinction between winter and summer, has been the center of Brazil's economic growth since the 1800s.

Minas Gerais, the only state in the region that does not have a sea coast, owes its early development to its mineral wealth. The red earth of Minas Gerais provides graphic testimony to its iron ore deposits. Part of Brazil's mammoth Pre-Cambrian shield area, Minas was the world's leading gold producer in the 18th century. In modern times, it has made Brazil a chief producer of iron ore and gemstones.

The south

The south is the smallest of Brazil's regions, accounting for only 7 percent of the total national territory. Like the southeast, it was blessed with rapid development in the second half of the 20th century and today is home to 15 percent of the nation's population. Located below the Tropic of Capricorn, the south is the only region of Brazil characterized by a subtropical climate with all four seasons, including frosts and occasional snowfall in winter. In part due to its climate, the three states of the southern region attracted large numbers of immigrants from Italy, Germany, Poland and Russia at the start of the 20th century.

The rolling farmlands of Paraná and Rio Grande do Sul have made these states, along with São Paulo, the breadbasket of Brazil, growing primarily wheat, corn, soybeans and rice.

The region is also Brazil's traditional cattle producer, although it has been losing ground to the center-west. In the western half of Rio Grande, pampas grasslands, or prairies, are home to many of Brazil's largest farms and cattle ranches. The eastern half of the state is marked by mountainous terrain with deep, forested valleys where Italian and German immigrants have established Brazil's wine and grape industries.

Besides its rich farmlands, the state of Paraná has benefitted from its vast pine forests, which have been a primary source of lumber for Brazil's construction industry, although they are now being rapidly depleted. Marking the state's western border is the Paraná River which, together with the Paraguay farther to the west, forms the country's third great river system. The force of these rivers has been harnessed to produce energy for the industries of the south and southeast, particularly the Paraná, where Brazil has built the world's largest hydroelectric project, the Itaipú Dam. ❑

LEFT: brahma cattle, a major source of wealth for the farmers of southern Brazil.

The Disappearing Rainforest

Being in the rainforest at dusk is an almost spiritual experience. As darkness falls, frogs and cicadas begin their chorus, while the eerie call of red howler monkeys can be heard echoing through the stillness of the twilight forest. The next generation may not have the opportunity to experience this firsthand because evolution's grandest experiment may soon be coming to a premature end, as the rainforest is burned and hacked to death for the sake of short-term economic gain.

When the first Europeans arrived in Brazil, it was blanketed with a huge rainforest that extended well beyond the Amazon basin, stretching all along the Atlantic coast from Recife south to Florianópolis. It covered about 1 million sq km (386,000 sq miles) and possessed the most diverse and distinct communities of plants and animals on the planet.

The shrinkage of the forest is a direct consequence of Brazil's ever-expanding population, particularly along its Atlantic fringes, now densely populated due to the productive soil. Moreover, fires started by peons and farmers to clear the land of fallen trees and brush, often rage out of control, destroying huge tracts of virgin forest. The most damaging recorded blaze, which occurred as recently as 1998, was described by the United Nations as "an environmental disaster without precedent on this planet".

Once, 200 species of mammals roamed or swung through the glades of the Brazilian forest. One thousand butterfly species fluttered through the forest canopy. Eight hundred species of trees, more than in the whole of North America, could be found in locations ranging from the Amazon river mouth to the highest mountain.

Amazingly, in view of the widespread destruction, Amazonia still tenaciously holds on to most of its plants and animals – and its secrets. Many of the species here are found nowhere else in the world. The rainforest canopy is one of the last great unexplored regions of the world and there may be anything from 10 to 30 million species of insects alone that are currently unknown to science. It is still the case that a scientist may stumble upon a new species within days or even hours of arrival in the forest.

But a huge loss of biological diversity is happening right now, and deforestation is the chief cause. No animal or plant can live in a void, and the rate of destruction of their forest habitat is staggering. If current levels continue, 90 percent of the rainforest will have disappeared by 2020. Between 1995 and 2000, 2 million hectares (4,942 million acres) were cut down each year; the equivalent of seven football fields a minute. Overall, an incredible 51 million hectares (127 million acres) have been deforested, mostly during the 1980s, which was dubbed the "decade of destruction". Although reforestation programs are in place, sponsored by organizations such as the World Bank, the rate of growth is still far exceeded by the rate of destruction. In the mid-1990s, an area equivalent to over 11 percent of the extent of the original rainforest was lost.

One sad result of this wholesale destruction is that the Amazon may soon lose some of its most distinguished denizens. The giant otter, for example, which was overhunted in the 1950s and 1960s, now clings to survival in rapidly shrinking habitats. The pet trade has driven several species of blue macaw close to extinction. Other endangered animals include the jaguar and black caiman crocodile. Catch sight of them while you can. ❑

RIGHT: *igapó* – flooded rainforest on the Río Negro.

Decisive Dates

COLONIAL ERA (1500–1822)

1494 The Treaty of Tordesillas, brokered by Pope Alexander VI, divides the non-European world between Portugal and Spain. Portugal gets present-day Brazil.

1500 Portuguese explorer Pedro Alvares Cabral, blown off course on his way to India and the Spice Islands, lands near Porto Seguro, and becomes the first European to set foot in Brazil. Although he names the continent Terra de Santa Cruz, it eventually takes the name Brazil, after *pau brasil*, a wood from which the Europeans extract red dye.

1501–02 Amerigo Vespucci sails along the Brazilian coast, naming places after the saints on whose days they were discovered.

1533 The colony is divided into 15 *capitanias* (captaincies), each governed by a Portuguese courtier.

1549 A central administration, based in Salvador and directed by a governor general, Tomé de Sousa, is put in place to oversee the *capitanias*. Conflicts arise between Jesuit missionaries, who convert the indians and settle them in villages, and colonists, who see indians as animals fit only for enslavement.

1549 A royal decree gives the Jesuits control over Christian indians, while colonists are allowed to enslave indians captured in warfare. Colonists import African slaves to boost their workforce.

1555 The French build a garrison in what is now Rio de Janeiro, but are driven out in 1565 by the governor general, Mem de Sá, who founds a city there in 1567.

1550–1800 Sugar cane, grown on huge plantations that are worked by African slaves, is the colony's most important crop, supplemented by tobacco, cattle and, in the 18th century, cotton and coffee.

1580–1640 Portugal and Spain are united.

1600s Great expeditions *(bandeiras)* of settlers, particularly from São Paulo, delve far into the interior in search of gold and indian slaves. There are frequent conflicts with indians and Jesuits, and a drastic reduction in the indian population through enslavement, European-introduced diseases and massacres.

1624–54 The Dutch West Indies Company conquers a large part of the northeast. A Dutch prince, Maurice of Nassau, rules "Dutch Brazil" (Pernambuco, in the heart of the rich sugar-cane growing region) from 1637–44.

1695 Discovery of gold (and, a few years later, diamonds) in Minas Gerais leads to rapid growth of gold rush towns in Brazil's interior.

1759 After years of disputes with both the colonists and the Portuguese government, the Jesuits are expelled from Brazil.

1763 Rio de Janeiro is made the capital city.

1789 An independence movement, known as the Inconfidência Mineira, springs up in Ouro Preto, spurred on by increased gold taxes. In 1792, its leader, Joaquim José da Silva Xavier, better known as Tiradentes, is hanged, and the movement collapses.

1807 King João VI of Portugal flees from Napoleon, and establishes his court in Rio. He introduces many reforms; Brazil, which previously could trade only with Portugal, is allowed to trade freely.

1821 King João returns to Portugal and names his son, Pedro, as Prince Regent and governor of Brazil.

THE EMPIRE (1822–1889)

1822 To prevent parliament from reversing his father's reforms, Pedro I proclaims independence from Portugal, and establishes the Brazilian Empire. The new nation is recognized by the United States, and in 1825, by Portugal as well.

1831 The autocratic and unpopular Pedro I abdicates in favour of his five-year-old son, also named Pedro. Political leaders run the country, and face numerous revolts and army rebellions.

1840–89 The reign of Pedro II sees the population increase from 4 million to 14 million. Wars with neighboring countries strengthen the status of the military, while the emperor's opposition to slavery makes him many enemies among the land-owning class.

1853 The importation of slaves ends.
1870–1914 Manaus becomes prosperous from the Amazonian rubber trade, but declines when Asia starts producing the crop, using seeds smuggled out of Brazil by the English botanist, Henry Wickham.
1871 All children born to slaves are declared free.
1888 The last slaves are freed.

REPUBLICAN BRAZIL (1889–1963)

1889 Pedro II is overthrown by the military and exiled.
1890s Coffee makes São Paulo the commercial center of the country – and the dominant power base.
1894 Prudente de Morais becomes the first elected civilian president.
1898–1902 President Manuel Ferraz de Campos Salles successfully re-negotiates Brazil's foreign debt.
1930–45 The military installs Getúlio Vargas as president. Vargas gives himself absolute power, and brings in a social security system and a minimum wage.
1942 Brazil declares war on Germany – the only Latin American country to take an active part in World War II.
1950–54 Vargas is again made president – this time thanks to a democratic election. In 1954, on the brink of a military coup, he commits suicide.
1953 Founding of national oil company, Petrobras.
1954 With Pelé on its side, Brazil wins World Cup in Stockholm.
1956 President Juscelino Kubitschek unveils a five-year plan for rapid industrialization.
1960 The new capital city, Brasília, is inaugurated.
1961 President Jânio Quadros resigns, after only six months in office.

MILITARY DICTATORSHIP (1964–1984)

1964–7 General Humberto de Alencar Castelo Branco rules as president after a military coup.
1968 General Arthur da Costa e Silva closes Congress and institutes a programme of repression.
1969–74 Under General Emílio Garrastazu Medici, state terrorism is used against guerrilla insurgents, but the economy soars. A massive program of road construction in Amazonia facilitates settlement.
1974–79 General Ernesto Geisel begins a gradual relaxation of the military regime.
1977 The first national conference of Brazilian indians.
1979 João Baptista Figueiredo becomes military president. Political rights restored to the opposition.
1982 Latin American debt crisis – Brazil has the largest national debt in the Third World.

1985–PRESENT

1985 Tancredo Neves becomes president, but dies six weeks later. José Sarney then becomes president.
1986 Sarney, with his economic package, the Cruzado Plan, attempts unsuccessfully to curb inflation.
1988 A new constitution is introduced, but without the long hoped-for land reform. Amerindians are granted full civil rights. Chico Mendes, defender of the rainforest, is murdered.
1989 Fernando Collor de Mello becomes president.

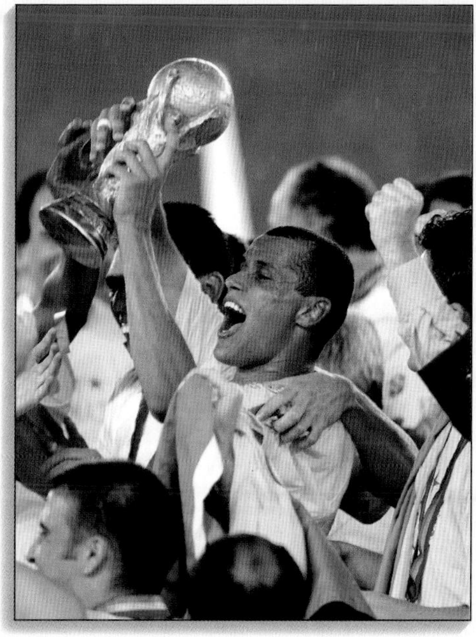

1992 UN Earth Summit is held in Rio, the largest ever gathering of heads of state and government.
1992 Collor resigns amid corruption scandals.
1994 Racing-driver and national hero, Ayrton Senna dies after a crash at the San Marino Grand Prix.
1994 Brazil wins the World Cup.
1994 Fernando Henrique Cardoso is elected president. His *Plano Real* brings inflation under control.
2000 Brazil's 500th anniversary as a country.
2002 Luiz Inácio Lula da Silva, popularly known as Lula, becomes the country's first left-wing president for 40 years. Brazil wins the World Cup for a record fifth time, with a 2–0 victory over Germany in Japan
2003 21 people killed in explosion of Brazilian satellite launch rocket at the Alcântara space center. ❑

PRECEDING PAGES: a naive painting of Bahia's capital, Salvador, by Calixto Sales.
LEFT: 1829 painting by Johann Moritz Rugendas, depicting Portuguese colonists and Brazilian indians.
RIGHT: celebrating Brazil's World Cup victory in 2002.

THE MAKING OF BRAZIL

Despite years of repressive dictatorships and one of the bloodiest conflicts in South American history, Brazil has managed to keep the peace at home

Fortunately, Brazil has not been marked by the type of violent upheavals that have occurred frequently elsewhere in Latin America. Change in the country has come peacefully, although not always quietly, a tribute to the ability of Brazilians to resolve their disputes through compromise rather than confrontation. Despite its size, Brazil has played only a secondary role in the shaping of the world today. Brazil does not possess a millennial culture with roots running back to a proud Amerindian past, à la Mexico and Peru, and it has remained on the sidelines in modern history.

The lack of a heroic past does not diminish Brazilian plans for greatness. Brazil is a country that is planted firmly in the present, with its eyes on the future and with very little sense of the past. It is even said that Brazil is a country without a memory.

However, Brazil's history sets it apart from the rest of South America. In addition to its size, which dwarfs that of its neighbors, Brazil stands out because of its language, Portuguese; its colonial period, in which it became the seat of government of the mother country; its mostly bloodless path towards independence and its largely peaceful relations with its neighbors.

Discovery and colonization

The discovery of Brazil in 1500 by explorer Pedro Alvares Cabral occurred during a series of voyages launched by the great Portuguese navigators in the 15th and 16th centuries. Cabral was sailing to India via the Cape of Good Hope and blown off course. At first, he thought he had discovered an island and named it Ilha de Vera Cruz. When it became obvious the island was the east coast of a continent, it was renamed Terra de Santa Cruz, which eventually evolved into Brazil after one of the colony's primary products, *pau brasil* or brazilwood, highly valued in Europe for red dye extract.

In 1533, the Portuguese crown made its first determined effort to organize the colonization of Brazil. The coastline, the only area that had yet been explored, was divided into 15 captaincies. These were given to Portuguese noblemen who received hereditary rights over them. The owners of captaincies were expected to settle and develop them, using their own resources in order to spare the crown this expense. The two most important captaincies were São Vicente in the southeast (now the state of São Paulo) and Pernambuco in the northeast, where the introduction of sugar plantations quickly made the area the economic center of the colony.

The captaincies, however, couldn't satisfy the needs of either the colonists or Portugal. Left to the whims and financial means of their owners, some were simply abandoned. Furthermore, there was no coordination among the captaincies, so Brazil's coastline fell prey to constant

LEFT: Petrópolis, the summer palace of Emperor Dom Pedro II, who reigned from 1840 to 1889.
RIGHT: portrait of Maria Leopoldina of Habsburg with her children (the future Emperor Pedro II on her lap), by Domenico Failutti.

attacks by French pirates. In 1549, King João III finally lost patience with the captaincy system and imposed a centralized colonial government on top of the existing divisions. The northeastern city of Salvador became the first capital of Brazil, a status it maintained for 214 years. Portuguese nobleman Tomé de Sousa was installed as the colony's first governor general.

With this administrative reform, colonization again picked up. From 1549 until the end of the century, a variety of colonists arrived – mostly noblemen, adventurers, and Jesuit missionaries charged with converting the Amerindians to Christianity. Several leading Jesuits, such as Father José de Anchieta in São Paulo, declared that Amerindians were to be protected, not enslaved, which put them in direct conflict with the interests of the colonizers. The Jesuits built schools and missions, around which Amerindian villages sprang up, in an effort to protect them from slave traders. It was because of the Jesuits and their initial success in preventing enslavement of the Amerindians that the colony turned to Africa for manpower. Soon slave ships were unloading slaves taken from the west coast of Africa.

French and Dutch occupations

In 1555, the French occupied what is now the city of Rio de Janeiro, the first step towards a major French colony in South America. But they were unable to attract European colonists to the area, and in 1565, the Portuguese drove them out. Two years later, the city of Rio was founded by the Portuguese.

This would be the last challenge to Portuguese control of Brazil until the Dutch West Indies Company sent out a fleet, which, in 1630, conquered the economically important sugar-growing region of Pernambuco in the northeast. This followed Portugal's alliance with the Spanish from 1580 to 1640, which brought Brazil under fire from Spain's enemies, Holland included. The Dutch established a well-functioning colony in Pernambuco that remained under their control until 1654, when they were driven out by a rebellion inspired and led by the colonists themselves with little help from Portugal.

The adventurers

In the same period, in the south of Brazil, bands of adventurers called *bandeirantes* (flag carriers) began to march out from their base in São Paulo in search of Amerindian slaves and gold. The great marches *(bandeiras)* of the *bandeirantes* took them west, south and north into the hinterlands. Some of these treks lasted for years. Through the *bandeirantes*, the colony launched its first effort to define its frontiers.

The *bandeirantes* clashed with the Jesuits over the Amerindians, but there was nothing the missionaries could do to stop the great *bandeiras*, which reached in the south to Uruguay and Argentina, in the west to Peru and Bolivia and in the northwest to Colombia. In the process, the *bandeirantes* crossed the imaginary line of the Tordesillas Treaty, which carved up South America into two empires. At the time, this had little significance, since Portugal and Spain were united, but after 1640, when Portugal again became an independent nation, the conquests of the *bandeirantes* were incorporated into Brazil against the protests of Spain.

As part of this period of nation building, Jesuit missionaries moved into the Amazon and the powerful landholders of the northeast expanded their influence and control into the arid backlands of this region. Uniting this huge colony was a common language and culture, Portuguese, a factor that made clear the distinction between Brazil and Spanish South America. The Treaty of Madrid with Spain in 1750 and succeeding treaties recognized the incursions of the *bandeirantes* and formally included these areas in the colony of Brazil.

Brazil in the 18th century had grown into a predominantly rural and coastal society. Wealth was concentrated in the hands of a few landholding families. The principal products were sugar, tobacco and cattle, but coffee and cotton were becoming increasingly important. Despite the Jesuit missions, the *bandeirantes* had managed to reduce drastically the Amerindian population through enslavement, disease and massacre. Meanwhile, the population of African slaves had increased sharply. Brazil traded only with Portugal and, other than the marches of the *bandeirantes*, had little con-

LEFT: *Founding of São Paulo, 1554*, by Oscar Pereira da Silva. **ABOVE:** *Independence or Death*, by Pedro Americo (1880).

GOLD SPAWNS NEW TOWNS

In the mountains of Brazil's central plateau, the *bandeirantes* finally found what they had been looking for – gold. In 1695, a gold rush brought thousands of settlers to what is today the state of Minas Gerais, the first mass settlement of Brazil's vast interior. Towns sprang up in the mountains, and by 1750, the city of Ouro Preto had a population of 80,000.

The gold found in Minas Gerais made Brazil the 18th century's largest producer of this precious metal. All the wealth, however, went to Portugal, a fact that was not lost upon the colonists who were already feeling more Brazilian than Portuguese.

The Golden Age of Pedro II

Pedro II reigned for 49 years, from 1840–89, using his extraordinary talents to give Brazil its longest continuous period of political stability. A humble man, Pedro felt uncomfortable with the traditional trappings of an emperor, but he was blessed with enormous personal authority. During the American Civil War, Abraham Lincoln remarked that the only man he would trust to arbitrate between north and south was Pedro II of Brazil.

Born in Rio de Janeiro, Pedro was classically educated. He married Teresa Cristina Maria, daughter of Francis I of Sicily, and fathered four children, though his two sons died as children. Fascinating illustrations of Pedro's character and scholarly interests are preserved in the modest but elegant neo-classical summer palace he built in Petrópolis *(see the chapter on Rio State, page 177)*.

Pedro was not only learned but also politically astute. He managed to keep regional rivalries in check and, through his own popularity, to extend the control of central government. Against this backdrop, Brazil was wealthy and economically stable, and technological progress was made. Yet, especially abroad, Pedro II also steadfastly pursued a series of risky and controversial policies. And whereas he was successful in restoring internal peace to the nation, his foreign policy put Brazil into armed conflict with its neighbors to the south.

Pedro was determined to maintain regional parity in South America, which led him to interfere with political developments in Uruguay, Argentina and Paraguay. As a result, Brazil fought three wars between 1851 and 1870. First, in 1851, to ensure free navigation on the vital River Plate and its tributaries, Pedro sent troops into Uruguay, gaining a quick victory and a new Brazil-friendly government, which he then allied with in order to overthrow the Argentine dictator Juan Manuel Rosas. This war also had a successful outcome.

A second incursion against Uruguay in 1864, however, provoked war with Paraguay. Allied with the losing side in Uruguay, Paraguay's ruler Francisco Solano Lopez struck back against both Brazil and Argentina. In 1865, the so-called triple alliance was formed, joining the apparently invincible forces of Brazil, Argentina and Uruguay against Paraguay. But after initial successes, the alliance suffered a series of surprising setbacks and the war dragged on until 1870, becoming in the process the longest in South America in the 19th century.

The consequent elevation to prominence of Brazil's military leaders meant that Pedro needed their support to remain in power – and when he lost it, he quickly fell from grace in spite of his popularity with the masses. Ironically, the issue that led to his demise was slavery, whose abolition, from today's perspective, was perhaps his greatest and most admirable achievement.

In the latter half of the 19th century, the Brazilian economy was still overwhelmingly agricultural, and slaves continued to play a major role, especially in the northeast. However, in the 1860s an abolitionist movement gathered pace, leading to the end of slavery in 1888. Although slavery was clearly doomed regardless of political side-taking (the slave population being in decline since the slave trade was ended, and Brazil being increasingly isolated in maintaining the institution), its abolition set the nation's landholders against Pedro.

By this time, the military, like the landholders, felt under-represented in government, and in November 1889, a military revolt led to a bloodless coup. Pedro II was deposed, and Brazil's most popular leader ever was forced into exile. He died in Paris, aged 66, where he was given a royal funeral. ❑

LEFT: Dom Pedro II.

tact with its neighbors. All of this, however, was about to change, thanks to the discovery of gold at the end of the 17th century.

The gold shifted the colony's center of wealth from the sugar producing areas of the northeast to the southeast. This led in 1763 to Brazil's capital moving from Salvador to Rio de Janeiro. At the same time, the captaincies were taken over by the crown, four years after the last Jesuits were expelled from Brazil.

Liberal ideas

Brazil was isolated, but not entirely shut off from the outside world. By the second half of the 18th century, the liberal ideas popular in Europe began to enter Brazil's consciousness. In 1789, the country experienced its first independence movement, centered in the gold rush boom town of Ouro Preto. The catalyst was a decision by Portugal to increase the tax on gold. But the *Inconfidência Mineira*, as it was called, ended badly, with the arrest of its leaders. One of these, Joaquim José da Silva Xavier, a dentist better known as Tiradentes, or tooth-puller, was hanged and quartered.

Other movements would probably have followed but for developments in Europe. In 1807, Napoleon conquered Portugal, forcing the Portuguese royal family into exile. King João VI fled to Brazil, making the colony the seat of government for the mother country, the only instance of such a turnaround during the colonial period.

Brazil's changed status led to the crown opening up commerce with other nations, in particular England, Portugal's ally against Napoleon. When King João at last returned to Portugal in 1821, he named his son, Dom Pedro, as regent, making him the head of government for Brazil. The Portuguese parliament, however, refused to recognize Brazil's new situation and attempted to force a return to the days of colonial dependence. Realizing that the Brazilians would never accept this, on September 7, 1822, Pedro declared independence from Portugal, in the process creating the Brazilian Empire, the first monarchy in the Americas.

With Portugal still recovering from the Napoleonic wars, Brazil faced little opposition from the mother country. Helped by a British soldier of fortune, Lord Alexander Thomas Cochrane, the Brazilian forces quickly expelled the remaining Portuguese garrisons. By the end of 1823 the Portuguese had left and the new nation's independence was secured. The following year, the United States became the first foreign nation to recognize Brazil, and in 1825 relations were re-established with Portugal.

Internal divisions

The ease with which independence was won, however, proved to be a false indication of the young nation's immediate future. During its first 18 years, Brazil struggled to overcome bitter internal divisions, which in some cases reached the point of open revolt. The first disappointment of the post-independence period was the emperor himself, who insisted on maintaining the privileges and power of an absolute monarch. Pedro I eventually agreed to the creation of a parliament, but fought with it constantly. Already widely disliked, he then plunged Brazil into a reckless and unpopular war with Argentina over what was then the southernmost state of Brazil, Cisplatina. Brazil lost the war and the area of Cisplatina, which is now Uruguay.

Pedro I abdicated in 1831 in favor of his five-year-old son and, from 1831 to 1840, Brazil was ruled by a triple regency of political leaders who ran the nation in the name of the young

RIGHT: Avenida Beira Mar in Botafogo, Rio.

Pedro. The next nine years were the most violent of Brazil's history, with revolts and army rebellions in the northeast, the Amazon, Minas Gerais and the south. Brazil appeared to be on the verge of civil war as regional factions fighting for autonomy threatened to tear the nation apart. In particular, the *farrapos* war, in the south lasted ten years and almost led to the loss of what is today the state of Rio Grande do Sul.

STATES IN CHARGE

From 1900 to 1920, Brazil's power base was described as "coffee and cream", since coffee producer São Paulo and dairy state Minas Gerais took turns in controlling the presidency.

Out of desperation, the country's political leadership agreed in 1840 to declare Pedro II

of age and hand over rule of the country to a 15-year-old monarch. They were right to do so *(see page 32)*, and it is ironic that Brazil's most successful emperor was also its last.

Debts of the military

The end of the monarchy in 1889 marked the arrival of what was to become Brazil's most powerful institution – the military. From 1889 to the present day, the armed forces have been at the center of almost every major political development in Brazil. The first two governments of the republic were headed by military men, both of whom proved better at spending than governing. By the time a civilian president took office (Prudente de Morais, 1894-98), the country was deep in debt. The problem was faced by the country's second civilian president, Manuel Ferraz de Campos Salles (1898–1902), who was the first to negotiate re-scheduling the foreign debt, and is credited with saving Brazil from financial collapse. Campos Salles and his successor, Francisco de Paula Rodrigues Alves (1902–06) put Brazil back on its feet and set an example that few subsequent presidents have matched since.

Alternating with good and bad presidents, Brazil went through a period of dramatic social change between 1900 and 1930, when large numbers of immigrants arrived from Europe. Economic power shifted to the southeast and so too did political power. While certain states, namely São Paulo and Minas Gerais, increased their power and influence, the federal government had very little of either, becoming a prisoner of regional and economic interests.

Economic woes lead to coup

After World War I, in which Brazil declared war on Germany but did not take an active role, economic woes again beset the country. Spendthrift governments emptied the public coffers, while rumors of widespread corruption led to public unrest. Military movements also resurfaced with an attempted coup in 1922 and an isolated revolt in São Paulo in 1924 put down with massive destruction by the federal government, whose troops bombarded the city of São Paulo at will. The dissatisfaction in the barracks was led by a group of junior officers who became known as the *tenentes* (lieutenants). These officers were closely identified with the emerging urban middle class, which was searching for political leadership to oppose the wealthy landholders of São Paulo state and Minas Gerais.

The political crisis reached its zenith following the 1930 election of establishment candidate Júlio Prestes, despite a major effort to mobilize the urban masses in favor of opposition candidate Getúlio Vargas, the governor of Rio Grande do Sul. The opposition refused to accept the election result. With the support of participants and backers of the lieutenants' movement of the 1920s, a revolt broke out in

Minas Gerais, Rio Grande do Sul and the northeast. Within two weeks, the army had control of the country, overthrowing Prestes and installing Getúlio Vargas as the new president.

The Vargas era

The rapid ascension of President Vargas signaled the beginning of a new era in Brazilian politics. A man linked to the urban middle and lower classes, Vargas represented a complete break from political control in the hands of the rural elite. The coffee barons of São Paulo and the wealthy landholders of other states and regions, the political power brokers of the Old Republic, were suddenly out. Instead of backroom politics dominated by a powerful elite, the focus of politics in Brazil was shifted to the common man in the fast-growing urban centers.

Ironically, this dramatic upheaval did not lead to increased democracy for the country. Intent on retaining power, Vargas initiated a policy marked by populism and nationalism that succeeded in keeping him at the center of Brazil's political life for 25 years. During this period, Vargas set the model for Brazilian politics for the remainder of the 20th century, which saw the country alternate between populist political leaders and military intervention.

Vargas' basic strategy was to win the support of the urban masses and concentrate power in his own hands. Taking advantage of the growing industrialization of the country, Vargas used labor legislation as his key weapon: laws were passed that created a minimum wage and a social security system, paid vacations, maternity leave and medical assistance. Vargas instituted reforms that legalized labor unions but also made the unions dependent on the federal government. He quickly became the most popular Brazilian leader since Dom Pedro II. In the new constitution, which was not drafted until 1934 and then only after an anti-Vargas revolt in São Paulo, Vargas further increased the powers of the central government.

With the constitution approved, Vargas' "interim" presidency ended and he was elected president by Congress in 1934. The constitution limited him to one four-year term, with elections for a new president scheduled for 1938, but Vargas refused to surrender power. In 1937, using the invented threat of a communist coup and with the support of the military, Vargas closed Congress and threw out the 1934 constitution, replacing it with a new document giving

LEFT: Getúlio Vargas (center, in riding boots).
ABOVE: Avenida Paulista in São Paulo, on its inaugural day in 1881, illustrated by Jules Victor André Martin.

him dictatorial powers. The second part of the Vargas reign, which he glorified under the title The New State, proved far more tumultuous than his first seven years.

Brazil at war

Growing political opposition to Vargas' repressive means threatened to topple him but the president saved himself by joining the allies in World War II, declaring war on Germany in 1942. Vargas sent a Brazilian expeditionary force of 25,000 soldiers to Europe, where they joined the allied Fifth Army in Italy, making Brazil the only Latin American country to take an active part in the war. Brazilian losses were light (approximately 450 dead), and the country's war effort served to distract the public and lessened the pressure on Vargas.

With the war winding down, however, Vargas was under threat from the same military that had put him in power, so he approved measures legalizing opposition political parties and calling for a presidential election at the end of 1945. But while he bargained with the opposition to prevent a coup, Vargas also instigated his backers in the labor movement to join forces with the communists in a popular movement to keep him in office. Fearful that Vargas might succeed, the military ousted him from power on October 29, 1945, ending a 15-year reign.

Vargas' exit, however, proved to be temporary. In the presidential election of 1945, his former war minister, General Eurico Gaspar Dutra, was elected president, serving a five-year term during which a new, liberal constitution was approved. Then in 1950, Vargas returned to power, this time elected by the people.

DEMISE OF A DICTATOR

During his final years in office following his 1950 election, Getúlio Vargas tried to safeguard his position by introducing nationalistic measures, such as the nationalization of oil production; nevertheless, he rapidly lost ground in the popularity stakes.

A political crisis sparked by an attempt on the life of one of his main political opponents, allegedly planned by a Vargas aide, finally brought the Vargas era to an end. When he was given an ultimatum by the military either to resign or be overthrown, Vargas instead chose a third route – on August 24, 1954 he committed suicide in the presidential palace.

Two men from the southeast

The eventual removal of Vargas from the political scene after his suicide in 1954 cleared the way for new faces to appear. The first to emerge came again from the twin poles of

Brazilian 20th-century politics, São Paulo and Minas Gerais. Juscelino Kubitschek from Minas and Jânio Quadros from São Paulo both used the same path to the presidency, first serving as mayors of their state capitals, and then as governors. Populism, nationalism and military connections, the three leading themes of modern Brazilian politics, all played a part in the careers of these men. Two new factors were the increasing linkage of economic growth with political developments and Brazil's growing economic and political ties with the outside world.

FAN OF COMMUNISM

Jânio Quadros shocked the military by giving a medal to Che Guevara, hero of the Cuban revolution.

Kubitschek, an expansive and dynamic leader with a vision of Brazil as a world power, was elected president in 1955. He promised to give the country "50 years of progress in five". For the first time, the country had a leader whose primary concern was economic growth. Under Kubitschek, there was rapid industrialization. Foreign auto manufacturers were invited to Brazil, providing the initial impetus for what was to become an explosion of growth in the city and state of São Paulo. Government funds and/or incentives were used to build roads, steel mills and hydroelectric plants, creating the precedent of direct government involvement in infrastructure projects. But Kubitschck's biggest project was the building of Brasília.

The idea of a new federal capital in the heart of the country came to obsess Kubitschek. Upon taking office, he ordered the plans drawn up, insisting Brazil would have a new capital before his term ended. He wanted to develop Brazil's near-deserted central plain by moving thousands of civil servants from Rio. Nothing existed at the chosen site, so Kubitschek faced enormous opposition from bureaucrats with no desire to leave the comforts and pleasures of Rio de Janeiro for an inland wilderness. From 1957 until 1960, construction continued at full speed and on April 21, 1960, Kubitschek proudly inaugurated his capital. But while Brasília became a symbol of Kubitschek's dynamism, it also became an unceasing drain on the country's treasury. Brasília and other grandiose public works projects meant the Kubitschek administration left office having produced not only rapid growth, but also a soaring public debt, high inflation and vast corruption.

The situation seemed readymade for Jânio Quadros, a self-styled reformer who used the broom as his campaign symbol, promising to sweep the government clean of all corruption. Instead, he embarked on a short but memorable administration culminating in an institutional crisis that ultimately brought an end to Brazil's experiment with democracy. Quadros was impatient, unpredictable and autocratic. Insisting that everything be done exactly his way (at one point he even banned bikinis from Brazil's beaches), he attempted to ignore Congress, sparking an open confrontation with the legislative branch, and surprised his followers by moving Brazil closer to the bloc of non-aligned nations. Finally, in a typical Quadros move, he resigned from the presidency without warning on August 25, 1961, seven months after taking office, citing the "terrible forces" which were aligned against him.

The resignation of Quadros created a crisis immediately, again bringing the military to the center of political developments. Top officials of

LEFT: president Juscelino Kubitschek at the ceremony inaugurating Brasília.

RIGHT: General Emílio Medici, president from 1969–74.

the armed forces threatened to prevent Quadros' leftist vice-president, João Goulart, from taking office. Goulart, though, had the support of military units in his home state of Rio Grande do Sul. Fearing a civil war, the military agreed to negotiate a solution to the impasse, permitting Goulart to assume the presidency but also instituting a parliamentary system of government with vastly reduced powers for the president.

Populist program

This compromise solution, however, failed to work in practice and, in 1963, a national plebiscite voted to return Brazil to presidential

rule. With his powers enhanced, Goulart launched a populist, nationalistic program that moved the country sharply to the left. He announced sweeping land reforms, promised widespread social reforms and threatened to nationalize foreign firms.

His economic policies, meanwhile, failed to stem inflation. The cost of living soared, contributing to a wave of strikes supported by Goulart's followers in the labor movement. Opposition grew, centered on the middle classes of São Paulo and Minas Gerais whose political leaders appealed to the military to intervene. Finally, on March 31, 1964, claiming that Goulart was preparing a communist takeover of the government, the military orchestrated a bloodless coup.

While the 1964 coup was the fourth time since 1945 that the military had intervened in the government, this was to be the only instance where the generals remained in power. For the next 21 years, Brazil was governed by a military regime, as the armed forces clamped down on civilian corruption and launched a bid to stamp out any leftist influence and transform the political system.

Five army generals occupied the presidency during this period. The first was Humberto de Alencar Castelo Branco, who concentrated on resolving the country's delicate economic situation. He introduced austerity measures to attack inflation and reduced government spending sharply. Thus the Castelo Branco government restored economic stability, setting the stage for the strong growth years that were to follow. His administration also adopted measures to limit political freedom – the existing political parties were suspended and replaced by a two-party system, one party (Arena) supporting the government and the other, the liberal Democratic Movement Party (PMDB) representing the opposition; mayors and governors were appointed by the military and the president's election was made indirect (all the presidents of the military regime were chosen in secret by the army).

Military repression

During the presidency of General Arthur da Costa e Silva, the successor of Castelo Branco, the military introduced a new constitution making Congress clearly subordinate to the executive branch. A wave of opposition to the military in 1968, including armed resistance, led Costa e Silva to clamp down. The closing of Congress and the severe restriction of individual rights marked the beginning of the most repressive years of the military regime. The doctrine of national security gave the government the right to arrest and detain without *habeas corpus*, and the military embarked on a war against "subversion." Organized guerrilla groups were crushed, government critics were arrested and often tortured and the press was censored.

Ruthless military repression peaked during General Emílio Garrastazu Medici's government. He assumed the presidency after Costa e Silva suffered a fatal stroke in 1969.

The Medici years were the most dramatic of the military regime not only because of the severe suppression of human rights but also due to the economic growth that Brazil enjoyed. While in power, Medici and his successor, General Ernesto Geisel (1974–79), saw the Brazilian economy surge ahead. These boom years brought unprecedented prosperity to the country, providing full employment for the urban masses and high salaries for middle-class professionals and white-collar workers. As a result, Brazilians were inclined to accept military rule and tolerate the lack of personal and political freedom. Brazil's increasing economic clout led the military to adopt a more independent foreign policy, breaking with the country's traditional adherence to US-backed positions.

THE BRAZILIAN MIRACLE

The dramatic economic upturn of the 1970s brought Brazil into the international spotlight and spurred the old dream of becoming a major world power.

Hard times

With the advent of the 1980s, however, the military regime fell on hard times. Economic growth first slowed then slumped. Following a debt moratorium by Mexico in 1982, the Latin American debt crisis exploded on the country. New foreign loans dried up and interest charges on previous loans outstripped the resources of the government.

General João Baptista Figueiredo – the last of the military presidents – who took office in 1979, promised to return Brazil to democracy and announced an amnesty for all political prisoners and exiles. The government moved ahead with other liberalizing steps. Press censorship was lifted, new political parties were founded and elections for governors and Congress were held. But the increasing political freedom did nothing to offset the sense of gloom in the recession from 1981 to 1983.

In January 1985, an electoral college composed of Congress and state delegates chose Tancredo Neves as Brazil's first civilian president in 22 years. A moderate who had opposed the military regime, he was acceptable to both conservatives and liberals. Brazil's transition to democracy, however, was marked by tragedy as Neves fell ill the night before he was to be sworn in and died a month later, once more plunging Brazil into a political crisis. Neves' vice president, José Sarney, a military-regime supporter, instantly assumed the presidency, but he was a conservative who had little support among the liberals who were now returning to power.

Once in office, Sarney attempted populist measures such as an ill-fated land reform program to secure the support of the liberals who controlled Congress. The country's economic difficulties, however,

worsened. Weighed down with foreign debt and lacking the resources for investments, the government was unable to provide effective leadership for the economy.

The Cruzado Plan

By the start of 1986, with inflation running at an annual rate of 330 percent, Sarney was facing a slump in popularity and pressure from the left for a direct presidential election to be held immediately. His response was the Cruzado Plan, an unorthodox economic package that froze prices while letting wages continue to rise. After years of seeing their spending power eroded by inflation, Brazilians

LEFT: impeached president Fernando Collor de Mello (1990–92).

RIGHT: supporters of Luiz Inácio da Silva campaign in front of Sugarloaf Mountain during the 2002 election.

threw themselves into the ensuing consumer boom. The president's popularity rose sharply; claiming co-responsibility for the plan, the politicians of the PMDB, who now supported Sarney, swept to landslide victories in the congressional and state elections of November 1986.

HYPERINFLATION

In 1993, Brazilian inflation peaked at an astonishing annual rate of 2,100 percent.

However, the long-term success of the Cruzado Plan depended on cuts in government spending, which Sarney, keen to hold on to his newfound popularity, was reluctant to make. Inflation returned with a vengeance, and was to survive a sequence of increasingly ineffectual

economic packages introduced throughout the remaining years of the Sarney administration.

The new constitution

The return of high inflation in 1987 coincided with the start of the National Constituent Assembly, charged with drafting a new democratic constitution. Announced in 1988, the Constitution's significant advances included the end of censorship, recognition of Amerindian land rights and increased worker benefits.

On the downside, powerful lobbies and the formation of an informal conservative majority within the Assembly blocked progress on controversial issues such as land reform. In addition, the upsurge in nationalism, which had contributed to Brazil's declaration of a moratorium on its debt with foreign banks in February 1987, led to the inclusion in the Constitution of measures directed against foreign capital.

By liberally distributing political favors and government concessions, President Sarney won Congressional approval to extend his term in office until March 1990. But his support dwindled as inflation accelerated and discontent grew.

Direct elections

In the municipal elections of November 1988, control of many state capitals (including Brazil's largest metropolis, São Paulo) was won by the left-wing Workers' Party (PT), a new political force based on the trade unions and free from any association with the old-style politicians. And when the long-awaited direct presidential elections were held in November 1989, the PT candidate, union leader Luiz Inácio Lula da Silva, emerged as a strong contender.

The traditional parties suffered overwhelming rejection of their candidates, while two "outsiders" ended up going through to the election's final round a month later. One of them was Lula. His opponent was the 40-year-old former governor of the insignificant northeastern state of Alagoas, running on the ticket of the virtually unheard-of National Reconstruction Party: Fernando Collor de Mello.

Mixing an appeal to youth and modernity with a moralizing discourse that reminded many of Jânio Quadros, and including a hefty dose of preaching against Lula's "communism," Collor beat the PT candidate by a narrow margin. Taking office in March 1990 with the authority of Brazil's first directly elected president in three decades, he immediately attacked inflation with a brutal fiscal squeeze that included an 18-month "compulsory loan," of 80 percent of the nation's savings.

Although these measures forestalled the threat of hyperinflation in the short term, they did not address Brazil's underlying fiscal malaise, and inflation soon began to creep back. When it came to light that Collor's closest associates had been milking the state of millions of dollars through a string of illegal scams, the middle classes rose up against him. They took to the streets in their thousands, demanding his impeachment.

Collor was replaced by his deputy, Itamar Franco. Although in many ways a lacklustre president, Franco soon won respect for his integrity. However, in 1994, at the end of Franco's term, they elected Fernando Henrique Cardoso as president by a clear majority in the first round. Cardoso's popularity was based on the success of his *Plano Real*, the financial plan he introduced as finance minister in Franco's government. This linked Brazil's latest currency, the *real*, to the US dollar in a relationship that retained the flexibility needed to accommodate international financial shocks, while giving the currency an anchor to prevent it being dragged back into a tide of rising inflation. Cardoso followed with a vengeance the path of privatization, started by Collor. He opened up the Brazilian economy, attracting substantial investment from overseas. In October 1998, Cardoso was re-elected for a second four-year term. He faced a setback at the beginning of 1999 when the *real* halved its value against the US dollar.

LEFT: Luiz Inácio da Silva, leader of the left-wing Workers' Party, who became President in 2002.
ABOVE: the Banco Mercantil of São Paulo, commercial and financial center of Brazil.

The first half of 2003 showed a contraction of the country's gross domestic product (GDP), while industrial output shrank by 3.7 percent, early indications of a possible recession.

Humble origins

Luiz Inácio Lula da Silva, one-time shoeshine boy and metal worker, won over 60 percent of the votes in 2002. A smarter image and streamlined policies ensured he won support from all sectors of society after losing three previous bids to gain power.

He has launched a nationwide program to eradicate illiteracy by 2006. Up to 20 million Brazilians cannot read or write. Lula represents the hope not just of a nation, but of the whole of South America. Brazil is the driving force behind Mercosul; the South American common market, and has taken a leading role in trade negotiations with other Latin American countries, the EU, and the US.

The new President has a commitment to increase the scope of Mercosul so that it is a political and cultural body and not just an economic one. Lula is adamant that rich countries cannot continue to preach free trade while practicing protectionism themselves. As he said when he took office: "Today, Brazil re-encounters itself." ❑

A COUNTRY OF THE FUTURE

Boom and bust cycles have finally been replaced with a period of sustained economic growth

Potential is Brazil's middle name. Born fully grown as the fifth largest nation on Earth, Brazil has since added people to its empty spaces, making it today not only the fifth largest in population (at around 175 million) but also one of the world's largest consumer markets. On top of this, Brazil possesses a vast store of natural resources, much of which is still untapped.

What amazes people most about Brazil is that it has managed to accomplish so much so quickly. The country's geographical position far from the news capitals of the world, its tendency towards isolation, and its propensity to undervalue its own achievements, have combined to keep the Brazil story under wraps.

Brazil's economic achievements (a few of which are highlighted on page 44) have provided it with a modern and diversified economy and put it on the threshold of graduation to the ranks of the economic heavyweights. With its large industrial base, its well-established and still growing domestic and foreign markets and its vast natural resources, Brazil's continued ascension in the rankings seems assured.

Progress for the country, however, has not been painless. Since colonial times, Brazil has gone through alternating cycles of boom and bust. Industrialization came late to Brazil. From colonial days until midway through this century, Brazil was primarily a rural society with a one-product economy. First it was timber, then sugar, shifting in the 18th century to gold. After the rubber boom, coffee emerged as the economy's work horse. As late as the 1950s, coffee still provided over half of Brazil's export revenue, 65 percent of the work force was farm-based and the main function of the banking system was to supply credit to farmers.

Modernization

World War II provided the first stimulus to Brazil's industry when the conflict cut off Brazil's supplies of manufactured goods, forcing the development of local substitutes. To expand further, however, Brazil's infant industries needed a strong push, and this was provided by the government – more specifically President Juscelino Kubitschek, who took office in 1955.

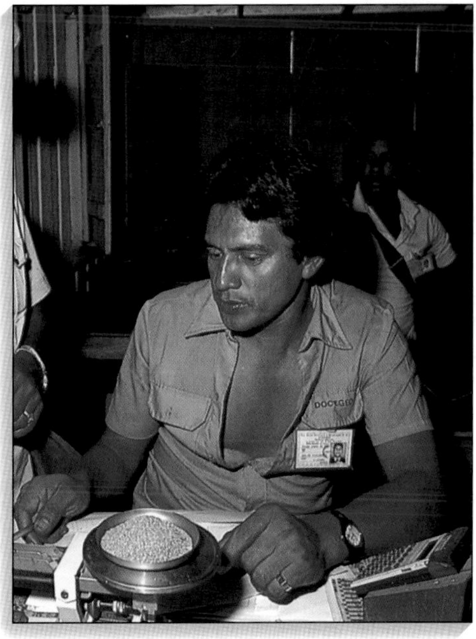

Kubitschek made economic growth the primary goal throughout his administration, and this policy has been followed by all succeeding governments. He also established the development model that was copied with modifications by his successors: it involved government intervention in managing the economy and an important role for foreign capital investment.

Kubitschek poured government money into infrastructure projects (highways and power plants) while inviting foreign auto makers to establish plants in São Paulo. Government loans also financed the private sector, with the result that for the period 1948–61, the Brazilian economy grew at an average annual rate of 7 percent.

LEFT: keeping Brazil's lines of communication open.
RIGHT: gold dealer weighing the booty.

At this point, however, two of the great evils of Brazil's 20th-century history – high inflation and political instability – ended the first spurt of economic growth. With the coup in 1964, Brazil's new military rulers turned to austerity measures to trim down inflation. By 1968, inflation was under control and the economy was poised for a historic takeoff.

Beginning in 1970, Brazil enjoyed four straight years of double digit economic growth that ended with a 14 percent expansion in 1973. Although the rate of growth then slowed, it never fell below 4.6 percent and averaged 8.9 percent a year between 1968 and 1980.

These boom years became known as the period of the Brazilian Miracle, and they changed the face of Brazil forever. Led by São Paulo, the country's major cities underwent rapid industrialization, and this attracted waves of peasant migrants fleeing their precarious existence in the nation's rural areas. Between 1960 and 1980, Brazil changed from a rural nation (55 percent of the population in rural areas) into a majority urban nation (67 percent of the population in the cities). By 2001, this figure had grown to 81 percent.

Nowhere was this more apparent than in the state of São Paulo. With São Paulo city receiv-

HIGHLIGHTS OF BRAZIL'S ECONOMY

With a gross domestic product of nearly US$600 billion (in 2003), Brazil is the world's eighth-largest economy, almost twice as big as that of South Korea, Brazil's main rival for the title of most developed emerging economy. Brazil's economic rankings in the world are:

- By far the most industrialized of the world's developing nations, with the most developed domestic consumer market.
- One of the world's major steel producers.
- The world's eighth-largest automobile manufacturer, fifth-largest aircraft manufacturer and fifth-largest arms exporter.
- Its hydroelectric potential surpasses that of any other nation, and Brazil has the world's largest hydroelectric plant.
- The largest producer of iron ore, sixth-largest producer of aluminum, and fourth-largest producer of tin. Also a top-ranking producer of manganese and gold.
- The largest exporter of coffee, the largest producer of sugar and orange juice, and the second-largest producer of soybeans. Brazil comes fourth in grain, fifth in cocoa production and second in meat production.

Agriculture, once dominant in Brazil's economy, accounts for just 7 percent of GDP; manufacturing adds up to 29 percent and services 64 percent. Coffee is no more the king of exports; industrial goods account for 64 percent of the total. Brazil exports cars, steel products, shoes and airplanes.

ing the bulk of new investments in the private sector, the state's industrial park exploded, emerging as the largest in Latin America and one of the most modern in the world. São Paulo's miracle has continued to the present day. Currently, the gross domestic product of São Paulo state is larger than that of any nation in Latin America except Mexico.

Loans finance wild ambition

But the miracle years brought more than dramatic social and economic changes. They also produced a profound effect on the national psyche. Accustomed to playing down both the value and potential of their country, Brazilians in the 1970s saw this sleeping giant suddenly begin to stir and climb to its feet.

Ecstatic with the success of their economic programs, the generals abandoned their initial goal of providing the framework for growth and embarked on a wildly ambitious scheme to turn Brazil into a world power. Moderation was abandoned and the military drew up massive development projects. The problem, however, was finding a way to finance these dreams. The government, the private sector and the foreign companies did not have the resources required. Clearly another partner was needed.

In 1974, that partner appeared. Following the 1973 oil shock, international banks were overflowing with petrodollars, so they sought investment opportunities in the developing world. And no other developing nation could match the growth record of Brazil, let alone its potential. It was a perfect marriage.

Soon, pin-striped bankers were flying down to Rio, Brasília and São Paulo from New York and London, followed shortly by their colleagues from Frankfurt, Tokyo, Paris, Toronto, Geneva, Chicago and Los Angeles. The rules of the game were disarmingly simple. The generals presented their blueprints for Brazilian superpowerdom and the bankers unloaded the dollars. There was no collateral.

In 1974, Brazil borrowed more money than it had in the preceding 150 years combined. When the decade finally bowed out five years later, a total of $40 billion had been transferred to Brazil. During these years, money poured into transportation (new highways, bridges and railroads across the country and subways for Rio and São Paulo), into industry (steel mills, a petrochemical complex and consumer goods factories), the energy sector (power plants,

LEFT: assembling electronic products at a factory owned by the Dutch giant Philips.
ABOVE: a robot at work in a Volkswagen car factory.

nuclear reactors, a program looking into alternative energy and oil exploration), communications (television, postal services and telecommunications) and, in some instances, into the pockets of generals and technocrats.

Then in 1979 the bubble burst. The second oil shock doubled the price of Brazil's imported petroleum while at the same time interest rates shot up and the prices of commodities on international markets came crashing down. Brazil's trade balance recorded a deficit in 1979 that was nearly three times that of 1978.

At first, however, neither the generals nor the bankers were willing to admit that the party was over. The borrowing continued, only now the incoming dollars went to pay for imported oil and to cover previous loans now falling due.

Lengthy recession

In 1981 the situation worsened, with a recession in the United States that was felt immediately by Brazil. Three years of recession forced Brazil into a lengthy depression. Many small and medium-sized businesses failed, throwing thousands into unemployment. Large industries laid off workers, leaving the poorest increasingly desperate, reliant on woefully inadequate and underfunded welfare provisions.

The decision by Mexico in 1982 to impose a moratorium on international loan interest triggered the so-called Latin American debt crisis. In response, international lending institutions cut off the flow of development loans.

The future looked grim. Twenty years of military government were drawing to a close, leaving the country with rampant inflation and a plethora of inefficient government-owned industries built on the largesse that the generals dispensed to appointees who presided over them. For 20 years the civil service had run amok, creating endless jobs of dubious worth, which nonetheless paid gold-plated salaries and bore a lifetime guarantee. By 1987, a staggering 60 percent of the economy was controlled by the government.

Brazil's manufacturing industries, built on import substitution policies pursued by successive governments after World War II, were soft-bellied and inefficient, often run by political appointees who were neither qualified nor experienced for the jobs they had been given.

ALCOHOL FUEL PROMOTES SELF-SUFFICIENCY

Brazil is unique in the world in having embraced a renewable energy source to power motor vehicles. The government-sponsored program to develop the use of home-produced sugar cane alcohol as a substitute for imported petroleum has been a great technical success and has taken Brazil to the forefront of ethanol fuel technology.

The program began in 1975 as a means of reducing expenditure on imported oil, gaining impetus during the international petroleum crises of the 1970s. As a result, a sustainable, renewable, low-pollution fuel was developed.

Yet the transformation of thousands of hectares of land from mixed agricultural production to sugar cane monoculture left thousands of rural workers landless, forcing them into low-paid seasonal jobs in the sugar industry. In 1990 the Pro-Alcohol Program collapsed due to a shortage of fuel and poor performance. Early 2003 saw a dramatic increase in the production of alcohol fuel and the government is currently trying to revive the scheme.

But production is expensive. Alcohol fuel was heavily subsidised from the start, and never became economically viable.

Remarkably, Brazil rose to the challenge. Before the debt crisis, exports had been dominated by raw materials and agricultural products, which provided the income to pay for imports of oil and capital goods. But during the 1980s, the overweight industries that had developed in the protected environment of import substitution began to slim down and become more efficient. The need to export opened up new, larger markets, which encouraged the expansion of manufacturing capacity beyond what the domestic market could support. Brazilians often refer to the 1980s as the "lost decade" but, in truth, it was a period of positive foundation building.

However, it was also a decade plagued by inflation, which held back the expansion of Brazil's industries. During these years, Brazil adapted to high inflation by index-linking virtually everything in the economy and, in the process, making market forces a hostage to government policies. All monetary contracts, from salaries and loans, to savings and time deposits, were indexed to inflation, receiving adjustments every month.

Financial manipulation

The Brazilian middle class became adept at manipulating their money, timing purchases to their best advantage and using an array of financial mechanisms to maintain their purchasing power. A topic of conversation often heard over breakfast in a business district café was the performance of the "overnight" – a financial mechanism known to most money dealers the whole world over but not normally indulged in by the salaried middle class.

During this period the government controlled everything. Prices were indexed, then they were controlled. Then they were frozen and then controlled again in a constant back and forth that left corporate planners dizzy. Wages, too, were at times frozen, at times linked to a government index which routinely left wage earners with less purchasing power. Exchange rates fluctuated daily, and most transactions, from the purchase of a refrigerator to multi-million dollar construction contracts, were priced in dollars.

At the corporate level, similar conditions prevailed. A company's principal activity became secondary to its financial planning, its profit primarily dependent on how adept it was at financial manipulation. Planning for the medium term became very uncertain, and long-term objectives were little more than wishes.

The financial uncertainties of the decade acted as a powerful disincentive to multinational firms who might otherwise have considered investing in Brazil. Curiously, those already well-established, such as Volkswagen, continued to make healthy profits, but Brazil needed new investment from multinationals to get its industry up to speed, and that would not happen until inflation was under control.

Brazil's first directly elected president, Fernando Collor de Mello, although removed from office in 1992 after only three years, set in motion many of the reforms that have brought Brazil into the mainstream of world trade. He instigated a program of privatization, selling off government-owned industries that were viable and closing down those that were not. He tore down many of the protectionist import tariffs and restrictions. And he began the taming of the rampant civil service, trimming the excesses of over-employment.

But his attempt to do the same with the economy failed. His financial plan went the same way as the four other attempts between 1986

LEFT: an oil rig off the Brazilian coast.
RIGHT: an industrial worker takes a break.

and 1995. Each was announced with a macho fanfare and a new currency, and each rapidly lost momentum as inflation returned with a vengeance, reaching a remarkable peak of more than 2,100 percent in 1993.

The Plano Real

There followed two years of continued financial mismanagement by provisional president, Itamar Franco, who had been Collor's deputy. Then, in July 1994, the *Plano Real* was introduced by the then little-known Finance Minister, Fernando Henrique Cardoso. He managed to link the new currency, the *real*, to the dollar in a way that left enough flexibility to enable it to withstand regional financial fluctuations without allowing inflation to get going again.

His election as president later the same year was in no small way a result of the effectiveness of the *Plano Real*. Throughout his first term, Cardoso and Finance Minister Pedro Malan exercised tight fiscal control, bringing inflation down to single figures. The new economic stability brought sighs of relief from both the industrialists and the ordinary citizens of Brazil.

Brazil's manufacturing industry experienced steady growth during the second half of the 1990s, attracting a rush of foreign investment. The election in October 2002 of left-wing Luiz Inacio Lula da Silva made the international capital markets jittery, but the new president is committed to sound financial management.

Brazil in the 21st century has acquired a new confidence. Its industry has survived the opening up of domestic markets to foreign competition, transforming itself into one of the most efficient in the world. Through Mercosul and other trade agreements, Brazil has become both a political and economic leader in the region, avoiding the political and economic meltdown suffered by other countries in the region. But the education system is signally failing to provide the majority of its young citizens with the skills they will need to prosper in the 21st century. This will leave Brazil's vital and growing industries with a damaging shortage of employees of the quality they will need to support their growth. Another major problem is the disparity between rich and poor, which leaves Brazil with huge social and economic problems.

Brazil's predominantly young population (over 60 percent of the population is under 29) is at once one of its major assets and potentially one of its costliest burdens. Well educated and employed, today's young Brazilians will be the driving force behind the country's future prosperity. Badly educated and possibly condemned to a life of poverty, they will instead become a huge financial and social burden.

The right environment

Industrialization is a messy business and Brazil is experiencing all the side-effects seen decades ago in Europe and the United States. Brazilians are well aware that they are getting plenty of criticism from abroad for the damage being done to the Amazon forest by mining companies, gold prospectors, ranchers, woodpulp factories and pig iron mills. And the country is slowly beginning to wake up to its responsibility as a protector of a huge tract of the Earth's surface.

However, although shocking scenes of flaming trees and polluted rivers appear on television in Brazil as frequently as they do elsewhere in the world, Brazilians' view of the problem is somewhat different from that of citizens of some more wealthy countries. Many people feel that they are being criticized for the same crimes as were committed by the rich nations during earlier decades and centuries.

Fortunately, both the government and concerned citizens' groups have taken steps to fight pollution, restrain the worst aspects of exploitation in the Amazon and try to improve the country's image internationally. To continue progressing Brazil will need aid, since priorities such as housing, healthcare and education demand first claim on the government's resources.

The environmental issue is helping to teach this young giant that, like it or not, Brazil cannot solve all its problems on its own. In addition, the world's new set of environmental priorities are giving the country a growing importance.

DON'T LECTURE US!

Brazilians defend themselves against charges of environmental destruction and human rights abuses by pointing to the way the United States has achieved world supremacy while slaughtering both animals and Amerindians, building dirty steel mills, and strip mining once-beautiful mountains.

LEFT: hoeing a sugarcane field.
ABOVE: harvesting coffee.

Future growth

Although in many ways a spectacular success, President Cardoso's government had difficulty in driving through some critical reforms designed to rein in the civil service and exert control over the vastly inefficient and extravagant social security system. This left Brazil with a large and intransigent public spending bill, resulting in a persistent budget deficit.

Meanwhile, Brazil is experiencing unprecedented levels of imports following the removal of trade barriers. Partly, this is due to the release of pent-up consumer demand. But the majority of imports are capital equipment, helping Brazil's industry to modernize and increase productivity. This will strengthen manufacturing output and allow the rapid growth in export sales to continue. The election in 2003 of President Lula, (53 million people voted for him) signaled a new era for Brazil's presence in international trade. He is committed to closer ties with the other members of Mercosul, and greater negotiations with other Latin American countries and the United States on the establishment of new trade agreements.

Minerals will continue to play a key role, having already placed Brazil in the select company of major mining powers. Brazil is a world leader in production of gold and iron ore, as well as "high-tech" minerals such as titanium, vanadium, zirconium, beryllium, niobium and quartz, which are now in great demand.

IRON ORE IN SPADES

Brazil's iron ore production is the highest in the world, with enough reserves in the Carajás region alone to satisfy the entire global demand for the next 500 years.

MERCOSUL: SOUTH AMERICA'S TRADING BLOC

The late 20th-century trend for regional trading blocs did not pass Brazil by. While North America has NAFTA and Europe has the EU, South America has Mercosul (or Mercosur, as it is known in Brazil's Spanish-speaking partner countries).

Mercosul grew out of a long history of ineffectual trade negotiations and treaties stretching back to the 1930s. Progress was impeded by economic and political factors, not least the macho posturing of dictatorial governments during the 1960s and 1970s.

Finally, the Treaty of Asunción of 1991 established the mechanism and institutional structure of Mercosul, a free trade area covering Argentina, Brazil, Paraguay and Uruguay. Like the European Union, this swept away customs posts, set standard external tariffs and outlawed restrictions on trade, effectively ending the post-war years of protectionism and import substitution policies favoured by the military regimes.

If all goes according to plan, negotiations due to be completed in 2005 will achieve the establishment of the South American Free Trade Area, which will include all the South American countries, with a market of 500 million people. Already both Chile and Bolivia have aligned themselves with Mercosul, extending the southern common market to six countries.

The years of rampant inflation filled the coffers of the banks, giving them the resources to develop their expertise and services. The banking system is well developed and stands to benefit enormously from the closer trading and financial links being established with other South American countries.

The single largest import bill for Brazil is oil, so the development of native oil reserves is essential. A major offshore oil exploration project already means that Brazil – one of the world's biggest oil importers in the 1970s – is now capable of producing approximately 60 percent of its needs. Substantial offshore reserves and large deposits in the Amazon, coupled with deregulation in the petrochemical industry, which is opening it up to international investment and expertise, will soon allow Brazil to become self-sufficient. Brazil is also one of the world's leading producers of hydroelectric power.

Decades of isolationism and protectionism have meant that for many people Brazil is associated only with the annual carnival (albeit a spectacular one) and the destruction of the rainforest. Despite having thousands of miles of glorious, sun-soaked, palm-fringed beaches, bountiful areas of natural beauty and good internal air transport, Brazil does not attract the number of tourists it deserves. The potential to develop tourism, particularly in the beautiful but grindingly poor states of the northeast, needs to be taken seriously.

Dubbed the Brazilian Blair for being something of a socialist-capitalist hybrid, President Lula da Silva's first 100 days indicated that he would follow sensible economic policies while not defaulting on the country's US$250 billion public debt. Just two days after his inauguration, he redirected US$760 million earmarked for new fighter jets into programs to help the poor, for which he has secured US$505 million in World Bank loans.

When the people of Brazil elected Lula they voted for change. His challenge is to meet their high expectations: to address poverty and hunger, control inflation, improve the country's industrial performance, and increase its negotiating power within global trade organizations. At the World Economic Forum, in Swwitzerland, January 2003, Lula pledged to awaken "the sleeping giant" that is Brazil. If he succeeds, the Country of the Future may finally become the Land of Today. ❑

LEFT: rail cars loaded with iron ore, Carajás.
ABOVE: waiting for the next wave of tourists to arrive, at the Hotel Tropical, Manaus.

COLORS OF BRAZIL

Patterns of conquest, slavery and immigration still affect race relations in subtle but important ways in this most heterogeneous of countries

Brazil is a diverse nation. Its people share only a common language and a vague notion of Brazil's cultural shape. They worship a dozen gods and their ancestors came from all over the globe. This melting pot is a legacy of Brazil's colonial past. Among the countries of the New World, it is unique. Where the Spanish-American colonies were ruled by rigid bureaucracies and the future United States by a negligent England, Brazil's colonial society followed a flexible middle course. The Portuguese colonists were not outcasts from their native land like the Puritans of New England. Nor were they like the grasping Spanish courtiers fulfilling a brief colonial service before returning home. They were men – and for decades, *only* men – who retained an allegiance to the old country but quickly identified with their new home.

Racial mixing

The Spanish grandees hated the New World, the Puritans were stuck with it, but the Portuguese *liked* Brazil – particularly its native women – and the colonizers' desire married with the beauty of the indigenous females to begin a new race. The first members of that race – the first *true* Brazilians – were *mamelucos*, the progeny of Portuguese white men and native Amerindian women. Later, other races emerged – the *cafusos*, of Amerindian and African blood, and the *mulatos*, of Africans and Europeans.

Octavio Paz, in his essay on the Mexican character, *The Labyrinth of Solitude*, notes his compatriots' ambivalence about race. There is not, in the whole of Mexico, a single monument to the conquistadors, he observes, and yet most *mestiços* (of European and Amerindian parentage) anticipate the time when their blood will be "purified" through miscegenation and their descendants will be able to pass legitimately as white.

PRECEDING PAGES: catching up with the news in Rio, *carioca* style; the colorful streets of São Paulo.
LEFT: white child with black nanny.
RIGHT: blonde European Brazilians.

In Brazil, the fusion of race is more complete. Pedro Alves Cabral is honored by all Brazilians as the country's "discoverer", yet the Amerindian past is not disdained. Diplomat William Schurz, in his 1961 book *Brazil,* notes that numerous Amerindian family names have been preserved. He lists *Ypiranga,*

Araripe, Peryassu and others, some of which belong to distinguished families in Pernambuco and Bahia.

The influence of the Amerindian language is also great. Schurz compiled a list of words from the Tupi-Guarani language that have influenced modern Portuguese and English: *abacaxi, urubu*, and *caatinga* are among the 20,000 indigenous words absorbed into Portuguese, while tobacco, hammock, tapioca, manioc, and jaguar are now in the English vocabulary.

In contemporary Brazil, Schurz might have pointed out, the Amerindian is only a shadow of the other races. Historians believe as many as four million Amerindians lived in the area at the time of the European discovery in 1500. According to Amerindian leader Ailton Krenak, approximately 700 tribes have disappeared from Brazilian soil since that time, having fallen victim to disease, extermination, or gradual absorption through miscegenation. Krenak believes about 180 tribes have survived, speaking 120 languages or dialects. They are mostly on government reservations in Mato Grosso and Goiás or in villages deep in the Amazon.

Brazil's *mestiço* population, meanwhile, has tended to melt into the white category. Only about 2–3 percent of Brazilians, mostly in the Amazon or its borders, consider themselves *mestiços*, but throughout the north and northeast, many nominal caucasians are really *mestiços*.

Gilberto Freyre, the Pernambucan sociologist, brings scholarly eloquence to the subject. In his epoch-making 1936 volume *Casa Grande e Senzala*, Freyre says "every Brazilian, even the light-skinned and fair-haired one, carries about with him in his soul, when not in soul and body alike, the shadow, or even the birthmark, of the aborigine or the negro. The influence of the African, either direct or remote, is everything that is a sincere reflection of our lives. We, almost all of us, bear the mark of that influence."

Starting in colonial days, entire portions of African culture were incorporated wholesale into Brazilian life. Today, they are reflected in

African culture

The history of African and the associated mixed-race people in Brazil has been highly complex. Despite now having the largest black population outside of Africa, Brazilians are known for being ambivalent about their black heritage. In the past, racism existed but was simply denied. In recent years, however, there has emerged an awareness of both Brazilian racism and the rich legacy that Africans have introduced to Brazil.

THE BLEACHING OF BRAZIL

The dominant white classes of Brazil hold deeply-ingrained racist views, yet their male heirs marry supposedly inferior, mixed-race Afro-Brazilian women. The country's unofficial ideology is "Brazilianization," which essentially means a whitening of the population. According to official census records, the Afro-Brazilian population has plunged from 14.6 percent in 1940 to 6.2 percent in 2000. Brazil's caucasian population has also declined. However, the proportion of mixed-race Afro-Brazilians has risen sharply, from 21.2 percent to 38.5 percent. Brazil was a black and white nation in 1940; today, it is increasingly a brown one.

the rhythmic music of samba, the varied and spicy cuisine of Bahia and the growth of African-origin spiritist religions, even in urban centers. And the mark of that influence, as Freyre said, goes far beyond mere religious and culinary conventions.

The Bahian writer Jorge Amado, in his masterly short novel *Tent of Miracles*, showed how strongly Brazilians felt about their racial heritage. He describes how Pedro Arcanjo, a medical assistant and amateur scholar of African and European descent, fought a tide of racism in the 1930s by proving that most of the "First Families of Bahia" had black blood in their veins, the fruit of Brazil's miscegenational heritage.

In the past, many Brazilians would have denied the mark of that influence. A turn-of-the-century painting, *The Redemption of Ham* by Modesto Brocos, is typical. The canvas depicts an elderly black woman sitting on a sofa next to her mixed-race Afro-Brazilian daughter and white son-in-law. The daughter is proudly holding a bouncing pink baby on her knee, while her mother lifts her eyes to heaven as if to say "Thanks be to God!"

Afro-Brazilians' heartland in Brazil is still Bahia. Salvador, one of the country's oldest and most fascinating cities, is a predominantly Afro-Brazilian state capital. Mixed-race Afro-Brazilians are more prominent in coastal regions north and south of Bahia and the vast interior state of Minas Gerais, west of Rio, where slavery was introduced during the 17th-century gold rush.

Change in racial views

Recent years have seen the rediscovery and redefinition of Brazil's African past, including the revision of racist views of history. Brazilian history books at the turn of the century often contained racist passages. One text portrayed Brazil's earliest African slaves as "accepting the most grotesque of fetishes." Another noted that "negroes of the worst quality, generally those from the Congo, were sent to the fields and the mines." The preamble of an early 20th-century immigration law said "it is necessary to preserve and develop the ethnic composition of our population by giving preference to its most desirable European elements."

LEFT: young street vendors.
RIGHT: a porter smiles under a heavy load.

Contemporary social scientists, beginning with Freyre, have catalogued the real achievements of Brazil's earliest black residents. In doing so, they have discovered that the Africans brought far more to the New World than their strong backs. For example, the Africans often possessed highly developed manual skills in carpenty, masonry and mining. Much of the best baroque carving that still graces the colonial churches of Bahia was done by Africans.

In Minas Gerais, the illegitimate son of a Portuguese builder and a black slave woman led Brazilian sculpture and architecture into the high baroque. Antônio Francisco Lisboa, called

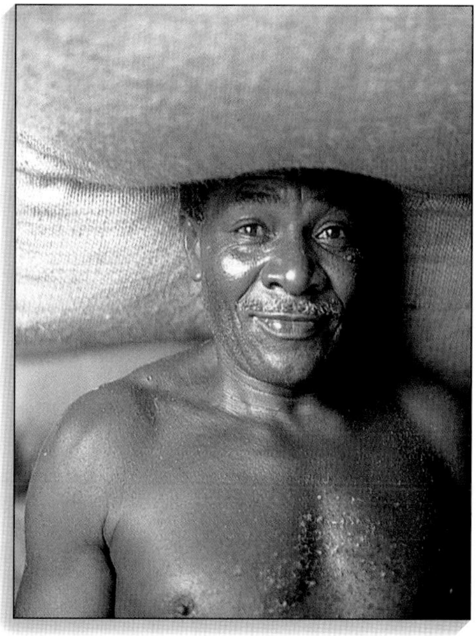

Aleijadinho (the little cripple) because of his deforming arthritis, started late in the 18th century with his elegant São Francisco church in Ouro Preto and the larger, more elaborate, São Francisco in São João del Rei. He also created 78 sinuous and life-like soapstone and cedar carvings at the Basílica do Senhor Bom Jesus de Matosinhos in Congonhas do Campo.

Aleijadinho's miracle is that he created an informed yet innovative artistic idiom at the edge of western civilization. During his 80-year lifetime he never studied art and never saw the ocean. Yet his Congonhas statues are numbered among the greatest collections of baroque art anywhere in the world *(see page 214)*.

In addition to their artistic attributes and economical skills, many Africans – especially the Yorubás of West Africa, who dominated in Bahia – also brought sophisticated political and religious practices to Brazil. Contemporary historians note that they practised Muhammadanism and were literate in Arabic. Their culture was rich in music, dance, art and unwritten but majestic literature. Writes Freyre, "In Bahia, many... were, in every respect but political and social status, the equal or superior of their masters."

FREEDOM OVERDUE

In 1888, Brazil became the last country in the western hemisphere to abolish slavery.

Rebellion against slavery

These proud Africans did not simply accept their bondage. Brazil's previous view of African slavery as "less rigorous than that practised by the French, English or North Americans" has been revised by historians, who note that nine violent slave rebellions rocked the province of Bahia between 1807 and 1835.

A German visitor to a Bahian plantation in the 19th century, Prince Adalbert of Prussia, reported that "the loaded guns and pistols hanging up in the plantation owner's bedroom showed that he had no confidence in his slaves and had more than once been obliged to face them with his loaded gun."

The story of Brazilian slavery is inevitably harrowing. Historians believe 12 million Africans were captured and shipped to Brazil between 1549 and the outlawing of the Brazilian slave trade in 1853. Of that number, about 20 percent, or 2 million people, died on the slave boats before they reached Brazilian shores.

Once in Brazil, white masters treated their slaves as a cheap investment. An African youth enslaved by the owner of a sugar plantation or gold mine could expect to live eight years. It was cheaper to buy new slaves than preserve the health of existing ones.

By 1835, the year of a bloody slave revolt in the interior of Bahia, there may have been more blacks in Brazil than whites. The rising tide of black consciousness and increasing violence against the white ruling classes led four Brazilian provinces to enact racial segregation laws against free men.

When not in revolt, enslaved Africans in the northeast were often in flight. Historians know of at least ten large-scale *quilombos,* or slave retreats, formed during colonial days in the deep interior of the northeast. The largest of these, Palmares, had a population of 30,000 at its peak and flourished for 67 years before being crushed by the colonial militia in 1694. Palmares, like the other great *quilombos* of the 17th and 18th centuries, was run along the lines of an African tribal monarchy, with a king, a royal council, community and private property, a tribal army and a priest class.

In some respect, however, Brazilian slavery was more liberal than its equivalents in other New World colonies. Owners were prohibited by law from separating slave families and were required to grant slaves their freedom if they could pay what was deemed a fair market price.

A surprising number of slaves were able to achieve this liberation, even in the earliest colonial days. Freed slaves often went on to form religious brotherhoods, with the support and encouragement of the Catholic church, particularly Jesuit missionaries. The brotherhoods raised money to buy the freedom of more slaves, and some of them became quite wealthy.

In Ouro Preto, one such Jesuit brotherhood built the magnificent baroque jewel, the Igreja da Nossa Senhora do Rosário dos Pretos, one of the most beautiful colonial churches in

Brazil. In a backlash against slavery and racism, Rosário dos Pretos discriminated against whites.

Brazilian slavery finally came to an end on May 13, 1888, when Princess Regent Isabel de Orleans e Bragança signed a law abolishing the institution. This law immediately freed an estimated 800,000 slaves.

Socio-economic development

Brazil's history of racism and slavery left its nonwhite population unprepared for the 21st century. Today, Afro-Brazilians lag behind in socioeconomic terms, creating a vicious circle that has resulted in persistent discrimination.

There is also a more subtle face to Brazilian racial discrimination. São Paulo's ex-State Government Afro-Brazilian Affairs Coordinator, Percy da Silva, said "while it may be true that blacks are no longer slaves, it is also a fact blacks do not have the same opportunities as whites. We are, to a great extent, stigmatized, seen as inferior. We must show a double capacity, both intellectual and personal, to be accepted in many places, especially the workplace." Thankfully, this has changed with the appointment by President Lula in 2002 of the first black cabinet officals, even though there remain few black diplomats, corporate leaders, or legislators. "The face Brazil shows the world," Percy da Silva said, "is a white face" even though Brazil is more than 40 percent black.

According to São Paulo human rights attorney, Dalmo Dallari, "we have, in our Constitution and laws, the explicit prohibition of racial discrimination. But, it is equally clear that such laws are merely an expression of intentions with little practical effect." Dallari and others point to persistent and widespread discrimination. Blacks barred at the doors of restaurants and told to "go to the service entrance" by doormen at high-rise apartment buildings are among many examples.

LEFT: European immigrants in southern Brazil's *Blumenau Oktoberfest.*

ABOVE: black is the predominant color of the *favelados,* the inhabitants of Rio's slums.

Statistically, the economic condition of Afro-Brazilians was amply documented in a 1999 report published by Brazil's official Geographic and Statistical Institute (IBGE). The report showed that whites formed 53.19 percent of the work force but they earned 71.1 percent of the personal income. Mixed-race Afro-Brazilians, on the other hand, constituted 40.1 percent of the work force but earned only 19.8 percent of personal income. Afro-Brazilians earned 5.2 percent of personal income while accounting for 6.8 percent of the work force. The study also found that 8.5 percent of all whites in the Brazilian work force had college degrees against only 1.1 percent of Afro-Brazilians and 2.7 percent of mixed-race Afro-Brazilians. Around 8.3 percent of whites were described as illiterate against 19.6 percent of Afro-Brazilians and 21.1 percent of mixed-race Afro-Brazilians.

In the past, some scholars have described Brazil as an emerging "racial democracy." This has been seriously questioned against the background of today's subtle discrimination and incipient racial tension. And even if the face Brazil presents to the world is white – 55 percent white, to be exact – there are many cultural groups making up that whiteness. Even in the white sector, Brazil is still a melting pot.

Like the United States, it is a nation of immigrants, and not just immigrants from Portugal, the original colonizing country. Rodrigues, Fernandes, de Souza and other Latin names dominate the phone book in some Brazilian cities. But, in others, names like Alaby or Geisel, Tolentino or Kobayashi, appear more than once.

European immigrants

The presence of many ethnic groups in Brazil dates from the 1850s, when the imperial government encouraged European immigration to help rebuild the labor force as the slave trade declined. The first immigrants were German and Swiss farmers who settled mainly in the three southern states of Rio Grande do Sul, Santa Catarina and Paraná, where the soil and climate were most similar to those in Europe.

For decades, some communities, such as Novo Hamburgo in Rio Grande do Sul and Blumenau in Santa Catarina, were more German than Brazilian. Protestant religious services were as common as Roman Catholic ones, and German rather than Portuguese was the first language of most residents. Such towns still bear the distinctive mark of their Teutonic heritage, with Alpine-style architecture dominat-

ITALIANS IN SÃO PAULO

From the 1870s, Italian immigrants flooded into São Paulo state. Many of them worked on the coffee plantations in the interior, while others entered the growing urban work force in São Paulo and neighboring cities. Within one generation, the Italians were established in the trades and professions; within two they were a new elite, with *nouveau riche* millionaire families such as the Martinellis and the Matarrazzos. One of Brazil's first skyscrapers was the Martinelli Building, built in São Paulo in 1929. A few years later, the 41-story Itália Building went up on Ipiranga Avenue – the tallest building in South America when it was constructed.

ing the landscape and restaurant menus offering more *knackwurst* and *eisbein* than *feijoada.*

Later in the 19th century, Italian immigration predominated, especially in the state of São Paulo. Unlike the first immigrants, many of the Italians were skilled workmen and a smattering were white-collar professionals.

By the turn of the century, Brazil was hosting immigrants from around the globe. According to records held by the foreign ministry, a total of 5 million immigrants arrived on Brazilian shores between 1884 and 1973, when restrictive legislation was adopted. Italians sent the greatest number, 1.4 million; Portugal sent 1.2 million people, Spain sent 580,000, Germany 200,000 and Russia 110,000, including many Jews who settled in São Paulo and Rio.

Asian immigrants

The call for immigrants reached far beyond the borders of Europe. Starting in 1908, with the arrival in Santos Harbor of the immigrant ship *Kasato Maru,* 250,000 Japanese transferred from their homeland to live permanently in Brazil. The descendants of those hardy Japanese, who were fleeing crop failures and earthquakes in their native islands, still live in metropolitan São Paulo, most visibly in the Japanese Liberdade district *(see pages 200–1)*.

The Middle East sent 700,000 immigrants, mostly from today's Syria and Lebanon, during the early 20th century. Two sprawling commercial districts in two towns – around Rua do Ouvidor in Rio and around Rua 25 de Março in São Paulo – feature hundreds of shops owned by people of Middle Eastern origin.

Regional diversity

Despite the impact of mass communications and the trend toward political centralization, the process of molding diverse populations into a single "Brazilian race" is far from complete. One result is the continued strength of regionalism in Brazil.

The nation's intricate pattern of ethnic heritage includes differences so pronounced that Euclides da Cunha, author of the seminal *Os Sertões* (a saga about the southern soldiers who marched in the 1897 Canudos campaign in Bahia), wrote, "they were in a strange land now, with other customs, other scenes, a different kind of people, another language even, spoken with an original and picturesque drawl."

Strangely, when regionalism comes to the fore, all the shades of the racial spectrum seem to blend together. The white *gaucho*, with his stoic Catholicism and diehard *machismo*, still stalks the southern plains. The aggressive *paulistas* (from São Paulo city) who practice religions ranging from Islam to Shintoism and have a varied ethnic origin, staff the nation's banks, industries, and offices. The *carioca* (from Rio de Janeiro) seems to practice all religions, but is actually agnostic.

The *mineiro* (from Minas Gerais), stolid and hard-working whether white, mixed-race, or black, is almost Puritanical in his worship, severe in his maleness, and infinitely patient and practical in his politics. The *nordestino* (from the northeast) is of brown or black skin, light of heart, colorful in personality, and practices a flamboyant blend of Catholic and African religions.

And finally, there is still the *sertanejo*, the man of the back country wilderness, whose religious beliefs may include a profound respect for the works of the Devil. His origins may reflect Amerindian, caucasian, and African roots. ❑

LEFT: São Paulo construction workers exemplify racial diversity. **RIGHT:** *favela* children.

BRAZILIAN FOOD AND DRINK

Reflecting its African, European and Amerindian racial mix, Brazilian cuisine has a delicious variety of tropical, exotic, hearty and spicy flavors

From giant Amazonian river fish to succulent beefsteaks, and with an abundance of tropical fruits and vegetables, Brazilian food offers something for all tastes and appetites. The most traditional dishes are variations on Portuguese or African foods, but the staple diet for many Brazilians remains rice, beans and *farinha*, dried and ground manioc.

Although few herbs are used, Brazilian food is seasoned and mild. Brazilians enjoy hot pepper *(pimenta)* and local malagueta chilies, but pepper sauce is served separately for personal choice.

REGIONAL SPECIALTIES

The spiciest Brazilian food is found in Bahia, where an African influence can be tasted in the dendé palm oil and coconut milk. Another Brazilian favorite is the *churrasco* or barbecue, which originated with the southern *gauchos* roasting meat over an open fire. Minas Gerais has hearty pork-and-bean cuisine and *queijo minas* cheese. A few exotic dishes can be found in the Amazon region, including those prepared with *tucupi* (manioc leaves, which numb the tongue). There are also many delicious varieties of tropical fruit, and river fish is the staple in the Pantanal. *Salgadinhos* are Brazilian savory snacks, served as appetizers with a round of beer. Most desserts are very sweet and are made out of fruit, coconut, egg yolk or milk.

▷ ***CACHAÇA***
Unique to Brazil, this strong liquor is distilled from sugarcane and often steeped with fruit and herbs.

▷ MARKET TRADING
Regular local markets, selling fresh fruit and vegetables, are perfect examples of the country's agricultural abundance.

△ RED PEPPER
Although cayenne pepper is readily available, it is only in Bahia state that food is spicy hot. The rest of the country uses just a "pinch", for a piquant flavor.

◁ FRESH FISH
Seafood is plentiful all along the coast, but the northeast region is particularly famed for its fish, shrimp, crabs and lobster. One of the tastiest varieties of fish is *badejo*, a sea bass with firm white meat.

▽ TROPICAL FRUIT
One of Brazil's finest features is the wonderful range of fruit, such as fresh guavas. There's always something exotic in season.

◁ ***FEIJOADA***
Brazil's "national dish" consists of black beans and a variety of dried, salted meats. It was originally made out of leftovers to feed slaves.

▽ **TEA BREAK**
Green tea *(chimarrão)*, sipped through a silver straw fitted with a strainer, is a *gaucho* tradition still favored in southern Brazil.

△ **ROASTED NUTS**
Cashew nuts grow in abundance in Brazil and are particularly popular in Bahian dishes.

▷ **SWEET SNACK**
Chunks of sugar-cane *(cana)* are sold on sticks as a snack, particularly popular with children.

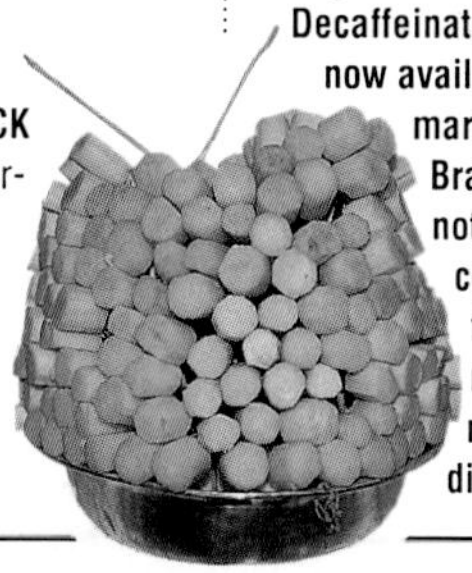

BRAZIL'S FAVORITE DRINK

Brazil and coffee *(café)* are two names synonymous with each other. Money earned from coffee sales did much to improve the country's economy in the early 20th century, and it is still one of Brazil's most successful exports.

Brazilian coffee is roasted dark, ground fine, prepared strong and drunk with plenty of sugar. Coffee mixed with hot milk *(café com leite)* is the traditional breakfast beverage in every region of Brazil.

Once breakfast is over, it is served black in tiny *demitasse* cups, and never with a meal. These *cafezinhos* or "little coffees", offered to visitors to any home or office, are served piping hot at all *botequins* – male-dominated stand-up bars where locals gather to chat and gossip. There are even *botequins* that serve only *cafezinho*. However you like it, Brazilian coffee makes the perfect ending to a good meal.

Decaffeinated coffee is now available in supermarkets, but as Brazilians do not favor the concept, finding it in restaurants may still be difficult.

National

THE AMERINDIANS

Today, the survival of Brazil's indigenous people hangs in the balance, all hopes pinned on the return of stolen and looted territories

"Do not trust the whites. They are the men who control the lightning, who live without a homeland, who wander to satisfy their thirst for gold. They are kind to us when they need us, for the land they tread and the rivers they assault are ours. Once they have achieved their goals, they are false and treacherous."

– Rosa (Borôro Amerindian), 1913

The first contact Brazilian Amerindians had with "white" civilization was in 1500, when the Portuguese explorer, Pedro Cabral, reached the shores of their country. Brazilian historians have long estimated that there were about four million Amerindians in Brazil at that time, but more recently, some anthropologists have begun to believe there might have been far more, possibly as many as 30 million. This is because many old Amerindian settlements are still being uncovered as new areas of Amazon rainforest are cut down.

Until recently, anthropologists also agreed that the ancestors of all Amerindians had migrated from Central Asia across the Bering Straits and down through the Americas about 10,000 years ago. However, ancient pottery finds in the Amazon and the wide variety of Amerindian cultures have led some experts to believe that Amerindians have lived in Brazil much longer, and may have come across the Pacific.

Tropical forest provides abundant timber but is a poor source of stone, and the Amerindians' shifting lifestyle left few lasting monuments that are considered the mark of advanced civilizations. Yet any assumption that Stone Age Amerindian culture was primitive has been challenged by the most recent archeological discoveries which suggest that substantial, permanent, and highly organized cities existed in pre-Columbian Amazonia. So, once again, the accepted view of Amerindian history is under new scrutiny.

LEFT: some Amerindians are tempted by modern cultural influences and technology.

RIGHT: a young Kayapo girl from the Amazon, with *genipapo* – vegetable dye body paint.

Mixed messages of white men

Early Portuguese explorers were greatly impressed by the Amerindians' innocence and generosity. One writer also noted: "Their bodies are so clean and so plump and so beautiful they could not be more so." They were regarded as "noble savages" and some Amerindians were

shipped to Europe to be paraded before royalty.

Thus, in the very early post-contact years, the Amerindians were relatively well-treated, but soon the colonizers' greed and the serious shortage of labor on their sugar plantations led them to overcome any moral scruples. Raiders – known as *bandeirantes* – traveled up from São Paulo to bring back Amerindians as slaves. Their brutality was legendary, and appalled Jesuit missionaries who opposed Amerindian slavery. At the same time, both groups of white men unwittingly introduced "white diseases", such as measles and influenza, against which the Amerindians had no immunity. Hundreds of thousands of Amerindians died as a result.

The Jesuits tried to protect and convert the Amerindians by forcing forest-dwelling tribes to live in *aldeias* or settlements. Their missions replaced Amerindian culture with Christianity and hard labor, yet at the same time, they encouraged the Amerindians to resist enslavement. There is still debate over whether Jesuit missions defended or helped crush the Amerindians.

Slavery and violence

In 1755, Portugal freed all Amerindians from slavery, but the effects were negligible. The Jesuits were soon after expelled and their missions in southern Brazil and Paraguay put under the control of lay directors who could make profits from the Amerindians' forced labor. Under the Jesuits, the seven Guaraní missions held 30,000 Amerindians. By 1821, only 3,000 survived. Amerindian labor became scarce, hence the importation of African slaves.

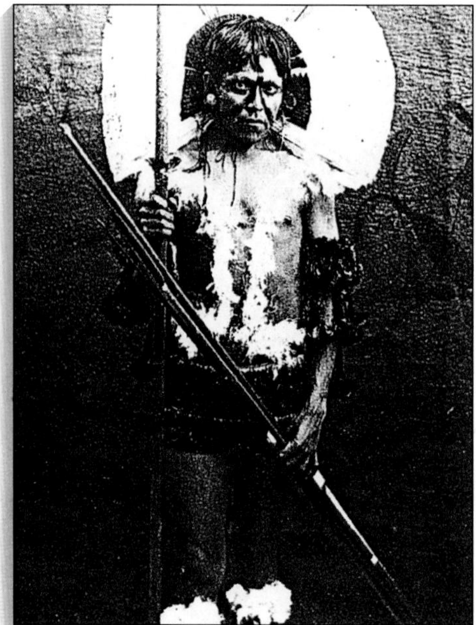

CONTEMPT OF THE COLONIZERS

By the 19th century, the few surviving Amerindians had failed to adapt to life in crowded, unhealthy *aldeias* (settlements), often laboring as debt slaves and at the mercy of alien diseases, such as influenza and smallpox, to which they had no resistance. Disease, slavery, and the introduction of alcohol had corrupted Amerindian culture, and whites consequently regarded the Amerindians as lazy, shiftless and incapable of integration. This attitude fueled the belief that they were an inferior race. "Immigration by a vigorous race will, in the struggle for survival of which Darwin speaks, annihilate them [the Amerindians] by assimilation," wrote a Brazilian intellectual.

The Amerindians worked on plantations or were forced to row expeditions up rivers, to work on road building or in royal shipyards. Accustomed to shifting agriculture and a forest existence, they responded to the harsh life imposed on them by fleeing up the tributaries of the Xingú and Madeira rivers to impenetrable sanctuaries – where some still survive today.

The advance of cattle ranchers across the northeastern plains and of gold miners to the south resulted in bloody conflicts. By the time the Portuguese royal family fled to Brazil in 1807, whites outnumbered Amerindians. A new edict was issued permitting enslavement of hostile Amerindians in the south. In 1845, the Amerindians were restored to mission life by the government, just in time for their labor to be exploited for extracting rubber from the rainforest. However, as the need for Amerindian labor declined, extreme racial "solutions" came to the fore. In 1908 Hermann von Ihering, director of São Paulo Museum, defended the extermination of all remaining Amerindians in the southern states of Santa Catarina and Paraná who threatened German and Italian immigrants. In the early 1900s, *bugreiros*, hunters hired by the colonists, prided themselves in poisoning, shooting or raping Kaingang Amerindians who attempted to stop a railroad line.

The fightback

Fewer than a million Amerindians survived, but public opinion began to turn. In 1910, the explorer and humanist soldier, Cândido Mariano da Silva Rondon – who instructed his troops: "Die if you must, but never shoot!" – formed the Indian Protection Service. It was nevertheless too late to stop the widespread destruction of Amerindian cultures. In 1960, anthropologist Darcy Ribeiro found that one third of the 230 tribes known to exist in 1900 had vanished.

Over the four centuries following Portuguese colonization, the new Brazilians have gradually occupied their vast country. As the agricultural frontier moved west and then north, the Amerindian population suffered greatly. One group after another became extinct, and the

Amerindian population dropped to 200,000. When, in the 1960s and 1970s, the government built a huge network of roads across the Amazon jungle and encouraged white settlers to move in, it seemed that the few remaining Amerindians would soon be exterminated. But since then they have staged a remarkably successful comeback.

The Panara

At the end of the 1960s, the Panara (or Krenakorore, as they were known at the time) were rumored to be giant Amerindians, fierce and elusive. They were seen as an obstacle in the drive to open up the interior of Brazil to economic development through the construction of a network of huge roads across the hitherto isolated Amazon basin. The Panara were contacted by anthropologists just days before the construction teams building the Cuiabá– Santarém highway reached their land.

Once contacted, the Amerindians were devastated by disease and reduced to begging beside the new road that cut their land in two. In February 1975, 79 demoralized survivors were taken by plane to the Xingú Amerindian reserve over 1,000 km (620 miles) away. This action caused outrage at home and abroad. The Panara – and other Amerindian groups that received similar treatment as a consequence of the government's Program of National Integration for colonizing Amazonia – were portrayed as "victims of the miracle", that is, groups of traditional people threatened with cultural, if not physical, extinction because of the military regime's obsesssion with obtaining high economic growth at almost any price.

With the help of a dedicated group of anthropologists, the Panara waged a campaign to regain their land. The political climate, in Brazil and internationally, changed so that their demands began to receive a more sympathetic hearing, and more than 20 years after their expulsion the wheel turned full circle. In October 1995, a small group of Panara Amerindians was taken by plane back to their traditional lands in northern Mato Grosso and southern Pará in the Amazon basin. They found much of the land devastated by gold mining, cattle ranching, and logging. Even so, the Panara are slowly reconstructing their old life, with its myths, rituals, songs, dances, and rhythms of work. At the same time, they have identified a large area comprising more than 490,000 hectares (1.2 million acres) of unoccupied forest, which was finally recognized in the Brazilian courts as their reserve in 1996.

Thus the attitude of the establishment has evolved since the creation of the Xingú Park, a natural "refuge" where several different tribes coexist. Yet the reserve, though flawed, could still be considered a success. The Xingú retain their tribal organization because contact with "civilization" is limited. That said, many of them have developed business activities and since 1982 when one of their leaders was elected to the national congress, many others have been elected as government officials.

LEFT: Capoyó indian dressed as chieftain, circa 1870.
RIGHT: a Kayapo man wearing a brilliantly colored feathered headdress.

Amerindian affairs are now under the juristiction of FUNAI (Fundação Nacional do Indio), a government agency, which is generally inefficient and has been found to have been guilty of corruption. FUNAI is responsible for demarcating Amerindian tribal land as protection against the tide of ranchers, miners, and loggers. Claims have been weakened, however, by Decree 1775, signed by the then president in 1996, which allows these very groups to challenge the demarcation process and, in the process, invade the Amerindians' land.

Staging a recovery

The Panara's return to their ancestral land is symbolic of a revival in the fortunes of Amerindian groups. After reaching their lowest point in the 1970s, they are gradually recovering. One of the surprises of the 2000 census was that numbers had increased by 138 percent since 1990; there are now 700,000 Amerindians in the country. Once the demarcation process is complete, Amerindian territories will cover about 10 percent of Brazil's total landmass.

However, sharp reductions in government funding have meant that demarcation, scheduled for completion by 1993, is still not complete.

And even when the land is marked out, there is no guarantee that the reserve will be respected, especially in view of the 1996 decree favoring the interests of non-indigenous land occupiers.

Gold panners frequently invade the large reserve allocated to the 27,000-strong Yanomami who live near the border with Venezuela. These illegal prospectors, known as *garimpeiros* – whom the government is either unable or unwilling to police – have brought with them violence, pollution, and disease epidemics.

Other Amerindian groups find it difficult to deal with the strains imposed by the modern world. There are about 25,000 Guarani-Kaiowa Amerindians in some 22 villages scattered over largely deforested scrubland in Mato Grosso do Sul in central Brazil. Without adequate provision of reserves to sustain them, many are forced to work as farm laborers. A large proportion of these Amerindians are unable to cope with the traumatic change this brings to their lifestyle and there has been an alarmingly high rate of suicides, even among children.

In recent years, however, even the Guarani-Kaiowa Amerindians have cautiously started to fight back. They have carried out a series of *retomadas* – retaking the lands from which they had been expelled. *Retomadas* are often difficult and violent, as the new occupants, predominantly cattle-rearers, struggle to retain their hold on the land. But the Amerindians are determined: in 2000, Amerindian groups throughout Brazil staged a well-publicized demonstration at the country's five-hundreth "birthday" celebrations.

Survival

Modern Brazilians are reminded of their country's indigenous roots daily, through place names, foods, the rituals of *umbanda* – and even the national passion for cleanliness. However, the unhappy history of Amerindian contact with whites means that today visitors are not welcome in reserves administered by FUNAI. Only bona fide researchers who are willing to apply in advance and wait months, will get through the bureaucratic curtain erected by FUNAI and Rio's Museu do Indio, which processes applications from foreigners.

Amerindians today throughout Brazil are in crisis. Many are at risk of losing their identity as traditional ways of life are eroded. Others – such as those in the Tapejana – are starving because they have no land. Some are taking desperate measures. In March 2003, the Cauruaia in the south west of Pará seized hostages in protest at miners on their reserve poisoning the rivers and wildlife with mercury in order to extract gold. In the same month, Amnesty International announced concern that a leader of the Xucuru community in Perambuco may have been killed.

Although indigenous groups welcomed the election of President Luiz Inacio Lula da Silva, 2003 saw a disturbing escalation of murders and attacks from North to South. ❑

LEFT: young Yanomami mother with baby.
RIGHT: Xingú men play long pipes in a reservation ceremony.

VENDE-SE
ESTA-CASA

RICH MAN, POOR MAN

Shocking surveys of wealth distribution and the living conditions of the poor paint a very unpleasant picture – but, at last, change may be on the cards

Although no map will ever show the distinction, there are two Brazils, inhabiting the same space and living side by side. One is a country of enormous potential, with vast human and natural resources, where an individual can discover a world of immense privilege and status. The second country is a land of deprivation, of blight and human misery. There are no opportunities in this second country and little hope – unless its inhabitants can escape to the other Brazil.

Since it became a nation, Brazil has been an imperfect, largely unjust society, sharply divided among social classes, with a small minority exercising complete control over political and economic life. Unlike other nations of the Americas, Brazil won its independence only to become a near carbon copy of its colonial past. Rather than rid itself of the trappings of monarchy bestowed by Portugal, Brazil embraced them. The country went from colony to empire, in the process replacing Portuguese noblemen with Brazilian clones and establishing elitist rule as a guiding precept.

Since that time, while the composition of the elite has changed (the nobles became landholders, then rubber barons, coffee barons, and today are the industrial and business lords of the southeastern states), the basic divisions of society have remained unchanged: a few on top, a few more on the next level and a great many more on the wide base of the Brazilian pyramid.

Huge inequalities

Brazil is one of the most unequal societies in the world. The richest 1 percent of the population earns 12 percent of the country's income, while the poorest 50 percent earns just 10 percent. According to a World Bank report published in 2001, only five other nations in the world – all in Africa – have greater income disparities.

PRECEDING PAGES: the wealthy secure their homes like fortresses. **LEFT:** improvised slum housing, built on wooden stilts and made of salvaged materials. **RIGHT:** poor Brazilian girl plays with a homemade kite.

Poverty in Brazil is not only relative but absolute. Over 40 million people live on US$48 or less a month and a third of the population survive on under US$1 a day. Some of them can be seen on the streets collecting cans for recycling. They earn three *reais* for one kilo (62 cans), normally a day's work.

About 32 million people in the country are starving. Education, when available, is through the underfinanced and often overcrowded public school system. Health care relies on a precarious public health system and housing conditions are deplorable, with millions living in shanty towns and tenement slums.

The rift between the world of the rich and the world of the poor is huge. Wealthy youngsters feel nothing in common – not even a shared humanity – with the very poor who scratch out a living in the shanty towns around Brazil's mega-cities. A wealthy, largely white elite lives in its own world of chauffeur-driven cars, luxury homes protected by heavily fortified fences and teams of security guards. Taking in a second layer of society, the 30 percent of Brazilian households that enjoy a middle-class or even higher standard of living have access to good health care, regular nutritional intake, decent schooling for their children and more than adequate housing. Their Brazil is a country of modern consumer goods, smart shopping centers, fashionable boutiques, high-rise apartment buildings, medical clinics, chic restaurants, new cars, private schools and university education. Meanwhile the poor, largely black population is employed as cheap labour, usually as maids, cooks and gardeners.

Social apartheid

The elite-driven nature of Brazilian society means that those on top have an authority that goes virtually unchallenged. There are white-collar crimes in Brazil but there are no white-collar criminals, for the elite is careful to protect its members. For the residents of the other Brazil, on the other hand, there are no protective barriers between themselves and the hardships of everyday life. The rift between the two worlds of rich and poor is as deep as the one found in South Africa before it started dismantling the apartheid system. For this reason, the phrase "social apartheid" was coined.

A MORALITY TALE

Very early one morning in Brasília, five young men were driving home from a night out on the town. They saw a figure whom they assumed to be a beggar, dozing at a deserted bus stop. The lads went to an all-night filling station and bought two liters of gasoline. They poured it over the beggar and – "just for a laugh" they later said – threw a match at him. The young men fled in their car. The beggar died from his burns.

Incidents like this are by no means infrequent, particularly in Brasília. But this time, the youths were brought to trial. A witness noted down the car's license plate, and the youths were identified. One was the son of a federal judge. Another's step-father was a former judge of the electoral tribunal.

The "beggar" turned out to be an Amerindian leader – Galdina Jesús dos Santos from the Pataxo tribe in southern Bahia. He had traveled to Brasília to take part in a big demonstration in support of the rights of indigenous people. Returning late, Galdino had fallen asleep while waiting for a bus back to his boarding house. One of the lads later said that he would not have mistreated the man if had realised that he was an Amerindian, "not a beggar."

Later, a federal judge in Brasília dismissed murder charges brought against the young men, saying that they had not intended to kill him.

Children's stories

The social divide is evident most dramatically in the lives of its children. UNICEF estimates that 7 or 8 million live or work on the streets, and that 36 percent of Brazilian children are poor. Claudio, is 11 years old; his brother, Felipe, is nine. They live in a tiny, one-room shack with eight other children and seven adults in the Rocinha shanty town in the south of Rio de Janeiro. At night, they all sleep together – siblings, cousins, mother, father, grandmother, aunt, and uncle – in two beds. The shack has no water, except for that seeping down the walls, and in common with neighboring huts, it gets its electricity from an illegal, improvised connection from an overhead power line.

There are, however, other children worse off than these. A few miles from Rocinha, in the smarter areas of Ipanema and Copacabana, live 12-year-old Roberto and eight-year-old Felipe. They follow the street markets, held each day in a different street, and survive from the tips they earn by pushing home shopping trolleys for middle-class customers. At night, they sleep under viaducts and are constantly sniffing glue, to which they are both addicted. They are "street kids", youngsters who have lost all contact with their parents. They are undernourished, have frequent attacks of diarrhea and suffer chronic skin complaints, including scabies.

The severe social crisis has spawned widespread violence. Foreign visitors – and Brazilians – are frequently robbed. Tradesmen in the big cities, exasperated by repeated lootings by adolescent boys too young to be sent to prison, have organized death squads to kill them. With more and more youngsters involved in drug-trafficking, boys frequently die in shoot-outs in the battle for territory in the big cities.

LEFT: gracious living for the wealthy.
ABOVE: a riverside slum in Bahia.

THE LANDLESS MOVEMENT

While a staggering 60 percent of Brazil's farmland lies idle, 25 million people seek out a living in poorly paid agricultural jobs. But the Landless Rural Workers' Movement (MST – *Movimento dos Trabalhadores Rurais Sem Terra*), established in 1985, has made huge headway.

The movement has become a major left-wing political presence, and MST members have taken to occupying non-productive lands belonging to big landowners.

Over 250,000 families have been given land titles to more than 6,070,000 hectares (15 million acres) as a result of MST iniatives.

The lives of rich children could not be more different. It is not uncommon for a rich Brazilian to spend over US$100,000 in a single night. This was what Luis Estevão de Oliveira Neto, a leading businessman, spent on a party to celebrate his daughter's 15th birthday. "Every father tries to provide the best for his daughter, according to his means," explained the proud, some would say misguided, father.

Birth control

On the issue of birth control, the poor themselves are taking the initiative, as Catholic principles are set aside in favor of common sense.

Women faced with overwhelming difficulties in trying to care for a big family, have begun to take control of the one factor in their lives over which they have ultimate power – reproduction.

As many as four out of ten Brazilian women of child-bearing age have been sterilized, usually after giving birth. This has become the preferred method of birth control in a country where less drastic means are among the most expensive in the world. But this option is often chosen because of a lack of information about other contraceptive methods – and, in the poorest areas of Brazil, politicians frequently offer women free sterilization in exchange for a vote. Many women subsequently regret their decision.

FEEDING TIME FRENZY

Picture a weekend afternoon in Brasília. Two teenagers were sitting in their car eating cheeseburgers at a McDonald's drive-in. To amuse themselves, they were casually tossing potato fries out of the window, as if feeding dogs. But instead, it was street children who were scrabbling on the ground after the food. Other customers watched, laughing.

Nevertheless, Brazil has experienced one of the fastest declines in population growth ever seen in the world, second only to China. Today the annual population growth across the country is estimated to have dropped to little above 1 percent, with the total figure now at around 150 million people.

Government aid

Over recent years, there have been the first timid signs of change for the better. Government initiatives in the 1970s and 1980s failed, largely because of economic instability and an inefficient bureaucracy. Then, an anti-inflationary plan, in 1994, put an end to runaway inflation and led to a significant improvement in the living standards of the poor. By 1998, the plan's primary objective was achieved, and had reduced the annual inflation rate down to 1.5 percent.

The present government, headed by President Lula, announced their "Zero Hunger" program, the aim of which is to feed the 46 million Brazilians who survive on less than US$1 a day. This program marks the first time that the near-starvation of many Brazilians has been given a priority over the country's foreign debt. The World Bank pledged US$5 billion to the initiative and its president, James Wolfensohn, said that he was extremely impressed by the government's commitment to curb spending.

Brazil hosted the World Social Forum in 2003, under the banner "Another World is Possible." The mood was highly optimistic, and Lula announced "Power is within the reach of the people... we need growth to redistribute income." ❑

LEFT: page-boy and bridesmaid at a society wedding in Rio de Janeiro.

RIGHT: Brazil's biggest and best-known shanty-town slum, Rocinha, Rio de Janeiro.

THE BODY BEAUTIFUL

From football to Carnival – the Brazilian celebration of physical beauty takes many forms and crosses all class barriers

Brazil was known as the land of beautiful people long before supermodel Gisele Bundchen strode onto the international catwalks. Images of gorgeous half-naked women in glitter and feathers, gyrating to samba, captured the global imagination long ago. And then there are those world-famous Brazilian bikini bottoms – two tiny triangles held together with string, giving them the nickname "dental floss".

Work that body

The cult of the beautiful people is rooted in the country's everyday life, and particularly in Rio de Janeiro. Dubbed the "marvelous" city, it is as if Rio's inhabitants aspire to be as physically perfect as her stunning geographical features. Every morning as soon as the sun rises, image-hungry creatures appear on Ipanema beach, the epicenter of chic.

Trim, tanned octogenarians in tiny trunks salute the sun in a series of yoga stretches. Hulking teenagers heave themselves off gym equipment on the beach as they study the sea. "Muscles for Everyone" screams a sign in enormous red letters in a gym window. In Brazil, the obsession with the perfect body is a democratic one, where age or poverty are no barriers in the quest for beauty. The philosophy is that if you want a good body, you have to work at it.

Cities in the south of Brazil rival those in the United States in terms of obsession about health. Health food shops are found throughout the country and "natural" restaurants are the latest craze. Wheatgrass (known locally as *clorofila*) is widely available as a supplement in fresh juices. Drunk for its health-giving properties, it is said to eliminate toxins and generally cleanse the body.

Spa resorts are a relatively new concept in the country, but the natural focus on the body and beauty, the incredibly scenic landscape, and the seemingly endless coastline make it an obvious setting for this kind of holiday.

LEFT: Brazilian model Roberta Close at Rio's carnival.
RIGHT: tall and tanned and young and lovely…

The Girl from Ipanema

The bossa nova song, "The Girl from Ipanema", released in 1963, has become a classic with a continuing resonance. Written by Antonio Carlos Jobim and Vinicius de Moraes, the two composers were inspired by a girl, or *garota,* who walked past their local bar in Ipanema every

morning on her way to the beach. Her lithe brown body spawned the now legendary words:

Tall and tan and young and lovely
The girl from Ipanema goes walking

Foreign visitors and Brazilians alike still flock to the bar "La Garota de Ipanema," – which was the composers' viewpoint, – to see if they can spot the young beauty.

The girl is now 55 years old, but her sex appeal has hardly faded and in 2003 she appeared on the cover of Brazilian *Playboy* magazine with her daughter. And Ipanema is still where the beautiful people live and congregate. Its beach is the beach to be seen at, its streets are filled with chic boutiques, and its restaurants, bars, and clubs are among the most fashionable in the country. Brazil has long been the designer center of South America. Gisele gave the fashion industry a huge boost and it has become a booming sector of the economy over the past few years, increasing by 24 percent in 2000.

Natural beauty

One of the disturbing aspects of Brazil's – or at least the Brazilian media's – portrayal of beauty is its endemic racism. Flick through the pages of any national magazine or look at the country's television programs and you will see a

white vision of beauty. Most models and actors are pale-skinned, with pale hair and light-colored eyes. Gisele is from the south of Brazil where there are a large number of German, Italian, and Polish immigrants and as such represents an essentially Caucasian vision of beauty.

Roberta lives in Cidade de Deus, the *favela* (shantytown; *see page 164*) made famous by the 2003 film. She is 18 years old and a model who has the cat-like good looks of a young Naomi Campbell. She is both stunning and spirited and has had the good fortune to have been educated by a cooperative that has given her modeling skills and a knowledge of fashion. But she has to battle the preconceptions of an industry that assumes that because she is black she is not marketable. Roberta works with four other models who have appeared in international magazines. It costs more than they can afford to produce the book of photographs needed to be a successful model, and although they have been lucky enough to have someone make a portfolio at a discounted rate, model agencies refuse to take them seriously.

"They think we are inferior because we come from a *favela*, and assume we are all drug traffickers". In response, they have set up a project known as *Lente dos Sonhos*, or "Lens of Dreams," and work at passing on the skills they have learned to other young hopefuls in their community.

Plastic pageants

Body fascism is the flip side of this phenomenon, in which individuals try, rather tragically, to live up to an ideal. It is virtually impossible to be a model, or even an actor, without plastic surgery. Brazil is the plastic surgery capital of the world, a country where men have manicures and teenagers have liposuction. Vinicius is 20 years old, handsome, and with a good body. He earns little, but pulls up his T-shirt to reveal a small scar where he has had liposuction. He is saving up to have the minor surgery perfomed again, even though he can barely pinch a centimeter from his stomach.

And in Brazil, botox can be bought and stored at home in the fridge, to be administered when needed. There is even a plastic surgery television show, "Before and After", which is shown daily throughout the country.

Interestingly, going under the knife is not perceived as an act of vanity, a betrayal of self, or a sacrifice, but as a human right. Hospitals offer free surgery for scars and the top plastic surgeon in Brazil – who operated on Nicki Lauda – provides free operations one day a week to the poor in Rio. Maids, and others in very poorly paid professions, pay for surgery by hire purchase, as those in the West would pay for the status symbol of a car.

In the run-up to Carnival, the country practically lines up for operations and surgeons work around the clock. In 2003, Brazil ran out of silicone, just as it does every year before Carnival when demand for breast and buttock implants reaches record levels. At Carnival, so many people want their bodies altered for the most extravagant celebration of the physical form anywhere on the planet.

Brazil also has an estimated 10,000 transsexuals, often known as shemales, who go under the knife regularly. Roberta Close is said to be the country's most beautiful woman, and she is in fact a man. She now lives in Switzerland where she is recognized as a woman.

Many of Brazil's shemales work in the sex industry and are often indistinguishable from women. There is an area in downtown Rio where so many of them congregate at night that it is known as Brazil's very own "Silicone Valley".

Julianna Borges, who competed in Miss Universe 2002, made no secret of the fact that she has undergone 19 surgical procedures.

One noticeable effect of globalization is the increasing demand from Brazilians for silicone breast implants. Traditionally, the focus has been on buttocks, but the Western ideal has started to filter through.

Sexual health

There is a darker side to the endemic physicality of Brazilians. Confident of their looks, they are also confident of their sexuality and sex is not a taboo in the way that it is in other parts of the world. The liberal attitude toward sex attracts foreign visitors who are willing to pay for the privilege, and the recent devaluation of the real has only worsened the problem.

Brazil, sadly, is the largest center of sex tourism outside Thailand. According to UNICEF it has one of the worst levels of child prostitution anywhere on the planet. Accurate figures are hard to come by, but they range from 500,000 to an astonishing 2 million children in the country. With one of the highest Aids rates in the world, Brazil has been forced to address the issue of sexual health. The country has aggressively pursued an anti-Aids program, involving the free distribution of needles and a bold educational campaign, which has become a model for the rest of the world. Condoms can even be found in the minibars of hotel rooms in major cities.

Furthermore, Brazil is the only country in the developing world in which free Aids treatment is provided. Bypassing the large pharmaceutical companies, the country produces its own generic copies of drugs for a fraction of the cost. As a result, the incidence of the disease has been cut by over half in the past ten years.

The Beautiful Game

Brazilian soccer players are famed the world over for their grace of movement when playing their national sport and commentators often remark how they seem to perform a kind of ballet around the pitch. Somewhat less well known are the *capoeira* martial art masters. *Capoeira* is rooted in the country's history; it was developed in the 18th century by slaves brought over from Africa. Forbidden to practice any form of aggression, they disguised their method of self-defense as a dance.

Capoeira is performed in a circle to music produced by a berimbau – a one-stringed, steel African bow – and a tambourine. It can be seen in tourist areas throughout the country and particularly in Salvador. Invariably men, the practitioners typically have muscular upper bodies due to the strength needed to carry out what has been described as a kind of Brazilian breakdancing. It involves athletic moves combining flying kicks, one-handed and jumping handstands, and balletic back-flips. Although a form of fighting, the emphasis is always on beauty of movement. ❑

LEFT: Brazilian models such as Gisèle Bundchen are in great demand on the international fashion circuit.
RIGHT: in search of a tan and a photographer.

SAINTS AND IDOLS

Brazilian religious beliefs are derived from an often bizarre blend of Amerindian, African, and European traditions, which feed the people's mystical tendencies

Visitors to Brazilian beaches in December, January and February often find flowers, cakes of soap still in their wrappers or perfume bottles tossed on a shore that is strewn with burnt-out candles. These are the offerings made by the followers of what is perhaps Brazil's largest "religion" after Catholicism: *umbanda*, which honors the African goddess of the sea, Iemanjá.

In the Vale da Aurora (Valley of the Dawn – christened after the movement of the same name), not far from Brasília, thousands of worshipers who believe in the imminent end of the world have set up a community under the protection of the spirits of Aluxá and Jaruá, with altars honoring Jesus Christ, White Arrow and the medium Aunt Neiva *(see page 91)*.

In the northeastern city of Juazeiro, women wear black every Friday, and on the 20th day of every month, they are in mourning over the death of Padre Cicero, who according to legend did not really die, but was translated (like Enoch, Elija and Santa Catarina) to heaven. It is widely believed that Padre Cicero's fingernail clippings possess therapeutic properties *(see page 89)*.

Also in the northeast, farmers draw magic circles around their sick cows and pray to Santa Barbara (or her African-cult equivalent, Iansã) that their cows will not die. The same farmers place six lumps of salt outside their homes on the night of Santa Lucia, December 12. If the dew dissolves the first lump, it will rain in December; if it dissolves the second lump, January; and so on. If no dew dissolves the salt, drought will plague the *sertão*, the backlands of the northeastern region.

Spiritual energy and diversity

The more time you spend in Brazil the more you discover that the country's inhabitants are charged with a spiritual energy that more often than not fails to fit into the patterns of the better-known world religions.

Brazil has the largest Catholic population in the world, and 11 million Evangelicals – twice the number of ten years ago. Yet millions of the faithful light candles at more than one altar without feeling hypocritical. It is also one of the few countries in the world in which you can choose the century in which you want to live. São Paulo, Rio de Janeiro and several other large cities offer a hectic urban lifestyle that is very much of the present day. However, small towns and rural areas have a way of life that differs little from that of 100 years ago. There are even pockets of the Middle Ages where religious cults live in communities and await the end of the world with varying degrees of anxiety or expectation. And should you wish to go back to the Stone Age, there are a few Amerindian groups living in the Amazon basin who have still not been introduced to metal tools.

LEFT: robed worshipers in supplication at Vale da Aurora outside Brasília.

RIGHT: Catholic priest in pensive mood.

Brazil is one of the few countries on Earth where you can choose one of several religions, or religious movements, and immerse yourself in all the internal and external expressions of it. You might choose the philosophy-based doctrines of existential Protestantism or the evangelical movement, or you might accept the liberation theology of rebel Catholic priests, or choose between modern and traditional Judaism.

Amerindian influence

The nation's Ameriindian heritage is partly responsible for the Brazilians' deep-rooted mystic beliefs. Even today, some Amerindian tribes continue to make religious artifacts, though such objects are losing their original meanings. The clay sculptures of the Carajá represent birth and death. The myth of the origin of medicinal plants is associated with the ritual flutes of the Nambiquara. The figures on Aparaí baskets represent the myths of that tribe, and the Borôro, Macro, Je, Urubu, and many other tribes wear diadems, bracelets, or necklaces made of feathers of birds emblematic of magic, health, disease, or death. Amazonian Amerindian men evoke dead ancestors rising out of totem tree trunks by painting their bodies with symbolic colors, wrestling, dancing to the music of giant flutes, and chanting day and night.

The tribal villages themselves assume a mythical configuration. The north huts and the south huts of the Borôro follow the trajectory of the sun, and to the west is a circular area called "Path of the Souls."

Cults of African origin

African rites are the second major influence in Brazil's religious culture. The most African of the rituals practised in Brazil is *candomblé*, which occurs primarily in the state of Bahia.

During a *candomblé* ritual, when priestesses are ordained they have their heads ceremonially shaved and having the blood of a hen or goat smeared on their foreheads along with chicken feathers. The ceremony is accompanied by *atabaque* drums, chants in various African languages and frenetic dancing that is kept up until the initiates fall into a trance.

Voodoo cults, similar to those still practiced in Haiti and elsewehere in the Caribbean, have developed roots in a few parts of Brazil. In Maranhão, situated in northeastern Brazil, and on the northern national border with the Guianas, the descendants of those slaves who managed to escape to freedom cultivated African tribal patterns and cults far removed from the domination of the white man. These practices continued until early in the 20th century.

Tracing ancestors

One by-product of Brazil's thriving African religious cults has been the maintenance of an oral history among the Afro-Brazilian community. It has been far easier for black people in Brazil to trace their ancestry back to Africa than for African Americans in the United States to do the same.

The leading priestesses of *candomblé*, such as the late Olga Olekatu and Mãe Menininha de Gantau, could recite the names of their African ancestors and the ancestors of members of their community, going right back to generations still in their African homeland. They described in detail how their ancestors were captured, bound and transported on slave ships to Brazil. The priestesses passed this knowledge on to the new spiritual leaders of the community, who memorized the vast genealogy.

This is similar to the system common in parts of Africa where, even today, spiritual leaders are the scribes and public notaries, learning by heart the genealogy of their people.

SPIRITUALIST BOOKS

Texts written by Brazilian spiritual leader, Chico Xavier – said to be transcodifications of messages from the life beyond – have sold to his followers in millions.

Religious blending

The mixture of Amerindian, African and European cults results in a unique form of syncretism or blending of religions in Brazil, where Catholic Santa Barbara is Iansã of the Afro-Brazilian cults, where Iemanjá, the goddess of the sea, often assumes the form of the Virgin Mary and Xango, the god of thunder, is transposed into St George the dragon slayer. Syncretist cults such as *umbanda* may also include the god of war, Ogun, god-like figures called *orixás*, and demon-like forces, *exus*, which are part of the *candomblé* and other African rituals.

Umbanda belongs to a mystic movement called "spiritism," which includes African-inspired figures as well as Brazilian semi-deities and mediums such as Pai João, Caboclo and Pomba Gira, plus the mystical theological concepts of Allan Kardec, a European. Some of the most popular images on *umbanda* and spiritist altars are St Cosme and St Damyan, St George slaying the dragon, Iemanjá in a white flowing dress, or the cigar-smoking figure of Pai João.

FAR LEFT: cult offering on a Rio beach.
LEFT: chicken blood is dripped on a *candomblé* initiate.
ABOVE: some follow both Christianity and African cults.
ABOVE RIGHT: parading a saint through Salvador.

Iemanjá is sometimes characterized as the Virgin Mary, sometimes as a sea goddess or a mermaid. Every December 13, in Praia Grande, São Paulo, and also every December 31 in Rio de Janeiro and February 2 in Bahia, Iemanja's worshipers offer flowers, perfume and face powder to the goddess at the edge of the sea (Iemanjá is a vain goddess, appeased only by flowers and cosmetics). If the offerings sink into the water or are carried out to sea, Iemanjá is said to accept them. If they return to shore, however, she has rejected them.

Religious imagery from Europe arrived with the first Portuguese colonizers, who brought

with them the most frequently worshiped of the Catholic saints and, above all, the crib nativity scene.

Every Christmas time for seven consecutive years, families were supposed to mount nativity scenes, or suffer divine retribution. Each year a new figure was introduced and new clothes were added to the old. In some crib scenes, Brazilian animals feature, including the armadillo and Amazonian butterflies.

Patron saint

The patron saint of Brazil is Nossa Senhora de Aparecida, the Virgin of the Conception. Three centuries ago, a broken terracotta image "appeared" in a fisherman's net in the Paraiba River between Rio and São Paulo.

Today the Basilica of Aparecida, located on the highway between Rio de Janeiro and São Paulo, houses the terracotta image and receives more than 5 million pilgrims a year. This incredible visitor record is exceeded only by the basilica of the Virgin of Guadalupe in Mexico and the shrine of Czechestowa in Poland. A number of legends, stories, superstitions, and presumed miracles have been woven around the image. In 1999, a religious theme park linked to the shrine was constructed at a cost of US$70 million.

In the late 1970s it was broken by a fanatic and restored by specialists from the São Paulo Art Museum. Every year on the saint's day, October 12, hundreds of thousands of worshipers will flock to the sanctuary, some crawling all the way on bleeding knees.

Another popular representation of the Virgin Mary is Our Lady of the "O", a euphemism for the pregnant Virgin. The upper clergy tried to suppress the cult of this figure in favor of Our Lady of the Conception (without a distended belly). Some Brazilians call Our Lady of the "O", "Our Lady of March 25," to mark Christ's conception nine months before Christmas. Due to the perils of childbirth, Our Lady of the "O" is worshiped by pregnant women.

Curative properties of saints

Other saints are believed to have therapeutic or healing properties. Santa Lucia is supposed to cure bad eyesight and blindness. Santa Barbara protects worshipers against lightning. Single girls pray to Santo Antonio to find them a husband. It is usual for the Santo Antonio idol to carry the Christ Child in his arms, but in a simplistic form of magic, a marriageable girl will remove the Christ Child to make the saint so upset he will do everything in his power – even find the girl a husband – to get little Jesus back again. Only after the wedding does the successful bride return the Christ Child to Santo Antonio's arms.

São Bras, the Bishop, protects those who pray to him against sore throats and choking on fish bones. Another popular saint, carved in wood or molded in plaster of paris, is Saint Jude, who always wears tall boots. This is the same Saint Jude who is known in Europe as the patron of lost causes.

Many images that once bore a religious connotation have survived without their former mystical aura. An example derives from *carrancas*, which were wooden figureheads attached to the prows of paddle-wheel steamers and other vessels sailing up and down the São Francisco River from 1850 to about 1950. Today, on the beach in Nazare, Portugal, fishermen paint eyes on the prows of ships to "see" the dangers underwater. Similar prow figures served the same purpose in Guiné and other parts of Africa.

EXTREME DEVOTION

It is said that one man walked 1,600 km (1,000 miles) carrying an enormous cross to fulfill a "promise."

The Brazilian *carrancas* were carved in the form of monsters, originally to frighten off the spirits of the waters that were a menace to shipping. The *carranca* gazed downward, and the crew aboard ship saw only the elaborate mane so as not to be "frightened" by its terrible features. The São Francisco River is rich with legends of water spirits, "the Water Bitch," "the Water Monster," and the *Caboclo da Agua* (the "Backwoodsman of the Water"), which send ships down to a watery grave.

Carved angels and saints

The spiritual force of wood-carving continues to this day in the São Francisco Valley and the Brazilian central plateau, where the Brazilian artist Geraldo Teles de Olivcira sculpts rings of winged forms mounted like spokes on a wheel, resembling the circular medieval representations of the hierarchies of angels. Oliveira's angels, however, look alike and have no differentiating features like the medieval distinctions between the cherubim, seraphim, archangels, thrones, powers, glories and dominations.

A popular subject for Brazilian artists through the centuries has been the crooked angel. Some of the carved and gilded angels in the São Francisco church and other churches in Bahia have malicious features – they are wall-eyed, cross-eyed, or presbyopic.

In a similar tradition, Maurino Araujo, a contemporary sculptor from Minas, creates his angels, priests, monks, and the centurions in the manger scene, with bulging guppy eyeballs, one of which looks north-northwest while the other looks south-southeast.

As well as angels, the arts and crafts fairs all over Brazil are literally flooded with sculptures of the saints. Among the most original of these are the no-neck images of Santa Ana made by wood-carvers from the northeastern state of Ceará.

Hundreds of wood-carvers have also sculpted images of the most famous religious figure

of the northeast, Padre Cicero, and literally millions of Plaster of Paris images have been sold throughout the country.

The cult of Padre Cicero

Some of Padre Cicero's followers honor him by wearing black on the day of his death (June 20). Cicero was considered a messiah who would turn the dry backlands into a green paradisiacal garden where hunger and poverty would cease. A verdant valley of the region was named the *Horto* or Garden of Gethsemane, and the city of Juazeiro was called the "New Jerusalem." Some of Padre Cicero's followers even collected his fingernail clippings,

LEFT: a living Iansã goddess-cum-*macumba* dancer taking part in the Carnival.
RIGHT: statue of Padre Cicero, 19th-century populist leader-cum-faith healer from the *sertão* of northeastern Brazil.

which were said to have magical properties.

Padre Cicero first gained fame when an elderly woman, Maria Araujo, received the host from his hands at Mass, then fell on the floor in convulsions. Blood in the form of the "sacred heart" was said to appear on the host. Balladeers wandered throughout the *sertão* singing the praises of the miraculous priest and the "miracle of the Sacred Heart."

More skeptical observers, suggested that Maria Araujo suffered from tuberculosis and had coughed up blood, or suffered from bleeding gums. One detractor, Pedro Gomes from nearby Crato, hinted that the host was made of litmus paper and that Padre Cicero's "miracle" was nothing more than an acid test known to every student of chemistry. Despite such cynicism, Padre Cicero's fame spread throughout the land like wildfire and one balladeer even went so far as to sing: "Padre Cicero is one of the three of the Holy Trinity."

The Canudos War

The "miracle of the Sacred Heart" (or "host") occurred in 1895, shortly before the outbreak of the Canudos War, in which troops of the newly founded Brazilian Republic were sent to crush a movement led by Antonio Conselheiro, a religious fanatic who prophesied a rain of stars and the imminent end of the world. The Brazilian government thought Conselheiro represented the deposed Brazilian emperor, while Conselheiro and his followers thought the leaders of the new republic represented the Antichrist because they refused to recognize religious marriages.

The republic sent thousands of troops to stamp out Conselheiro's community in Canudos, in Bahia state. Conselheiro's men repelled four government incursions, but in 1897 the army got the upper hand and slaughtered thousands of Conselheiro's followers, including women and children. Some of those who survived wandered to Juazeiro and swelled the ranks of Padre Cicero's worshipers.

Through wood-carvings, songs and poems published in chapbook form, the Padre Cicero legend has been carried forward. A statue of the priest was built in Horto in the 1960s and his church has become a popular shrine that annually manages to attract thousands of followers.

JUZEIRO'S VOTIVE OFFERINGS

The church in Juazeiro is filled with *ex votos* (votive offerings) carved in wood in the shape of injured limbs or parts of human bodies. When someone is cured of an illness they fulfill a promise by carving an image of the wounded part of their body and, after making a pilgrimage to Juazeiro, hang the carving in the *ex voto* chamber of the church as a token of gratitude.

Churches in Caninde and Salvador are filled with *ex votos*, the more recent ones made of wax at the encouragement of the priests, who melt them down and sell them as candles. There are delicately carved femurs, tibias, hands, elbows, pockmarked heads, eyes, perforated abdomens, and so on.

One elderly woman who watched over the *ex voto* room in Juazeiro was famed for the curses she hurled at anyone who tried to steal the votive offerings: "Steal those eyes and Padre Cicero will blind you. Steal those lungs and Padre Cicero will give you tuberculosis. Steal that leg and Padre Cicero will curse you with leprosy."

One of the most famous Padre Cicero woodcuts is called "The Girl Who Turned into a She Dog Because She Cursed Padre Cicero on Good Friday." Metamorphosis, or the transformation of a human into an animal, is a punishment frequent in Brazilian chapbooks, doled out when someone violates the moral and religious codes of the region.

Since the death of Padre Cicero, numerous messianic cults have appeared, of which the most famous is found in the northeast and centered around Frei Damião, a Calabrian priest who arrived in Brazil in his youth and who preaches with the same fire and brimstone images used by other prophetic figures over the past three centuries.

Brasília's millennium sect

Thought by believers to be the center of a magnetic field giving off cosmic energy, the city of Brasília has attracted various modern religious cults. The best known is the Valley of the Dawn movement, based in a nearby valley of the same name.

The believers have built an enormous temple filled with new deities and religious figures that include Aluxá, Jaruá, White Arrow – an Amerindian deity – and the medium Aunt Neiva, the founder of the movement. About 60 km (35 miles) from Brasília, the Valley of the Dawn is currently the largest such center in Brazil.

Aunt Neiva founded the movement in 1959 and moved to the town of Planaltina in 1969. Today the Valley has 27,000 inhabitants, schools, restaurants, a very simple hotel and two police officers assigned by the Brasília police department.

On arriving at the Valley of the Dawn, visitors will see dozens of women in long robes decorated with silver sequins shaped as stars and quarter moons. The men wear brown trousers, a black shirt and ribbons that cross their chests, and they carry a leather shield. These are the mediums who lead thousands of the sect.

Aunt Neiva believed that there were about 100,000 Brazilians with the powers of a medium, and she herself registered 80,000, according to her follower Mario Sassi. "Two thirds of humanity will disappear at the end of the millennium, but we, here in the Valley of the Dawn, will be saved," Aunt Neiva preached. The millenium has past and they are still there. They believe that the third millennium started many years ago, and we are now in a period of improvement and transition.

The Valley of the Dawn is the latest in a long line of messianic movements all over Brazil. It is a nation that has always been synonymous with mystic forces and religious hope. ❑

LEFT: dazzling gilt altar of the Igreja da Ordem Terceira de São Francisco, Salvador da Bahia. **ABOVE:** paying tribute to the saints at Bom Jesus da Lapa, Bahia state.

CARNIVAL AND OTHER FESTIVALS

Rio's Carnival has a history as interesting as its parades are spectacular, and the party continues during all manner of festivals throughout the country

Brazilians are some of the world's most musical, fun-loving people. This image has for decades drawn tourists, ever since Fred Astaire and Ginger Rogers danced *The Carioca* in the breezy 1933 Hollywood musical *Flying Down to Rio*. Brazil's many attractions, including Carnival, "The Biggest Party on Earth," are deeply rooted in the nation's ethnic and racial heritage.

Carnival's roots are European, although experts disagree over the origin of the name. According to one school of thought, the word *carnival* comes from the Latin *carrum novalis,* a Roman festival float. Another opinion is that it stems from the Latin *carnem levare*, "putting away meat," since Carnival marks the last days before Lenten abstinence.

The Romans had more than 100 festivals during their year, of which the most famous was the December Saturnalia, marked by the temporary disappearance of class distinctions. Slaves and masters dined at the same table, drank the same wine and slept with the same women. Elements of Saturnalia were incorporated into Christmas and Carnival. The latter disappeared during the Dark Ages. When it came back, it was better than ever. Again, it was sexual license and the inversion of social roles that typified Carnival.

The prankster's festival

In Brazil, pre-Lenten observances have existed since colonial days. However, until the 20th century, they were a time for the prankster rather than for good-natured celebration. This aspect of Carnival was called *entrudo* and featured stink bombs and water balloons. *Entrudo* was so bad, decent citizens spent Carnival locked in their homes. One of those who didn't was architect Grandjean de Montigny, who died of pneumonia in 1850 after being doused with water during Carnival. It wasn't until the early 1900s that a stop was finally put to *entrudo.* The indiscriminate tossing of confetti and streamers, still a part of Carnival, is all that remains of the bad old days.

The fancy-dress ball was part of European Carnival as early as the 18th century. Paris and Venice had the best masked Carnival balls. This custom hit Rio in 1840 with a chic event at the Hotel Itália on Praça Tiradentes, but that ball lost money, and it wasn't until 1846 that a second one was held, this time in the uppercrust district of São Cristóvão.

The first modern Carnival ball was the High Life, at a Copacabana hotel in 1908; guests danced the polka and Viennese waltzes. The formal City Ball was inaugurated in 1932 at the Teatro Municipal. By then there were a hundred fancy-dress balls in Rio de Janeiro at Carnival time.

For Rio's working class, music, dance and drink were, and still are, the main Carnival

PRECEDING PAGES AND LEFT: the Carnival generates energy and excitement.
RIGHT: children dress up as country bumpkins for the Dia de São João party.

diversions. A Portuguese immigrant, José Nogueira Paredes (nicknamed Zé Pereira), is credited with originating the first Carnival club. One of his ideas was to get everybody in the club to play the same kind of drum, creating a powerful, unified sound. This technique became the basis for the modern samba school *bateria* or percussion section.

The working- and middle-class clubs, called *blocos*, *ranchos* or *cordões*, played European-origin ballads known as *choros*. In the 19th century, they often had charitable or political aims, and were also active off-season. Many of these predominantly white clubs still exist,

including the Clube dos Democráticos, which annually kicks off the downtown street Carnival.

Carnival parade

One of the main contributions of the clubs to modern Carnival was the parade, complete with elaborate costumes, wheeled floats, and appropriate musical accompaniment. Parade themes stressed Bible stories, mythology, and literature.

The first parade was organized in 1855 by a group grandly named *O Congresso das Sumidades Carnavalescas*. They marched before an elite audience including the emperor. Featured were overdressed Cossacks and tableaux depicting scenes from French history and *Don Quixote*. By 1900 the annual downtown parade of such groups, called *Grandes Sociedades*, had become the highlight of Carnival.

Black people first became involved in Carnival in the late 19th century. This was partly due to the northeast drought of 1877, which brought many freed slaves, along with their music and dance traditions, to Rio in the 1890s. Today's celebration of Carnival in Rio has three main features: frenzied street events, traditional club balls, and the samba parade.

The parade was taken off the streets in 1984 when the Sambódromo, designed by Oscar Niemeyer, was completed.

Street Carnival draws thousands of revelers, many dressed as clowns, television personalities or animals. The most common sight is men dressed as women; for example, the *Bloco das Piranhas* is a group of men who always turn up kitted out as prostitutes. A few years ago the Carnival costume prize was awarded to *The Young Widows*, a group of men splendidly dressed as middle-class women.

Carnival nights belong to the club balls. Among events attracting both *cariocas* and tourists are nightly bashes at the Sírio-Libanês, Flamengo, Fluminense, Scala and Monte-Líbano clubs. The contest for best costume is held at several balls and features outrageous get-ups which depict everything from medieval troubadours to Roman Catholic archbishops.

The samba centerpiece

But the undisputed centerpiece of any Rio de Janeiro Carnival is the main Samba School Parade. The samba parade is the most African of the Carnival events due mainly to the popularity of the dance, which is a mix of European folk influences and African techniques.

Modern samba music dates from the 19th century, when the crude tones of the former slaves met the stylized European sound of Rio. The word "samba" is believed to derive from the Angolan *semba* describing a ceremony in which tribesmen were allowed to select female partners from a circle of dancers. In Brazil during colonial times, the rhythmic music of *semba* and the dance that accompanies it were prohibited by the Jesuits as excessively erotic.

Today the main samba schools that parade in the Sambódromo are judged by a government-appointed jury. Each school's presentation must have a central theme, such as an historical event or personality, or a Brazilian Indian legend. The theme embraces every aspect of the school's presentation. Costumes must accord with historic time and place. The samba song must recount or develop the theme and the huge floats that push ponderously down the avenue must detail it through the media of papier-mâché figures and paintings. In 2000 it was agreed that the central theme for all the top samba schools would be the 500th anniversary of Brazil's discovery by the Europeans.

Each school's presentation includes the "opening wing," the *Abre-Alas*, consisting of a group of colorfully costumed *sambistas* marching next to a large float. The float depicts an

LEFT: a patterned sea of dancers at the Rio parade.
ABOVE: performers in luxurious feathered costumes float past the packed grandstand.

SAMBA HISTORY

The first samba school was called *Deixa Falar (Let Them Talk)*, founded by the black residents of Rio's Estácio District in 1928, and its first parade was in 1929. Participants followed no fixed route and were poorly organized, but their size and the cleverness of their routines made them different.

It wasn't very long before other black districts set up rival organizations. By 1930, there were five groups and so many spectators that police had to clear a special area around Praça Onze for their parade. These early groups practiced on school playgrounds, hence the name samba "schools".

open book or scroll and is, in effect, the title page of the school's theme. Behind the *Abre-Alas* is a line of formally dressed men, the *Comissão de Frente*, or Board of Directors, who are chosen for their dignified air.

The real event begins with the appearance of the *Porta Bandeira* (Flag Bearer) and the *Mestre Sala* (Dance Master), dressed in lavish 18th-century formal wear. The *Porta Bandeira* is a female dancer who holds the school flag during an elaborate dance routine with her consort. The bulk of the samba school follows on behind, including the small army of percussion enthusiasts known as the *bateria*. Their role is

to maintain a constant rhythm in order to help the other members of the school keep up with the tempo of the samba song.

Behind the *bateria* are the major samba school *alas*. These groups of *sambistas* illustrate aspects of the school's theme through their costumes. If the theme is an Amazon myth, one of its main *alas* might be *sambistas* dressed as Indians; another could have its members dressed as Amazonian animals. The compulsory *ala das Baianas* group consists of dozens of elderly women dressed in the flowing attire of Bahia. They honor the earliest history of samba.

In between the major *alas* are lavishly costumed individuals depicting the main characters of the school's theme. They are known as *Figuras de Destaque* (Prominent Figures), and they are often played by local celebrities. The preferred personalities for these roles are voluptuous actresses. There will also be groups of dancers known as *passistas*. These are agile young men and women who often stop to perform complicated dance routines.

Visual extravaganza

Finally, there are the giant Carnival floats called *Carros Alegóricos*, created from papier-mâché and styrofoam, which present the major motifs of the school's theme. The impact of

the floats is primarily visual, and critics argue that these extravaganzas detract from the music which, they insist, should be the mainstay of the parade.

The man who practically invented the form taken by the contemporary samba parade, Joãozinho Trinta, attacked the "folkloric" view a few years ago in a famous comment: "Intellectuals want poverty, but the public doesn't. It wants luxury." Later, he pointed out that the strong visual elements were needed to make the parade appeal to foreign tourists and, more especially, local television viewers.

Besides the glitz and glitter of the floats, Joãozinho Trinta invented what was for a while another popular aspect of the modern parade, the presence of beautiful, topless young women on the Carnival floats.

The announcement of the winning schools is made on the Wednesday after Carnival, and this is one of the biggest events of the year in Rio. Losing schools are rarely satisfied with the results and cries of fraud are common. Meanwhile, the winners go back to the clubhouse for a celebration that lasts until the following Saturday when the top scoring schools get to parade again.

Carnival in the northeast

Rio is not the only Brazilian city with a tradition of fervent Carnival revelry. Many experienced travelers prefer Carnival in the northeast's coastal cities of Salvador and Recife, where non-stop street action is the highlight.

The centerpiece of Carnival in Salvador (capital of Bahia State) is a glittering music festival on wheels called *Trio Elétrico*. The celebration started in 1950 when a hillbilly singing act called *Dodô and Osmar* drove a beat-up Chevy convertible through the city during Carnival week playing pop and folk tunes for anyone who would stop to listen. In subsequent Carnivals the concept was perfected. Instead of convertibles, Bahian musicians started using flat-bed trucks with flashing lights, streamers and elaborate sound systems, and they added a third performer.

Today, there are dozens of *Trio Elétrico* groups, with carefully planned schedules and three routes. Praça Castro Alves was the traditional headquarters of Bahian Carnival but increasingly the Barra-Ondina stretch is becoming the focus. The *Trio Elétrico* repertoire is dominated by samba, a hopped-up northeast dance music called *frevo*, and a new style called *deboche*, which blends traditional Carnival sounds with rock-and-roll.

The preeminent Carnival music of Recife (capital of Pernambuco state, population 1.4 million) is *frevo*. Described by folklorists as recent, *frevo* is a corruption of the Portuguese word for boiling *(fervura)*. *Frevo*, in other words, it ignites the passions of its listeners.

While Carnival in Bahia moves horizontally, as fans follow their favorite musicians through the city streets, in Pernambuco the movement is vertical – dancers seem to leap up and down like ballerinas in double time.

Frevo may have evolved as a musical accompaniment to *capoeira*, the devilishly complex northeastern dance style which is also a martial art. But modern *frevo* has been simplified musically and its listeners freed to invent their own dance routines. The result is that Recife Carnival revelers dance a myriad of tortured styles, some of which have gained fame and peculiar nicknames such as "The Crab" and "The Screwdriver."

FAR LEFT: a young performer dazzling the crowds.
LEFT: animal faces of Carnival.
RIGHT: pounding out the samba rhythm.

THE ALTERNATIVE CARNIVAL

Followers of African-origin religions bring a darker, more mysterious element to Carnival in the northeast. In Salvador, performers of the *afoxé* conduct subdued, reverent processions during the four days of Carnival. They dress in flowing satin robes and carry banners and canopies. Monotonous music, often sung in African languages, provides the eerie accompaniment.

In Recife, too, Afro-Brazilians maintain a parallel Carnival tradition. *Maracatu*, like *afoxé*, is a procession that mixes theatrical and musical elements. The central figure is a queen protected by a canopy and surrounded by elaborately costumed consorts.

Skilled *frevo* dancers are called *passistas* and they all wear knee britches, stockings, a floppy shirt and a colorful umbrella. The attire is a throwback to colonial days, when a variety of African cultural elements combined to create *capoeira*. The umbrellas probably derive from the ornate canopies once used by African kings.

Christmas in Brazil

Although Carnival is probably the world's most exhausting holiday, Brazilians do muster enough energy for the other major dates on the Roman Catholic calendar. Befitting the world's largest Catholic country, Christmas is Brazil's chief religious and family observance.

Most Brazilian children believe that Santa Claus (called Papai Noel in Brazil) distributes gifts to families around the world on Christmas Eve. He enters each home through an open window, and leaves presents in shoes that have been left for this purpose on the floor or the window sill. He wears his familiar red suit and travels in an enormous sled drawn by reindeer.

The Brazilian belief in Santa Claus is remarkably similar to that of the Europeans and the North Americans because of relatively recent influences. Brazilian Christmas in the 19th

FESTIVALS IN THE SALVADOR DE BAHIA

At New Year, while the rest of Brazil is honoring Iemanjá, Salvador (Brazil's former capital) celebrates the colorful festival of *Bom Jesus dos Navegantes*. A procession of small craft burdened with streamers and flags carries a statue of the Lord Jesus of Seafarers from the harbor to the Boa Viagem church. Thousands line the beaches to watch. Legend has it that sailors participating in the event will never die by drowning. (A similar procession takes place on the same day in Angra dos Reis, 150 km/90 miles south of Rio.)

In mid-January, Salvador prepares for another spectacle unique to this city that so loves pageantry – the *Festa do Bonfim*. Central to the event, which takes place in a Salvador suburb, is the Washing of the Steps at the Bonfim Church. Scores of Bahian women, dressed in traditional flowing garments, scour the stairs of the church until they are sparkling white. Crowds throng the tree-shaded church square to witness the women's labor. Visitors may take part in a Bahian tradition by buying colorful Bonfim ribbons from hawkers in the square. Tie the ribbon around your wrist with several knots, each knot being a wish. When the ribbon accidentally breaks, your wishes will be granted – but only if the ribbons were a gift, so the trick is to buy and then exchange them.

Iemanjá, the festival of the Queen of the Seas, is celebrated in Salvador on February 2.

century was a more religious and family oriented celebration than it is today. The custom was to serve a lavish Christmas Eve supper, then attend midnight mass followed by a procession. Instead of a Christmas tree, most families displayed a nativity scene, called a *presépio*.

The contemporary celebration of Christmas in Brazil had its origin in the turn-of-the-century influence of German immigrants, who introduced the Christmas tree, gift-giving and Santa Claus. The usual commercialism, including the department-store Santa Claus, pushed the trend. One aspect of Christmas hasn't changed, however – the Christmas Eve supper. Turkey, *rabanada* (a kind of French toast) and ham still adorn many dinner tables as main courses. Brazilian families also consume a variety of nuts and dried fruits, including figs, chestnuts, almonds, hazelnuts, raisins and dates.

Brazil's most popular New Year's Eve celebration takes place in Rio de Janeiro, where crowded club balls are a rehearsal for Carnival. An elaborate firework display splashes brilliant many-colored hues across the velvet sky at midnight.

New Year's wishes

The best place to observe the New Year's celebration is on one of Rio's beaches, especially Copacabana. Hundreds of *Filhas-de-Santo*, white-robed priestesses of Brazil's African religions, launch makeshift wooden vessels on the waters. The tiny boats are filled with flowers and gifts for Iemanjá, the Queen of the Seas. When the tide carries one of the gift-laden boats to sea it means Iemanjá will grant the gift-giver's wish. If the vessel washes the gifts back, the wish has been rejected.

Another colorful event from the Roman Catholic calendar is the *Festa do Divino*, held just before Pentecost Sunday. Two of Brazil's most strikingly beautiful colonial-era towns – Alcântara in the northeast state of Maranhão and Paraty, 250 km (150 miles) on the coast south of Rio – feature some classic *Festa do Divino* celebrations.

Townspeople dress in colonial attire, with many of them playing roles of prominent figures from Brazilian history. The climax is a visit from the "emperor," who comes for a procession and mass held in the church square. In a gesture of royal magnanimity, he frees prisoners from the town jail. Strolling musicians, called *Folias do Divino*, serenade the townsfolk day and night.

LEFT: Dida Banda, an *afoxé* carnival group, Salvador.
ABOVE: samba band performing with perfect balance.

The June festivals

Soon after Pentecost begins one of Brazil's most interesting celebration cycles, the June festivals. Feasts of Saints John, Anthony and Peter all fall in June – a good excuse for an entire month of festivities.

The feast of Saint Anthony, patron of lost possessions and maidens in search of a husband, begins on June 12. Strictly religious observances dominate this saint's day, but feast days for Saints John and Peter are festive. Saint John's days are June 23 and 24, and are characterized by brightly illuminated balloons filling the skies and bonfires blazing through the night. Saint Peter's feast days are last, June 28 and 29. Fireworks, ample food and drink and folk music are the elements for celebrating this occasion. The saint is especially honored by widows, who place lighted candles on their doorsteps during the festival.

Most June festivities take place outdoors. Participants dress up like country people, or *caipiras*. Country music, square dancing and mock wedding ceremonies (at which the bride may appear pregnant) feature at the most authentic June festival parties.

In the São Paulo suburb of Osasco, Brazil's largest bonfire, measuring some 20 meters (70 ft) high, is lit during the last week of June. Consisting entirely of long-burning eucalyptus logs, the fire takes a week to burn itself out.

October celebrations

October in Brazil is also a month-long cycle of religiously inspired celebrations, including three of Brazil's most characteristic festivals. One of these events, Nossa Senhora de Aparecida, on October 12, is also a national holiday.

In October 1717, "the miracle of Aparecida" occurred in Guaratingueta, situated about halfway between Rio and São Paulo. The colonial governor of São Paulo was passing through the town at lunchtime when he stopped at a

fisherman's cottage demanding a meal for his party. The fisherman and two friends hurried to their boats on the Paraíba River but failed to catch any fish. So they prayed. When they cast their nets again, they pulled a small black statue of the Blessed Virgin Mary out of the river. With the image aboard their craft, they landed a catch that nearly burst their nets.

This story quickly spread to the surrounding countryside, and in 1745 a rustic chapel was built to house the statue. Mainly because of the shrine's strategic location on the Rio–São Paulo highway, the cult of Our Lady of Aparecida grew and, in the mid-19th century, a church more grand than the first was built.

The idea of building a third church was suggested as early as 1900, when a Vatican-decreed Holy Year brought 150,000 pilgrims to Aparecida. The coronation of the original statue in 1931, as the Vatican-anointed patron saint of Brazil, made Aparecida the country's chief religious shrine. This increased the desire to build a bigger church, and by 1978, the main outlines of the cathedral were completed.The second church still stands on a hill overlooking the newer one.

The latter basilica is a massive structure out of proportion with its surroundings. The more modest 19th-century shrine would fit easily inside the vast new church. However, this cathedral, with its enormous nave and network of chapels and galleries, is visited every year by about 8 million pilgrims. About one million visit Aparecida in October alone.

In comparison, the pretty Igreja de Nossa Senhora da Penha in Rio is hardly imposing, but it has an unusual history. Located atop a 92-meter (300-ft) cone-shaped hill, Penha represents one of Brazil's oldest lay religious organizations.

The order of Penha was founded in the 17th century by a Portuguese landowner called Baltazar Cardoso, who believed he had been saved from death in a hunting accident by divine intervention. The accident took place in Portugal, near a mountain called Penha. Later in the century, the lay order that Cardoso founded as a result of his experience transferred its activities to Brazil, and it found a rocky cone in Rio – Penha – that was a small-scale copy of Cardoso's Penha in Portugal.The first church was built on the rock in 1635 and two more later went up on the same site. The third edifice, built in 1871, now plays host every year to the Penha October festivities.

Penha festivities are unique in Rio's religious calendar. Not only do worshipers participate in religious ceremonies every Sunday of October, they can also enjoy a lay festival at the base of the hill, which is reknowned for its good food, abundant beer and live music.

Festival in the Amazon

October also marks the chief religious observance of the Brazilian Amazon – the festival of Círio de Nazaré in the city of Belém, at the mouth of the Amazon. Belém annually attracts tens of thousands of penitents and tourists for the remarkable procession, a four-hour cortege along 5 km (3.1 miles) of downtown streets on the second Sunday of October. A thick rope, several blocks long, is used to drag a colorfully decorated carriage bearing the image of Our Lady of Nazareth. Pilgrims who succeed in grabbing hold of the rope believe they are granted favors by the saint. When the image reaches the basilica, a 15-day festival, similar to Penha festivities in Rio, begins.

The Círio de Nazaré story tells of a mulatto hunter named José de Sousa, who found the

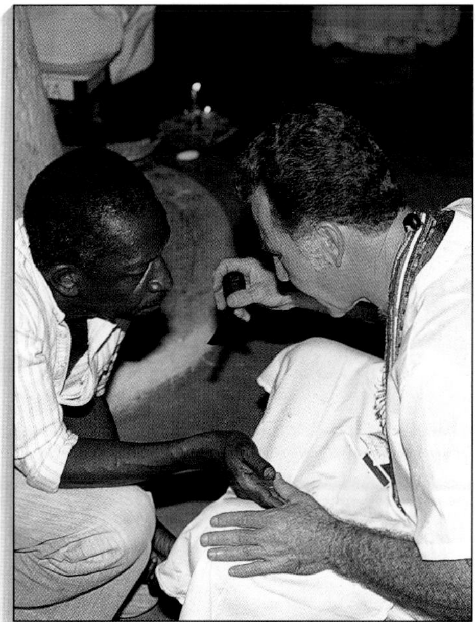

image lying in the forest. Sousa felt the image brought him luck, and it was later placed in a chapel where it was said to bring miraculous cures for his ailing neighbors. The first procession displaying the image took place in 1763. The rope was added only in the 19th century.

Festivals like Círio de Nazaré, Bom Jesus dos Navegantes, and even Carnival have some important aspects in common: they are all observed on important dates on the Roman Catholic liturgical calendar; they all possess central themes with traditional and folkloric elements; and perhaps what makes them most typically Brazilian, their participants all have an uproarious good time. ❑

LEFT: Filhos de Gandhi, an *afoxé* group in Salvador.
RIGHT: a devotee and a *pãe de santo* (priest) at an *umbanda* (Afro-Brazilian cult) ceremony.

14

A PASSION FOR SOCCER

In a game played and loved in nations across the world, Brazil – the only five times winner of the World Cup – is pre-eminent

Brazilians did not invent soccer, they just perfected it. Today Brazil is probably as well known around the world for its unique style of soccer as it is for its coffee or Carnival.

The game arrived in Brazil just before the turn of the 20th century, brought to São Paulo by a young Brazilian-born Englishman named Charles Miller. Upon Miller's return to Brazil as a young adult, he taught soccer at São Paulo Athletic Club (SPAC), a British community club. In 1901, a city-wide soccer league was formed, of which SPAC were champions in 1902, 1903 and 1904.

But 1904 was the last time a soccer trophy in Brazil was won by British descendants. Brazilians were quick to learn the game, and were soon beating the British at their own sport.

Passion of millions

Today soccer is an all-consuming passion for millions of fans, and a frenzied peak is reached every four years when soccer's World Cup is played. Many factory managers now install television sets on the production lines in a mostly futile effort to keep absenteeism to a minimum on match days. Most businesses, however, simply close down during play – and for the subsequent celebration if Brazil wins.

Known as *futebol*, soccer in Brazil is so hugely popular that some of the world's largest stadia have been erected here. Rio de Janeiro's gigantic oval Maracanã is able to seat 120,000 people. Morumbi Stadium in São Paulo can hold up to 70,000 onlookers and five other Brazilian stadiums can easily handle 80,000–100,000 fans.

One of the reasons for soccer's popularity in Brazil is that it is a sport readily accessible to all, as no expensive equipment is required and makeshift pitches can be set up anywhere. The game has attracted many players from Brazil's slums, who see soccer as a ticket out of poverty. Indeed there are many rags-to-riches stories of kids who have excelled at the game.

LEFT: Brazil's Ronaldo is feted after scoring against Germany in the 2002 FIFA World Cup.

RIGHT: a supporter helps create a carnival mood.

Soccer's greatest player

The richest and most famous of these is Edson Arantes do Nascimento, known to the world as Pelé. A frail-looking boy from a small city slum in Minas Gerais, Pelé had never even owned a pair of shoes when he was contracted at the age of 15 to play for the Santos Soccer Club.

One year later, in 1958, he helped the national team to Brazil's first World Cup win. Four years later, together with another national soccer legend, Garrincha (Manoel Francisco dos Santos), he propelled Brazil to its second consecutive win of the world's most prestigious soccer trophy.

Pelé was injured during the 1966 World Cup Finals, staged that year in England, as a result of foul play, but in 1970 he was back and once again Brazil won the World Cup title, for a record third time.

The dream of millions of youths is to follow Pelé's example and play for one of the major metropolitan clubs. And the ultimate honor for any player is to be picked for the national team. *Gods of Brazil*, a film released in 2003 which uses archive footage, suggests that Garrincha, rather than Pelé, was the world's greatest footballer of all time.

RECORD GOAL TALLY

By the time he retired in 1977, Pelé had scored an extraordinary 1,300 goals. To date, no other player has even reached 1,000.

In fact, the entire mood of the country can be altered by the success or failure of the national team. In 1970, the national squad's third World Cup win gave a tremendous boost to the previously unpopular, dictatorial military government headed by Emílio Garrastazu Medici.

The 1970 "dream team"

Many distinguished soccer commentators consider the 1970 squad the best ever. Soccer fans around the world were enthralled by the fluid attacking, skillful ball handling and clever playmaking of the Brazilians in Mexico. The names of many great players on the team – including Pelé, Tostão, Gerson, Jairzinho and Carlos Alberto – are still invoked nostalgically today. The win was the zenith of Brazilian soccer.

When Brazil won its fourth World Cup title, in the 1994 championship, the country went crazy. Despite the indifferent quality of the final against Italy, which Brazil won on penalties, the team's players were national heroes again.

Disappointment

Inevitably, as the 1998 World Cup Finals approached, the Brazilians were favorites, for their squad not only included many of the star players of 1994 but, crucially, the 21-year-old striker, Ronaldo, who had been voted World Player of the Year for the previous two years. But this time, victory was not theirs. Brazil scraped through to the final against host nation France – but then lost, 3–0. Ronaldo was sent on to the field despite suffering a mystery convulsion only hours before the match, and was clearly unfit. However, Brazil went on to win the Copa América, the South American Championship, in 1999.

Fifth time victorious

Just months before the 2002 World Cup, Brazil's team was considered one of it's weakest ever. But Ronaldo more than made up for his poor performance in 1998 by scoring both goals in the 2-0 victory against Germany in the final in Japan. In fact, he scored eight times in the tournament – the most in the World Cup since 1970. Brazilians celebrated in typically wild style and chanted "*Penateam peo*," which means fifth-time champions, at the team who had won the World Cup title for a record fifth time.

One of the unmissable attractions of a visit to Brazil is a soccer league classic match, such as Rio's Flamengo versus Vasco da Gama in Maracanã Stadium. Even if the game is dull, the spectacle of the fans is worth the price of admission; at a big match, the fans are as much a part of the action as are the players.

At the end of the Brazilian national championship, which takes six months and involves up to 44 teams, the day of the final game is effectively a national holiday. If you are visiting the hometown of the national champion on the evening the title is won, prepare yourself for an unforgettable experience. Hundreds of thousands of fans will emerge into the streets for a night of carousing and merrymaking.

The South American Football Federation (CSF) voted to back the country as its candidate to host the 2014 World Cup, which Brazil look certain to fulfil. ❑

LEFT: "sand lot" soccer players begin young.

Motor Racing Mania

A dream shared by many Brazilians, rich and poor, is to gain international fame through world championship motor racing, which has an especially enthusiastic following in Brazil. For that reason, the death of one of Brazil's most celebrated sons, Ayrton Senna, during the San Marino Grand Prix at Imola in May 1994, was bitterly felt – but it didn't put an end to the dream. It is fitting that São Paulo, Senna's home city, continues to host the Brazilian Formula One Grand Prix at Interlagos.

Senna broke more records than any other Brazilian motor racing driver in history. He was second only to Alain Prost in the number of Formula One victories (he won 41 times against Prost's 51) and in the total number of Formula One championship points. He earned more pole position starts than anyone in Formula One history (a total of 65), and led more championship races for more miles than any other driver. In all probability, if his life had not been cut short so tragically, he would have broken all the records. He was only 34 when he died.

But Ayrton Senna was not the only superlative driver from Brazil in the history of Formula One. The names roll off the tongue: Emerson Fittipaldi, Nelson Piquet, Mauricio Gugelmin, Raul Boesel... And even before Senna's death, the next generation of young turks from Brazil was making its mark; Rubens Barichello was already the youngest driver ever to qualify for a Formula One race with pole position. Now, several years on, Barrichello is considered one of the world's best drivers.

Many Brazilians participate in the US-based Indycar and Champcar series, including Gil De Ferran, Helio Castroneves, and Roberto Moreno. Cristiano Da Matta is the reigning Champcar driver and the third Brazilian to win the title.

In 2003, the top three places in the Indianapolis 500 were secured by Brazilian drivers – De Ferran, Castroneves, and Tony Kanaan, following in the footsteps of De Ferran in 2000 and 2001, and Emmerson Fittipaldi in 1989. Fittipaldi and Castroneves are also two-time winners of the Indianapolis 500. But no one has yet taken on the mantle of Senna, and it is unlikely they ever will.

Despite being one of the few developing nations on the World Championship Grand Prix circuit, Brazil always seems to have drivers in the top ranks. Without the wealth of the upper strata there would be no world-class drivers emerging from Brazil, but of course world champions are not made by money alone.

The dedication, the belief in their own abilities, the keenness of reactions, and the sympathy with the machines they drive are all part of the essential make-up of a great driver, and the character of the young Brazilian male makes him likely to succeed in this specialist field. He is lively, fit, and quick-witted, and his reactions and timing are

RIGHT: Ayrton Senna – the legend lives on.

honed by a childhood rich in soccer, volleyball, and music. There is also more than an element of arrogance in the Brazilian male, plus sheer bloody-minded tenacity. These are traits that could be seen as essential for a Formula One driver.

One motivating factor for Brazilian drivers must be that Brazilians worship success, and world-conquering sportsmen become instant national heroes. Yet it cannot be denied that, when it is at its best, Brazilian driving, like Brazilian soccer, is nothing short of magical. And that magic is more than capable of galvanizing the Brazilian crowds into a frenzy whenever a local driver wins at home, in the Brazilian Grand Prix on São Paulo's Interlagos circuit. ❑

JKT-2034

MUSEU
DA CIDADE

Zildjian
RUDE

SONG AND DANCE

Compelling musical styles and fusions, shaped by Brazil's ethnic inheritance, are the vital forces behind Carnival and integral to the lifestyle of every Brazilian

On a Saturday night in any sizeable Brazilian town, a vast musical choice presents itself. Will you tap cutlery to a samba *pagode* in a tile-floored bar or dance hip-to-hip to the simple rhythm of the *forró*; try the tango-like ballroom virtuosity of the *gafiera*, or converse over the twinkling swirls of the *choro* played on mandolins and violas? Or even risk the decibels of techno-rock, Brazilian style?

In the nightclubs, jazz takes its turn with the melancholy of the Portuguese *fado* or Brazilian torch singers. In contrast, the simple nostalgia of *duplas sertanejas* (country duos) strikes a universal chord. One popular duo, Millionário e José Rico, sells briskly as far afield as China, whereas the death in 1998 of 36-year old Leonardo, the younger half of the Leandro and Leonardo duo, set off nationwide mourning and the suicide of one young fan – found poisoned, alongside her CD player, set on repeat play of their top-seller *Pense em Mim* (Think of Me).

Lambada was a craze that swept Brazil one steamy summer in the late 1980s: a raunchier, Brazilian version of the clingy, hip-swaying dances of Spanish America. Once hips had grown used to the feel of Latin swing (rather than samba flick) Brazilians dived into learning *salsa* and *merengue*.

Regional music is still very much alive. In Rio Grande do Sul, *gauchos* sing along to accordion music much as their German forebears did 100 years ago. In Mato Grosso do Sul, *boleros* are sung with all the drama of the Spanish culture just across the border in neighboring Paraguay. Northeastern rhythms like *baião*, *forró* and *maracatu* in the interior and the faster *frevo* on the coast, especially Recife, dominate not only in those regions but wherever the northeasterners have migrated.

The heterogeneity of the nation explains why so many genres of popular music coexist with equal vigor. Successive waves of immigration have left their imprint, beginning with the Portuguese colonists, the Jesuit missions, and the forced immigration of the slaves, and culminating with the economic and political refugees from 19th- and 20th-century Europe and Asia.

Culturally mixed and socially hierarchical, Brazil has one foot in the computer age and the other in the 17th century. It is over 80 percent urban, yet so recently urban that large sectors of the city population retain the cultural habits of the *sertão*; still a predominantly oral culture, yet one exposed to the rest of the world through radio, television and the Internet. These days, it does not take long for the latest international releases to reach the furthest corners of the country, yet folk music is still very much alive.

Rhythm makers

It is a tired old cliché that Brazil has rhythm. What it actually has is *rhythms*, in the plural, together with an openness that leads to the blending of genres, known as "fusions."

PRECEDING PAGES: *capoeira* dancers in Salvador.
LEFT: afternoon rock concert in a Rio park.
RIGHT: spontaneous dancing in the street.

The first fusion was indian/Jesuit. In the 16th century, the missionaries perceived the indians' response to music and used it as an instrument of conversion, adapting Catholic liturgy to indian ritual song and choreography. Today, with the total indian population reduced to about 300,000, the Catholic church takes a back seat. Yet traces of the past remain – in the northwest of Amazonas state, near the Venezuelan border, indians of the Tucano tribe still sing Gregorian credos and glorias.

The music of Brazilian indians focuses on rhythm rather than melody. Its principal instruments are maracas, rattles and sometimes simple

flutes and pan pipes. Song is considered so sacred that its use is often restricted to ritual, the principal exception being lullabies, which are sung softly and sweetly by indian women.

Certain animist ceremonies practised by non-indians today, such as the *catimbo* in the interior of the northeast of Brazil and the *pajelança* in the northern Amazon, owe a great deal to indian ritual. And some surviving country folk dances, such as *caiapos* and *caboclinhos*, are directly inspired by indian dance.

But for four centuries the colonizers of Brazil, the Portuguese, were the dominant influence. They defined Brazilian harmonic tonalism and established the four-beat bar and the syncopation that would later blend so well with African rhythms. They brought the *cavaquinho* (similar to the ukulele, but usually steel stringed today), the *bandolin* (mandolin), the Portuguese guitar (like a large mandolin, an indian sitar or a Greek bazuki, with five pairs of strings), the Portuguese bagpipes and the piano, viola and harp.

Curiously it was not the Portuguese guitar that was destined to become the backbone of Brazilian popular music, but the Spanish. Likewise with the Italian accordion. In the northeast, the accordion player is the mainstay of country parties, traveling from village to village and in huge demand during June for the traditional feasts of São João (Saint John).

Folk dance

The Portuguese provided the basis of Brazilian folk dance, from children's ring and maypole dances to the so-called "dramatized dances". Most of the latter are linked to the Catholic religious calendar, such as the *reisados* (performed on the sixth day after Christmas to celebrate the visit of the Magi to the infant Jesus), *pastoris* (nativity plays) and *Festa do Divino* (performed at Pentecost). Yet the liveliest are profane. *Bumba meu Boi* is thought to be a comic representation of the *tourinhos* – Portugal's bullfights. Today, this dance is colorful, rhythmic and essentially African, most popular in Pernambuco, Maranhão and Bahia states.

While the Portuguese provided the lyrical-poetic framework, and the range of themes and emotions present in Brazilian popular music, we must look to Africa for its "axe" (a Yoruba word meaning joy and strength).

The majority of Brazil's slaves came from

NORDESTINO ACCORDIONISTS

Over the years, northeasterners have developed their own accordion technique. Bahian Pedro Sertanejo, who owns a *forró* dance hall in São Paulo, recalls the reactions on his band's European tour: "They stared at us open-mouthed, wondering how we got all that rhythm into the accordion."

The undisputed king of the accordion is the late Luis Gonzaga (1912–89), inventor of the *baião* rhythm. His songs recount the hardships of northeastern life. *Asa Branca* (named after a bird, the whitewing), the haunting lament of a peasant farmer driven off his land by drought, has become an unofficial anthem.

Angola, followed by the Congos and Sudan. Unlike in the US, where little survives of African animist ritual, Brazilian plantation owners broadly tolerated these people's rhythmic dance and trance rituals. It was later, when the freed slaves tried to organize their religion in the towns, that police repression was unleashed against them and they had to resort to disguising their forest gods as Catholic saints, a process known as syncretism.

Origins of samba

For the Afro-Brazilian, music is both social and religious. The same instruments are used (although to different rhythms) for their religious ceremonies *(candomblés)* and for infor-mal parties: *atabaque* (drums), *ganza* (a metal rattle), *cuíca* (a skin in a small drum is pulled to make a hoarse rasping noise), *agogo* (a single or double conical bell, beaten with a stick or metal rod). With the addition of the guitar or *cavaquinho*, these instruments were to form the basis of what has become Brazil's national music: the samba.

It is thought that the word "samba" comes from the Angolan *semba*, a synonym for *umbigada* – literally a belly button thrust. Africans formed a circle, clapping, singing and beating percussion instruments while one dancer at a time twirled and gyrated in the middle. When his time was up, the dancer would stop in front of someone in the circle and, with an *umbigada*, they would swap places. Versions of *umbigadas* survive virtually unchanged today in Afro-Brazilian communities all over Brazil, known variously as *samba de roda*, *jongo*, *tambor-de-crioulo*, *batuque* and *caxambu*.

Black rhythms made their first, tentative, foray into the salons of white urban society in the late 18th century in the form of the *lundu*. This toned-down creation was danced in pairs and with the addition of viola and sitar. Domingos Caldas Barbosa, born in Rio de Janeiro around 1740 to a black mother and white father, was to become the most renowned and prolific composer of *lundus*, and also of *modinhas*.

By the mid-19th century, *modinhas* had become the favorite of the court, rarefied to a unique form of near-classical chamber music, with opera-like arias. Yet, at the end of that century, they had descended again to street level, to the gaslit *serenatas*, or serenades, of wandering guitarists.

Slave music

In the second half of the 19th century, the slave bands playing on country plantations and in city ballrooms were obliged to copy fashionable European dance rhythms, such as the polka and the mazurka. When playing for themselves, however, these bands let rip, endowing polka's lively jig with their own sensuous thrusts and swings. The result was *maxixe*, an extravagant, rhythmic form of tango. As with

lundu, *maxixe* was first condemned and then began a gradual ascent to high society.

At the turn of the century, a now largely forgotten musical genius made an appearance: Ernesto Nazaré (1863–1934). Weaving folk melody with classical technique, Nazaré's piano compositions sound startlingly similar to the piano rags of American Scott Joplin.

What Ernesto Nazaré was to popular music, Heitor Villa-Lobos (1887–1959) was to classical. His *Bahianas Brasileiras* (composed from 1930–34) infiltrated Bach's form with Brazilian *joie de vivre* and haunting echoes of folk song. A prolific composer, tireless performer and inveterate traveler, Heitor Villa-

LEFT: Gilberto Gil, and **RIGHT:** Caetano Veloso, the 1960s inventors of *tropicalismo*, the fusion of native Brazilian sounds with Western rock music.

Lobos formed two great musical friendships – with Milhaud and Arthur Rubinstein.

A failed Brazilian dentist, Lopes de Amorin Diniz, known as Duque, became a huge success in Paris in the early 20th century as a dancer and teacher of *le vrai tango bresilien*. In 1913 he performed for Pope Pius X, who remarked that it reminded him of an Italian dance, the *furlana*. Ironically, back in Brazil, the *maxixe* was still being combated tooth and nail by church leaders. By the time Fred Astaire danced a version of the *maxixe* in the 1933 Hollywood film *Flying Down to Rio*, the dance was dying out in Rio, being replaced by the less complex *sambas* popularized by Carnival parades. Today there are still dance halls, known as *gafieras*, where glued-together couples dance *maxixes*, *habaneras*, *choros* and *sambas* with all the extravagant virtuosity of the Duque in his heyday.

KILLJOY OVERRULED

In 1907, the prudish army minister, Marshal Hermes da Fonseca, banned military bands from playing *maxixe* tunes. But five years later, his wife performed a *maxixe* at an official party.

The rise of samba

Samba's official history began in 1916, when the composition *Pelo Telefone* was registered in a Rio notary's office by a lower-middle class *carioca* composer, Donga. The following year, *Pelo Telefone* was the success of the Carnival, becoming the first samba to be recorded. Soon the new genre put an end to the ragbag of rhythms that had characterized Rio Carnival up until then – polka and stately *marcha-ranchos* for the upper classes, rhythmic *afoxé* and *lundu* for the Afro-Brazilians.

The best-known form of samba is the exhilarating spectacle of Rio's Carnival. Known as the *samba enredo*, or story-samba, it is sung by one amplified voice, accompanied by a guitar and *cavaquinho*, to which thousands of voices in the parade harmonize. The rhythm sections in the biggest samba schools can consist of between 300 and 400 drummers.

Yet that is only one of samba's many subgenres. There is the pure *samba do morro*, played with percussion instruments only; *samba do breque*, which stops abruptly, often for a wry interjection, before picking up again; and the *bebop samba* of the 1940s and 1950s. And then there's the perennial ballad version, *samba-canção*, the Frank Sinatra of sambas. With musical frontiers blown wide open and fashions flashing by at increasing speed, samba's fusions seem virtually limitless – samba-rock, samba-funk, samba-reggae, samba-rap.

Yet, today, it is one of the most traditional styles of samba – the *pagode* – that is proving a record-breaker, with an album by the group Só Para Contrariar becoming the first-ever Brazilian recording to sell over three million copies.

Mid-20th century styles

Brazilians celebrated two important birthdays in 1998 – the 40th anniversary of *bossa nova* and the 30th anniversary of *tropicalismo*. *Bossa nova* hit the world on November 22, 1962, when the classically trained pianist and composer Tom Jobim held New York's Carnegie Hall in thrall to *The Girl from Ipanema* and *Samba de uma nota só*. It took shape several years earlier, a result of the quest of Jobim and other young *carioca* intellectuals for a calmer samba, an answer to US cool jazz.

They found it in João Gilberto, a shy young man from Bahia, who played a wholly original, self-invented style of guitar, mixing jazz harmonies with a chunky, persistent, offbeat rhythm extracted from the guitar itself. Poet and former diplomat, Vinicius de Moraes, an inveterate bohemian, became the movement's high priest, writing lyrics such as the exquisite *Eu sei que vou te amar* (I know that I will love you).

Bossa nova – which means roughly, "new thing" – was developed in the apartments and bars of Rio's chic Zona Sul rather than in the hillside shacks, a middle-class taste that never fully filtered down. It requires considerable skill to play, as one musician described it, "like talking in a long sentence, but one in which you switch language every two words."

Tropicalismo was a reaction against the cool of *bossa nova* and the socially committed "protest sambas" that succeeded *bossa nova* in the later 1960s. The latter were aptly defined by literature professor Walnice Nogueira Galvão as the songs of *o dia que virá* – the day that will come. It was the period of the military regime, when there was increasing censorship and repression. In 1968, Geraldo Vandré, composer of the anti-military protest song *Pra não dizer que não falei de flores* (So as not to say I didn't speak of flowers) was arrested, tortured and sent into exile.

Tropicalismo was born when *baianos* Gilberto Gil and Caetano Veloso, presented, respectively, the songs *Domingo no Parque* (Sunday in the Park) and *Alegria, Alegria* (Joy, Joy) at a São Paulo music festival. They shocked the purists in much the same way as Bob Dylan did when he appeared on stage with an electric guitar. The *baianos* used all the resources of pop-rock – electric guitars and a backing group called the Beat-boys (the Beatles were then the idols of Brazilian youth).

Tropicalismo was loud, anarchic and irreverent, mixing concrete images of Brazil with international junk culture in striking juxtapositions. Once they got over the shock, Brazilian audiences were driven to delirium. In 1969, the alarmed military government arrested Veloso and Gil, and forced them into exile in England. By the time they returned, in 1972, the breakthroughs of *tropicalismo* had become the norm and every group had electric instruments.

Enduring popularity

Along with *tropicalismo*'s 30th birthday came talk of the emergence of a "*novo tropicalismo*" in time for the 21st century, headed by bright new artists such as the Pernambucan Chico Cesar. Yet the original creators of *tropicalismo* still dominate the more sophisticated reaches of Brazilian popular music: Caetano Veloso, with his sinuous melody and poetic wit, always one step ahead of the collective consciousness, and Gilberto Gil,

LEFT: Renaissance man Chico Buarque.
RIGHT: Milton Nascimento, still immensely popular.

an Afro-Brazilian and now Brazil's culture minister, playful, rhythmic and mesmerizing. The third great popular musician from that generation is Chico Buarque – a singer, composer, musician, librettist, novelist and political activist.

Indeed, the Brazilian generation of popular musicians born in the 1940s (to name a few – Jorge Benjor, Milton Nascimento, Baby Consuelo, Moraes Moreira, Maria Bethania, Djavan, Egberto Gismonti and Gal Costa; the *sambistas* Paulinho da Viola, the late Tim Maia, Bete Carvalho, and the "granny" of Brazilian rock, Rita Lee) is a vintage unlikely to be seen again. It is rather like expecting the

Left: Olodum drum group from Salvador, who shot to fame in collaboration with US songwriter Paul Simon.

Beatles, Jimmy Hendrix, and the Rolling Stones still to be producing their best work 30 years on.

Brazilian rock has always had a certain sweetness to it, and has concentrated on incorporating international trends – from the earliest, teenage, mini-skirted singers of the mid-1960s who sang "ie-ie-ie" (after the Beatles "Yeah, yeah, yeah") onwards. However, an innovative element originating in the 1980s has been Brazilian rock's direct, urban and often mocking or humorous language – a far cry from the traditional romanticism. In the 1990s, rap artists continued in this vein by tinging their lectures with humor.

Re-Africanization

However, for musical innovation in the 21st century one must look to the city of Salvador, where an unprecedented "re-Africanization" has taken place.

It began in the late 1970s when *afoxés*, groups of dancers linked to the city's *candomblés*, began to make their presence felt during Salvador's Carnival. Dressed in flowing white robes, they paraded, not to the frenetic *trio elétrico* or samba, but to the African rhythms of the *agogos*. They became the nerve centers of a growing black consciousness movement.

Simultaneously, imported Bob Marley records, not available then in the shops, found their way to Bahia. *Baianos* immediately identified with reggae and Gilberto Gil gave a spine-tingling concert with Jamaican artist Jimmy Cliff.

Salvador's Carnival became charged with a momentum which each year generated a new dance and new singing stars. Some didn't last the season; others, like Margareth Menezes, Carlinhos Brown and Daniela Mercury, found their way to national and international renown.

The drumming group Olodum was founded in the early 1980s and provided the backing for Paul Simon's hit single *The Obvious Child* from his *Rhythm of the Saints* album. Many of its 280 permanent members were street kids who discovered identity and pride in Olodum. Soon the band was running classes in Yoruba, Portuguese and computing, and workshops in metalwork and carpentry.

"In Bahia, the drum has become the synonym of employment, education, social ascension, and, of course, polemic," decreed leading news magazine *Veja* in June 1998. When Carlinhos Brown launched his third solo album *Bahia do Mundo*, in 2001, he described it as the product of a Bahia "that is being born all the time," and paid tribute to the country's black musical traditions. "Drum and bass, house, and even funk exist because of samba schools, and trance only exists because of Brazilian Carnival." With funds from UNICEF, Brown built a school to teach young drummers music, literacy, and math. His latest vision is to create recording studios in the larger *favelas* as a means of nurturing this vital source of musical talent. As Brown puts it, "It is a revolution, but an elegant one." ❑

The end of an era, if not an empire

When President Lula declared three days of mourning in August 2003, it was to mark the death of Roberto Marinho, not a previous state leader, or even a politician, but a media mogul. Dubbed the Brazilian Citizen Kane for his news and entertainment empire, the tycoon died aged 98, at a time when his network reached 99.9 percent of Brazilian homes. Marinho was the head of the nationwide Globo television network,

whose soap operas attract a huge following in Brazil and sell in large numbers around the world. The company is the fourth most prolific producer of television programs in the world.

One of Latin America's richest men, Marinho's career spanned almost eight decades. The key to Globo's domination of Brazil, probably unequaled in any other country, is its presence in all media. Globo's stranglehold on the market has been seen by some as a threat to the nation's democracy and, at election time, stations are often accused of a lack of objectivity.

ABOVE: live reporting of local and national news has long been a feature of Brazilian television.

Most of Brazilian television is at best crass and at worst manipulative. Pride of place on the small screen goes to the legendary short-run soap operas known as *novelas*. The most successful can hold the entire nation spellbound, from smart lawyers in the rich suburbs of Sao Paulo to penniless *favelados* (slum dwellers) in remote Manaus.

Between 1995 and 2000, the number of owners of television sets shot up by a staggering 30 percent in Brazil. Today, 90 percent of homes have a TV and for the lower classes it is their major source of information. Because the government is responsible for licensing radio and TV, this is often used by politicians for their own means. Many believe that in the 1989 presidential elections Globo's coverage ruined the political prospects of the then left-wing candidate Luis Inacio Lula da Silva.

The Globo network boasts nearly 75 percent of prime-time viewers. However, with a debt of $1.4 billion, even the mighty Globo has been affected by the country's economic problems. New hope came in December 2002 when a new law was introduced that allows foreign investors to invest up to 30 percent in Brazil's media.

For the housewives, soap opera stars and high-ranking politicians who attended Marinho's funeral, it was certainly the end of an era, although it seems certain that his death does not mean the end of his empire. ❑

ART AND ARTISTS

Brazilian art has blossomed since 1922, from the abstract work of the mid-20th century to today's vibrant mix of traditional and avant-garde

Contemporary Brazilian art is wonderfully hard to categorize. At first glance, it appears resolutely international and less identifiably Brazilian in character than, for example, Mexican art is identifiable as Mexican. Yet it does have a Brazilian flavor, albeit surprisingly subtle. Brazilian scholar Ivo Mesquita appoints a certain lightness of touch as the defining feature: "The ability to parody others as well as ourselves separates us from the tragic sensibility of our Hispanic neighbors." And, he could add, a playful delight in the new.

Brazilian artists are among the liveliest participants at the big international shows (the Venice, São Paulo and Sydney Bienals, and the Kassel Documenta). And there is much to-ing and fro-ing, or *intercâmbio*, both by Brazilian artists who do stints abroad and foreign ones who settle in Brazil.

"The richest, liveliest and most varied range of conceptual and site-specific art has been produced in Brazil," writes the art historian Edward Lucie Smith, comparing Brazilian avant-garde favorably with that of the rest of Latin America. "Site-specific art" – usually large sculptures or installations – might include: the cascading plastic curtains of Leda Catunda (b. 1962); the giant hair plaits of Tunga (b. 1952); the eery silhouettes of Regina Silveira (b. 1937), painted on walls and ceilings; and the large but restrained sculptures of José Resende (b. 1945), with their elegant shapes made physical by arresting surface textures, such as rust on a steel curve.

In painting, there are the thick and vibrant abstract-expressionist brush strokes of Jorge Guinle (1947–87) and José Roberto Aguillar (b. 1941), the atmospheric city streets of Gregorio Gruber and the eroticism of Ivald Granato. In 1996, Ana Maria Pacheco became the first ever non-European to be appointed Artist in Residence at Britain's National Gallery, with a brief that involves developing art that makes reference to works in the national collection.

The birth of modernism

Given the élan and confidence of Brazilian artists today, it might seem surprising that, before the early 20th century, the fine arts in Brazil were in the grip of an antiquated European academicism, as dictated by Rio's Academia Imperial de Belas Artes, founded in 1826.

The rebellion took place in São Paulo, a city that in the early 20th century was growing vertiginously, fuelled by the wealth of the so-called coffee barons. Unfettered by tradition, these nouveaux riches sunk their money into industry, monuments and mansions, and put São Paulo at the cutting edge of new cultural trends.

The "Week of Modern Art", held in São Paulo in 1922, was the watershed. By today's standards, the event was relatively modest – an art exhibition in the foyer of the Municipal Theater and three days of poetry readings and lec-

LEFT: *A bicicleta com copos de leite*, a naïve painting by Ivonaldo.
RIGHT: detail from sculpture of the apostles by the 18th-century sculptor, Aleijadinho.

tures. But art in Brazil was never to be the same again. The exhibition was the gateway into the "-isms" of the age: the angles and refractions of cubism, art deco stylism, Italian futurism and the metaphors of symbolism and surrealism.

Six years later, the poet Oswald de Andrade coined the term *antropofagia* (cannibalism) to describe how Brazilian art had begun to relate to international trends. The word referred to the belief of some Brazilian Amerindian tribes that cooking and eating the bodies of enemies they had killed in battle would endow them with the strength and bravery of the vanquished. Applied to art, this idea was extremely liberating. Brazilian artists dipped into the art world's "isms" without becoming dominated by them.

Two women played key roles in the modernization of Brazilian art. Anita Malfatti (1889–1964) had studied at the Berlin Academy under Lovis Corinth, and in New York, before returning to Brazil and holding a groundbreaking exhibition in 1917, showing canvasses that sung with Cezannesque colors and boldness. The younger generation loved her work, but Malfatti was crushed by a damning newspaper review written by Monteiro Lobato, a well-known novelist, from which she never fully recovered.

Tarsila do Amaral (1886–1973) wrote to her parents in 1923 from Paris, where she was studying under Fernand Léger: "I want, in art, to be the little country girl from São Bernardo, playing with straw dolls." She achieved her aim by means of a uniquely sophisticated yet simple style that owed much to the uncorrupted eye of the child. A major restrospective in São Paulo in 1998 put her in the front rank of Brazil's 20th-century painters.

Emiliano di Cavalcanti (1897–1976), a prolific painter and vigorous draughtsman, also did a stint in Paris as correspondent for a Brazilian newspaper, where he mixed with the great cubists, Picasso, Léger and Braque. Returning to Brazil, he spent the next 50 years affection-

MANET'S INSPIRATION

Brazilian legend has it that the sparkling quality of the light reflected in Rio's Guanabara Bay provided the inspiration behind impressionism. This belief is based on the occasion when a French frigate carrying 16-year-old Edouard Manet, the "father of impressionism," docked in Rio de Janeiro harbor for three months in 1849.

Manet, whose art was characterized by lively scenes and bright colors, later wrote: "I learned a lot in Brazil. I spent endless nights looking at the play of light and shade in the ship's wake. And in the daytime, from the upper deck, I would keep my eyes on the horizon. That's how I learnt how to capture a sky."

ately portraying the mixed-race *mulata* woman in a variety of styles, most notably a decorative form of cubism.

Europe's Art Deco movement directly influenced two other distinctive stylists: Italian-born sculptor Vitor Brecheret (1891–1957) and Vicente do Rego Monteiro (1899–1970). Brecheret's impressive *Monument to the Bandeirantes* (Pioneers) in São Paulo's Ibirapuera Park dwarfs even the Mussolini school in monumentalism. Monteiro's paintings, often of biblical or indigenous scenes, have the feel of Egyptian bas-reliefs.

José Pancetti (1904–58), perhaps Brazil's best-loved impressionist, was a tubercular ex-sailor whose moody landscapes and seascapes reflected the state of his mind more than the bright scenery about him.

Portinari

Candido Portinari (1903–62) is Brazil's Diego Rivera. His *War and Peace* fresco adorns the United Nations Building in New York, and his *Discovery and Colonization* painting is hung in the Library of Congress in Washington. Unlike Ribera, however, he never became a fashionable ambassador for his country. Indeed, he painted so intensively that he contracted cancer from his highly toxic paints and died young.

Born into a family of poor Italian immigrants who worked in the coffee plantations of São Paulo state, Portinari had a deep empathy with uneducated Brazilian laborers. He intentionally exaggerated the size of their hands and feet as if to say, "These are my only assets. When these are used up, I, too, am tossed aside." In his youth, Portinari joined the Brazilian Communist Party. In maturity, he painted a searing series on the *retirantes* – peasant farmers driven from their land by drought and debt.

Portinari's influence on other artists was such that his style of social realism became known as "Portinarism." His followers include Orlando Teruz (1902–84), Thomaz Santa Rosa (1909–56), Enrico Bianco (b. 1918) and Proença Sigaud (1899–1979) .

Carlos Scliar painted in the "Portinarist" fashion for some time, reflecting the conditions of rural workers in Rio Grande do Sul. Gradually, however, he eliminated social elements from his paintings and concentrated on landscapes with geometrical forms and planes. His best-known work of art is a pastel toned teapot, with a flattened perspective and minimal use of light and shade.

LEFT: a Portinari fresco in Pampulha, Minas Gerais.
ABOVE: *Fishermen* by Emiliano Di Calvacanti, 1951.

By contrast, Orlando Terluz's (1902–84) countryside is a rich loamy brown and the rural inhabitants of his paintings are full of a beatific innocence. Fulvio Pennacchi also concentrated on country pleasures, such as church fairs and parties. His migrants look like happy families on a pilgrimage, and his villages sometimes reflect the style of those in his native Tuscany.

Another Tuscan émigré, Alfredo Volpi (1896–1988), began his career with paintings of country scenes such as religious *festas*. But by the late 1950s he had reduced his pictures to just one element: the strings of colorful bunting that festoon rural church fairs. Volpi was known as the "flag painter" and his work was widely reproduced as silk-screen prints. The artist himself always claimed that his overuling interest was color.

The birth of abstract art

At the end of World War II, Brazil was enjoying increased prosperity. The São Paulo Museum of Modern Art (MASP) was built in 1948, Rio's Museum of Modern Art (MAM) opened in 1949 and, in the midst of São Paulo's Ibirapuera Park, the vast, custom-built Bienal Pavilion, designed by Oscar Niemeyer, went up – which hosted the first Bienal in 1951.

The Bienal is held on odd years and lasts three months, from September to December. It involves thousands of exhibits and hundreds of events. In the early days, it seemed that the greatest impact was caused by works brought in from abroad, which included Picasso's *Guernica*, Francis Bacon's triptychs and the vast canvasses of the US abstract expressionists. These days, there is a far more equal exchange.

The birth of the Bienal ushered in a phase of abstraction. The rivalry between São Paulo and Rio raged hotly, with artists in the former favoring art that was strictly about color and shape, and the Rio group, who dubbed themselves the "neo-concretists", permitting some symbolic associations with reality.

Ligia Clarke (1920–88) and Helio Oiticica (1937–80), two *cariocas*, were among the most influential abstract sculptors of their generation. Clarke created one series of tactile *borrachas* (rubber grubs), and another of feisty, hard metal *bichos* (animals). Oiticica's work often had the throwaway feel of a Carnival prop.

JAPANESE-BRAZILIAN ARTISTS

The post-war period saw the emergence of a school of Japanese-Brazilian artists, led by Manabu Mabe (1924–1997). First contracted to work as a field hand, Mabe moved to São Paulo city, where his reputation grew steadily and his work became more abstract. His stunning colors and forms mingle Oriental harmony with bold Brazilian chromatic tones and light. Every painting of Mabe's is a sheer visual delight, with brush strokes of white daringly exploding in a field of stark reds, blues and greens.

Far more cerebral and geometrical, using only two or three colors, is the work of Tomie Ohtake (b. 1915). Ohtake began painting professionally relatively late, after her family, also indentured farm workers (like Mabe and Portinari), moved to São Paulo. Her stage designs for *Madame Butterfly* at Rio de Janeiro's Municipal Theater are a landmark in Latin American scenography.

Mabe's son, Hugo, began his career painting landscapes with an expressionist vigor, and over the years has gradually reduced them to abstracted form and color. A similar artist is Taro Kaneko, whose mountains and bays of Rio, and São Paulo's Jaragua Peak, are barely perceptible in his intense, thickly massed oils with explosive, unexpected colors. Kaneko's seas are gold or red, his skies green or orange, and his mountains are yellow or black.

The Bahian-born Rubem Valentim (1922–92) used symbols from Afro-Brazilian *candomblé* ritual to create exuberant, geometrically patterned canvases, often of a mesmeric intensity.

The regions

While São Paulo and Rio monopolize the art trade and are the main centers for international exhibitions and ideas, many artists are rooted in their native regions. Indeed, though they are becoming fewer in number, Brazil still has a class of uneducated rural artisans from which, every now and again, an artistic genius emerges.

It is this that can make the São Paulo Bienals so exciting, bringing together the internationally focused, Internet and video-art set with simple country artists who may never have been out of their home villages, and indigenous artists working in feather, bone and wood.

Minas Gerais has a tradition of breeding imaginative wood carvers and potters. Carver Maurino Araujo has been compared to the nation's greatest sculptor, the 18th-century Aleijadinho. He specializes in myopic, crook and one-eyed angels, archangels, cherubim and seraphim. From the same region comes Geraldo Teles de Oliveira (often known as GTO, 1913–90), whose mandala-like wood-carvings exemplify the best in folk art sculpture.

In Goiás, near Brasília, Siron Franco portrays wild animals with magical energy and blazing color. Snakes and the *capivara*, a native rodent with a round snout, are among his favorites. His human and animal faces have bold white, yellow or fluorescent lines about the eyes. (Siron's father, a sharecropper, was so distraught when he lost his land, that he lay down and stared into the sun until he went blind.)

At the end of the 1980s, a bizarre and tragic accident occurred in Goiás. An illiterate man stole a discarded piece of hospital equipment containing a capsule of radioactive material. Fascinated by the blue glow emitted by the Cesium 137, he took it home and passed it around his family, most of whom susequently died in protracted agonies of radioactive poisoning. Franco produced a stunning series of paintings based on the incident that briefly turned his quiet town into a hive of international reporters and scientists.

LEFT: *Equador No. 2*, a 1973 painting by Manabu Mabe. **RIGHT:** detail of *Tabôa na lagoa*, naïve painting by Ana Maria Dias.

In the 1960s and 1970s, the new city of Brasília attracted artists from all over Brazil to complete the decoration of Oscar Niemeyer's superb architecture. Bruno Giorgi's meteors adorn the lake before the Itamarati Palace. Ceschiatti's bronze sculpture of two seated females combing their hair sits in the pool of the President's Palace, while his mobile of streamlined angels floats permanently beneath the soaring ceiling of Brasília Cathedral, framed by Niemeyer's boomerang-shaped columns.

Recife is solidly represented by João Camara, who first caught the public's attention with his figures with tortured, non-anatomical limbs in *A Confession*, a protest against the repression of the military government in the early 1970s.

In the neighboring town of Olinda, Gilvan Samico draws on the *literatura de cordel* (chapbook) tradition of woodcut engraving. He has illustrated the ballads of Charlemagne and local legends such as those of the charismatic Padre Cícero and the bandit heroes Lampião and Maria Bonita. Samico's engravings are highly prized by museums, being several grades above the folk art of the north eastern wood engravers.

Aldemir Martins, who was born in Ceará, paints the flora and fauna of his native northeast. His subjects include exotic fruits such as *jenipapo*, jackfruit, *jabuticaba*, cashew and the wrinkled *maracujá* (passion fruit).

The best of Bahian art can be found in the sculptures of Mario Cravo Junior, who experiments in wood and pigmented polyester resin for such creations as *Germination I*, *II* and *III*. His son, Mario Cravo, creates wrinkled, untitled forms from materials such as polyester resin and fiberglass.

Rio Grande do Sul is noted for its sculptors, particularly Vasco Prado, who is fascinated by pregnant mares. Francisco Stockinger's warriors of bronze and other metals have an ominous air, with limbs and faces merely suggested.

LEFT: *Praia do Barbosa*, a naïve painting by Dila.

Crafts and photography

The Tangiers-born Madeleine Colaço (1907–2001) has invented a form of tapestry stitch registered at the international Tapestry Museum in Lausanne as the "Brazilian Stitch." She and her daughter, Concessa, use flora and fauna motifs. The French-born Jacques Douchez and São Paulo's Norberto Nicola, on the other hand, have modernized Brazilian tapestry with their abstract designs and novel use of non-embroidered elements, including native plant fibers.

One Brazilian photographer is in a class of his own. Sebastião Salgado lives in Paris and works for Henri Cartier-Bresson's picture agency, Magnum. He came to world prominence in the late 1970s with his photographs of Serra Pelada, a vast open-cast gold mine in the Amazon region. Whether photographing Bolivian tin miners, Ruhr valley steel workers or the crowds at football matches, Salgado has a truly compassionate eye.

The sophisticated *naif*

For decades, Brazil's art critics have been arguing about whether "primitive" or *naif* (naive) art can rank as art at all. Sooner or later, one feels, they will be forced to admit that not only is it art but it is currently enjoying a glorious heyday. Indeed, in its range of subject matter, styles and techniques, Brazilian *naif* has become supremely sophisticated.

Rodolfo Tamanini (b. 1951), whose paintings are hung in São Paulo's stock exchange, brings *naif* technique to contemporary reality. His subjects range from city scenes, such as a block of flats with incidents on every balcony, to luminous coastal vistas of virgin forest, sea and sky. In direct contrast, Ernani Pavanelli (b. 1942), a former systems analyst, specializes in nostalgic snatches of daily life from a bygone era, his formally atired couples and family groups painted in Seurat-style pointilism.

Ivonaldo (b. 1943) uses strong colors and wry humor – his country people (and animals) all have vividly expressive eyes, whether they be bikini-clad sunbathers, weary cane cutters or shy lovers. Dila (b.1939), from the interior of Maranhão, paints detailed portraits of backland life, particularly open-air markets, with much haggling and mountainous piles of fruit.

Isabel de Jesus (b 1938), a former nun, is internationally recognized for her dream-like fantasies in delicate goaches. Her palette of turquoises, purples, yellows and crimsons blends over delicate line drawings of cats, dogs, fish, horses, children, stars, wolves, and so on.

Several of the *naifs* concentrate more on vegetation than people. Francisco Severino paints landscapes from his native Minas Gerais with botanical accuracy. Ferreira, a fisherman, and Edivaldo, a former commercial artist, create luxuriant seascapes and riverscapes in which people are dwarfed by their environment.

The best collection of *naif* art in Brazil – and possibly the world – is in the Museu Internacional do Brazil in Rio de Janeiro. ❑

Modern Architecture

A select group of Brazilian architects – the creators of a fresh "tropical" aesthetic and several new techniques – are among the most honored leaders of their profession today. The urban planner Lúcio Costa, the tropical landscape magician Roberto Burle-Marx and the architect Oscar Niemeyer have left dozens of monuments in Brazil's major cities. Niemeyer also counts among his achievements the sweeping French Communist Party Headquarters in Paris, the National University Campus in Algeria and the facade of the United Nations Building in New York.

The culmination of these architects' talents is undoubtedly the gleaming capital of Brasília, founded in 1960, but the first seeds of modern Brazilian architecture were sown in 1931, when the legendary French architect Le Corbusier gave a lecture series in Rio on functionalism.

Le Corbusier's key themes of simplicity in design, economy in materials, and open spaces made their first appearance in Brazil in the Education Ministry building in Rio de Janeiro, the Palácio Capanema, built 1937– 45 by a team including Costa, Niemeyer, Affonso Reidy and Roberto Burle-Marx, who landscaped the broad esplanade. The ministry incorporates a patio made possible by raising the main structure by 9 meters (30 ft) on concrete pillars called *pilotis*. Inside, the floor spaces were left entirely open for flexibility. A sense of open space and a magnificent view of Guanabara Bay were achieved by nearly doubling the normal window size.

Juscelino Kubitschek, then mayor of Belo Horizonte, brought the same team together again in the 1940s to create what is acknowledged as Brazil's most pleasing park – Pampulha. With its expansive recreational area built around an artificial lake, Pampulha is a unique combination of the landscaper's art together with the discreet placement of public buildings. These include an art museum, a dance pavilion and the Capela de São Francisco.

Niemeyer, fascinated by the "plasticity" of concrete, erected in Pampulha elegant monuments using curves, ramps and undulating roofs. His low-rise, subtropical constructions included great stretches of ground floor patios and breezy esplanades. The overall effect is an architecture of fresh, light structures that seem to hover over the green parkland and blue waters of the lake. Kubitschek was delighted and critics stood in awe.

As Brazil's president in the 1950s, Kubitschek reunited the Pampulha team for an even bolder project, for which he had a persional vision – a new capital city for Brazil. An international competition was held to select the best urban plan for Brasília. But, said Burle-Marx, "everybody knew in advance who was going to win."

Costa's submission consisted of only a few sketches scratched on notepaper. However, as predicted, this crude effort was enough to win him the contract. Kubitschek himself recruited Niemeyer to design the main public buildings.

The new capital represented the last stage in Niemeyer's march towards austere design and spare construction. The searing white walls of the main buildings on the Plaza of Three Powers emulate the texture of the clouds in the sky above. Great fields of glass reflect the sky to create a similar effect. City and sky seem to be one.

"I sought forms distinctly characterizing the buildings, giving them lightness, as if they were only tentatively attached to the ground," said Niemeyer years later. Niemeyer is still Brazil's premier architect, responsible for Rio's Sambodrome and the Contemporary Art Museum in Niterói. He designed the Serpentine Gallery Pavilion in London in 2003, his first UK project. ❑

RIGHT: Niemeyer's stunning museum in Niterói.

COURO
BAHIA

CASA DE COUROS

PLACES

A detailed guide to the entire country, with main sites and attractions clearly cross-referenced with the maps

As its size suggests, Brazil is a giant package with a multitude of gifts. Travelers looking for warm water, white sand, and tropical beauty will be overwhelmed by the Brazilian coastline – the longest, if not the most beautiful, of any country in the world. In an area that could swallow up all the beaches of the Riviera and Hawaii with hundreds of miles left over, the options range from isolated, palm-fringed inlets to miles-long straightways backed by sand dunes. Brazilians will argue eternally over which of the country's beaches is the best, but reach no consensus.

In the north and northeast, colonial monuments dot the state capitals, most of which are located on the water. Salvador and Recife offer the best combination of beach and history. In addition, Salvador has developed a particularly rich culture from its special mix of African and Portuguese influences.

The succession of beautiful beaches continues south, reaching its zenith in the all-time leading beach city of the Americas, Rio de Janeiro. But Rio is more than the sum of its beaches. It is spectacular scenery (mountains and sea), samba, Carnival, and a relaxed, carefree existence. By contrast, in São Paulo, Brazil stops playing and gets down to the serious stuff. The center of the developing world's largest industrial park, São Paulo is the most dynamic city in South America, its hodgepodge of nationalities making it a wonderful Brazilian version of New York.

The further south you travel in Brazil, the more European are the influences, culminating in the states of Paraná, Santa Catarina, and Rio Grande do Sul, where Italian, German, and Polish settlers have left their mark. Here, too, the accent is on sand and water but, of course, not all of Brazil is located on the coast. Inland travelers will discover some of the world's most remarkable natural wonders. Occupying one-third of the nation's territory is the Amazon rainforest, and below the Amazon region, in an area drained by its rivers, is the Pantanal, a natural sanctuary for fish, birds, and animals. In the south, the wildly beautiful Iguaçu Falls is considered by many to be the greatest natural attraction of Brazil.

Opening times: Opening hours for museums and other attractions change frequently in Brazil. Most museums close Monday and during lunch (noon–2pm). There is usually a modest admission charge to enter museums, whereas public gardens and nature reserves are generally free. You are advised to check details at your hotel. ❑

PRECEDING PAGES: Brasília's cathedral of light; colonial architecture in Salvador, capital of Bahia; Rio's Baía de Guanabara sparkles by night.

LEFT: wild flowers on a mountainside near Petrópolis in Rio de Janeiro state.

Bogotá
COLOMBIA
Buenaventura
Cali
Cordillera Central
Río Magdalena
Cordillera Oriental
Río Guaviare
Tumaco
Pasto
Esmeraldas
Cabo de San Francisco
Quito
Caráquez
Manta
ECUADOR
Chimborazo 6310
Guayaquil
Salinas
Golfo de Guayaquil
Puerto Bolívar
Cuenca
Talara
Punta Parinas
Sullana
Paita
Piura
Punta Negra
Chiclayo
Puerto Eten
Trujillo
Chimbote
Puerto Huarmey
Callao
Lima
Pisco
Ica
PERU
A N D E S
Cordillera Central
Cordillera Occidental
Cordillera Oriental
Río Marañón
Río Napo
Río Putumayo
Iquitos
Río Ucayali
Pucallpa
Huánuco
Huancayo
Huancavelica
Ayacucho
Cuzco
6613
Volcán Misti
Arequipa
5821
Mollendo
Juliaca
Nevado Ancohuma 6308
Lago Titicaca
La Paz
BOLIVIA
Cochabamba
Nevado Sajama 6542
Oruro
Lago de Poopó
Sucre
Potosí
Pulacayo
Salar de Uyuni
Tarija
Santa Cruz de la Sierra
Trinidad
Río Beni
Río Mamoré
Puerto Maldonado
Tacna
Arica
Iquique
Tocopilla
Mejillones
Antofagasta
Taltal
Desierto de Atacama
Cerro Zapaleri 5648
Cerro Rincón 5594
Salar de Arizaro
CHILE
Copiapó
Ojos del Salado 6880
Vallenar
6880
6250
La Serena
Coquimbo
6252
Cerro Aconcagua 7021
Vina del Mar
Valparaíso
Santiago
Mendoza
Córdoba
Salinas Grandes
Santiago del Estero
Río Salado
ARGENTINA
Rafaela
Santa Fe
Rosario
Río Paraná
Río Uruguay
Resistencia
Corrientes
Posad
PARAGUAY
Concepción
Asun
Villarric
Chaco Boreal
Bela Vista
Corumbá
PACIFIC OCEAN
Isla San Félix
Isla San Ambrosio
(Chile)
Islas Juan Fernández
(Chile)
Isla Alejandro Selkirk
Isla Róbinson Crusoe
Puerto Ayacucho
VENEZUELA
Mount Roraima 2810
Boa Vista
R o r a i m a
GUYANA
Río Essequibo
SURI
Río Branco
São Gabriel da Cachoeira
Río Uaupés
Río Negro
Río Japurá
Río Içá
Río Solimões
A m a z o n a s
Manaus
Río Amaz
Leticia
Río Jurua
Río Purus
Río Madeira
Porto Velho
Acre
Rio Branco
Guayaramerín
R o n d ô n i a
Serra do Parecis
Diamantino
Cuiabá
B R
U R U G
Santana Livrame
Paysar

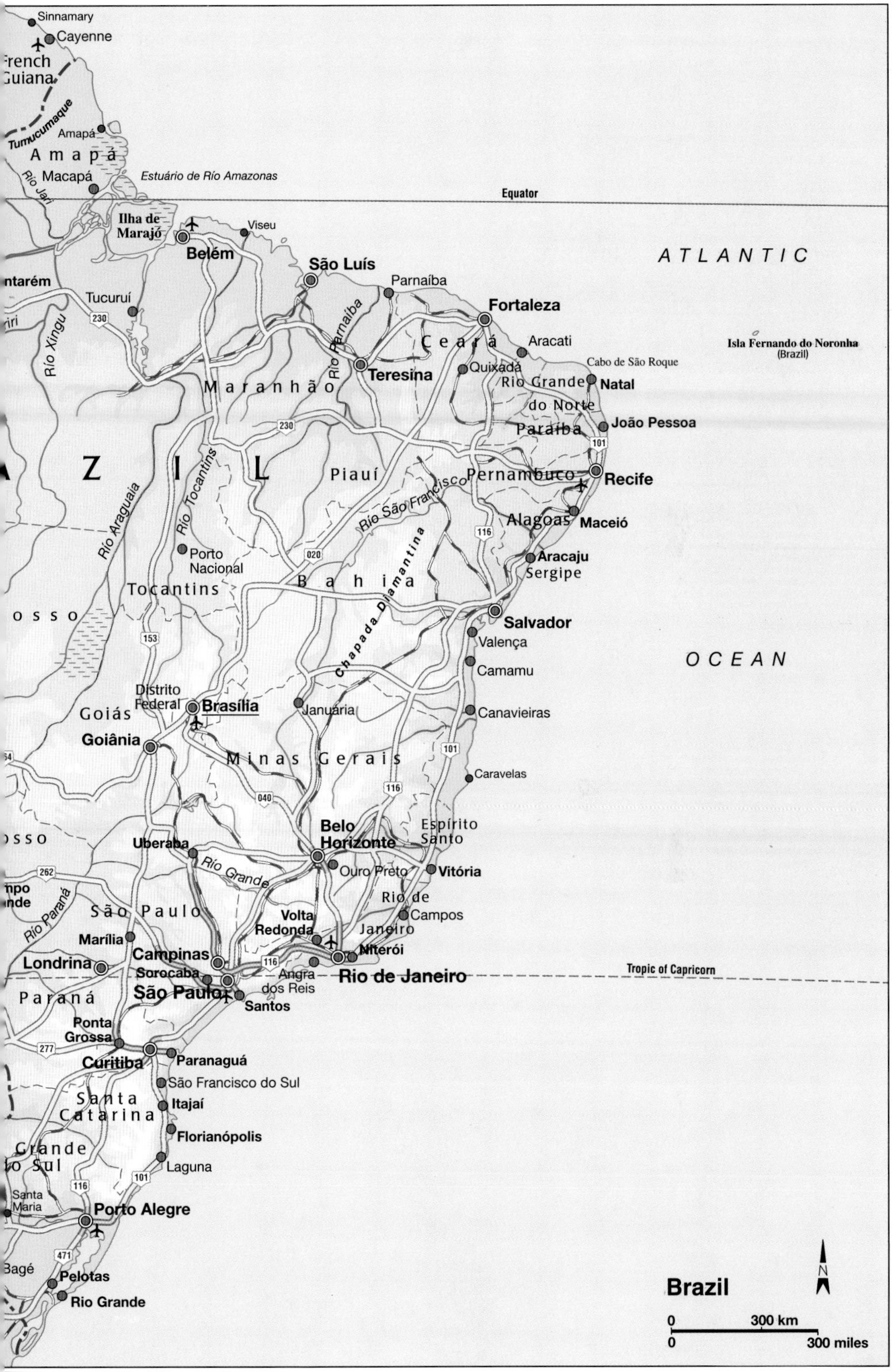
Sinnamary
Cayenne
French Guiana
Tumucumaque
Amapá
Amapá
Macapá
Rio Jari
Estuário de Río Amazonas
Equator
Ilha de Marajó
Viseu
Belém
São Luís
Parnaiba
ATLANTIC
Santarém
Tucuruí
Fortaleza
Rio Xingu
Rio Parnaiba
Ceará
Aracati
Isla Fernando do Noronha (Brazil)
Quixadá
Cabo de São Roque
Teresina
Rio Grande do Norte
Natal
Maranhão
Paraíba
João Pessoa
Piauí
Pernambuco
Recife
Rio Tocantins
Rio São Francisco
Alagoas
Maceió
Rio Araguaia
Chapada Diamantina
Aracaju
Sergipe
Porto Nacional
Tocantins
Bahia
Salvador
Valença
OCEAN
Camamu
Distrito Federal
Brasília
Januária
Canavieiras
Goiás
Goiânia
Minas Gerais
Caravelas
Belo Horizonte
Espírito Santo
Uberaba
Rio Grande
Ouro Preto
Vitória
Rio de Janeiro
Campos
Rio Paraná
São Paulo
Volta Redonda
Marília
Niterói
Campinas
Londrina
Sorocaba
Angra dos Reis
Rio de Janeiro
Tropic of Capricorn
Paraná
São Paulo
Santos
Ponta Grossa
Curitiba
Paranaguá
São Francisco do Sul
Santa Catarina
Itajaí
Florianópolis
Grande do Sul
Laguna
Santa Maria
Porto Alegre
Bagé
Pelotas
Rio Grande
Brazil
0 300 km
0 300 miles
N

THE SOUTHEAST

This region contains Brazil's largest city, São Paulo, and the world-famous beach city of Rio de Janeiro

Though not large by Brazilian standards, this region contains the nation's most important metropolitan centers and, with its superior infrastructure, services, and leisure facilities, is economically streets ahead of the rest of the country. Partly because of this, and because of the allure of sun and sea, the southeast is also Brazil's premier tourist destination.

The industries that have generated wealth and First-World lifestyles for many people in the region, operate mainly inside a triangle of three state capitals – also the three most populous cities in Brazil – Rio de Janeiro, São Paulo, and Belo Horizonte.

Alongside the manufacturing successes of São Paulo in particular, agriculture (from coffee plantations to cattle ranches) is still a major player in the southeast's economy. Sugarcane was the region's first money-spinner in the 16th century, followed by gold and diamonds in Minas Gerais, coffee in Rio (and banking in the former capital city of Brazil) and, most recently, soybeans. The mines of Minas Gerais now yield mainly iron ore, feeding the region's steel industry and securing the port of Vitória as the world's biggest exporter of the mineral. The downsides to all this, however, are pollution and shocking social inequality.

For visitors, the southeastern experience is likely to consist of one or more of three chief attractions. These comprise two natural assets of the region: the hundreds of beautiful beaches along the coast, coupled in Rio with an appealing laid-back lifestyle; and, by contrast, lush forested mountains above. And in landlocked Minas Gerais, there is history and culture to lure those with a yearning to relive the romance of the pioneering days. The colonial towns of this state are showcases for the best of Brazil's baroque art and architecture, a legacy of spectacular riches amassed by mineral prospectors. ❑

LEFT: one of the hundreds of secluded coves in the resort of Angra dos Reis, on Rio state's Costa Verde – the Green Coast.

BODYBOARD

XYZ
XYZ
HOTEL

RIO DE JANEIRO

Though no longer Brazil's capital, Rio is undoubtedly its most beautiful city, where everything from its spectacular landmarks to its brash and glitzy beach scene must be seen to be believed

Maps:
City 142
Area 146

Sprawling in majestic disarray across a strip of land between granite peaks and the South Atlantic ocean, Rio de Janeiro is the final victory of fantasy over fact. Each day, Rio's streets and sidewalks support 9 mil-ion people transported by a million cars, trucks, buses, motorcycles, and cooters, all competing for room in a space designed for less than one-third heir number. This spectacular chaos, though, is normal and does nothing to lampen the enthusiasm of the *carioca*, Rio's imperturbable native son. For he *carioca*, all things are relative, except for one – the wonder and beauty f Rio de Janeiro.

There are about 6 million *cariocas*, the residents of Rio proper, but an dditional 5 million live in suburbs ringing the city. Many are poor by American r European standards – as many as 70 percent. But there is the beach and there s the samba and there is Carnival. And, not least of all, there is the comforting resence of Rio's extraordinary beauty.

Nothing quite prepares you for Rio, not the postcards, not the films, not the omments, nothing, not even living in Rio really does it. There are other cities hat have grown up backed by mountains and fronted by the sea, but there are one where the play of light, the shifting of shadows, the mix of colors and ues are so vibrant and mobile. Each day in Rio is lightly different from the previous one and all are trikingly beautiful.

PRECEDING PAGES: a place in the sun on Copacabana Beach.
LEFT: a statue of Christ the Redeemer at the apex of Corcovado.
BELOW: an Ipanema artist.

arly history

he first tourists officially arrived in Rio on January , 1502. They were part of a Portuguese exploratory oyage headed by Amerigo Vespucci. He entered what he thought to be the mouth of a river, hence the ame Rio de Janeiro or January River. Vespucci's iver was in reality a 380-sq km (147-sq mile) bay, till known by its Amerindian name, Guanabara or Arm of the Sea."

As the Portuguese slowly settled their colony, they oncentrated on regions to the north and south of io, leaving in peace the Tamoio Amerindians who t that time inhabited the land surrounding the bay. his peace was eventually broken by raids launched y French and Portuguese pirates who prowled the razilian coast in search of riches.

In 1555, a French fleet arrived with the intention f founding France's first colony in the southern half f South America. The efforts to colonize the coast-ne were largely unsuccessful and, in 1560, the ortuguese attacked, driving out the last remnants f the French colony in 1565.

From then on, Rio de Janeiro received increasing ttention from Brazil's Portuguese masters. In 1567,

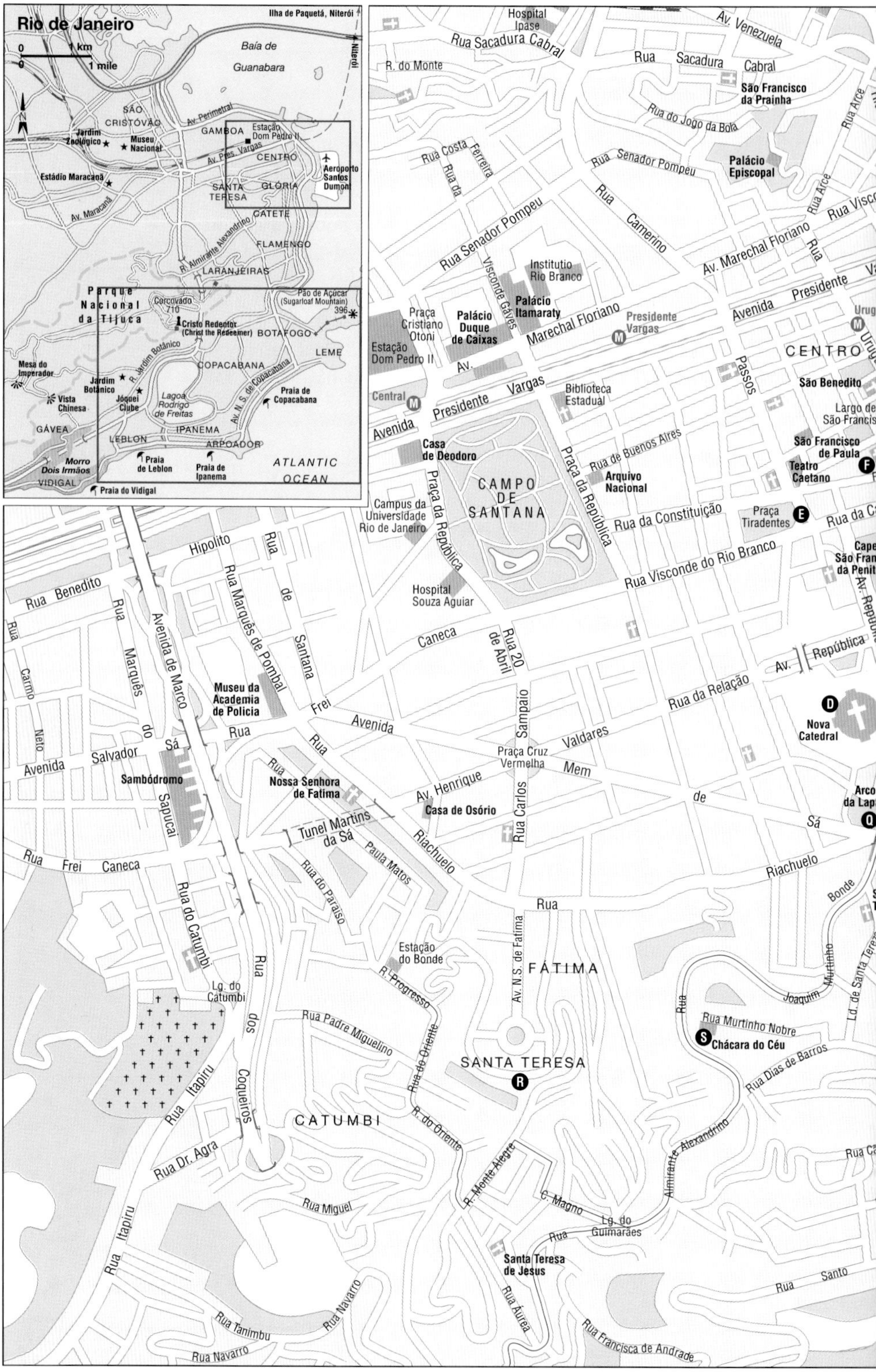
Rio de Janeiro
0 1 km
0 1 mile
Ilha de Paquetá, Niterói
Niterói
Baía de Guanabara
SÃO CRISTÓVÃO
Jardim Zoológico
Museu Nacional
Estádio Maracanã
Av. Maracanã
GAMBOA
Estação Dom Pedro II
Av. Perimetral
Av. Pres. Vargas
CENTRO
Aeroporto Santos Dumont
SANTA TERESA
GLÓRIA
CATETE
FLAMENGO
R. Almirante Alexandrino
LARANJEIRAS
Parque Nacional da Tijuca
Corcovado 710
Cristo Redentor (Christ the Redeemer)
Pão de Açúcar (Sugarloaf Mountain) 396
BOTAFOGO
LEME
R. Jardim Botânico
COPACABANA
Mesa do Imperador
Jardim Botânico
Jóquei Clube
Lagoa Rodrigo de Freitas
Av. N.S. de Copacabana
Praia de Copacabana
Vista Chinesa
GÁVEA
IPANEMA
LEBLON
ARPOADOR
Praia de Leblon
Praia de Ipanema
Morro Dois Irmãos
VIDIGAL
Praia do Vidigal
ATLANTIC OCEAN
Hospital Ipase
Rua Sacadura Cabral
Av. Venezuela
R. do Monte
Rua Sacadura Cabral
São Francisco da Prainha
Rua do Jogo da Bola
Rua Arce
Rua Costa Ferreira
Rua da
Rua Senador Pompeu
Palácio Episcopal
Rua Camerino
Rua Senador Pompeu
Visconde Gávea
Institutio Rio Branco
Palácio Itamaraty
Av. Marechal Floriano
Rua Visc
Praça Cristiano Otoni
Palácio Duque de Caixas
Estação Dom Pedro II
Av. Marechal Floriano
Presidente Vargas
Avenida Presidente Vargas
CENTRO
Passos
São Benedito
Largo de São Francis
Central
Avenida Presidente Vargas
Biblioteca Estadual
Casa de Deodoro
Praça da República
Rua de Buenos Aires
São Francisco de Paula
Teatro Caetano
CAMPO DE SANTANA
Arquivo Nacional
Campus da Universidade Rio de Janeiro
Praça da República
Rua da Constituição
Praça Tiradentes
Rua da C
Hipolito
Rua de Santana
Rua Marquês de Pombal
Rua Visconde do Rio Branco
Cape São Fran da Penit
Hospital Souza Aguiar
Av. Repúblic
Rua Benedito
Rua Carmo Neto
Rua Marquês do Sá
Avenida de Marco
Caneca
Rua 20 de Abril
Av. República
Museu da Academia de Policia
Frei
Rua da Relação
Avenida
Sampaio
Nova Catedral
Avenida Salvador Sá
Rua
Rua
Praça Cruz Vermelha
Valdares
Mem
Sambódromo
Rua Nossa Senhora de Fatima
Av. Henrique
Casa de Osório
Rua Carlos
de
Arco da Lap
Sapucaí
Tunel Martins da Sá
Riachuelo
Sá
Rua Frei Caneca
Paula Matos
Rua do Paraiso
Riachuelo
Rua
Bonde
Rua do Catumbi
Estação do Bonde
Av. N.S. de Fatima
FÁTIMA
Lg. do Catumbi
R. Progresso
Rua
Joaquim Murtinho
Ld. de Santa Teres
Rua dos Coqueiros
Rua Padre Miguelino
Rua do Oriente
Rua Murtinho Nobre
Chácara do Céu
SANTA TERESA
Rua Dias de Barros
Rua Itapiru
R. do Oriente
CATUMBI
Almirante Alexandrino
Rua Dr. Agra
R. Monte Alegre
Rua C
C. Magno
Rua Miguel
Lg. do Guimarães
Rua
Rua Itapiru
Santa Teresa de Jesus
Rua Santo
Rua Navarro
Rua Áurea
Rua Tanimbu
Rua Francisca de Andrade
Rua Navarro

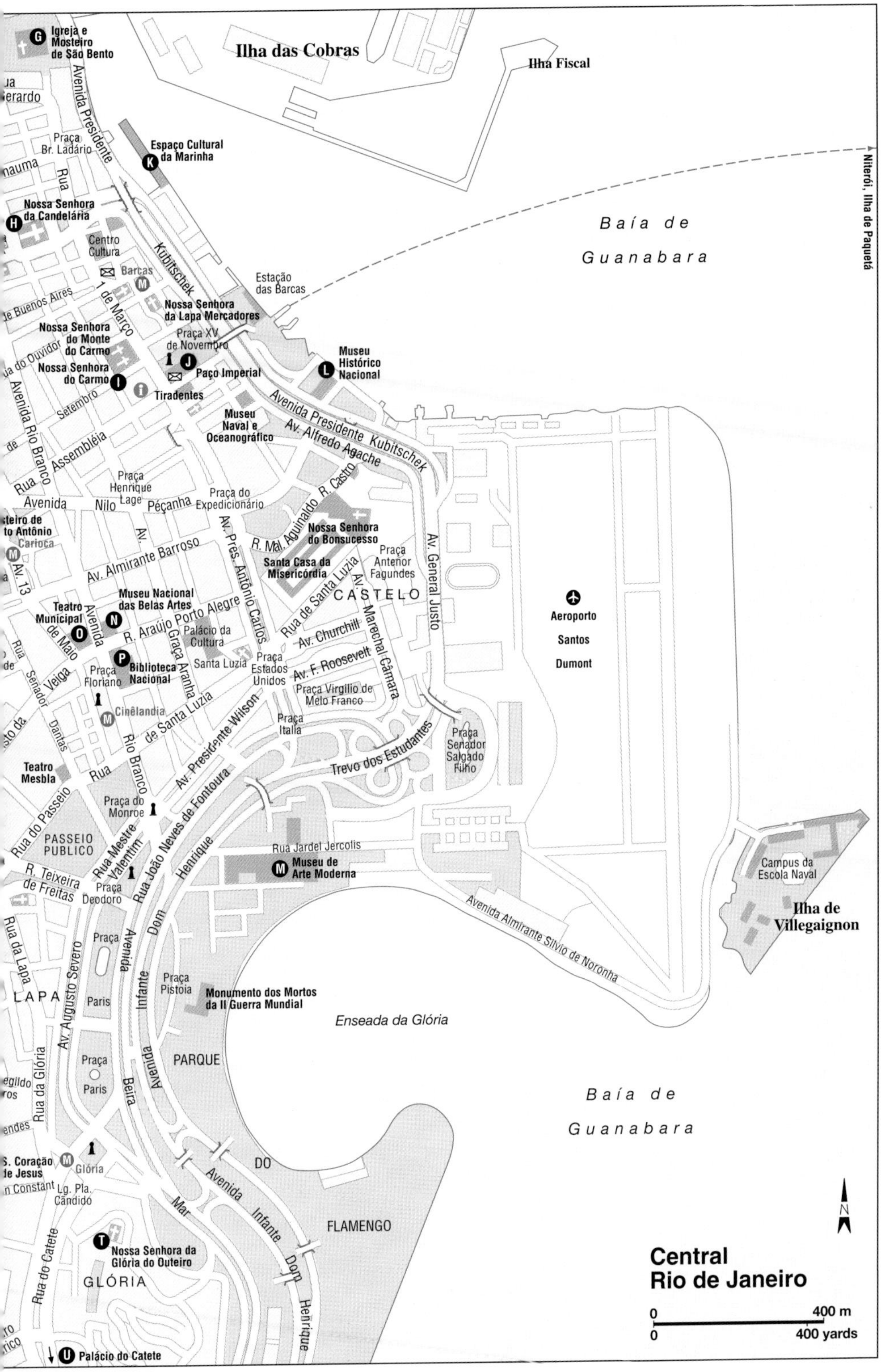
Central
Rio de Janeiro
0
400 m
0
400 yards
N
Ilha das Cobras
Ilha Fiscal
Niterói, Ilha de Paquetá
Baía de Guanabara
Baía de Guanabara
Enseada da Glória
Igreja e Mosteiro de São Bento
Avenida Presidente Kubitschek
Espaço Cultural da Marinha
Praça Br. Ladário
Rua
Nossa Senhora da Candelária
Centro Cultura
Barcas
Estação das Barcas
1 de Março
Nossa Senhora da Lapa Mercadores
Nossa Senhora do Monte do Carmo
Praça XV de Novembro
Paço Imperial
Nossa Senhora do Carmo
Tiradentes
Museu Histórico Nacional
Museu Naval e Oceanográfico
Avenida Presidente Kubitschek
Av. Alfredo Agache
Setembro
Avenida Rio Branco
Rua Assembléia
Praça Henrique Lage
Avenida Nilo Péçanha
Praça do Expedicionário
R. Mal. Aguinaldo
R. Castro
Nossa Senhora do Bonsucesso
Praça Antenor Fagundes
Santa Casa da Misericórdia
Carioca
Av. 13
Av. Almirante Barroso
Av. Pres. Antônio Carlos
Rua de Santa Luzia
Av. Marechal Câmara
CASTELO
Av. General Justo
Aeroporto Santos Dumont
Museu Nacional das Belas Artes
Teatro Municipal
Avenida 13 de Maio
R. Araújo Porto Alegre
Palácio da Cultura
Graça Aranha
Av. Churchill
Av. F. Roosevelt
Praça Estados Unidos
Santa Luzia
Biblioteca Nacional
Praça Floriano
Senador Dantas
Veiga
Cinêlandia
de Santa Luzia
Praça Virgílio de Melo Franco
Praça Itália
Av. Presidente Wilson
Trevo dos Estudantes
Praça Senador Salgado Filho
Teatro Mesbla
Rua
Rio Branco
Rua do Passeio
Praça do Monroe
PASSEIO PUBLICO
Rua Mestre Valentim
Rua João Neves de Fontoura
Rua Jardel Jercolis
Museu de Arte Moderna
R. Teixeira de Freitas
Praça Deodoro
Campus da Escola Naval
Ilha de Villegaignon
Avenida Almirante Silvio de Noronha
Rua da Lapa
Av. Augusto Severo
Praça Paris
Avenida Infante Dom Henrique
Praça Pistoia
Monumento dos Mortos da II Guerra Mundial
LAPA
Praça Paris
PARQUE DO FLAMENGO
Rua da Glória
Avenida Beira Mar
Avenida Infante Dom Henrique
S. Coração de Jesus
Glória
Lg. Pla. Cândido
Rua do Catete
Nossa Senhora da Glória do Outeiro
GLÓRIA
Palácio do Catete

Maps:
City 142
Area 146

the city of São Sebastião de Rio de Janeiro was founded. While named in honor of St Sebastian (having been established on his feast day), the city soon became simply Rio de Janeiro.

By the end of the 16th century, Rio was one of the four largest population centers of the Portuguese colony, and from its port sugar was exported to Europe. Its importance grew steadily over the next 10 years, challenging that of the colony's capital, Salvador, in the northeastern state of Bahia.

In the 18th century, a gold rush in the neighboring state of Minas Gerais turned Rio into the colony's financial center. Gold became the main export item and all of Brazil's gold went through Rio to Portugal. In 1763, the colonial capital was transferred from Salvador to Rio as recognition of Rio's newly won status.

Capital city

Until the 1950s, Rio was Brazil's pre-eminent city. When the Portuguese royal family fled from Napoleon's conquering army in 1808, Rio became capital of the Portuguese Empire. With Brazil's independence in 1822, Rio's title shifted to capital of the Brazilian Empire, changing again in 1889 to capital of the Republic of Brazil. Throughout these years, the city was the economic and political center of Brazil, home to the pomp of the monarchy and the intrigue of the republic.

But the 20th century brought a surge of economic growth in the state of São Paulo. By 1950, São Paulo surpassed Rio in population and economic importance, a lead that it has never relinquished. Then, in 1960, Rio suffered the ultimate humiliation when president Juscelino Kubitschek formally moved the nation's capital to the city he had founded in the center of the country, Brasília.

Since losing its number one status, Rio has floundered. Its previous rankings as the country's leading industrial and financial center had already been taken over by the upstart São Paulo and, although Rio's upper crust still refuses to admit it, the city has become dependent on tourism to a large extent. But, even in the uncomfortable role of number two, Rio

Left: Copacabana Beach with Sugarloaf mountain rising behind.

remains at the heart of the nation's unending political intrigue. Decisions may be made in Brasília and São Paulo, but as the *cariocas* note with some pride, the plots are still hatched in Rio de Janeiro.

TIP

Most of the museums in Rio and the Jardim Botânico *(see page 158)* are closed on Mondays and during Carnival – namely, from the Friday before Carnival up to and including Ash Wednesday.

The remains of history

For visitors to Rio, there is little sense of the city's historical past – a result of sporadic construction booms and the *carioca's* insatiable thirst for the new and modern. With space limited by the contours of the city, something must usually come down before something else can go up. The wrecking ball has done away with much of the original Rio, but there are still unique treasures hidden along the old downtown streets.

In the heart of Rio de Janeiro's downtown area, at the **Largo da Carioca** Ⓐ, is the **Mosteiro de Santo Antônio** Ⓑ. This monastery was built over several colonial periods starting in 1608. The main church was completed in 1780 and next to it stands the 1739 **Capela de São Francisco da Penitência** Ⓒ, whose interior is rich in gold leaf and wood carvings.

South of the Largo da Carioca is a modern area dominated by the Roman Catholic **Catedral Metropolitana** Ⓓ on Avenida Chile, which was inaugurated in 1979. This huge cone-shaped structure can cram in up to 20,000 people. Four 60-meter- (197-ft-) high stained-glass windows throw jewel-bright rainbows of light on the interior.

Situated directly north of the cathedral is **Praça Tiradentes** Ⓔ, a public square where Brazil's most famed revolutionary, Tiradentes, was hanged in 1793 after the Portuguese uncovered his plot to win independence for the colony. Urban decay has removed the square's historical aura, a problem

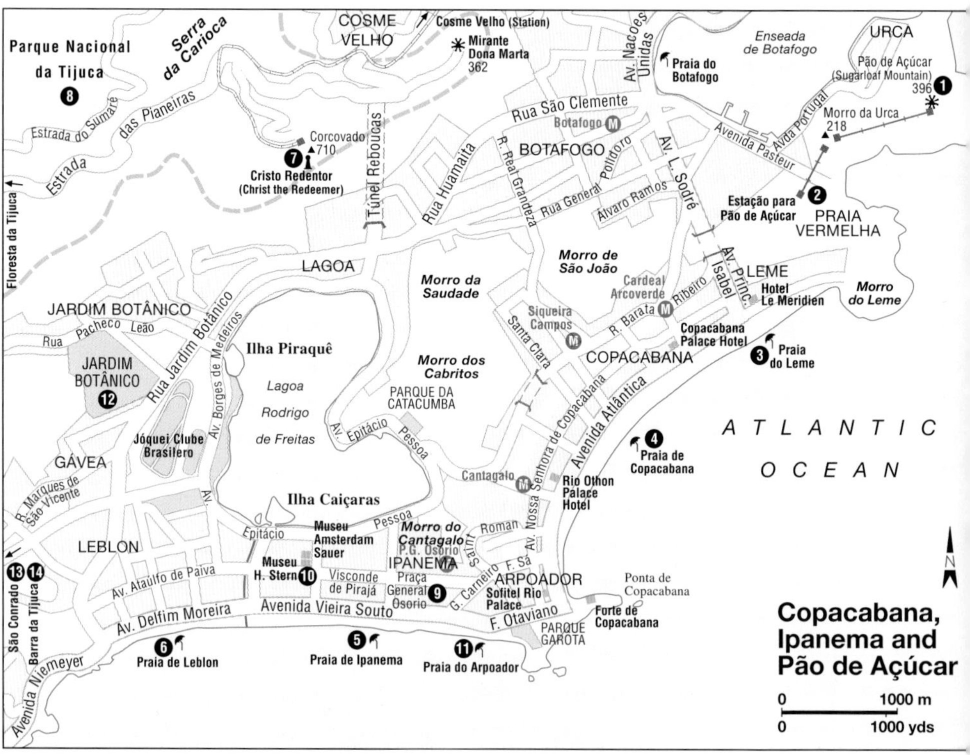

that has also affected the **Largo de São Francisco**, located behind Tiradentes.

On the south side of the Largo, behind the rows of buses that hug the square's contours, is the **Igreja de São Francisco de Paula** (F). With a rococo design on the outside, the church's interior chapel is well known for its paintings by baroque artist Valentim da Fonseca e Silva.

One kilometer north, on Avenida Rio Branco and up a hill, is the **Igreja e Mosteiro de São Bento** (G), dating from 1663. This monastery overlooks the bay, but more impressive and spectacular than the view from the hill is the real splendor of the monastery's gold-leaf wood carvings.

The hill on which the monastery stands is one of the few that survive in downtown Rio. The others that existed during the colonial period have fallen victim to one form of *carioca* progress – a penchant for removing hills to fill in the bay. The most tragic example of this trend took place in 1921–22 when the downtown hill of Castelo was carted off together with most of Rio's remaining 16th- and 17th-century structures. Before the hill disappeared it formed a solid backdrop to Rio's most elegant street, Avenida Central.

Rio's most striking church, the **Igreja da Candelária** (H), is situated three blocks south of the Mosteiro São Bento, along Avenida Rio Branco. Built between 1775 and 1811, the domed Candelária stands like a timeless guardian at the head of Avenida Presidente Vargas. This church once stood close to the water, but is now far removed, thanks to land fills formed by dirt from flattened hills.

Continuing parallel to the curve of the bay, you will come to the church of **Nossa Senhora do Carmo** (I), on **Rua Primeiro de Março**, which was completed in 1761. This spectacular church was the site of the coronations of both

Map on page 142

Grand colonial mansion, Rio de Janeiro.

BELOW: the Candelária church, downtown Rio.

of the Brazilian emperors, Pedro I and Pedro II. Next door, separated by a narrow passageway, is the **Nossa Senhora do Monte do Carmo** church, which was completed in 1770.

One block east, in a neighborhood containing a maze of streets that are always crowded with business executives, shoppers, and an army of office boys, is **Praça XV de Novembro**. This square is home to the **Paço Imperial** **J**, a classic structure that dates from 1743 and first served as the capital building for Brazil's governor generals and was later used as the imperial palace. Restored in the 1980s, the Paço is now a cultural center incorporating a theater, movie house, library, exhibition spaces, and restaurants. Across Rua da Assembléia is the recently restored **Tiradentes Palace**, seat of the State of Rio de Janeiro parliament. Admission is free and there are displays in English. The building is an impressive example of the belle-époque style – don't miss the Grand Salon.

TIP

Pick up a copy of *Nomad*, a free guide to the city, from certain shops and hotels. Updated every two months, it has good maps and lots of detailed, practical information

Fine museums

Further north, situated on the bay, is an area designated the **Espaço Cultural da Marinha** **K**, a floating museum in the torpedo-boat *Bauru*. The center includes the **Museu Naval e Oceanográfico** south of the Praça XV (Avda Alfredo Agache; open Mon–Fri noon–5.30 pm, Sat, Sun and hols 9am–5.30pm), with finely detailed models of ships. Some 500 meters (550 yards) southeast of the naval museum is the **Museu Histórico Nacional** **L** (Praça Marechal Ancora; open Tues–Fri 10am– 5.30pm, weekends and holidays pm only), whose collection of colonial buildings holds Brazil's national archives of rare documents and colonial artifacts along with a collection of photographs by

BELOW: Praça XV, with Ilha Fiscal and Niterói.

Spaniard Juan Gutierrez, who documented Rio at the end of the 19th century.

The **Museu de Arte Moderna** Ⓜ (Parque do Flamengo; open Tues–Sun noon–6pm) is on the Glória Bay beside the downtown airport. The museum complements its own national collection with a series of visiting international exhibits. It is also the venue for the city's annual jazz festival in October.

Most of Rio's principal museums are either downtown or nearby, such as the **Museu do Indio** (Indian Museum), in the Botafogo neighborhood 10 minutes from downtown – an excellent source of information on Brazil's indigenous tribes (Rua das Palmeiras 55; open Tues–Fri 9.30am–5.30pm, weekends pm only). **Casa Rui Barbosa**, near the Indian Museum, was home to one of Brazil's famous scholars and political leaders.

Fifteen minutes by car from downtown is the **Museu Nacional** (Quinta de Boa Vista; open daily except Mon), the residence of the Brazilian Imperial family during the 19th century. The palace is impressive and houses exhibits on natural history, archaeology, and minerals. It is located next door to Rio's zoo.

One of the most impressive buildings on the Avenida Rio Branco, five blocks north of the **Museu de Arte Moderna**, is the **Museu Nacional das Belas Artes** Ⓝ (Museum of Fine Arts; open Tues–Fri 10am–6pm, Sat–Sun 2–6pm), where the works of Brazil's greatest artists are on display.

The Rio Branco was inaugurated in 1905 as the Avenida Central, in response to President Rodrigues Alves' vision of a tropical Paris. Unfortunately, Alves the visionary overlooked the fact that downtown Rio de Janeiro, unlike Paris, had no room to grow other than vertically. Through the years, the elegant three- and five-story buildings of Avenida Central were replaced by 30-story skyscrapers. In the process, the avenue also underwent a name change.

Map on page 142

TIP

A warning: the Santa Teresa trolleys are the targets of petty thieves and pickpockets. Hold on to your purses, cameras, and wallets.

BELOW: the Santa Teresa trolley packs them in.

TIP

Forró music, originally from the northeast of Brazil, has become very popular in the southeast. Try the Forr do Ballroom on Rua Humait 110 on Thursdays, or Xote Coladinho on Arcos da Lapa on Tuesdays.

Of the 115 buildings that flanked Avenida Central in 1905, only 10 remain. These include the **Museu Nacional das Belas Artes**; the adjacent **Teatro Municipal** **O**, a splendid replica of the Paris Opera (open Mon–Fri 10am–5pm; three guided tours a day; tel: 21-226 2359), and the **Biblioteca Nacional** **P** (National Library; open Mon–Fri 9am–8pm, Sat 9am–3pm), an eclectic mixture of neoclassic and art nouveau holding around 9 million works.

Mountain trolley to Santa Teresa

Departing from downtown in front of the **Petrobrás** building (Brazil's state oil company) are open-sided trolley cars that make the picturesque climb up the mountain and along the surprise-filled streets of the **Santa Teresa** neighborhood. The highlight of the trip is the crossing of the **Carioca Aqueduct**, known to locals as the **Arcos da Lapa** **Q**, one of downtown Rio's most striking landmarks. Built in the 18th century to carry water from Santa Teresa to the downtown area, the aqueduct became a viaduct in 1896 when the trolley car service began operating. The Santa Teresa trolley offers one of the most interesting day trips in Rio.

Only a few minutes from Rio's crowded downtown streets, **Santa Teresa** **R** is a tranquil nest of eccentricities perched atop the mountain spine that presses against the city down below. According to legend, black slaves used Santa Teresa's mountain trails to escape to freedom during the 18th century, when Rio was Brazil's leading slave port. The neighborhood began to receive more permanent residents when a yellow fever epidemic forced the city's population to flee to the hills to escape from the mosquitoes carrying the disease. By the end of the 19th century, Santa Teresa became a privileged address for Rio's wealthy

BELOW: a view of Niterói, painted by Herni Nicolas Vinet in the 19th century.

whose Victorian mansions sprouted from its hillsides. Intellectuals and artists were also attracted by its cool breezes and tranquil setting, which were at the same time removed yet close to the hectic downtown area.

One of the neighborhood's most famous 20th-century residents – certainly its most notorious – was the "Great Train Robber" Ronnie Biggs *(see page 164).*

Map on page 142

Distinctive districts

Today, hanging from its hillsides and flanking its winding, cobblestoned streets, the architectural hodgepodge made up of Santa Teresa's homes is one of Rio's most distinctive features. Gabled mansions with wrought-iron fixtures and stained-glass windows stand beside more staid and proper edifices, all perfectly at home atop a mountain that provides a spectacular vista of the **Baía de Guanabara** below. Views are as plentiful as flowers and greenery in Santa Teresa. The best are from the second trolley station.

There are several public stairways that lead from Santa Teresa's streets to the neighborhoods of **Glória** and **Flamengo** hundreds of feet below; and the grounds of the **Museu Chácara do Céu** **S** (Little House in the Sky Museum) that look out over the city, the aqueduct and the bay.

The museum itself (Rua Murtinho Nobre 93; open Wed–Mon noon–5pm) is one of Santa Teresa's main attractions. It contains a superb collection of works by Brazilian modernists, including paintings by Brazil's greatest modern artist, Candido Portinari, as well as those by European masters Modigliani, Dalí, Matisse, Monet, and Picasso.

A curvaceous statue on Sugarloaf mountain, said to emulate Rio's sweeping bays.

In the Glória neighborhood east of Santa Teresa, there is, perched on a hilltop overlooking Guanabara Bay, a precious architectural gem, the **Nossa Senhora da Glória do Outeiro** chapel **T**, popularly known simply as the Glória church. This petite 1720s construction, with its gleaming white walls and classic lines, is one of the best-preserved examples of Brazilian baroque and a landmark of downtown Rio.

BELOW: a *carioca* beach bum.

Nearby in **Catetc** is the **Palácio do Catete** **U**, the former residence of Brazilian presidents, which now houses the **Museu da República** (Rua do Catete 153; Tues–Fri noon–5pm, weekends and holidays 2–6pm) exhibiting historical paintings. Adjoining it is the **Museu do Folclore Édison Carneiro** (Folklore Museum; open Tues–Fri 11am–6pm, Sat and Sun 3–6pm, closed Mon) with interesting displays on everyday life and popular religion in Brazil.

The bay

Ever since its "discovery" in 1502, Rio de Janeiro's **Baía de Guanabara** has delighted visitors. One Charles Darwin wrote in 1823: "Guanabara Bay exceeds in its magnificence everything the European has seen in his native land." In modern times, however, the bay has become a massive refuse dump for the *cariocas*, with an estimated 1½ million tons of waste poured into it daily, making it a virtual cesspool. Despite this, views of the bay are beautiful, accented by the two forts, one from the 17th century and the other from the 19th, which guard its entrance.

TIP

Try to avoid visiting Sugarloaf between 10 and 11am and between 2 and 3pm when a lot of the tourist buses arrive. The best time to go is an hour before sunset, to see the city by day and by night. Visit on a clear day for the best views.

Trips across the bay to the city of **Niterói** on the far side or to the islands within the bay offer spectacular vistas looking back at Rio. The cheapest trip is by ferry boat, but more comfortable aerofoils also make bay trips (both the ferry and the aerofoils leave from Praça XV de Novembro). Schooner trips take in various tourist points and leave every Sunday at 10am, also from the Praça XV. Two-hour sunset trips of the bay depart daily at 3pm and 5pm from the Glora Marina. Within the Baía de Guanabara, the favorite stop is the **Ilha de Paquetá**, largest of its 84 islands. Visitors may rent bicycles or take a magical trip around the island by horse-drawn buggy, but swimming in the bay is definitely to be avoided.

Although *cariocas* can be dismissive about Niterói, the city does have attractions: the **Parque da Cidade**, at the end of a winding uphill road through a tropical forest, provides stunning views of the bay and the mountains. At the foot of this hill is the Praia Itaipú, a beach that offers the same panoramic views of Rio. Niterói is also the site of the **Museu de Arte Contemporânea** (open Tues–Sun 11am–6pm). Designed by Oscar Niemeyer, the spaceship-like building is the attraction, rather than its rather mediocre exhibits. See it at night, when it is spectacularly lit.

Sugarloaf

Undoubtedly the most famous landmark of Guanabara Bay is **Pão de Açúcar** ❶, the solid granite prominence that rises 270-meters (887-ft) high at the bay's entrance, and known to the world as Sugarloaf. The Amerindians called this singularly shaped monolith *Pau-na-Acuqua*, meaning high, pointed, isolated peak. To the Portuguese this sounded like *pão de açúcar* (sugarloaf) and its

BELOW: the cable car ride to the top of Sugarloaf Mountain.

Map on page 146

shape reminded them of the clay molds used to refine sugar into a conical lump called a sugarloaf. In 1912, the first cable car line was built from **Praia Vermelha ❷** at the base of Sugarloaf to its top in two stages, the first stopping at the rounded **Morro da Urca** (Urca Mountain) at the foot of Sugarloaf.

Visitors are whisked up in Italian-made bubble-shaped cars, which each hold up to 75 passengers and offer 360-degree vision. Each stage takes just 3 minutes, with cars starting out from the top and the bottom simultaneously and zipping past each other in the middle of the ride. Departures from the Praia Vermelho station, where tickets are sold, are every half hour from 8am to 10pm.

From both the Morro da Urca and Sugarloaf, visitors have excellent views on all sides, with paths leading to viewpoints. To the west lie the beaches of **Leme ❸**, **Copacabana ❹**, **Ipanema ❺**, and **Leblon ❻** and the mountains beyond. At your feet are **Botafogo** and **Flamengo** leading to downtown, with **Corcovado** peak and the statue of Christ the Redeemer behind. To the north, the high bridge across the bay connects Rio de Janeiro and Niterói, with the latter's beaches stretching away toward the east. At any hour of the day or night, the view from Sugarloaf is extraordinarily beautiful.

The Copacabana Palace Hotel, which opened in Rio in 1923, was South America's very first luxury hotel.

The beaches

While the bay's waters are not fit for swimming today, the beaches that encircle it were once the principal attraction for *cariocas*. At the start of the 20th century, tunnels were constructed linking bayside Botafogo with the ocean beach of Copacabana, and Rio's beach life found a new home. Since then, the *cariocas'* endless search for the best beach has carried them constantly south, first to Copacabana, then to Ipanema and Leblon, then São Conrado, Barra da Tijuca and beyond.

BELOW: volleyball on the beach.

With the passage of time, a day on the beach has evolved from a tranquil family outing into an all-encompassing cradle-to-grave lifestyle of its own. Today, the beach is not part of the life of Rio, it *is* the life. The beach is a nursery and a school yard, a reading room, a soccer field, and a volleyball court. It serves as a singles bar, restaurant, and rock concert hall; an exercise center and office all at the same time. Occasionally, someone goes into the water, but only for a refreshing pause before returning to more important beach-based activities.

Cariocas read, gossip, flirt, jog, exercise, dream, think, and even close business deals on the beach. On a glorious summer weekend, nearly the whole of Rio spends some time on the beach. And this isn't to say they aren't on the beach during the week as well. One of the great mysteries of Rio is how anything ever gets done on a warm, sunny day.

The great equalizer

Carioca sociologists claim that the beach is Rio's great equalizer in addition to being its great escape valve. According to this theory, the poor who make up the majority of the city's residents, the inhabitants of its mountainside *favelas*, its housing projects and northern slums, have equal access to the beach and are therefore satisfied even though they are poor. Surprisingly enough, there is some truth to this simplistic and romantic notion, although a rising crime rate indicates that not all of the poor are satisfied. The beach, though, remains open to all and it is free.

But while they are democratic and integrated, Rio's beaches are not entirely classless. A quick passage along the sands of Copacabana and Ipanema will take you past small "neighborhoods" of bathers each congregating in its own social type or group – gays, couples, families, teenagers, yuppies, celebrities, and so on. If you return the next day, you will find the same groups in exactly the same places. These "beach corner societies" have become a permanent characteristic of life in Rio de Janeiro.

TIP

To get two views over the city from Corcovado for the price of one, go up around 3pm in daylight, and descend again after seeing the city light up at dusk. The last train leaves the top at about 6pm.

Copacabana

Although aged, somewhat the worse for wear, and the concentration of large, upmarket hotels having made the area a target for crime, **Praia de Copacabana** remains the centerpiece of Rio de Janeiro's beaches. Its classic crescent curve anchored at one end by the imposing presence of Sugarloaf has made Copacabana a world-class picture postcard scene for decades. Copacabana beach first gained fame in the 1920s after the opening of the high-class **Copacabana Palace Hotel**. It was also in the early 1920s that gambling was legalized in Brazil and Copacabana subsequently became home to many of Rio's liveliest casinos.

With gambling and the continent's best hotel, Copacabana evolved into an international watering hole for the world's most glamorous celebrities. Black tie evening at the Copa, as the hotel was baptized by the *cariocas*, became *de rigueur* for internationally famous figures, including such luminaries as Lana Turner, Eva Perón, Ali Khan, and Orson Welles. Even John F. Kennedy dropped in for a visit once in the 1940s.

BELOW: relaxing in a hammock made for two.

Casino gambling was finally outlawed in Brazil in 1946, but the party rolled on into the 1950s. Copacabana suffered a slump in the 1960s, but with the construction of three major hotels and the refurbishing of others, including the landmark Copacabana Palace, the beach staged a comeback in the 1980s. Today, Copacabana beach has been widened by landfill, although Ipanema is an altogether more attractive and safer neighborhood to stay in.

Across its steaming sands on hot summer days pass literally hundreds of thousands of sun and water worshipers. Hawkers of beverages, food, suntan lotions, and hats sway across the beach, adding a musical accompaniment to the flow of colors with their singsong voices and the frantic rhythms with which they beat on small drums and whirl metal ratchets. Bathers linger beneath multicolored beach umbrellas or canopies, then briefly wet themselves in the ocean before parading across **Avenida Atlântica**, the beach drive, for a cool beer at one of the sidewalk cafés.

On any given summer weekend, up to a half-million *cariocas* and tourists will descend on the locale to promenade on Copacabana. The crush of the beach is an extension of the crush beyond the beach. The quintessential Rio neighborhood, Copacabana is made up of 109 streets on which more than 350,000 people live, squeezed close together into high rises by the mountains at their back and the Atlantic in front. For this urban mass, the beach is their final backyard escape into open spaces.

Map on page 146

Christ the Redeemer

Overlooking Rio's beach life is the world-famous statue of **Cristo Redentor** ❼ (Christ the Redeemer), standing with his arms outstretched atop **Corcovado** or Hunchback Mountain. To reach the 710-meter (2,330-ft) summit you may go by rented car or taxi, but the most recommended means is the 3.7-km (2.3-mile) Corcovado Railroad with trains leaving every 30 minutes (daily 8am– 7pm) from a station in the **Cosme Velho** neighborhood, halfway between downtown and Copacabana. The scenic ride climbs through tropical foliage with views of the mountain and city below. From the upper station, a recently installed escalator takes visitors the short distance to the summit, where there is a café.

On the top, the granite statue is visible day and night from most parts of Rio. Standing 38 meters (125 ft) tall, it is the work of a team of artisans headed by French sculptor Paul Landowsky and was completed in 1931. Since then it has competed with Sugarloaf for the titles of symbol of Rio and best viewpoint. One decided advantage that Corcovado has over Sugarloaf is that it provides the best view possible of Sugarloaf itself. Towering over the city, Corcovado looks down at Sugarloaf, Niterói, the southern ocean beaches – Copacabana and Ipanema – and the beautiful Lagoa Rodrigo de Freitas, known to *cariocas* simply as the Lagoa (Lagoon). For an even more spectacular panorama, take to the skies in a helicopter. Helisight, tel: 2511-2141, has 4 helipads and 8 different flights available.

A ceramic tile map of Tijuca National Park.

BELOW: swan pedalos at Lagoa Rodrigo de Freitas.

Enveloping Corcovado is one of Rio's least known but most enchanting natural attractions, the **Parque Nacional da Tijuca** ❽, a tropical reserve that includes 100 km (60 miles) of narrow, two-lane roads, winding through the forest's thick vegetation interrupted periodically by waterfalls. Along the way are several excellent viewpoints not to be missed. The **Mesa do Imperador**, according to legend, is where Dom Pedro II brought his family for royal picnics where they could look down directly at the lagoon and southern neighborhoods. The **Vista Chinesa** (Chinese View) looks toward the south with a sidewise glance at Corcovado. The **Dona Marta Belvedere**, at 362 meters (1,190ft), just below the summit of Corcovado, looks directly toward Sugarloaf.

TIP

Jeep tours through the Tijuca National Park are offered by Jeep Adventure Tours, tel: 21-226 8055, cell: 21-998 5750

Maracanã Stadium

This is the country's temple of soccer, where Pelé scored his one-thousandth goal in 1969 and where major games take place on Sunday afternoons and Wednesday evenings. Trips to matches and to the stadium's hall of fame (on non-match days) can be arranged through "Be a Local", tel: 21-9643 0366.

Ipanema

Along much of its route, the main road through the **Tijuca National Park** provides often spectacular glimpses of the beach and neighborhood of **Ipanema** ❾, its extension, **Leblon**, and the **Lagoa Rodrigo de Freitas**. This is the money belt of Rio, home to a mixture of traditional wealth and the *nouveaux riches*. Ipanema (an Amerindian name meaning dangerous waters) began as an adventure in land development in 1894, marked by dirt roads running through the existing sand dunes with a handful of bungalows along the sides of the roads. The neighborhood was mostly ignored until the crush of Copacabana became too much for its well-to-do residents and they moved to the next beach south.

From the 1950s to the present day, Ipanema has undergone an extraordinary real-estate boom and population explosion and since the 1960s, a surging army of high-rises, which have turned the Ipanema skyline into a smaller version of Copacabana.

In the 1960s, the neighborhood was swept by a highly romanticized wave of liberalism. Rio's bohemians and intellectuals gathered at Ipanema's sidewalk cafés and bars to philosophize over the movements of the decade – the hippies, rock 'n' roll, the Beatles, drugs, long hair, and free love. Humor was also present, expressed monthly through a satirical newspaper that proudly announced the founding of the Independent Republic of Ipanema. Two of the Republic's prominent members were the poet Vinícius de Moraes and the songwriter Tom Jobim. One day, Jobim, in the spirit of the period, became enchanted with a beautiful schoolgirl who walked by his habitual perch in an Ipanema bar. Each day for weeks, he followed her daily passage, and even invited his pal Moraes to join him. Inspired by her beauty, the two put their feelings in to words and music, the result being the pop classic, *The Girl from Ipanema.*

BELOW: a bikini vendor on the beach does a roaring trade.

Map on page 146

This mystical blend of Camelot and Haight Ashbury received a severe blow with the 1964 military coup and the subsequent crackdown on liberals. Today, Moraes and Jobim are both dead and the girl, Heloisa Pinheiro, is a middle-aged businesswoman and mother of four. However, the story of the song's origin is commemorated in place-names: the street down which Heloisa walked is now named after Moraes and the bar is called *A Garota de Ipanema* (The Girl from Ipanema).

Despite its brevity, this period defined the modern *carioca* spirit – irreverent, independent, and decidedly liberal toward matters of the flesh and spirit. It also propelled Ipanema into the vanguard in determining *carioca* style, pushing Copacabana back into second-class status.

Today, Ipanema is Rio's center of chic and sophistication. If it's not "in" in Ipanema then it's simply not in. The city's poshest boutiques line the streets of Ipanema and Leblon, which are essentially the same neighborhood – a canal linking the lagoon with the ocean divides the two, giving rise to separate names but a shared identity.

Selling drinks on Ipanema beach.

The trendiest of Ipanema's famed boutiques are located on the neighborhood's main street, **Visconde de Pirajá**, and on adjoining side streets running in both directions, of which **Rua Garcia d'Avila** is the best. Ipanema's shops cater to all tastes and all ages, offering leather goods and shoes in addition to clothing and gifts. Although this is not the cheapest area to shop in the city, prices are very reasonable compared to Europe and the United States.

Ipanema in recent years has become Rio de Janeiro's center for jewelry. Brazil is the largest producer of colored gemstones in the world, and samples of every variety and hue can be found on the block of Visconde de Pirajá

BELOW: dusk over Botafogo Bay.

Showing the way to the Botanic Gardens.

between Garcia d'Avila and Rua Anibal Mendonça. This block is home to seven jewelry stores, including the world headquarters of H. Stern, Brazil's leading jeweler and one of the largest in the world. The **Museu H. Stern** ⓾ Rua Garcia d'Avila 113, 3rd Floor; open Mon–Fri 8.30am–5.30pm, Sat 8.30am–12.30pm; admission free and free taxi to museum from major hotels) houses a fascinating exhibition about everything to do with jewelry, and a free guided multilingual tour is available. There is also the option to buy exclusive jewelry at H. Stern prices.

The beach of the beautiful people

At the Copacabana end of Ipanema beach is a section called **Arpoador** ⓫, which is famed for its surfing. At the far end, standing sentinel, is the imposing **Dois Irmãos** ("Two Brothers") mountain – a feature in one of Rio de Janeiro's most spectacular natural settings. In the morning, joggers and cyclists rub shoulders, the former on the sidewalk and the latter in the *ciclovia* (cycle lane) that runs the length of the beach, while exercise class participants go through their public gyrations. During the day, and for much of the evening, the beautiful people of the city hang out here. A wonderful, tension-relieving massage can be had from Amarilton, who can be found every day on the beach between the two rainbow flags.

Palm trees add to the special, intimate setting of Ipanema. At sunset, the sidewalk is crowded with lovers of all ages, often strolling along hand in hand. Ipanema is less boisterous than the beachfront of Copacabana, and it preserves the romance of Rio more than any of the city's 22 other beaches.

BELOW: Christ the Redeemer looks down on Rio.

Away from the beaches

Inland from Ipanema is another of the symbols of Rio de Janeiro's romantic side, the **Lagoa Rodrigo de Freitas**, often referred to simply as Lagoa. This natural lake, originally part of a 16th-century sugar plantation, provides a breathing space from the crowded southern beaches of the city. Around its winding shore, joggers, walkers, and cyclists beat a steady path, while at the same time enjoying the best of Rio's mountain scenery – Corcovado and the Tijuca Forest, Dois Irmãos Mountain and the distant flat top of Gávea Mountain.

Toward the mountains on the side of the lagoon farthest from the beach is Rio's **Jardim Botânico** ⓬ (Botanical Garden), an area of 140 hectares (340 acres) containing 235,000 plants and trees representing over 8,000 species (open daily 8am–5pm). Created by Portuguese prince regent Dom João VI in 1808, the garden was used to introduce plants from other parts of the world, including tea, cloves, cinnamon, and pineapples. Many species of birds and other wildlife can also be seen. The tranquil garden is a refreshing respite from the heat and urban rush and tumble of Rio, and it deserves a long, studied walk through its many and varied examples of tropical greenery. The majestic avenue at the garden's entrance is lined with a double row of 134 royal palms all more than 160 years old.

The outlying beaches

More beaches extend south of Ipanema. The first, **São Conrado**, rests in an idyllic natural amphitheater, surrounded on three sides by thickly forested mountains and hills – including the **Pedra da Gávea**, a massive block of granite more impressive in shape and size than Sugarloaf.

São Conrado beach closes the circle on this small, enclosed valley and is popular among the affluent youth of Rio. São Conrado can be reached from Ipanema by a tunnel underneath Dois Irmãos Mountain but a far more interesting route is **Avenida Niemeyer**, an engineering marvel that was completed in 1917. The avenue hugs the mountain's cliffs from the end of Leblon to São Conrado. At times, it looks straight down into the sea with striking vistas of the ocean and Ipanema looking back. But the best view is saved for the end, where the avenue descends to São Conrado and suddenly, the ocean, the beach and the towering presence of Gávea emerge into sight. In Rio de Janeiro, the spectacular can become a commonplace, but this is a view that startles with its suddenness and unmatched beauty.

Notwithstanding the beauty of São Conrado, the growth of the city southward and the presence of shanty towns in the vicinity have turned it into one of the most polluted beaches in Rio.

On the cliff side of Avenida Niemeyer is the neighborhood of Vidigal, an eclectic mix of the super rich and those who live in abject poverty. The mountain-side homes of the former have been surrounded slowly by the advancing shacks of the Vidigal *favela*.

Space and the absence of the crush of Copacabana and Ipanema are the main factors that separate the outlying beach areas from their better-known

Map on page 146

TIP

To find out how the other half live in Rio, go on a guided tour of a *favela*. Contact Favela Tour 021-3322 2727, or 9989 0074

BELOW: magnificent giant Vitoria Regis water lilies in Rio's Botanic Garden.

neighbors. Although it is compact in area, the lack of people means São Conrado has an uncrowded openness that is further guaranteed by the 18-hole **Gávea Golf Course**, which runs through the middle.

São Conrado

One of the city's more exclusive addresses, **São Conrado** ⓭ is also a near perfect microcosm of Rio society. On the valley floor live the middle- and upper-middle-class *cariocas* in luxurious apartments, houses, and condominium complexes, which line the beachfront and flank the golf course. The privileged location of the links makes it one of the most beautiful in the world and adds to the dominating presence of greenery in São Conrado.

But as lush as São Conrado is, the beauty of the whole area is marred by a development that contrasts starkly with its wealthier face. There is a swath cut out of the hillside vegetation where **Rocinha**, South America's largest *favela* *(see page 166)*, spreads like a blight across the mountain from top to bottom. In this swarming anthill of narrow alleys and streets, at least 150,000 people live – and some estimates are double this number. Most of them inhabit tumbledown brick houses and shacks, pressed tightly together side by side.

At the end of São Conrado, a highway surges past the massive **Gávea**, where hang gliders soar overhead. On the right, another road leads to the Tijuca National Park and Corcovado, passing through the thick tropical forest and providing memorable views of the beaches below. You may wish to experience the exhilarating sensation of jumping off a runway 510 meters (1,680 ft) above sea level, soaring above the bay, and then gliding down to the beach. To fill this need, several of Rio's more experienced and trustworthy hang-glider pilots

Rio's motor racing circuit, the Autódromo Nelson Piquet, located behind the Barra, now hosts the Champ Car series' race and the Brazilian Motorbike Grand Prix.

BELOW: Lagoa Rodrigo de Freitas,

Map on page 146

offer tandem rides. It is safer not to take rides with hang-gliders touting on the beach. Paulo Celani has over 15 years' experience, tel: 21-226 8055, cell: 21-998 5750.

From São Conrado, an elevated roadway continues on to the far western beaches, twisting along the sharply vertical cliffs where the mansions of the rich hang suspended at precarious angles. Emerging from a tunnel, you are suddenly face to face with the **Barra da Tijuca** ⓮, firmly established as a prestigious middle- and upper middle-class suburb.

Over the past 15 years, the height of the buildings in the Barra, as it is commonly known, increased dramatically. Prestigious high-rise blocks march toward the mountains on the western horizon. It is now a North American-style city within the city, dubbed Brazil's Miami. Everything is more expensive here, and a car is pretty much a necessity for getting around. The Barra is also where Latin America's largest shopping center, **Barra Shopping**, is located. This is a thriving, opulent consumer paradise that acts as a magnet for Rio's discerning shoppers.

Barra's 18-km (11-mile) beach fills up during the weekend. All along the beach drive, **Avenida Sernambetiba**, the traffic is bumper to bumper as Rio's middle classes seek to escape the dust and pollution of the city.

At night, like the other Rio beaches, the Barra comes alive. Nuts and People are currently two of the most popular nightclubs in the neighborhood, along with the Hard Rock Café Rio. There are also plenty of excellent places to eat, from smart international restaurants to fast-food outlets, to the multitude of shacks and trailers that line the Avenida Sernambetiba.

BELOW: faster than four-wheeled transport.

The Barra's trailers

The Barra's answer to Copacabana's sidewalk cafés are the nondescript trailers that sell cold drinks and hot food during the day to bathers. But on weekend nights these same trailers become convivial meeting points for both couples and singles. Large crowds gather around the more popular trailers, some of which are converted at nights into samba centers called *pagodes*.

Originally confined to back yards in the city's lower-class northern neighborhoods, *pagodes* were no more than samba sing-alongs where musicians, both professional and amateur, engaged in midnight jam sessions. In the move to the affluent southern zone of Rio, the *pagodes* have maintained their purist samba qualities but have acquired commercial overtones, becoming in effect open-air samba bars.

For romantics, however, there can be no quibbling over the splendid image of the Barra's beachside trailers. With the surf crashing behind them, guitar and percussion instruments pounding out the samba in the night and scores of fun-seekers singing along, it is just right for an evening out in Rio de Janeiro.

Dozens of motels have sprung up in the Barra region over the years. In Rio – as in the rest of the country – motels are designed for lovers, and rooms are rented out by the hour and furnished with all the facilities a loving couple might desire, including saunas, whirlpools, and mirrored ceilings. Some of the Barra's motels outshine even the city's five-star hotels for unadulterated luxury and sheer indulgence.

At the end of the Barra is the **Recreio dos Bandeirantes**, a small beach with a natural breakwater creating the effect of a quiet bay. From Recreio the road climbs sharply along the mountainside, descending to Prainha, a beach that is popular among surfers, and then to **Grumari**, a marvelously isolated beach where part of the movie *Blame It On Rio* was filmed.

TIP

The beaches west of Barra Da Tijuca can be almost deserted during the week. Avoid them at weekends, though, when they can become very crowded.

From Grumari, a narrow, potholed road climbs straight up the hillside. At the top you will be treated to another of Rio's unforgettable views – the expanse of the **Guaratiba** flatlands and a long sliver of beach stretching off into the distance, the Restinga de Marambaia, a military property that is unfortunately off limits to bathers.

Down the hill is **Pedra da Guaratiba** (60 km/37 miles southwest of Rio), a quaint fishing village with excellent seafood restaurants (Candido's and Quatro Sete Meia). From Barra to Guaratiba is an exhilarating day trip that can be topped by a leisurely two-hour lunch of shrimp or fish dishes at any of the Guaratiba restaurants, the favorites of the Rio in-crowd.

Out on the town

For all *cariocas* an evening out is serious business. For many, in fact, it is more serious than the working day. To be in step with Rio time, a night out begins with dinner at 9pm or later. Most popular restaurants are still receiving dinner guests into the morning hours on weekends.

Meals fall into two categories: small and intimate or sprawling and raucous. For an intimate dinner, French restaurants with excellent views are favored.

BELOW: hang-gliding over São Conrado.

For the sprawling, raucous evening, you will be best served by Brazilian steak houses called *churrascarias*, where *cariocas* gather with small armies of friends around long tables practically overflowing with food and drink. At night, Copacabana is traditionally the king of Rio. The lights along the curve of the beach and the darkened profile of Sugarloaf in the background are sufficient for anyone's night of romance.

The beach itself is an excellent starting point. Sidewalk cafés run the length of Avenida Atlântica, and they act as gathering points for tourists and locals where cold draft beer is the favorite order. Copacabana at night is like a Persian bazaar. Street vendors will be hawking souvenirs, paintings, wood sculptures, and T-shirts along the median of the avenue. Prostitutes (female, male, and transvestite) prowl the broad sidewalk, with its serpentine designs.

The famous Copacabana Palace Hotel, known affectionately among the inhabitants of the city as "the Copa," was sympathetically refurbished in the 1990s, returning it to its glory days in the 1920s and 30s, when it attracted the rich and famous from all over the world *(see page 154)*. Don't miss the chance to indulge in a cocktail by the pool, even if you can't afford to stay here. The Sofitel Rio Palace also has a cocktail bar, from where you can watch the sun set over Ipanema.

Between Copacabana and Leme is the infamous red-light district. In the dark bars and clubs, and even on the sidewalks, you will see Western men openly curb-crawling – seemingly oblivious to the risk of Aids, the desperation that causes individuals to become prostitutes, and the fact that many of the most attractive women working here are, in fact, men. Lapa was once a red-light district, that has over the past few years become an exciting area studded

Map on page 146

An ecstatic and exhausted samba dancer.

BELOW: a novel approach to sunbathing.

with live music bars. The crowd tends to be fairly young, and you shouldn't stray from the main streets to be absolutely safe. Recommended venues include Carioca da Gema, Semente, and Rio Scenarium, which should not be missed for their varied program of Brazilian music from samba to bossa nova in atmospheric settings. For an authentic, Brazilian night out, try Night Life Tours, tel: 2552-9204 or 9721-0594.

Fish and seafood feature on many a restaurant menu in Rio.

For full-scale extravaganzas, Rio's leading show houses are Canecão, located next to the Rio Sul Shopping Center, close to Copacabana, and in Barra the ATL Hall, which showcase the best in Brazilian and international attractions, while Plataforma I, in Leblon, presents a nightly review of Brazilian song, dance, and Carnival.

Popular nightclubs include Baronneti on Rua Barão da Torre, Ipanema; Bukowski on Rua Paulo Barreto, Botafogo; Six on Rua das Marrecas, Centro; The Ball Room on Rua Humaitá, Botafogo; and Terraço Rio Sul and Fun Club in the Rio Sul Shopping Center. For jazz and bossa nova the best call is Mistura Fina on Avenida Borges de Medeiros, Lagoa; and Vinicius Bar on Rua Vinicius de Moraes, Ipanema.

Dining out

Rio de Janeiro's cuisine, with a few exceptions, is uniform in one respect only: it is delicious. Otherwise, it is as varied as the multitude of nationalities that pass through the *Cidade Maravilhosa*. French, Italian, Japanese, Chinese, and Lebanese restaurants vie with the more traditional Brazilian *churrascarias* (grill houses), which serve an unlimited supply of perfectly cooked beef, sausage, fish, and chicken. There are also a plethora of fish and

BELOW: transport to the beach.

RIO'S GREAT TRAIN ROBBER

Rio de Janeiro was for 30 years the home of the "Great Train Robber" Ronnie Biggs. A small-time crook from London, Ronnie was a member of the gang that carried out an audacious robbery in August 1963, stopping a mail train in England and making off with a haul amounting to more than £2.6 million sterling (worth £30 million today).

Although a substantial amount of the loot was never recovered, Ronnie and 12 other gang members were convicted; three others were never caught. Biggs escaped from Wandsworth in 1965, arriving in Brazil via Paris and Australia, having undergone plastic surgery to change his appearance. He lived openly in fashionable Santa Teresa, since there was no extradition treaty with Britain, and kept clear of any criminal activity. Jack Slipper, the Scotland Yard detective in charge of the case, visited Rio several times, and attempts were made to have Biggs deported, but they were thwarted by the birth of Ronnie's son to a Brazilian woman.

In May 2001, aged 71, he returned voluntarily to the UK (Britain's tabloid newspaper, the *Sun*, paid for his flight) and was immediately imprisoned on his arrival. His son Michael continues to press for his release on the grounds of his failing health.

seafood restaurants, specializing in both Portuguese and northeastern Brazilian dishes, which attract the custom of tourists and *cariocas* alike.

Rio's restaurants, though, are more than just places to eat. Brazilians have refined the practice of eating out, making it a major form of recreation. When they go out to a restaurant, which is often, they do so to meet friends, to show off their latest clothes, cars, and girl/boyfriends, and to be *seen*. But, most of all, they go to have a good time. Many restaurants have communal tables, where you may be seated next to a pop star, a senator, or a bank clerk. It doesn't matter who it is, you'll usually find yourself caught up in the *carioca* passion for life. Leaving the restaurant several hours later, you will be sure you have met everyone in Rio, and that they are all your very best friends.

All tastes are catered for. Some of Rio's restaurants are intimate and discreet, others are large and brash. In Rio, it is always easy to find somewhere to eat that fits the mood; more often, the problem is how to choose.

Map on page 146

Going shopping

Although Rio de Janeiro's first shopping center wasn't constructed until the 1980s, *cariocas* quickly switched to shopping in air-conditioned malls away from the summer temperatures, which average around 95°F (35°C). Nowadays, many of the city's best shops and boutiques are gravitating away from Ipanema and heading toward the city's top malls and shopping centers. The principal shopping centers in Rio de Janeiro are as follows:

- **Rio-Sul** (open Mon–Sat 10am–10pm, Sun 3–9pm; free buses from Copacabana's hotels) is located in the neighborhood of Botafogo, a short distance from Copacabana. It has recently been completely refurbished and has high-level security. The Rio-Sul is a good option for entertainment, too: it has a nightclub, food courts, and several cinemas.
- **Barra Shopping** (open Mon–Sat 11am–9.30pm, Sun 3–9pm; free buses to and from hotels), Latin America's largest shopping center is in Barra da Tijuca. Looks like an American suburban mall.
- **Cassino Atlântico** (open Mon–Fri 9am–9pm, Sat til 8pm) is situated on Copacabana's beachfront drive, Avenida Atlântica, at the Sofitel Rio Palace Hotel. It is small but has a good selection of souvenir and antique shops, as well as art galleries.
- **São Conrado Fashion Mall** (open Mon–Sat 11am–10pm, Sun 3–9pm) is not far from the Sheraton and Inter-Continental hotels in São Conrado. It is smaller but more stylish than most of the others, and has boutiques, restaurants, and art galleries.
- Souvenir hunters should also check out the **Ipanema Hippie Fair** at Praça General Osorio (open Sunday 9am–6pm). The fair is a lingering reminder of Ipanema's flower-children days of the 1960s, and it has a wide variety of woodcarvings, paintings, hand-tooled leather goods, and other assorted gifts, including a large selection of Rio's multicolored T-shirts. Many of the fair's vendors can also be found selling their wares at night-time along the median of Copacabana's Avenida Atlântica. ❑

BELOW: serious cooking for a carnival party.

Rio's *Favelas*

The *favela*, or shantytown, has become so much a feature of life in Rio that some tourist guides even include a visit to Rocinha, the largest of the *favelas*, in their itineraries. Rocinha first sprouted in the 1940s and is now a swarming anthill of narrow alleys, built on the side of a steep hill. Up to 300,000 people live in Rocinha, most of them in shacks.

In many ways the *favela* is the heartbeat of Brazil's cities, a hotbed of musical talent and home of many of its most creative residents. The cultural input of the *favela* is rarely acknowledged. In fact, the country's world-famous Carnival would not exist if it were not for these communities. All the main samba schools, which are the focus of the celebrations, come from and are named after, Rio de Janeiro's *favelas*. In the run-up to Carnival, *favelados* furiously practice their samba routines and prepare their costumes of plumes, sequins and satins.

The *favelas* in Rio are the most visible, but all Brazilian cities have them. Often, as in São Paulo, they are hidden away and casual visitors only glimpse them when driving past, between the airport and city center.

Favelas sprang up as a response among the poor to the chaotic expansion of the city. Property prices exploded, making it impossible for a poor family to buy or rent a house downtown. At the same time, increases in bus fares made it exorbitantly expensive for poorly paid workers to take the two or three buses required to travel in from the cheaper suburbs. So, in the early 1900s, poor families began to build illegally on the steep hillsides that were regarded as unsuitable sites for more expensive properties.

Around 70 percent of the people who live in Rochina are from the impoverished north east of Brazil. They live in similar conditions to the European immigrants who arrived in New York at around the same time.

Often a family of six will live in one room with one bed for the adults, while the children sleep on the floor. Almost all houses have a color television and telephone, however, and most have a stereo. Some 80 percent of people in Rocinha are employed, and the vast majority have nothing to do with the drugs and violence for which their community is famous.

Tours to Rio's *favelas* can be done in a four-wheel drive vehicle, by foot or on a motorbike. Only some offer the chance to interact with the residents. The better agencies are allied with charitable organizations and plow at least a fraction of their profits back into social projects, such as schools and teaching handicrafts. A visit can be an enlightening experience.

Today, there are about 700 *favelas* in Rio. About 3 million people in the city live in them. Over the years, many of the *favelados* have improved their property, so that some today have electricity and running water. There is even a thriving property business within the *favelas*, with richer *favelados* moving on to better houses and selling their rougher shacks to newcomers.

A handful of *favelados* have become national figures. Benedita da Silva, Brazil's first black woman senator, and now a minister, still lives in the Chapeu Mangueira shantytown in Rio de Janeiro. Like most shantytowns, it is located on a hillside and you have to climb up 56 steps to reach Benedita's house. Her mother was a washer-woman and she

LEFT: *favela* shacks cling precariously to the mountainside.

remembers delivering laundry, as a child, to the house of President Juscelino Kubitschek.

Favelas are not safe to visit unaccompanied. Drug-traffickers, armed with sophisticated, modern weapons have moved into many *favelas*, not infrequently resulting in gun battles with police troops sent in after them. Innocent bystanders, including children, have been killed by stray bullets. Life expectancy is low – just 48 years, compared to the national average of 68 years. Illnesses such as bronchitis are common, and although medical care is available at no cost, essential medicines are not.

What makes the Rio *favelas* extraordinary is their close proximity to some of the world's richest neighborhoods. Sprawling across a mountainside, Rocinha looks down on five-star hotels, luxury condominiums, and sophisticated restaurants. For decades, the rich, largely white, elite has been unable to banish entirely the nightmare vision of poor, largely black, *favelados* storming down from their shacks to overthrow their "oppressors," but the arrangement has its advantages: the *favelas* provide their rich neighbors with cheap labor, working as maids, doormen, and restaurant staff.

There is some irony in the fact that most middle-class Brazilians would never dream of going anywhere near a *favela* even though they are happy to employ their residents as nannies to look after their children. Their stance is partly due to a fear generated by the national media which is quick to pounce on the more dramatic, invariably negative, aspects of these communities.

Cidade de Deus (City of God) blasted onto cinema screens in January 2003. Set in a real *favela* on the outskirts of Rio, the film is a brutal but human portrayal of drugs, crime, and violence. The fact that *Cidade de Deus* won great critical acclaim from around the world was particularly impressive as none of the actors was professional, but recruited directly from the slum communities. The film, and President Lula's announcement in 2003 that he will provide *favela* residents with much-needed resources and education, perhaps signals that these communities are finally receiving the respect they deserve. ❑

BELOW: about 3 million people live in Rio's *favelas*

RIO DE JANEIRO STATE

Along the Rio coast are a string of perfect tropical seaside destinations, while in the cool mountains above nestles the charming and civilized imperial city of Petrópolis

Map on pages 170–71

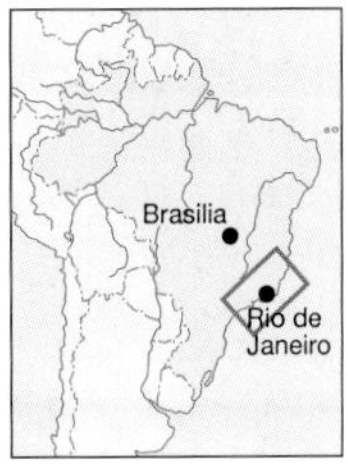

While the city of **Rio de Janeiro** ❶ has captured most of Brazil's glory through the decades, the state of which it is the capital (also called Rio de Janeiro) is replete with attractions of its own. Like its capital, the state of Rio is an exciting contrast of forested mountains and sun-drenched beaches, all located within a few hours of the city.

The Bardot connection

According to the history books, **Búzios** ❷ was "discovered" by the Portuguese at the beginning of the 16th century. Locals, however, know better. Búzios was actually discovered in 1964 by the actress Brigitte Bardot. Convinced by an Argentine friend, Bardot spent two well-documented stays in Búzios, parading her famous bikini-clad torso along the unspoiled beaches and, in the process, spreading the fame of Búzios across the globe. The town hasn't been the same since.

Búzios is used to describe the main town of Armação de Búzios (once a tranquil fishing village fronting the lapping waters of a bay and the peninsula on which it stands. After Bardot, it became a synonym for all that splendor in the tropics is supposed to be – white sand beaches, crystalline water, palm trees and coconuts, beautiful half-naked bathers, and a relaxing, intoxicating lifestyle of careless ease.

What is amazing about Búzios is that all of this is true. It is one of only a handful of super-hyped travel destinations that doesn't delude or disappoint. It is not just as good as the posters. It is even better.

LEFT: diving from the high prow of a *saveiro* (fishing boat) near Angra dos Reis.
BELOW: one of Búzios' idyllic *pousadas* (inns).

Paradise found

Located 190 km (115 miles) east of Rio along what is known as the Sun Coast (Costa do Sol), Búzios has been compared to the Spanish island of Ibiza. It is a sophisticated, international resort that for most of the year manages to retain the air of a quiet fishing village. The exception is the high summer season, just before, during and after Carnival, when even tranquil Búzios is overrun by tourists, its population of 20,000 swelling to 100,000. It is best avoided at these times.

For the remaining nine months of the year, Búzios is the type of beach town most travelers suspect exists only in their dreams. Unlike many popular resorts in Brazil, including Rio de Janeiro itself, Búzios has not lost control of its growth. It is a favorite retreat of Rio's social column set.

Búzios has undergone a major real-estate boom since the 1970s but, fortunately, the city fathers have kept a firm hand on developers. Strict zoning laws limit building heights, with the result that Búzios has escaped the high-rise invasion that has scarred many

Don't be surprised to find tanned, blond-haired surfers along the coast of Rio state.

TIP

Take a trip on one of the schooners to decide which beach is your favorite. You can either return by bus for a day trip, or find accommodation there.

Brazilian beaches. The fashionable homes that dot the Búzios beach-scape for the most part blend in with the picturesque homes of the fishermen. Many of the accommodations in Búzios are foreign-owned *pousadas* or inns, quaint and small, although very sophisticated and often with pools.

The beaches

Altogether, there are 23 beaches in the Búzios area, some fronting quiet coves and inlets, others the open sea. The main distinction, though, is accessibility. Beaches close in to the town or nearby, such as **Ossos, Do Canto**, and **Ferradura**, are easily reached on foot or by car.

As might be expected, the best beaches are those that require the most effort to reach: in the case of Búzios either via long hikes, sometimes over rocky ground, or by a drive along a potholed dirt road. At the end are treasures like **Tartaruga**, **Azeda**, and **Azedinha**, **Brava**, and **Forno**, known for their beautifully calm waters as well as for their equally gorgeous near-naked sunbathers.

Visiting all the beaches by land is not only tiring but also unnecessary. The fishermen of Búzios have become part-time tour operators, and tourists can rent their boats by the hour or by the day. Sailboats can also be hired, as can cars and dune buggies, bicycles, motorcycles, and horses. Enthusiastic divers will find they can rent all the necessary equipment in town.

A typical Búzios day begins late (few people wake up before 11am) with a hearty breakfast at a *pousada*. Daytime activities center around the beach. Swimming, long leisurely walks, or the exploration of distant beaches can be enjoyed, with the occasional break for fried shrimp or fresh oysters washed

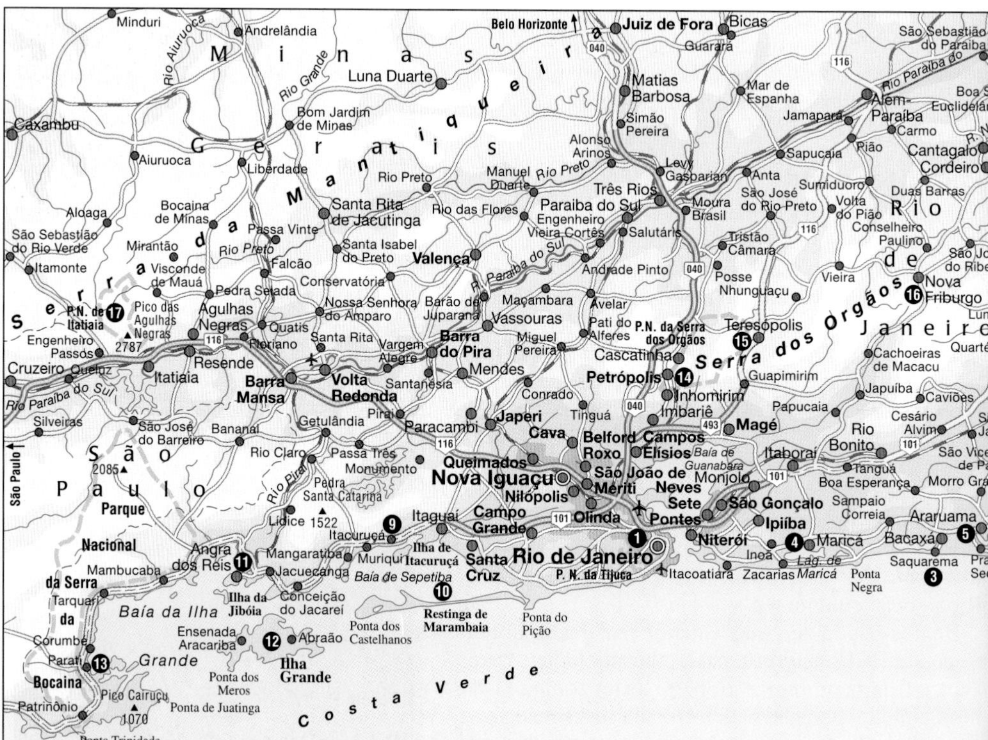

down with ice-cold beer or *caipirinhas*, Brazil's national drink, which is composed of lime slices, ice, and sugarcane liquor.

Shopping-wise, there are a variety of fashionable boutiques along cobblestoned **Rua José Bento Ribeiro Dantas**, better known as **Rua das Pedras**, or Stone Street, and also on **Rua Manuel Turibe de Farias**.

Map: see below

Nightlife in Búzios

At night, the bohemian spirit of Búzios takes charge. Though small in size, the city is considered to be one of the best in Brazil for dining out, with over 20 quality restaurants, some of which are rated among the country's finest. Gourmets have a wide array of cuisines from which to choose, including Brazilian, Italian, French, and Portuguese, as well as seafood and crêpes – a local favorite.

Estância Don Juan (barbecued meats), Cigalon (French), and Satyricon (seafood) are considered the best of Búzios' restaurants. Other small eateries are constantly popping up, and many are superb. A word of caution, though: the bargain prices of Rio's restaurants are not to be found these days in Búzios.

After an inspiring meal, the in-crowd of Búzios gravitates to the city's bars, many of which have live entertainment. Both bars and restaurants in Búzios are as well known for their owners as for their offerings. The city's numerous charms have waylaid dozens of foreign visitors since Bardot's first promenade. She left but many of the others have stayed, opening inns, restaurants, and bars and providing Búzios with an international air. Natives of Búzios have been joined by French, Swiss, Scandinavian, and American expatriates, who vow they will never leave.

BELOW: children play in the ocean near Búzios.

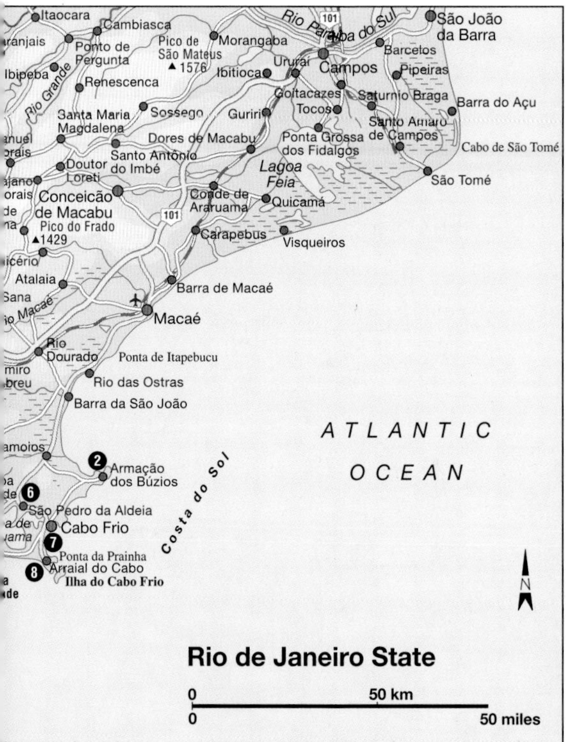

The lake region

Between Rio and Búzios are several beautiful beach areas, starting with what is known as the lake region: a series of lagoons separated from the sea by lengthy sand bars. The sea along this unbroken coastline east of Rio is marked by strong currents and large waves, making it a favorite area for surfers.

Major surfing competitions are held in **Saquarema ❸**, one of the four beach resorts in the lake region. Here, horseback riding through scenic countryside is offered at Nosso Paraìso (tel: 022-9906 8172 or 022-2653 6278).

Near **Maricá ❹** is the **Ponta Negra** beach, a spectacular, nearly deserted stretch of white sand and wild blue water. **Araruama ❺** and **São Pedro da Aldeia ❻** are popular among *cariocas* during vacation periods (especially Carnival) when the lake region's hotels and numerous campgrounds are filled to overflowing. Salt flats are also visible off the side of the road along this stretch, culminating in a large area of flats at **Cabo Frio ❼**, officially the end of the lake region and the beginning of the Sun Coast.

Located 29 km (18 miles) from Búzios, Cabo Frio is famed for the white, powdery sand of its beaches and dunes. In vacation season, Cabo Frio's population of 110,000 swells with *cariocas* on holiday. Unlike Búzios, Cabo Frio is a historic city. Its 17th-century ruins include the **Forte São Mateus** and **Nossa Senhora da Assunção** church (both built in 1616), and the **Nossa Senhora dos Anjos** convent (built in 1686).

BELOW: Praia do Forte beach in Cabo Frio.

Undiscovered paradise

Only 18 km (11 miles) from Cabo Frio is **Arraial do Cabo ❽**, next to Búzios the most beautiful attraction of the Sun Coast. Arraial has been discovered by

the tourist trade. Once vacationers preferred to stay in Búzios and Cabo Frio, and just make day trips to Arraial, but now there is a range of *pousadas* and hotels to choose from.

Arraial has the clearest water in southern Brazil, making it the preferred site of scuba divers and spear fishermen. The city is located at the tip of a cape with a variety of beaches, some with quiet waters and lush green mountain backdrops, while others, the surfer beaches, are swept by strong winds that drive the waves high up the beach.

Off the coast is the **Ilha do Farol**, site of a lighthouse but better known for the **Gruta Azul**, an underwater grotto with bright blue waters. The island, accessible by boat, also offers excellent views of the mainland.

Like Búzios, Arraial began as a fishing village and is still known for the quality of the fresh catches brought in each day. The local fishermen climb to the top of sand dunes, from where they look into the water below in search of schools of fish, a testimony to the unspoiled clarity of the waters.

Map on pages 170–71

The Green Coast

On the western side of the city of Rio are a string of beaches and islands known collectively as the **Costa Verde** (Green Coast). Named for the dense vegetation that dominates the coastline and descends to the sea, the Costa Verde is nature at its best: a splendid tropical mix of mountains, rainforest, beaches, and islands. Green, in every imaginable shade, surrounds you, invading even the sea with a soft turquoise hue.

Access to the Green Coast is along coastal highway BR 101, known locally as the **Rio–Santos Highway** after the two port cities that it connects. The scenic

BELOW LEFT: a fisherman and his boat.
BELOW: a leisurely boat excursion in the bay.

TIP

Avoid driving on the BR 101 coastal route at night. Not only will you miss the scenery, but in the dark, the highway – with its sharp bends, unmarked shoulders, and frequent, poorly lit construction sites – can become extremely dangerous.

drive compares with the one down Spain's Costa Brava or California's State Road 1. At times, it seems almost as if you are going to take flight as the road rises high up a mountainside for a wide panoramic view, before winding steeply back down to the shoreline. This memorable route takes you past a national park, a nuclear power plant, tourist resorts, fishing villages, ocean liner tanking stations, cattle ranches, a shipyard, and also the town of Parati – a stunning monument to Brazil's colonial past.

The most enticing attractions along the 270-km (160-mile) extension of the Green Coast are the beaches. Some are small, encased by rocky cliffs, with clear, tranquil lagoons, while others stretch on for miles, pounded by rough surf. The entire area is a haven for sports enthusiasts, offering everything from tennis, golf, and boating to deep-sea fishing, diving, and surfing.

Although it is possible to see the Green Coast in a single day, to explore it thoroughly and truly enjoy its beauty, plan on two to three days. Over the past 20 years, tourism has become the leading activity of the region and there are a growing number of fine hotels and restaurants, even on some of the islands.

Tropical islands

The Green Coast begins 100 km (60 miles) outside of Rio de Janeiro city at the town of **Itacuruçá** ❾ (pop. 3,700). From the town's harbor, schooners holding up to 40 people depart every morning for one-day excursions to the nearby tropical islands in the surrounding **Baía de Sepetiba** ❿. The trips are reasonably priced and you can buy a seafood lunch for an extra fee. The schooners stop at several islands, such as **Martins**, **Itacuruçá**, and **Jaguanum**, to allow passengers to swim or snorkel. Some of the smaller islands can be visited by hiring a

BELOW: picturesque colonial Parati.

boat and guide, usually a local fisherman (the islands of **Pombeba** and **Sororoca** are recommended). Also, for visitors who wish to stay on the islands, there are several good hotels, including the Hotel Elias C and the Hotel do Pierre.

The highway continues past **Muriqui** to **Mangaratiba**, site of a large Club Mediterranée. Further down the road is **Angra dos Reis** ⓫ (Kings' Cove), the Green Coast's largest city (pop. 130,000), which sprawls across a series of hills at the beginning of a 100-km long (60-mile) gulf.

The **Angra Gulf** has over 370 islands, 2,000 beaches, seven bays, and dozens of coves. The water is warm and clear, a perfect sanctuary for marine life. Spearfishing on the rocky shores and fishing in deeper waters are favorite pastimes. The tourist information center, across from the bus station near the harbor, provides maps and information on hotels and boat tours. The Hotel do Frade has the Green Coast's only golf course, a scenic 18 holes, where international tournaments are held every June and November.

Some 90 minutes from Angra by boat is the paradisiacal **Ilha Grande** ⓬, a nature reserve with spectacular flora and fauna and beautiful beaches. Body and Soul Adventures offers a unique program of sea kayaking and hiking through the island's spectacular trails, along with yoga and massage. The island can be reached by ferry boats that operate from Mangaratiba and Angra and disembark at **Abraão**, the only town on the island.

In Abraão, small boats can be rented if you wish to visit the more distant beaches, such as **Lopes Mendes**, **Das Palmas**, and **Saco do Céu**. There are several campsites on the island and a range of *pousadas* (inns), some of which are very sophisticated.

History preserved

From Angra, the coastal highway flanks the gulf, running past the nuclear power plant and the picturesque fishing village of **Mambucaba**. At the far end of the gulf, three and a half hours from Rio (265 km/165 miles), is **Parati** ⓭ (pop. 30,000), a colonial jewel that in 1966 was declared a national monument by UNESCO and today delights visitors from around the world.

Parati was founded in 1660, and in the 18th century gained fame and wealth as a result of the discovery of gold and diamonds in the neighboring state of Minas Gerais. The precious stones were transported by land to Parati and from there either on to Rio de Janeiro or by ship to Portugal. The city also served as the main stopping-off point for travelers and commerce moving between São Paulo to the south and Rio de Janeiro. For more than a century, Parati flourished and its citizens prospered. Opulent mansions and large estates attest to the wealth of its residents.

After Brazil declared independence in 1822, the export of gold to Portugal ceased and a new road was eventually built, bypassing Parati and connecting Rio to São Paulo directly. Parati lost its strategic position and was forgotten, and its colonial heritage was consequently preserved. Today, that heritage awaits visitors in the form of colonial churches and houses in the relaxed, laid-back atmosphere of a town trapped contentedly in a time warp.

Map on pages 170–71

TIP

Live bands (usually very good) play at many of Parati's restaurants. You will pay for the pleasure, though, in the form of an (often unannounced) cover charge.

BELOW: lush greenery adorns the old houses in Parati's narrow streets.

A decorative old mail box in Parati.

BELOW: cheerful colors in Parati.

Standing out among Parati's churches is **Santa Rita dos Paredos** (built in 1722), a classic example of Brazilian baroque architecture which was built for the freed mulatto population. Today the church also houses the small **Museu de Arte Sacra** (Museum of Sacred Art; Largo Santa Rita; open Wed–Sun).

All of Parati's streets contain hidden surprises: art galleries, handicraft shops, quaint *pousadas*, and colonial houses. From the outside, the *pousadas* look like typical whitewashed Mediterranean-style houses, with heavy wooden doors and shutters painted in bright colored trim. Once inside, however, they open up on to delicately landscaped courtyards with pots of ferns, orchids, rosebushes, violets, and begonias. Porto, next to the Pousada do Ouru hotel, is one of Parati's best restaurants: French/Brazilian fusion dishes are served in an elegant colonial house. Superb cocktails and an impressive wine list complete the experience (tel: 024-3371 1058).

Parati is not known for its beaches, but schooners such as the 24-meter (80-ft) *Soberno da Costa* make day trips to the nearby islands. There are about 65 islands and 200 beaches to choose from. Hotels and travel agents sell tickets for trips out. The 18th-century Gold Trail, or **Caminho do Ouro**, was opened to visitors in 1999. Teatro Espaço offers trekking trips along the trail to an old toll-house with sweeping views of Parati's bay. Teatro Espaço, on Rua Dona Geralda 327, also puts on a world-class puppet show on Wednesday and Saturday, which is well worth seeing. August 2003 saw the first international Literary Festival.

Into the cool mountains

Dedicated as they are to beach life, Rio's residents also feel an occasional need to get away from it all and escape to the cool, refreshing air of the mountains.

BRAZIL'S COLONIAL FAZENDAS

In the 19th century, when Brazil's major export was coffee, production was centered on large farms, or *fazendas*, in the hinterland behind Rio de Janeiro; land was often hacked out of the lush Atlantic rainforest of the Paraiba valley by slaves. The wealth generated turned the coffee barons into a new elite, who established luxurious and beautiful homes. When coffee production in the area began to decline in the 1880s, to be gradually replaced by cattle, many *fazendas* changed hands, surviving as seats for new owners with independent incomes.

Some of the handful of opulent *fazendas* remaining in the valley have been converted into country hotels and restaurants that offer an experience very different from the hot, fast life of Rio city. Set in extensive grounds, they provide relaxation and comfort, with delicious home-produced food served in the silver-plate style of a bygone age. Several have facilities for pursuits such as horse riding and canoeing. Recommended are Pousada Fazenda São Polycarpo (tel: 024-452 1029), a hotel-*fazenda* beautifully decorated with 19th-century furniture and objets d'art, and Fazenda Pau d'Alho in Valenca (tel: 024-453 3033), which has no accommodation but serves incomparable colonial-style afternoon teas (reserve).

This urge has existed since the first days of the Brazilian nation and was the principal reason behind the founding of Rio's two leading mountain resorts, Petrópolis and Teresópolis. The pastel hues and green gardens of these two *carioca* getaways are a 19th-century imperial inheritance left by independent Brazil's first two rulers, emperors Pedro I and Pedro II.

Petrópolis ⓮, a city of 280,000 only 65 km (40 miles) from Rio, is a monument to Pedro II, emperor of Brazil from 1831 until his exile in 1889 (he died in France two years later). The city was first envisioned in the 1830s by Pedro I, who purchased land in the spectacular **Serra Fluminense** mountain range for a projected summer palace. But it was his son, Pedro II, who actually built the palace and the quaint town surrounding it, starting in the 1840s. The idea was to maintain a refreshing refuge from the wilting summer heat of Rio.

The road to Petrópolis is itself one of the state of Rio's prime scenic attractions. An engineering marvel, its concrete bridges soar over green valleys as the road curves around mountains and the flatlands below. From sea level in Rio, the highway climbs 810 meters (2,660 ft) during the hour-and-a-quarter drive. Along the way, visitors can still glimpse traces of the old Petrópolis Highway, a perilous, cobblestoned roadway that used to keep workers busy the whole year round making repairs.

Life in Petrópolis is centered around two busy streets, **Rua do Imperador** and **Rua 15 de Novembro**, the only part of town with buildings over five stories tall. Temperatures are lower here than in Rio and the city's sweater-clad inhabitants give it an autumnal air during the cool months from June to September.

Perpendicular to Rua do Imperador is the Avenida 7 de Setembro, the city's lush boulevard that was used by Brazilian kings of the past. The partially cobbled avenue is divided by a slow-moving canal, and horse-drawn carriages lined up for rent by the hour form an attractive old-fashioned taxi stand on its sun-dappled stones.

The area around the former royal Summer Palace, which is now called the **Museu Imperial** (open Tues–Sun 11am–5pm), is crowded with trees and shrubs and is crisscrossed by carefully kept pathways. The rose-colored palace, fronting Avenida 7 de Setembro, is one of Brazil's most interesting museums. Visitors are asked to wear specially provided felt slippers, which pad quietly over the gleaming *jacarandá* and brazilwood floors. The museum's humble furnishings, as well as its outward appearance, attest to the less-than bourgeois character of Pedro II, who for the most part avoided the traditional trappings of nobility. Its second-floor collection of kingly personal artifacts, including a telescope and a telephone, is a reminder of Pedro's scientific dabblings.

Among other items of interest in the palace museum are the spectacular **crown jewels** – a glistening frame of 77 pearls and 639 diamonds – and the colorful skirts and cloaks of the emperor's ceremonial wardrobe, including a cape of bright Amazon toucan feathers. Royal photographs on the second floor, however, show that independent Brazil's last two emperors felt more at home in their conservative business suits than in flowing robes.

Map on pages 170–71

TIP

Parati gets very crowded at weekends and during holidays, when it is best avoided.

BELOW: the Museu Imperial, Petrópolis.

Regal dwellings

Across the square from the palace is the royal guesthouse, which is now the res idence of Pedro II's heirs. Dom Pedro de Orleans e Bragança, Pedro II's grea grandson, is the home's owner and also the chief representative of monarchisn in Brazil. Although the house is closed to the public, Dom Pedro himself ca sometimes be seen walking in the square chatting with local residents.

A few blocks up Avenida 7 de Setembro is the French Gothic-style **Catedra de São Pedro de Alcântara** (open Tues–Sun). Begun in 1884, this imposin structure took 55 years to complete.

The city is notable for its delightful, rose-colored houses, including man that were once the dwellings of members of the royal family. Petrópolis is als known for its many overgrown private gardens and public parks and the simpl beauty of its streets. **Casa de Pétropolis – Instituto de Cultura** in Rua Ipirang is one of the few mansions open to the public. Go to marvel at its exquisit interior, to view its quality art exhibitions and to have a coffee or lunch in it lovely restaurant.

A few blocks beyond the cathedral, on Rua Alfredo Pachá, is the 1884 **Palá cio de Cristal** (Crystal Palace), a glass-and-iron frame still used for gardenin and art exhibits. The palace was built almost entirely of panels shipped fron France. Nearby is the unusual **Casa de Santos-Dumont** (Rua do Encanto 22 open Tues–Sun 9am–5pm), which displays a collection of eccentricities reflect ing the unusual personality of its former owner, the pilot and inventor *extraor dinaire*, Alberto Santos-Dumont. The house, which he designed himself, has jus one room, no tables or kitchen (his meals were delivered by a hotel), and no inte rior staircases. There are all kinds of shelves, each designed for a specific pur pose, and a special chest of drawers that the invento used as a bed.

BELOW: the home of Alberto Santos-Dumont.

Other Petrópolis attractions include the sprawlin Normandy-style **Hotel Quitandinha** (open Tues–Sun) a luxuriously appointed structure completed in 194 to be Brazil's leading hotel casino. Unfortunately, onl a few months after its inauguration, gambling wa outlawed and has remained so ever since. Today, th still striking complex, which is located on th Rio–Petrópolis Highway 8 km (5 miles) from down town Petrópolis, is a combination condominium an private club.

Teresópolis

Just 57 km (35 miles) from Petrópolis, at the end of a one-hour drive along steep and winding mountai roads, is Rio de Janeiro's other mountain gem, **Ter esópolis** (pop. 125,000) ⓯. Named after Pedro II's wife, the empress Tereza Cristina, Teresópolis was planned in the 1880s but only incorporated in 1891, two years after the royal couple's exile.

The picturesque town, which is 92 km (57 miles) from Rio on the broad **Rio–Teresópolis Highway**, clings to the edge of the **Serra Fluminense** at 870 meters (2,850 ft). The main attractions, besides the cool air, are an encompassing, though distant, view of Rio's **Baía de Guanabara** and the city's proxim ity to the spectacular **Parque Nacional da Serra** dos **Orgãos**. The park, landscaped with broad lawns, masonry, fountains, and patios, is dominated by a ridge of sharp peaks. The tallest, **Pedra do Sino**, is :,260 meters (7,410 ft) above sea level. But the range's most striking summit s the rocky spike called **O Dedo de Deus** (The Finger of God). On clear days, the chiseled profile of the Serra dos Orgãos can be seen from many points in Rio itself.

Map on pages 170–71

Nova Friburgo ⓰ (pop. 180,000), a Swiss outpost in the heart of the tropics, is situated 78 km (48 miles) east of Teresópolis. The city was founded in 818 by exiled Portuguese king João VI, who authorized the immigration of 400 Swiss families from the canton of Freibourg. Upon arrival, the immigrants settled in the mountains and called their adopted home "New Freibourg". The city s notable for its rich green parks and alpine architecture.

On the state border, 240 km (150 miles) west of Teresópolis (174 km/108 miles from Rio), is the **Parque Nacional de Itatiaia** ⓱ (off Via Dutra, the main Rio–São Paulo highway). This beautiful nature reserve on the slopes of he Mantiqueira mountain range was established in 1937. It was Brazil's first national park and has a good infrastructure for tourists. Its forests are rich in wildlife, orchids, and bromeliads; it is a paradise for bird watchers and has beautiful waterfalls and lakes.

Higher up in the mountains, the vegetation changes to grassland and brush, hen to the lunar rocky landscape of the **Pico das Agulhas Negras** (2,787 meters/9,150 ft). This is a great place for rock-climbing and trekking. Near the park entrance, there is a natural history museum (open Tues–Sun 10am–4pm). Good places to stay are the Hotel Simon (tel: 024-3352 1122) and the Hotel do Ypê (tel: 024-3352 1453). ❑

A portrait of Alberto Santos-Dumont.

ALBERTO SANTOS-DUMONT

The downtown Santos-Dumont Airport in Rio commemorates Brazil's most famous inventor. The son of wealthy coffee grower, Alberto Santos-Dumont moved o Paris at the age of 17 in 1891 to study engineering. There he led the life of a playboy until in 1898 he took his first flight in a balloon. Santos-Dumont was enthralled and went on to design a series of airships. He won the Deutsch prize for flying from Saint-Cloud, round the Eiffel Tower and back – and gave half his winnings to the poor.

Later, he built 14-bis, an ungainly aircraft resembling a series of linked box kites. In this craft, on October 23 1906, he made the first official heavier-than-air flight in Europe and, in fact, the first self-powered flight, since he Wright Brothers used a catapult system to get their craft airborne three years earlier. Santos-Dumont subsequently designed a monoplane, but lost interest n aviation soon afterward. Sometimes, he used his inventions to visit friends in the Paris suburbs, and he would tether a small airship to convenient lampposts near bars he wished to visit.

Santos-Dumont spent his last years back in Brazil. Tragically, he committed suicide in 1932, unable to come o terms with the use of aircraft in war.

BELOW: freshly picked bananas for sale on a mountain highway.

ASSICURAZIONI GENERALI

banespa

SAO PAULO: CITY AND STATE

Map on page 198

As a modern, cosmopolitan, industrial metropolis, São Paulo has its good and bad sides. But it is a vibrant, go-ahead city, and you can escape to beach and mountain resorts nearby

While there may be two Brazils – one a dynamic developing country, the other scourged by poverty and drought – there are many São Paulos, one for each of this city's multitude of ethnic and social groups. The New 'ork of Latin America, **São Paulo ❶** is home to more ethnic communities than ny other city in the region. Its 18 million inhabitants, 10 percent of Brazil's population, make it the third-largest city on Earth, smaller only than New York and 'okyo. Its vast industrial park, one of the biggest and most modern in the world, ttests to the force of the São Paulo dynamo, just as it's elegant apartment buildıgs and mansions demonstrate the wealth of its powerful business elite.

São Paulo is a city of contrasts. While it is the country's industrial and financial enter, it is also saddled with teeming slums. Five million *paulistanos*, as resients of the city are called (*paulistas* are inhabitants of the state), live in tin-and-'ood hovels or shabby tenements called *cortiços,* where a hundred people may ıare a bathroom and children play with garbage in the backyard. A hilly ring of ıburbs is ill-lit, badly paved, and stinks from the effluence of a thousand miles of pen sewers. Half the population survives on a total family income of only US$100 month or less. Yet, even for its poor, São Paulo is a "carousel," according to one f the city's most respected journalists, Lourenço Diaféria. "São Paulo is a migrant ity," he notes. "Many people manage to rise here, if nly because their origins were so humble."

PRECEDING PAGES: the huge sprawl of São Paulo.
LEFT: Banespa Bank building, São Paulo.
BELOW: dealers with walkie-talkies in the São Paulo stock exchange.

thnic makeup

bout 2½ million *paulistanos* are of Italian descent, ıaking up one of the largest communities outside aly; another 1½ million are of Spanish or Spanishpeaking Latin origin. Large communities hail from ermany (100,000), Russia (50,000), and Armenia 50,000), with another 70,000 from Balkan and Cenal European immigrant groups.

As in North American cities, the ethnic population mainly working and middle class, while refugees 'om blighted rural areas have become the legion of rban poor. About 4 million *paulistanos* are migrants r decendants of migrants from Brazil's impoverished ortheast area.

Of São Paulo's important non-Caucasian population oout 1 million are of Japanese heritage, with another 00,000 of diverse origins elsewhere in Asia. In conast to other big Brazilian cities, black and mixed-race eople make up less than 10 percent of São Paulo's opulation.

São Paulo is one of Brazil's least Roman Catholic ities, with one-third of its population following other ligions. These include Shinto and Buddhism among ıe sizable Oriental population, and Islam among the million-strong Lebanese-origin community. The city

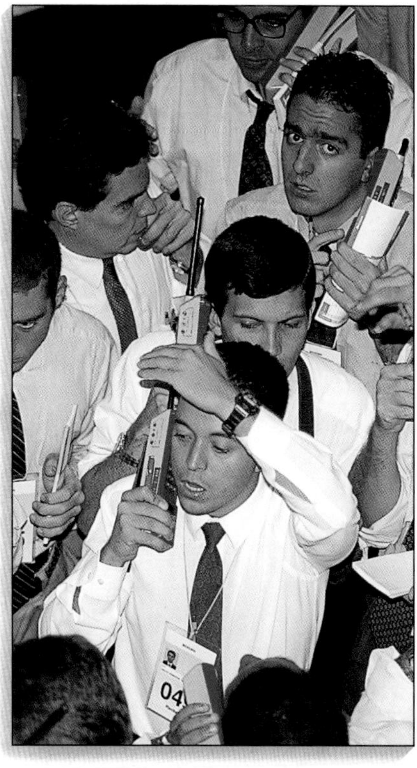

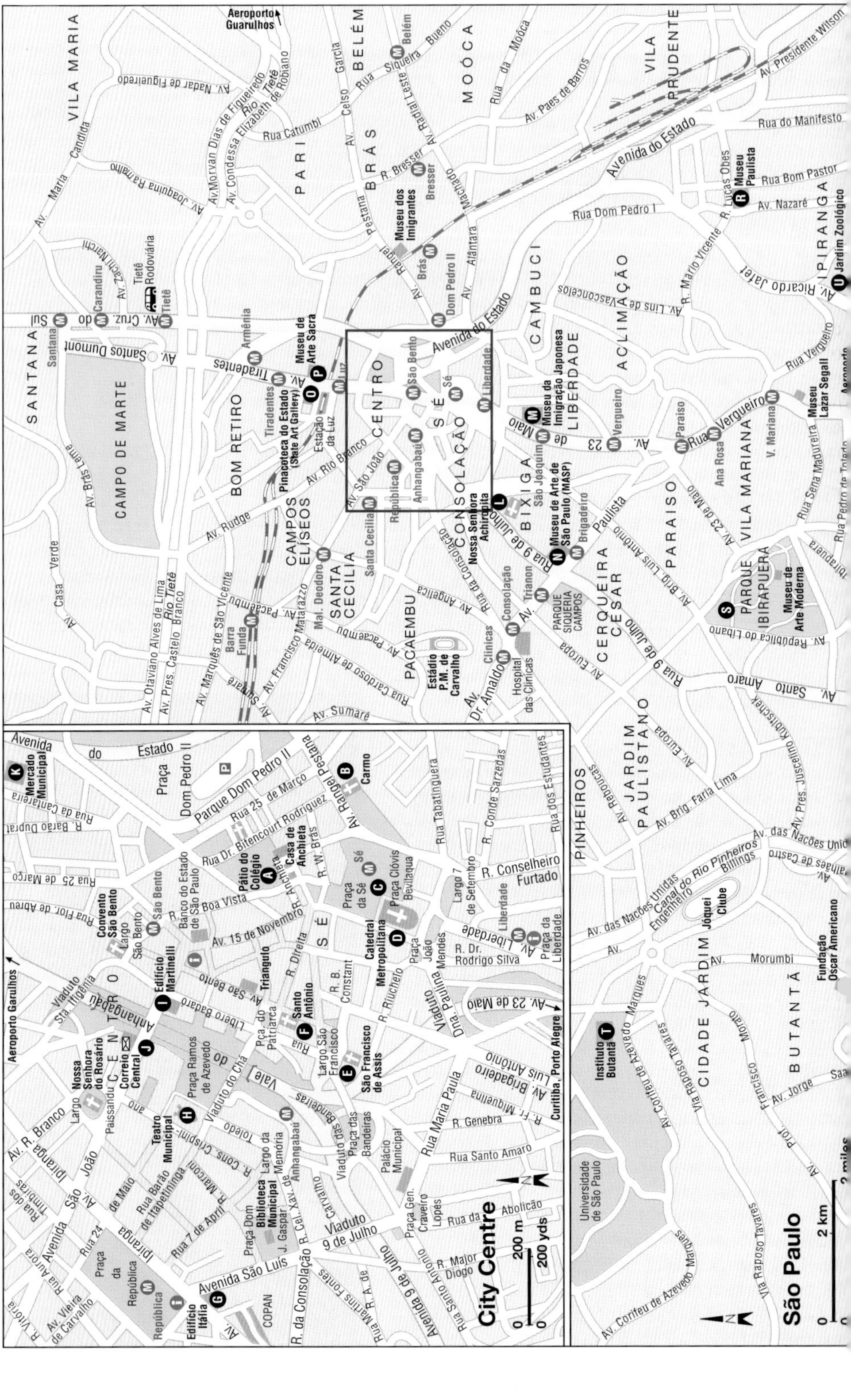
São Paulo
City Centre
2 km
2 miles
200 m
200 yds
Aeroporto Guarulhos
VILA MARIA
SANTANA
CAMPO DE MARTE
BOM RETIRO
PARI
BRÁS
BELÉM
MOÓCA
VILA PRUDENTE
CENTRO
SÉ
CONSOLAÇÃO
CAMPOS ELÍSEOS
SANTA CECÍLIA
PACAEMBU
BIXIGA
LIBERDADE
CAMBUCI
ACLIMAÇÃO
IPIRANGA
PARAISO
VILA MARIANA
CERQUEIRA CESAR
JARDIM PAULISTANO
PINHEIROS
CIDADE JARDIM
BUTANTÃ
Museu dos Imigrantes
Museu de Arte Sacra
Pinacoteca do Estado (State Art Gallery)
Estação da Luz
Museu da Imigração Japonesa
Museu de Arte de São Paulo (MASP)
Nossa Senhora Achiropita
Estádio P.M. de Carvalho
Hospital das Clínicas
PARQUE SIQUEIRA CAMPOS
PARQUE IBIRAPUERA
Museu de Arte Moderna
Museu Lazar Segall
Museu Paulista
Jardim Zoológico
Jóquei Clube
Fundação Oscar Americano
Instituto Butantã
Universidade de São Paulo
Avenida do Estado
Av. Paulista
Rua 9 de Julho
Mercado Municipal
Carmo
Pátio do Colégio
Casa de Anchieta
Convento São Bento
Banco do Estado de São Paulo
Edifício Martinelli
Correio Central
Nossa Senhora do Rosário
Teatro Municipal
Praça da Sé
Catedral Metropolitana
Santo Antônio
São Francisco de Assis
Biblioteca Municipal
Edifício Itália
COPAN
Praça da República
Praça da Liberdade
Palácio Municipal
Viaduto do Chá
Vale do Anhangabaú
Avenida São Luís
Avenida Ipiranga
Curitiba, Porto Alegre

has approximately 100,000 Jewish worshipers. Even among Roman Catholics there is diversity. At last count, Sunday Mass was conducted in 26 languages.

Surrounding the city is the state of São Paulo – Brazil's largest (pop. 35 million), most economically diverse, and wealthiest. The state of São Paulo includes a little bit of everything, from the smoky industries of São Paulo city to beach resorts that rival Rio; from a string of pleasing mountain resorts to a fertile farm area that is the most productive in Brazil.

Map on page 184

The state of São Paulo is Brazil's economic powerhouse and as such provides 30 percent of the GNP for the country. It accounts for federal tax revenues well in excess of the average per capita in Brazil, and a disproportionately high consumption of such items as electrical power. Half of all Brazilian manufacturing concerns are members of the state industrial federation (FIESP) and around half of Brazil's 50 biggest privately held corporations and private banks are headquartered in the state. The most striking element of São Paulo's modern development has been its startling velocity. During the first three and a half centuries of European Brazilian history São Paulo was a backwater, home to a few mixed-race traders and pioneers.

Paulistas are proud of the fact that Brazil's verbal declaration of independence was made by the prince regent, Pedro I, on São Paulo soil – at Ipiranga, on September 7, 1822.

First settlements

São Paulo's story is as old as Brazil's. The coastal settlement of São Vicente was founded in 1532, the first permanent Portuguese colony in the New World. A generation later, in 1554, two courageous Jesuits, José de Anchieta and Manuel da Nóbrega, established a mission on the high plateau 70 km (42 miles) inland from São Vicente. They called the colony **São Paulo de Piratininga**.

Much of São Paulo's traditional dynamism can be traced to the early isolation of settlements like São Vicente and Piratininga, located far away from the administrative and commercial center of the colony in the northeast region.

Since few European women were willing to accept the hardships of life on the wind-blown plateau, male colonists took Amerindian women for concubines. They fathered hardy, mixed-race children who were accustomed to the privations of a frontier life and felt little attachment to Portugal.

Within two generations, the remote colony had produced its own brand of *bandeirante* (frontiersman). On his Amerindian side, the *bandeirante*'s heritage included pathfinding and survival skills. From his Portuguese father, he inherited a thirst for gain and a nomadic streak that would send him roaming across half a continent.

Bandeirante individualism was carried over to the political arena during the 19th century. Pedro I was greatly influenced by his *paulista* advisers, led by José Bonifácio de Andrada e Silva, and later in the century, *paulistas* led the fight against slavery and helped to establish the 1889 republic.

Economic growth

But São Paulo's true vocation was business. Attracted by the growth of British textile manufacturing, *paulista* plantation owners first cultivated cotton in the early 19th century. Lacking a large slave popula-

BELOW: São Paulo Hilton amid city center skyscrapers.

tion, however, the state's plantations soon faced a manpower shortage and cotton production fell behind the American competition. So, with money from the cotton boom, they diversified into coffee, a product enjoying increased world demand but little producer competition. São Paulo's climatic conditions and the fertile red soil called *terra roxa* proved ideal for the finicky coffee bush and the stage was set for the state to become Brazil's richest.

Within a decade, coffee surpassed cotton as São Paulo's chief cash crop. Meanwhile, the labor shortage problem was solved with large-scale European immigration, which began in the 1870s following a systematic campaign to attract settlers. Between 1870 and 1920, the campaign successfully attracted some 5 million immigrants. About half settled in São Paulo, most working for set contractual periods as coffee plantation laborers.

Industry and migration

Coffee money rebuilt the once-sleepy outpost of São Paulo de Piratininga. At the same time, the coffee barons began to look for investment hedges to protect themselves against a drop in world coffee prices. Their chief strategy, as in the past, was diversification, this time into manufacturing.

Key elements were: an innovative, dynamic business elite; ready capital from booming coffee exports; an enviable network of railroads; a first-class port; skilled, literate workers from the ranks of European immigrants; and, because of the web of rivers flowing down the coastal mountains, the Serra do Mar, ample sources of cheap hydroelectric power.

The stage was set for São Paulo's leap toward becoming both an industrial and financial giant. World War I was the spark: lack of European manufactured

BELOW: looking across the bay toward the port of Santos.

imports left a vacuum eagerly filled by a rising class of entrepreneurs. The 1930s depression began a process of internal migration that further satisfied the rapidly industrializing state's hunger for labor and made São Paulo city the world's fastest-growing major city during most of the 1960s and 1970s, with as many as 1,000 new residents arriving per day.

The velocity of São Paulo's growth can be seen in comparative population figures. In 1872, São Paulo was Brazil's ninth-largest municipality, a village of 32,000. Rio de Janeiro was a metropolis with a population of 276,000. Even in 1890 São Paulo still had only 65,000 people. But the expansion of manufacturing spurred by World War I made São Paulo into a working- and middle-class city of 579,000 by 1920, number two behind the 1.1 million-population of Rio de Janeiro. In 1954, São Paulo surpassed Rio to become Brazil's biggest city. By 1960, it had 3.8 million residents, and in 2002 São Paulo passed the 18 million mark, including 8 million in its endless suburbs against Rio's 11 million.

Independent streak

Meanwhile, São Paulo's tradition of political and intellectual independence continued into the 20th century. One of the first stirrings against the conservative old republic was a 1924 São Paulo barracks revolt led by young army officers. In 1932, the entire state mobilized in a three-month civil war against federal intervention in state affairs.

Paulistas were also at the forefront of a nationalist intellectual movement that erupted in 1922. That year, Brazil's government organized an exhibition in Rio de Janeiro marking the 100th anniversary of independence. A group of

Map on page 184

Brazil's favorite beverage.

BELOW: Avenida Paulista from the sky.

São Paulo artists and writers boycotted the official event, staging a parallel **Modern Art Week** at São Paulo's **Municipal Theater**.

This generation of intellectuals – the painter Anita Malfatti, novelist Mário de Andrade, critic Oswald de Andrade, sculptor Victor Brecheret, and composer Heitor Villa-Lobos – came to dominate 20th-century Brazilian arts and literature, and the continued mix of disparate elements, old and new, foreign and indigenous, is probably São Paulo's greatest charm.

Historical center

The hard knot marking the center of São Paulo is a breezy esplanade and a handful of white-walled structures called the **Pátio do Colégio** Ⓐ. It was here that the hardy Jesuits Anchieta and Nóbrega founded the São Paulo de Piratininga mission in 1554. The houses and chapel were substantially reinforced during restoration work in the 1970s. The **Casa de Anchieta** is now a cramped museum (open daily 9am–noon and 1–5pm except Mon) displaying artifacts belonging to the village's earliest settlers.

It took nearly 100 years to add the first ring around São Paulo's humble settlement. In 1632, the **Igreja do Carmo** Ⓑ was built about 200 meters (660 ft) from Anchieta's chapel, just behind the historic square, **Praça da Sé** Ⓒ. The Mannerist facade of the Carmo church is well-preserved, although largely hidden by office buildings and a fire station. On the south side of the Praça da Sé, the present **Catedral Metropolitana** Ⓓ, whose Gothic facade and 100-meter (330-ft) spires were built in 1954, replaced a tottering 18th-century cathedral that was torn down by the city's Roman Catholic diocese in 1920.

BELOW: colorful colonial facade at Embu, on the city outskirts.

In 1647, another appealing Mannerist facade was built at one of the outlying points of the village – the pretty **São Francisco de Assis** Ⓔ church, located about 400 meters (1,320 ft) from the Pátio do Colégio. A convent was attached in 1676. The complex is still bustling and displays colonial-era woodcarvings and gold-leaf decoration.

Finally, in 1717, the **Igreja de Santo Antônio Church** Ⓕ was completed about halfway between the Pátio do Colégio and São Francisco. Recently restored, Santo Antônio's bright yellow-and-white facade is a pleasing contrast to the gray office towers that rise around it.

New building frenzy

The 20th century brought a sweeping transformation to the old downtown. The peak coffee year of 1901 coincided with the inauguration of the brick-and-iron Luz train station, marked by an English-style clock tower and expansive gardens. The post-war years brought the **Banco do Estado de São Paulo**, modeled after New York's Empire State Building and, later, one of the most potent symbols of the new São Paulo, Latin America's tallest office building. The 42-story **Edifício Itália** Ⓖ, three blocks northwest of Santo Antônio church, was built in 1965.

Two blocks east, on Rua Toledo, is the **Teatro Municipal** Ⓗ, an eclectic building (Italian Renaissance and Art Nouveau), designed by the noted architect Francisco Ramos de Azevedo. It was inaugurated

Map on page 184

in 1911. Isadora Duncan, Anna Pavlova, and Enrico Caruso performed under the one-and-a-half-ton Swiss crystal chandelier and must have been impressed by the marble, bronze, and onyx decor. The spirit of an Italian opera singer is said to belt out forlorn solos from an upper window as his equally ghostly girlfriend clasps a lily and weeps.

Nearby, on **Avenida São João**, is the 30-story office building, the **Edifício Martinelli** Ⓘ. The first great status symbol of São Paulo's Italian population, it was inaugurated in 1929. Just the other side of the tunnel stands the imposing **Correio Central** Ⓙ (Central Post Office), which was built in 1920.

The depression year of 1933 saw the completion of another Azevedo building, the sprawling German-Gothic **Mercado Municipal** Ⓚ, at the northeastern edge of the city center behind Praça Dom Pedro II. This market is still in use, and worth a visit for its pretty stained-glass windows and wonderful displays of fresh produce.

In 1989, the **Memorial da América Latina** designed by Oscar Niemeyer, was built next to Barra Funda metro station. The rather unattractive buildings house a small display of Latin American crafts and temporary exhibitions.

Bela Vista owes its rather unappealing nickname of Bixiga (meaning 'bladder' in Portuguese) to an early 20th-century market that sold tripe to immigrants who couldn't afford anything better.

City expansion

Until the mid-19th century the quadrilateral of churches, embracing a dozen or so streets of mostly one-story dwellings, was the full extent of the "city" of São Paulo. The 1868 inauguration of the Jundiaí–Santos railroad to transport the cotton crop changed the face of São Paulo forever. Red brick and wrought iron crept into the city's previously rustic architecture. Workshops and warehouses grew up around the train station, near today's Luz commuter rail terminal.

The rise of coffee presaged even more growth. From 1892, when the first iron footbridge was flung across the downtown **Anhangabaú Valley**, through the 1920s, São Paulo added another ring of busy business districts and colorful neighborhoods. The coffee barons themselves were the first to build on the north side of the Anhangabaú, in a district called **Campos Elíseos**. Some of their Art Nouveau mansions, surrounded by high iron gates and gleaming with bronze and stained-glass finishings, can still be seen although, overall, the neighborhood today is a shabby remnant of its glittering past. Later, more mansions were erected in nearby **Higienópolis** and then in an elegant row along **Avenida Paulista**.

Meanwhile, thousands of immigrants poured into working-class neighborhoods that sprouted up around São Paulo's old downtown. Vila Inglesa, Vila Economizadora, and others, their rows of red-brick houses and shops still neat and tidy, were civilized efforts to meet the city's urgent housing needs. But they didn't work.

By the time São Paulo's World War I industrial expansion began, Italian, Japanese, and Portuguese immigrants were crowded into cheek-by-jowl tenements in a ring of slums – **Brás, Bom Retiro, Bela Vista**, and **Liberdade** – circling the historic downtown. Even today these neighborhoods contain shabby tenements with strong ethnic communities.

BELOW: São Paulo's Catholic University building.

A hot-dog seller waiting for business on the city streets.

Distinctive communities

Bela Vista (popularly known as **Bixiga**) is São Paulo's colorful Little Italy. **Rua 13 de Maio**, Bixiga's heart, is a row of green and red *cantinas* and pretty little two-story houses. The parish church of **Nossa Senhora Achiropita** Ⓛ is a squat, mini-basilica graced by ornate columns and topped by an oversized dome. Achiropita is the site of an annual festival (which takes place during the weekends of August) celebrating wine, pasta, and music. Rua 13 de Maio is roped off as thousands gather for dancing, drinking (5,000 liters of wine) and eating (three tons of spaghetti and 40,000 pizzas).

Liberdade, just behind Praça da Sé, has kept its Japanese origins intact to the point where street signs use Oriental characters and movie houses show Japanese films *(see page 200)*. The **Museu da Imigração Japonesa** Ⓜ (Japanese Immigration Museum) at Rua São Joaquim 381 (open pm daily except Mon) opened in 1978 while Brazil was celebrating 70 years of Japanese immigration. On display are some 1,000 items comprising mainly works of art and religious objects and vestments.

Bom Retiro, near the Luz train station, retains vestiges of its past as São Paulo's Arab and Lebanese Christian neighborhood. Twisting Rua 25 de Março packs fabric and rug stores in a noisy bazaar. Jewish, Muslim, and Christian merchants sip coffee and chat as if Middle East tensions never existed.

Beyond Bom Retiro, surrounding the cavernous Roosevelt commuter train terminal, is **Brás**. Predominantly Italian at the turn of the 20th century, today's Brás is a vast slum, housing thousands of migrants from the impoverished northeast. They are São Paulo's bus drivers, sun-seared road workers, and construction laborers. Their culture, rich with the sap of Brazilian folklore, can be seen on every street corner. *Nordestino* (northeastern) accordion players perform nightly at the shabby north end of Praça da Sé. During the day, *repentistas* (guitar players who make up clever, rhyming lyrics on any subject suggested by onlookers) hold forth on the breezy **São Bento** esplanade. Bahian *capoeira* (Afro-Brazilian fighting dance) performers move to the eerie sound of the single-string *berimbau* outside the Anhangabaú subway station, and at Praça do Patriarca, a *nordestino* herb salesman deals in alligator skins, colorless elixirs, and Amazon spices sold from burlap sacks spread on the sidewalk.

From the 1940s, São Paulo added more and more commercial and residential rings as it spiraled outward. **Higienópolis** and the **Jardins**, south of **Avenida Paulista**, became middle- and upper-class high-rise apartment neighborhoods. Later, offices, apartments, and shopping centers formed another ring around elegant **Avenida Faria Lima**, just to the south of Paulista. In the 1970s, São Paulo jumped the **Pinheiros River** to start an even glitzier ring in hilly **Morumbi**, where strikingly landscaped mansions include the official residence of the state governor.

BELOW: the Japanese Liberdade district.

Art museums

While São Paulo's citizens are known as workaholics, the city boasts the best cultural attractions in the country, and excellent parks.

Map on page 184

MASP, the **Museu de Arte de São Paulo** Ⓝ (Avenida Paulista 1578; open daily 11am–5pm; except Mon), is São Paulo's cultural pride, with nearly 1,000 pieces originating from ancient Greece and contemporary Brazil. The unique display arrangement – rows of paintings encased in smoked-glass slabs – was designed chiefly as a teaching aid. Detailed explanations on the back of each display put the artist and their work into historical perspective.

The museum is like an art history book – but offering the real thing instead of color plates. Rafael, Bosch, Holbein, Rembrandt, Monet, Van Gogh, Goya, Reynolds, and Picasso are just a few of the artists representing major European trends. The museum also includes a survey of Brazilian art from 19th-century court painters, Almeida Júnior and Pedro Américo, to 20th-century modernists Portinari, Di Cavalcanti, and Tarsila do Amaral.

Behind the Luz train station and park is the **Pinacoteca do Estado** Ⓞ (State Art Gallery), a beautiful neo-classical building designed by Ramos de Azevedo in 1905 (Avenida Tiradentes 141; open daily except Mon; 10am–6pm). What MASP does for Western art, the state gallery's 5,000-piece collection does for its Brazilian counterpart. Highlights include sculptures by Vitor Brecheret, creator of the *Bandeirantes Monument*, and Júnior's *A Leitura*, a portrait of a girl reading against a background of palm trees and striped awnings.

Across Avenida Tiradentes from Pinacoteca do Estado is São Paulo's most important collection of colonial art and artifacts. The **Museu de Arte Sacra** Ⓟ (open daily 11am–6pm, except Mon) contains 1,000 pieces displayed in the former cloisters and chapel of the labyrinthian **Luz Monastery**. The main baroque structure was completed in 1774, although portions date from the late 17th century. The collection is completed by oil portraits of São Paulo's first bishops, gold and silver altar accoutrements, carved gold-leaf fragments of churches torn down by the juggernaut of 20th-century progress, and rare wood carvings by Brazil's great 18th-century sculptor Antônio Francisco Lisboa, better known as Aleijadinho *(see page 215)*.

Across from the imposing state governor's palace in Morumbi, on the southwestern side of the city, the **Fundação Oscar Americano** Ⓠ (Avenida Morumbi 3700; open Tues–Fri 11am–5pm; from 10am weekends) is São Paulo's most bucolic setting for art appreciation. Oscar Americano was a noted architect and collector who willed his estate to the public as an arts foundation when he died in 1974. The discreet glass-and-stone mansion displays works by Di Cavalcanti, Portinari, Guignard, 17th-century Dutch painter Franz Post, and many others against a lush background of broad lawns and landscaped woods. A tea room overlooks the ground-floor patio and is open until 6pm. String quartets and soloists perform in a small auditorium on Sunday afternoons.

Imperial reminders

Located in the Parque da Independência, in the tranquil suburb of Ipiranga, the sprawling **Museu Paulista** Ⓡ (open daily except Mon; 9am–4.45pm) marks the spot where Pedro I declared Brazilian independence. An equestrian monument stands on the site

BELOW: the Obelisk, a 1932 monument to the *tenentes* revolt in 1924.

where Pedro shouted "Independence or death!" before a small entourage. The emperor's remains are buried beneath the bronze and concrete landmark.

On a nearby bluff is the massive, neo-classical museum building. Inside is a hodgepodge of historical and scientific exhibits. One wing displays artifacts of Pedro and his family. Another includes furnishings, farm implements, and even horse carts from São Paulo's colonial past. Research by the **University of São Paulo** on Brazil's Amerindians has yielded material for several galleries, including a display of pre-Columbian pottery from the Amazon island of **Marajó**. Other exhibits honor aviation pioneer Alberto Santos-Dumont and the state militiamen who fought in the 1924 *tenentes* military revolt *(see page 34)*. A separate gallery displays Pedro Américo's 1888 painting *O Grito do Ipiranga*, a romanticized portrayal of Pedro I's famous "independence or death" declaration.

Parks and animals

São Paulo's most important park, **Ibirapuera** ❸, is a huge area of trees, lawns, and handsome pavilions, completed to celebrate São Paulo's 400th anniversary in 1954. Today, a half million *paulistanos* use its playgrounds, picnic areas, and sports complex on sunny weekends. In front of the park are two of São Paulo's most noted monuments: the 72-meter (235-ft) **Obelisk and Mausoleum** honoring heroes of the 1932 civil war and Vitor Brecheret's **Bandeirantes Monument**, a tribute to the 17th-century pioneers *(see pages 30–31)*. Ibirapuera's low-slung curving pavilions, designed by Niemeyer, constitute São Paulo's most important cultural center. The main showcase is a three-story rectangle of ramps and glass, which hosts São Paulo's prestigious Bienal art shows.

BELOW: monument to the city of São Paulo.

Held since 1951, the São Paulo Bienal is the world's largest regularly scheduled arts event, bringing together all that's new, experimental, and even weird in the worlds of art and music, for a two-month extravaganza. The pavilion also hosts industrial and cultural fairs. The third floor displays a permanent collection of contemporary Brazilian paintings. Linked to the Bienal Pavilion by an undulating breezeway is São Paulo's **Museu de Arte Moderna** (open Tues, Wed, Fri–Sun 11am–6pm, Thur 2–8pm), with changing exhibits of work by Brazil's 20th-century sculptors and painters.

The **Instituto Butantã** Ⓣ (Avenida Vital Brasil 1500; open daily except Mon; 9am–4.45pm), founded in 1901, is one of the world's leading centers for the study of poisonous snakes. The slithery reptiles are everywhere – coiled behind glass in ornate kiosks, piled one on top of the other in grassy habitats, stuffed and mounted in display cases next to hairy spiders and scorpions. Altogether, there are some 1,000 live snakes on the premises. Periodically, staff members will milk venom from their fangs.

São Paulo has one of the world's largest zoos, with no less than 3,500 specimens occupying primarily natural habitats. Noted for its tropical bird collection, the **Jardim Zoológico** Ⓤ (Avenida Miguel Stéfano 4241; open daily except Mon 9am–5pm) annually attracts several million visitors.

Map on page 184

The **Horto Florestal**, also known as Parque Alfredo Lefgren (Rua do Horto 931; open daily 6am–6pm), was founded in 1896. A pleasant place to spend an afternoon, the park has a playground, walking trails, and the Pedra Grande viewpoint, offering a beautiful view of the north of São Paulo city. Located inside the park is the **Museu Florestal Octvio Vecchi**, displaying a huge variety of native wood samples.

On the same street as the zoo is the **Jardim Botânico** **V** (Botanic Garden; open Wed–Sun 9am–5pm). There is public access to 360,000 sq meters (430,000 sq yards) of gardens, with two glasshouses containing hundreds of delicate plant species including an orchid collection. The Botanic Institute here educates the public on the various ecosystems of Brazil.

Local art for sale in the market at Embu.

Dining and shopping

For most *paulistanos*, as well as foreign visitors, São Paulo is above all else a restaurant city. Food is king in São Paulo – buffet tables burst with it, waiters fuss over it, grills and spits sputter with it, and a priesthood of critics and gourmets argue over it.

Paulistanos love food – in all its flavors, shapes, and ethnic varieties – more than any other urban population in Brazil. With its many ethnic communities, each with their own national dishes and restaurants, São Paulo has raised food appreciation to the level of worship. For the *paulistanos*, the substitute for Rio's beach life is an active nightlife centered around wine and dinner at one of the city's many restaurants – *see* the *Where to Eat* section in *Travel Tips*.

When *paulistanos* are not working or dining out, they are usually shopping. **Rua Augusta**, around Rua Oscar Freire in Jardim Paulista, is the traditional headquarters for fashionable but pricey men and women's wear. Forum, Zoomp, and Ellus are famous boutiques. There are more boutiques in various galleries spread along Rua Augusta. **Rua Oscar Friere** and its surroundings (Rua Bela Cintra and Rua Haddock Lobo) are known as São Paulo's "5th Avenue," where you can find designer names including Versace, Fendi, Montblanc, Armani, Kenzo, Thierry Mugler, Cartier, and Tommy Hilfiger.

A narrow gallery of handicraft stores at **Augusta 2883** leads to São Paulo's leading arts corner – **Rua Padre João Manuel** and **Rua Barão de Capanema**. A dozen art galleries, of which the **Dan** and the **Renot** are the largest, display the best in contemporary Brazilian painting and sculpture.

But the *paulistano*'s first love is the shopping center. The priciest is **Morumbi**, featuring top boutiques and designer stores. The oldest, the most elegant and, for many, the best, is **Iguatemi**, on Avenida Faria Lima, noted for its traffic congestion, pedestrian ramps, water clock, and four movie theaters.

Almost as traditional is **Ibirapuera**, a boxy structure near the park. But the biggest shopping center is **Eldorado**, a huge glass enclosure of splashing fountains and towering mirrors with its own entertainment plaza and the **Monica Park** for children. The newest is **Shopping Light**, an upmarket mall with boutiques and eateries.

BELOW: a tempting fruit stall in the city.

Nightlife

São Paulo has a seemingly infinite number of nightclubs and discos. The choice of where to go depends on taste, money, season, age, and what is or is not currently trendy. São Paulo's nightlife comes alive around midnight. Be warned that instead of an entrance fee, many venues use a card with a pre-set minimum amount that you pay at the end of the night. Even soft drinks can be expensive and some places also charge an "artistic cover" to pay for the cost of the band.

Popular with the "old money" are members-only clubs like The Gallery in the Oscar Freire area. Less sedate and more varied nightlife can be found in Itaim Bibi and Vila Olímpia, and to a lesser extent, Bixaga. Top musical acts perform at Tau Brasil in Vila Olímpia. Check local press for details. In Centro, Bar Brahma (Avda Sao Joao 677) opened its doors in 1948 to a crowd of original bohemians. Completely restored in 1998, it has a 24-hour café too. Bars on Rua da Consolaçâo (between Alameda Jacé and Alameda Tietê) cater to a gay clientele.

Cigar aficionados should head for the Havana Club in the Hotel Renaissance (Alameda Santos 2233, Cerqueira César) – a comfortable cigar lounge and bar with its own dance floor. For cowboys and cowgirls (even the Brazilian ones, of whom there are many), there is Jardineira Beer (Avenida dos Bandeirantes 1051, Vila Olímpia).

São Paulo club crawlers who don't want to go deaf also have plenty of options to choose from. A row of bars and restaurants located on **Vila Madalena** and neighboring **Rua Henrique Schaumann** in Pinheiros lean toward Brazilian pop and folk music, with a preference for *choro* and *pagode*, traditional ballads played with a touch of Tin Pan Alley. Popular spots are the Clube do Choro and the Cathedral do Choro.

TIP

Happy Hour is an institution in Sao Paulo, when from 6–8pm office workers fill the bars for half-price drinks. Things do not liven up again until after 11pm. Thursday is a big night out as many locals leave the city for the weekend.

BELOW: the alpine-style resort of Campos do Jordão.

Diverse entertainments

Piano bars are a *paulistano* favorite. The Baiuca on Faria Lima is the most popular among singles. One of the prettiest, for its smoked-glass decor and soft lights, is the San Francisco Bay in Jardim Paulista. The noisy Executive Piano Bar, on the top floor of the Itália Building, is noted mainly for its view. You could also try Piano Forte, on Rua Groenlândia 513, in Jardim América.

São Paulo's post-war growth (and money) has made it a magnet for world-class performers. A typical season might bring the Bolshoi Ballet, the New York Philharmonic, James Taylor, and many other stars to venues including the **Anhembi Convention Center**, the state-of-the-art **Credicard Hall**, **Ibirapuera Gymnasium**, the **Teatro Municipal**, or the **Direct TV Music Hall** in Moema. The **Alfa Real Theater**, next to the Transamérica Hotel, offers modern and comfortable facilities for the performing arts.

São Paulo competes head to head with Rio when it comes to X-rated entertainment. Glitzy strip bars featuring explicit "erotic" acts start on Rua Augusta near the Caesar Park Hotel, extending all the way to Rua Nestor Pestana downtown. Others are located on Rua Bento Freitas near the Hilton. In Itaim, near Ibirapuera, there is also the renowned Café Photo.

Mountain resorts

Like the residents of Rio de Janeiro, São Paulo residents can vacation in the mountains or on the shore without leaving their home state. At 1,700 meters (5,600 ft), in a lush valley of the Mantiqueira Range, **Campos do Jordão** ❷ is São Paulo's chief mountain resort with alpine chalets and winter weather. Its month-long July Music Festival at the modern **Municipal Auditorium** features

Maps:
City 184
Area 198

BELOW: a chip off the old block, Embu market.

classical and popular programs. Next door is the pleasantly landscaped **Felícia Leirner sculpture garden**. On display are magnificent bronze and granite works by the Polish-born artist whose name it takes.

The hub of Campos do Jordão's busy downtown is a row of chalet-style restaurants and shops. Local products include metal, wood and leather crafts, woolens, and rustic furniture. Primitive arts are on sale. Nearby is a tranquil lake circled by horse-drawn carriages for hire. Yellow and brown trollies carrying tourists occasionally rattle past.

Ringing the downtown area are around 50 hotels and dozens of summer homes belonging to the *paulistano* elite. The largest such abode, bearing the impressive name **Palácio Boa Vista**, is the state governor's winter retreat. A portion of this Tudor-style mansion has been converted into a museum (open Wed–Sun 10am–noon and 2–5pm). Attractions include 19th-century furnishings and oil paintings by *paulista* artists, including Tarsila do Amaral, Di Cavalcanti, and Portinari.

About 12 km (7 miles) from downtown, Itapeva Peak offers an impressive view of the Paraíba River Valley, where São Paulo coffee bushes first took root more than a century ago.

Resorts close to the city

The only problem with the state's most bucolic resort, **Campos do Jordão**, is its distance from São Paulo, which is 167 km (103 miles) away. Closer to the big town, 60 km (40 miles) away traveling toward the coast, is a quaint railroad outpost frozen in time – **Paranapiacaba ❸**.

BELOW: "Immigrants Road" bridge en route to the coast.

Built in 1867 by British railroaders, the brick-and-board station and row houses are a portrait of Victorian England. The tall clock tower is reminiscent of Big Ben at Westminster. At a height of 800 meters (2,500 ft), Paranapiacaba (Sea View in Tupi-Guarani) was the last station on the Jundiaí–Santos line before the breathtaking plunge down the Great Escarpment.

A half-hour train ride, on a creaking, huffing engine, will bring tourists through tunnels and across narrow viaducts to the edge of the sheer mountainside for a spectacular view of the Santos lowlands. Paranapiacaba offers few amenities, however. There are no hotels or restaurants, only a few fruit and soft drink stands. A museum (open weekends only) displays 19th-century train cars and memorabilia.

Also close to São Paulo, 60 km (40 miles) on the Fernão Dias Highway, but better organized for visitors, is the mountain resort of **Atibaia ❹**, São Paulo's peach and strawberry capital. A winter festival honors the lowly strawberry, selling everything from strawberry jam to pink strawberry liquors.

At 800 meters (2,600 ft) above sea-level, Atibaia's crisp, clean air contrasts with São Paulo's smog, and it calls itself the Brazilian Switzerland.

The city's delightfully landscaped Parque Municipal features mineral water springs, lakes, and a railway museum (open weekends and holidays 10am–6pm). Near the center is Atibaia's white-walled **Museu Municipal João Batista Conti** (Praça Bento

Paz; open Wed–Sat noon–5pm, Sun 9am–5pm), dating from 1836. The sacred art objects contrast with the erotic pieces displayed by local sculptor Yolanda Mallozzi in a second-floor gallery.

Just outside Atibaia are two noted resort hotels, the Village Eldorado and the Park Atibaia, offering sports and leisure facilities. São Paulo residents are attracted here for the fresh air.

Day trips

Quaint, prosperous **Itu ❺**, 100 km (60 miles) from São Paulo on the Castelo Branco Highway, is another fresh-air paradise. The town's delights include 18th- and 19th-century row houses on pretty pedestrian streets, and a handful of cluttered antique stores. The **Museu Republicano da Convenção de Itu** off the main square (open daily except Mon; 10am–5pm) exhibits colonial and imperial-era furnishings and artifacts. A small **Museu da Energia** tells the story of electricity.

Closer to São Paulo, 28 km (17 miles) on the Regis Bittencourt Highway, is the state handicrafts capital of **Embu ❻**. The town's two main squares and a network of pedestrian streets linking them become a vast primitive arts, handicrafts, and Brazilian food festival every Sunday. Wooden stalls sell ceramics, leather- and metal-worked handicrafts, woolen goods, lacework, knitted items, and colorful batiks. On Largo dos Jesuitas, wood carvers practice their craft in the open air. Rows of quaint 18th-century houses serve as antique and rustic furniture stores. The rather primitive chapel of **Nossa Senhora do Rosário** was built by Amerindians in 1690. In the annex is a musty sacred art museum.

Visitors can sample Bahian delicacies like *vatapá* (a seafood or chicken stew) or coconut sweets at outdoor stalls; or choose from among a dozen interesting restaurants. Nearby, the **Orixás** serves Bahian delicacies and *feijoada*, the pork and black bean stew that is Brazil's national dish. The **Patacão** also specializes in Brazilian cuisine; its long, dark-wood tables and fireplace recall a colonial-era tavern.

Beaches

São Paulo state is not famous for its beaches. Nevertheless, there are over a hundred along the 400 km (240 miles) of coast, which are regular retreats for wealthy city workers during weekends and holidays.

Ubatuba ❼, only 70 km (40 miles) from Parati in southern Rio de Janeiro *(see pages 175–6)*, is convenient for both São Paulo and Rio, although its charms are low key rather than picturesque. A total of 85 km (50 miles) of beaches curl around Ubatuba's inlets and islands. Boat trips take visitors to the Anchieta Prison ruins on one of the main islands, then up the coast to the eerie remains of Lagoinha Sugar Plantation, which was partially destroyed by fire during the 19th century.

Caraguatatuba ❽, 50 km (30 miles) south of Ubatuba on State Highway 55, has almost as many beaches but fewer historical attractions than its northern neighbor. A first-class resort hotel, the **Tabatinga**,

Map on page 198

In the 1970s, Itu's town fathers tried to boost tourism with the campaign slogan, "Everything is Big in Itu." To prove it, they installed an immense public telephone – still standing – in the town square, and an oversized traffic light nearby.

BELOW: São Paulo's pristine coastline.

offers complete sports facilities, including golf. Caraguatatuba is a springboard for visiting São Paulo's largest off-shore island – **São Sebastião ❾**, 30 km (18 miles) south on Highway 55.

Ferry boats regularly take visitors from the quaint town of São Sebastião on the mainland to the village of **Ilhabela** on the island. The startling mountain scenery, waterfalls, beaches, and azure sea have made the island popular with São Paulo's rich set.

Another 100 km (60 miles) down Highway 55 is peaceful **Bertioga ❿**. The **Fortress of São João**, with blazing white walls and miniature turrets, guards a narrow inlet. Its ancient cannons bear down on passing pleasure craft. The fort dates from 1547.

Thirty kilometers (18 miles) south of Bertioga is São Paulo's elite resort of **Guarujá ⓫**, so-called pearl of the Atlantic. **Enseada** is the most popular beach, a horseshoe of spray, sand, and gleaming hotels recalling Copacabana. Nearby is the more isolated **Pernambuco** beach. São Paulo's monied elite have made this their Malibu. Mansions of every architectural style – surrounded by broad lawns and closed in by fences, hedges, and guards – look out on surf, and green and gray offshore islands.

Like São Paulo, only 90 km (nearly 54 miles) away, Guarujá is a city for restaurant-goers. Highly recommended are Il Faro for Italian cuisine and Rufino's for seafood, and the bar and restaurant of the Casa Grande Hotel, a sprawling colonial inn on **Praia da Enseada**.

Just a few blocks from the Casa Grande is the narrow area of **Praia de Pitangueiras**. Streets near the beach have been pedestrianized so people can browse unhindered among dozens of boutiques, handicraft and jewelry stores.

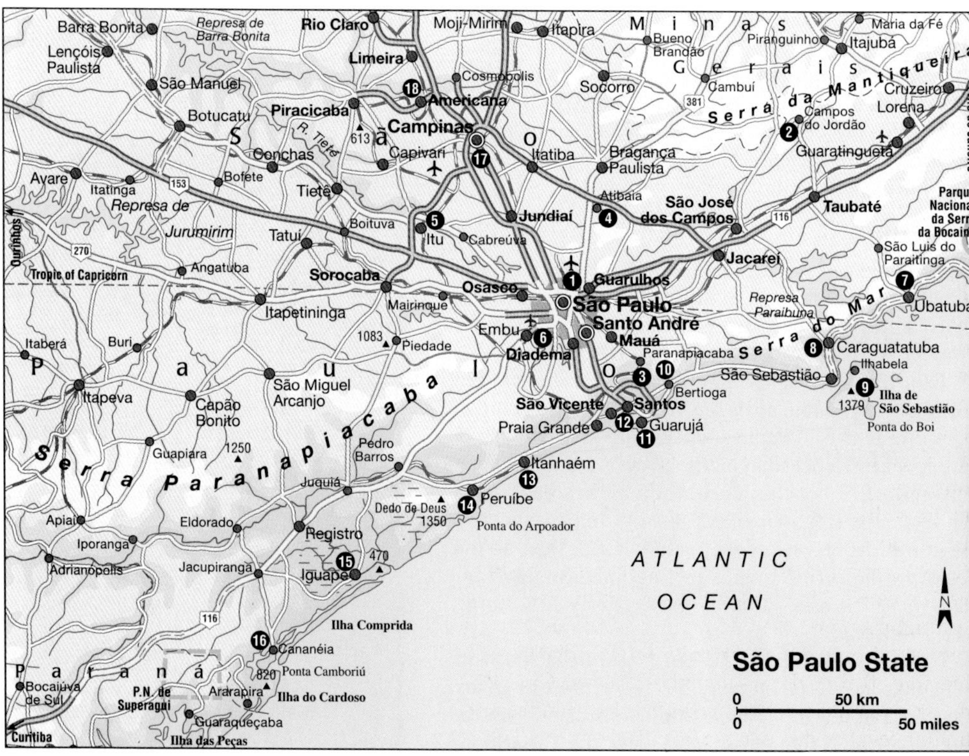

Island port

Map on page 198

From downtown, visitors can catch the car ferry across an oily inlet to **Santos** ⓬, São Paulo's chief port. *Santistas* take little pain to hide the business end of their island – hulking tankers ply the narrow channels spewing oil; freight containers are piled in ugly pens or next to dilapidated warehouses. Unfortunately, this decay has spread from the port to the city's old downtown area. Historic **Igreja do Carmo**, with portions dating from 1589, is a gray facade next to a broken-down train station. Nearby, a slum district has sprung up around the 17th-century **São Bento** church and its **Museu de Arte Sacra** (Rua Santa Joana D'Arc 795; open daily except Mon; 2–5.30pm). The recently restored **Bolsa oficial de Café** in Rua 15 de Novembre houses a small but interesting coffee museum and café.

The ocean side of Santos, however, shows the same whitewashed face as Guarujá. The **Museu do Mar** (Sea Museum), on Rua República do Equador 81 (open daily 9am–6pm, weekends until 8pm) near the Guarujá ferry landing, exhibits stuffed sharks killed in nearby waters, an immense 148-kg (325-pound) sea shell, aquatic plantlife, and bizarre coral formations.

Santos also has a lovely orchid garden, **Orquidário Municipal**, in the José Menino District near **São Vicente**, Brazil's oldest settlement. The main **Gonzaguinha** beach is lined with white and pastel-colored apartment houses and bars and outdoor restaurants.

São Vicente is the gateway to Brazil's most crowded beach – **Praia Grande**, an endless stretch of spray, grayish-brown sand, tourist buses, and bobbing human bodies. But another 60 km (35 miles) south on Highway 55 is yet another scene, the slow-moving **Itanhaém** ⓭, one of Brazil's oldest settlements. Parts of Itanhaém's gray, spooky Nossa Senhora da Conceição chapel date back as far as 1534.

Other beach towns south of São Vicente include picturesque **Peruíbe** ⓮ (80 km/50 miles); **Iguape** ⓯ (200 km/120 miles), on the quiet inlet formed by Ilha Comprida; and remote **Cananéia** ⓰ (280 km/170 miles), which has a nature reserve and also offers boat excursions out to nearby islands, which have some isolated beaches.

BELOW: the road to São Vicente beach, Santos.

Northern towns

Two urban centers in the northern interior of São Paulo state are worth visiting briefly (if you are passing that way). One is industrial **Campinas** ⓱ (pop. over 1 million; 100 km/60 miles from São Paulo), which became wealthy from sugar and coffee and is now the site of one of Brazil's best universities, Unicamp (13 km/8 miles from downtown), which was a refuge for left-wing teachers during the years of military repression. The city has a fine cathedral, the neo-classical **Catedral Metropolitana** (1883) on Largo do Rosário, and the **Centro de Convivência** (Praça Imprensa Fluminense) is the main cultural venue, with a noted symphony orchestra.

Nearby **Americana** ⓲ (pop. 175,000) was the most successful Brazilian community to be settled by Confederates fleeing the southern US after the Civil War, drawn by cheap land, religious freedom and the continuing legality of slave labor in Brazil. ❑

Liberdade: Tokyo Town

A towering red portico, called a *tori*, straddles the main business street. Next to it is a tiny, expertly manicured garden, lush with dark green shrubs and graced by an arching footbridge, called a *hashi*. Beyond the portico, 450 smaller gateways, each bearing a white strobe light, march toward the urban horizon.

Along the side streets, movie theaters advertize in Japanese. Itinerant merchants, with Oriental faces wreathed by scores of wrinkles, hawk fresh flowers in carefully tied bunches. Signs on low-rise, concrete buildings announce centers for acupuncture and meditation. Classes in judo, flower arranging, and the tea ceremony are also available here.

Welcome to Liberdade, São Paulo's lively Japanese neighborhood, home to 1 million Japanese, the largest population outside Japan itself.

Liberdade residents can choose from three Japanese-language community newspapers and shop at neighborhood grocery stores for Oriental delicacies. Some say Liberdade is more Japanese than Tokyo, which, they claim, has become excessively Westernized. Liberdade is lost in both time and space.

The sprawling neighborhood, centered around Rua Galvão Bueno, behind São Paulo's Roman Catholic cathedral, originated in 1908. On June 18 of that year, the immigrant steamer *Kasato Maru* docked at Santos Harbor with 830 Japanese on board.

The immigrants, almost all of them farmers, were fleeing crop failures and earthquakes in their native islands. Using loans supplied by a Japanese development firm, most of the 165 families set up modest truck-farming operations in the interior of São Paulo. Later, some moved to Mato Grosso and the Amazon. Over the next five decades, a quarter of a million Japanese followed in their footsteps. Their story is recounted at Liberdade's **Immigration Museum** on Rua São Joaquim.

BELOW: East meets West on the busy streets.

Liberdade became São Paulo's Oriental section in the 1940s, when the descendants of early settlers took up urban trades and professions. Today, about 100 Japanese shops cater to neighborhood and tourist needs.

Crowded emporiums such as **Casa Mizumoto** and **Minikimono** sell a wide range of artifacts, from cheap stone or plastic Buddhas to expensive, delicately carved ivory figures, hand-painted vases and *furins*, or "Bells of Happiness," which drive away evil spirits. Brazilian semi-precious stones are another mainstay of the gift and specialty trade.

Sampling the neighborhood cuisine is probably the highlight of any visit to Liberdade. Good Japanese restaurants include: Yamamoto (Rua Américo de Campos 84; dinner only), with a charming Japanese garden; inexpensive Sushi Yassu (Rua Tomás Gonzaga 98), which has recently expanded its menu to include a variety of eels; and intimate Sushi Lika (Rua dos Estudantes 170), offering beautifully prepared dishes and Japanese music.

Larger restaurants, including Yamamoto, normally have their own sushi bars, which are a kind of smorgasbord of Japanese delicacies offered to guests seated around a semi-circular counter. The most complete sushi and restaurant services are at Liberdade's Banri, Osaka and Nikkey Palace hotels on Rua Galvão Bueno.

First-time samplers of Japanese cuisine usually stick with choices such as *Okonomi Yaki*, a shrimp, pork, or fish pancake; *Sukiyaki*, a meat and vegetable dish soaked in gravy; or *Lobatazaki*, fish or meat broiled on a spit. The more daring might try exotic dishes such as *Unagui*, stewed eel served in sweet sauce, or *Kocarai*, raw carp. Shrimp, raw fish, marine algae patties, mushrooms, and salmon are typical appetizers in Liberdade.

Although the neighborhood is overwhelmingly Japanese, people of Chinese, Vietnamese and Korean origin have been moving into the area over the past few years. This trend can be seen in the local restaurants and shops selling exotic produce.

One of the best ways to sample Liberdade cuisine is to try one delicacy at a time at the Oriental Street Fair every Sunday morning at **Praça Liberdade** (by Liberdade subway station). Dozens of stalls serve shrimp, fish, and meat tidbits from spits that sputter on open grills. The fair sprawls over the plaza and into neighboring streets, where stalls also sell a range of edibles similar to those that are on offer in the emporia. Imports, however, are restricted – a measure that is designed to stimulate local handicraft production.

At first glance, Liberdade nightlife seems surprisingly subdued, with few pedestrians and little traffic around. The action is all indoors. Some of the larger restaurants feature soothing Japanese music performed by brightly costumed players using acoustic instruments, while multi-course banquets can stretch through an entire evening.

The great Japanese past-time of karaoke is well represented in Liberdade. Try Karaoke Subaru, Karaoke Forever, and Karaoke Roppongi. On Avenida Liberdade, the plush Liberty Plaza Club offers a surprisingly eclectic mixture of erotic entertainment, rock 'n' roll, a sushi bar, and billiards.

Day or night, Liberdade is full of life, color, and surprises. Visitors typically have only one complaint – they find it hard to believe they're in the heart of South America. ❑

Right: proud resident of Liberdade.

MINAS GERAIS AND ESPIRITO SANTO

Map on page 204

Minas Gerais got rich quick and gave enduring substance to an artistic vision, while its adjoining coastal strip, despite considerable natural assets, has stayed out of the limelight

Minas Gerais is a Brazilian giant. It covers 587,000 sq km (352,200 sq miles), is the fifth-largest state in the area and has nearly 19 million inhabitants. It is rugged and isolated.

The central plateau rises sharply from an escarpment that rims the entire eastern frontier. The land of this once heavily wooded province is ragged now. *Minas* means mines. Everything from gold and diamonds to iron has flowed from its mineral ore veins to the world. Even today, the streets of its quaint, ancient towns are pink with iron ore dust and its rivers red with it.

Folklore contrasts the *mineiro* sharply with the extravagant *carioca* and the industrious *paulista*. The *mineiro* is said to be stubborn, cautious, hardworking, and thrifty. He is also an assiduous preserver; he has kept not only the music box churches of his baroque past, but also saved family heirlooms and trinkets, which clutter his attic rooms. São João del Rei residents have preserved the music and even the musical instruments of the 18th century, performing a liturgy of baroque orchestral pieces every Holy Week. Yet the *mineiro* is both conservative and progressive. While the *mineiros* boast Brazil's best-preserved colonial towns, they also built the nation's first planned city, Belo Horizonte. And a group of *mineiros,* led by president Juscelino Kubitschek, built Brasília.

Much of the *mineiro* traditionalism can be traced to the state's isolation during colonial times. Minas Gerais was established only when the gold rush began in 1695 *(see page 31)*. The only line of communication with the rest of the world until the 19th century was by way of mule down the perilous escarpment.

Isolation was so great that the *mineiros* started their own farms and cottage industries. This versatility gave many of them a vocation for democracy. The French traveler Saint Hilaire noted that "there were scarcely any absentee landowners in Minas. The landowner worked side by side with his slaves, unlike the aristocratic owners in the rest of Brazil." And *mineiro* poet Carlos Drummond de Andrade said: "Minas has never produced a dictator and never will."

Gold and diamond fever

In the 18th century, the gold of Minas Gerais was a colossus bestriding the world of commerce. About 1,200 tons of it were mined from 1700 to 1820. This fantastic amount made up 80 percent of all the gold produced throughout the world during that period.

Prospectors became spectacularly wealthy almost overnight. There were even slaves who enriched themselves by clandestinely clawing the earth from under-

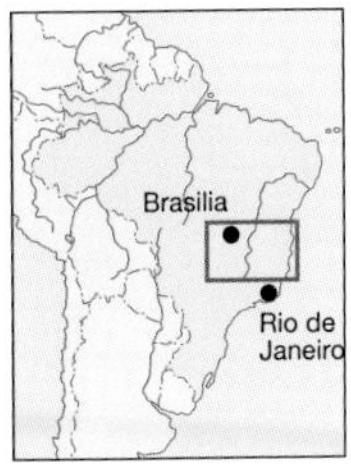

LEFT: *Prophet*, Aleijadinho sculpture in Congonhas do Campo.
BELOW: Matriz Santo Antônio, Tiradentes

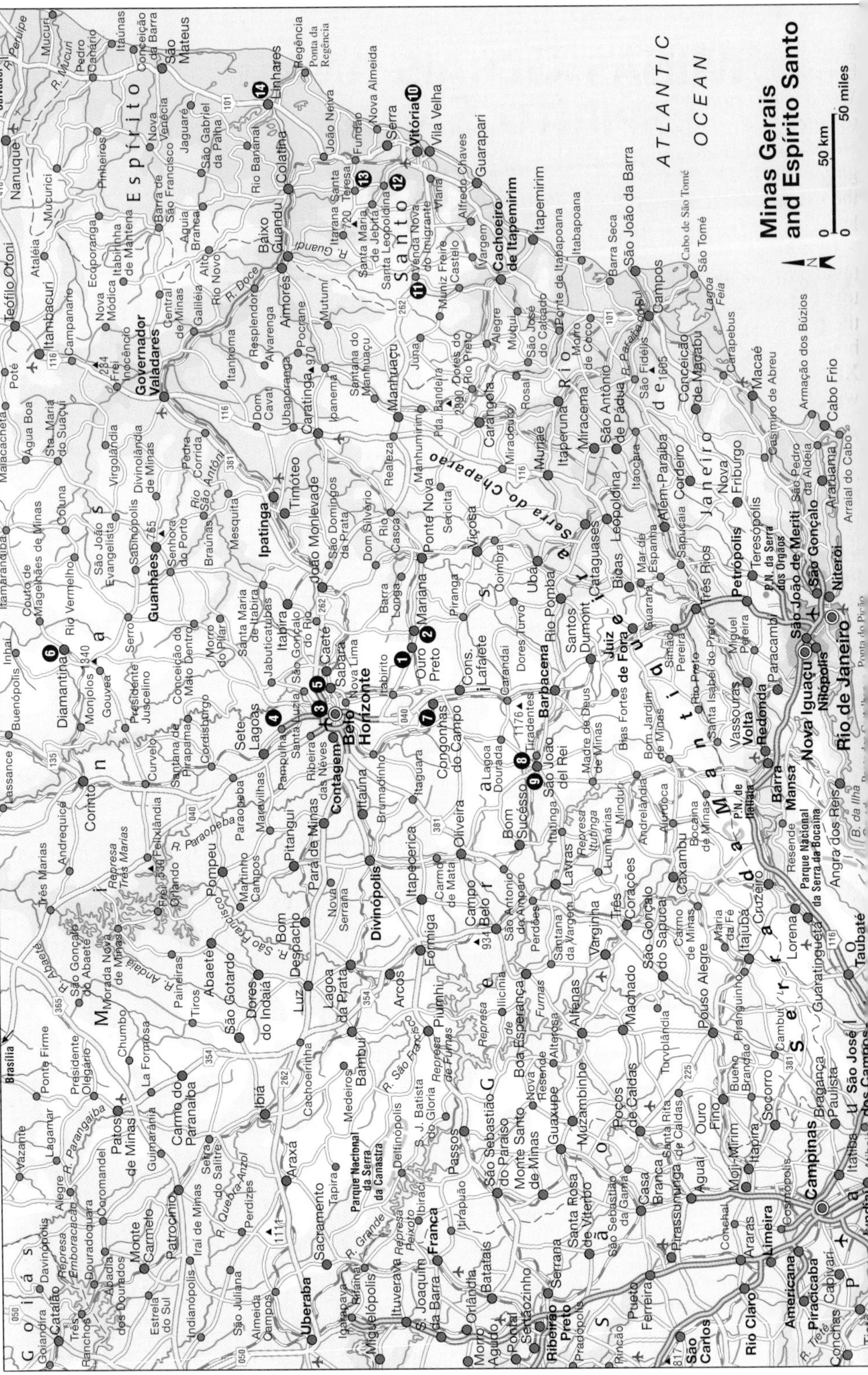
Minas Gerais and Espírito Santo
0 50 km
0 50 miles
ATLANTIC OCEAN
Minas Gerais
Espírito Santo
Rio de Janeiro
São Paulo
Goiás
Serra do Chaparão
Serra da Mantiqueira
Serra do Mar
Belo Horizonte
Contagem
Ouro Preto
Mariana
Vitória
Vila Velha
Governador Valadares
Ipatinga
Uberaba
Juiz de Fora
Rio de Janeiro
Niterói
Petrópolis
Campinas
Ribeirão Preto
Diamantina
Congonhas
São João del Rei
Tiradentes
Linhares
Colatina
Cachoeiro de Itapemirim
Campos
Cabo Frio
Salvador
Brasília

ground mines. The legendary Chico Rei, who was a king in Africa before being brought to Brazil as a slave, vowed he would recover his crown in the New World. That's exactly what he did, working feverishly in order to earn enough gold to purchase his own freedom and that of his large brotherhood.

The gold rush in Minas had ramifications abroad. Lisbon was flooded by gold coins minted at Ouro Preto's Casa dos Contos. But instead of investing their newfound wealth securely, the kings frittered away the fortune on opulent "improvements."

By the time Brazil's gold rush gave way to diamonds a few years later, Portugal had learned its lesson. The Tijuco diamond mines were closed to prospectors. A governor was appointed and a garrison sent to back up his decrees. But the plan didn't work. Governors like João Fernandes – who spent a vast sum building an artificial lake and a Portuguese sailing ship for his slave mistress, Xica da Silva – dealt in contraband. The diamonds themselves brought renewed wealth for only a short time.

"Black gold" town

Although the riches disappeared, the art remained. Today, the best place to see it is **Ouro Preto ❶**. Located 100 km (60 miles) from the state capital, Belo Horizonte, Ouro Preto was the center of the late 17th-century gold rush. First known as Vila Rica, it was just a mountain village when bands of adventurers from the Atlantic coast came in search of slaves and gold. Near Vila Rica they found a strange black stone and sent samples to Portugal. In fact, they had unwittingly discovered gold (the black coloration was from iron oxide in the soil). Vila Rica was swiftly renamed Ouro Preto (black gold) and the gold rush was underway.

Map on page 204

Surveying the streets of Ouro Preto.

BELOW: Ouro Preto, nestled among green hillsides.

"At the epicenter of the golden hurricane there was madness. Prospectors and buyers dressed their slaves in gold and drenched them in diamonds. They decorated their homes in lace and silver, their mistresses in gems."
– 18TH-CENTURY TRAVELER

By 1750, Ouro Preto had a population of 80,000, at that time larger than that of New York City. Jesuit priests also arrived, bringing ideas and artistic concepts of Europe; they insisted that their churches, financed by the gold from the mines, be built in the baroque style. Today, Ouro Preto has Brazil's purest collection of baroque art and architecture. Six museums and 13 churches among low hills and picture-book cottages make Ouro Preto a Grimm Brothers' fairy-tale town. In 1981, UNESCO declared Ouro Preto "a world cultural monument."

Art and history on display

At the center of town is spacious **Praça Tiradentes** Ⓐ, fronted by the imposing **Museu da Inconfidência** Ⓑ (open daily, except Mon; noon–5.30pm). The cobbled plaza is rich in history. The severed head of patriot Joaquim da Silva Xavier (nicknamed Tiradentes, "the tooth-puller") was displayed on a pole there in 1792. Xavier and six of his co-conspirators had plotted Brazilian independence. But spies exposed the plan, which led to Xavier's execution.

The museum once served as the town hall. Art and history are its current focuses. A macabre exhibit displays portions of the gallows used for Tiradentes' execution. Nearby is a copy of his death warrant. Some of Tiradentes' fellow conspirators are buried beneath masonry slabs on the first floor. In a separate gallery are eccentric, richly detailed wood carvings by Ouro Preto's other colonial hero – the sculptor and architect Antônio Francisco Lisboa (1738–1814). He was nicknamed Aleijadinho, "little cripple," because of a debilitating disease he had contracted in midlife. Of particular note is the moving *Christ at the Pillar.*

More of Aleijadinho's work can be viewed at the impressive church **Nossa Senhora do Carmo** Ⓒ, also on the plaza (open daily except Mon, noon–5pm),

BELOW: souvenir shop with typical local figurines, Ouro Preto.

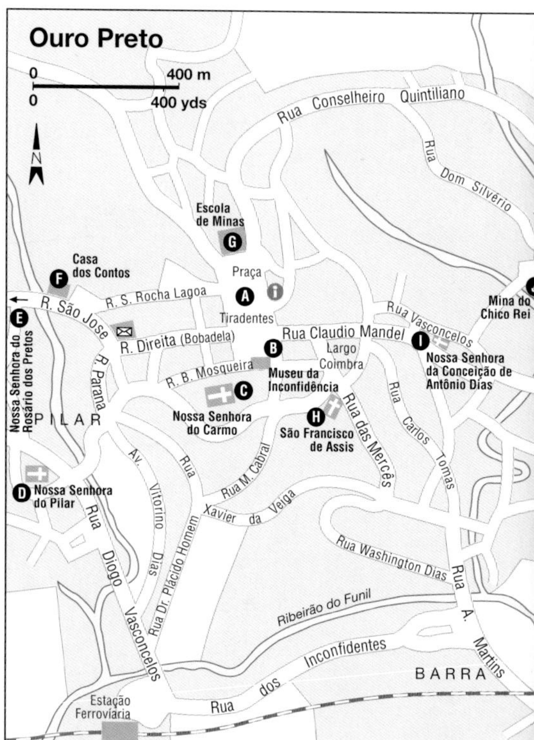

and at the sacred art collection in the nearby **Museu do Oratório** (open daily 9.30–11.50am and 1.30–5.30pm). This sturdy edifice was designed in 1766 by Aleijadinho's father, the engineer Manuel Francisco Lisboa. Aleijadinho altered the plan while work was underway in 1770, incorporating the bell towers into the facade and adding an elegant archway over the main door. The changes were a compromise between conservative Mannerist traditions and the emerging baroque style that Aleijadinho championed. Of particular note are the exuberant stone carvings of curlicues and soaring angels above the main entrance.

Next to the church is Carmo's richly endowed sacred art collection. Aleijadinho's wood carvings are prominent, along with illuminated manuscripts and gleaming gold and silver altar accoutrements. A piece of bone labeled "Saint Clement" floats eerily in a glass and gold reliquary.

Golden decor

Three blocks west of Carmo is the deceptively simple parish church of **Nossa Senhora do Pilar** Ⓓ. The squarish facade hides Ouro Preto's most extravagant baroque interior. Partly the work of the sculptor Francisco Xavier de Brito, Pilar's walls explode with rosy-cheeked saints and angels, their garments fluttering against the gold-leaf background.

Nossa Senhora do Rosário dos Pretos Ⓔ, in the Rosário district farther west, produces the opposite effect. Its bold baroque facade houses a nearly bare interior. Rosário was built by slaves, who had just enough gold to erect its stunning shell. But what a shell; its convex walls, curved facade, and shapely bell towers make Rosário Brazil's most brashly baroque architectural monument. Two other museums mark the route along cobbled streets back to Praça Tira-

Map on page 206

It is said that 400 kg (880 lbs) of gold dust was mixed with paint to adorn the interior of Nossa Senhora do Pilar in Ouro Preto.

BELOW: at home in a colonial-era house in Ouro Preto.

dentes. The **Casa dos Contos** Ⓕ (open Tues–Sat 12.30–5.30pm; Sun 9am–3pm), at the base of steep Rua Rocha Lagoa, was the tax authority during the gold rush. Gold coins, and the surprisingly sophisticated foundry for minting them, are displayed. At the high end of the street is Ouro Preto's sprawling **Escola de Minas (College of Mine Engineering)** Ⓖ. The mineralogy museum inside (open daily pm, except Mon) has a very interesting collection of precious stones, ores and crystals – 23,000 pieces in total.

TIP

If you are only visiting Ouro Preto for a day, avoid Mondays when the museums and churches are all closed. But try to spend at least one night here so that you can enjoy the town without the crowds.

Aleijadinho's masterpiece

Just east of Praça Tiradentes is an Aleijadinho architectural masterpiece, the jewel box chapel of **São Francisco de Assis** Ⓗ (open daily except Mon, 8.30–11.45am and 1.30–5pm). The church's baroque lines resemble those of Rosário dos Pretos. Extravagant relief work above the main entrance is a continuation of similar works at Carmo. Inside are rare wood and soapstone carvings by Aleijadinho, characterized by the almond eyes, shapely anatomical features and ruffled garments of the high *mineiro* baroque. The wall and ceiling paintings are by Manuel da Costa Athayde (1762–1837), whose works feature distorted human figures and realistic backgrounds. Painted surfaces and architectural features blend at the margins as if the painted sky ceiling could open up for God's inspection.

Two blocks east of São Francisco chapel is Ouro Preto's monument to Aleijadinho, the museum and church of **Nossa Senhora da Conceição de Antônio Dias** Ⓘ (open Tues–Sat 8.30am–11.30pm, 1.30–4.45pm; Sun noon–4.45pm). Aleijadinho is buried beneath a wooden marker near a side altar. The galleries behind the sacristy display his wood and soapstone carvings and the richly illustrated bibles and missals he used to study European artistic models.

BELOW: Capela de São Francisco, Pampulha, designed by Niemeyer.

Maps:
Area 204
City 206

Still in Ouro Preto, you can visit the **Mina do Chico Rei** ❶ (Rua Dom Silvério 108; open daily 8am–5pm), a gold mine built by slaves in 1702, which fell into disuse following the abolition of slavery in 1888. A small stretch of the 1,300-meter (4,265-ft) gallery is accessible to visitors.

Between Ouro Preto and Mariana (8 km/5 miles from Ouro Preto) is the more interesting **Mina da Passagem** (open daily 9am–5pm; substantial admission charge), which was in use until 15 years ago, where demonstrations are held of the processing of gold ore. This mine was dug out in the 18th century and has a 11-km (7-mile) gallery, going down to a depth of 120 meters (394 ft). Visitors can go down into the gallery by train as far as an underground lake.

The fascinating colonial town of **Mariana** ❷, birthplace of Athayde, is 12 km (7 miles) from Ouro Preto. The twin chapels of **Carmo** and **São Francisco** and the magnificent **Catedral de Nossa Senhora da Assunção** are smothered in the dark colors and mulatto figures of Athayde's opulent art. Especially noteworthy is *The Passion and Death of Saint Francis*. Athayde is buried under a wooden marker at the rear of Carmo. The cathedral has a German organ, built in 1701 and dragged by mule from Rio de Janeiro. Concerts are held on Fridays at 11am and Sundays at 12.15pm. Behind the cathedral is Mariana's sacred art museum, **Museu Arquidiocesano de Arte Sacra** (Rua Frei Durão; open daily except Mon; 9am–noon and 1.30–5pm), which contains the largest collection of baroque painting and sculpture in Minas Gerais.

Tours from Belo Horizonte

Ouro Preto was Minas Gerais' capital until 1897, when *mineiro* statesmen inaugurated Brazil's first planned city, **Belo Horizonte** ❸. Compared to Ouro Preto the bustling metropolis with a population of 2.4 million possesses little for sightseers, but it is a good base for visiting surrounding historic towns.

In chic **Pampulha** ❹, is the striking **Capela de São Francisco**, with its undulating roof and blue tiles, designed by Oscar Niemeyer in collaboration with Brazil's greatest modern artist, Cândido Portinari, who is responsible for the starkly painted images of St Francis and the 14 Stations of the Cross *(see page 121)*.

In a wooded valley 23 km (14 miles) north of Belo Horizonte is another baroque treasure, **Sabará** ❺. A leafy suburb hides the town's bizarre, musty jewel, the oddly shaped chapel of **Nossa Senhora do O**. O's humble exterior belies its exuberant decor; every inch of wall and ceiling space is covered by wood carvings, gold leaf, darkly mysterious paintings that depict various bible stories, and delicate gold-hued Oriental motifs. The Far Eastern figures reflect the experiences of Portuguese Jesuits in the Orient.

A few blocks from the chapel is Sabará's larger **Nossa Senhora da Conceição** parish church. Its squarish facade is redeemed by an explosion of rich interior decoration. The Oriental theme is frequently used, especially on the design-crowded sacristy door.

Presiding incongruously over Sabará's main square is the ghostly stone shell of the **Igreja do Rosário dos Pretos**, which was abandoned when the gold mines ran down. A few blocks away is precious **Igreja do**

BELOW: an expressive fountain dating from 1752.

Baroque-style painted wooden frieze, Igreja de São Francisco, Ouro Preto

Carmo, a rich treasure trove of Aleijadinho works, including intricate soapstone pulpits and a bas-relief frontispiece. A pair of muscular male torsos, bulging with wood-carved veins, hold the ornate choir loft in place.

Diamantina

About 280 km (175 miles) north of Belo Horizonte is a rugged hamlet many consider the equal of Ouro Preto in austere beauty and history – **Diamantina ❻**. Bordering Brazil's semi-arid *sertão*, Diamantina is surrounded by iron-red hills rising to a rocky plain. This area is particularly rich in orchids. The town's white-walled cottages and churches cascade down an irregular slope, producing a stark profile of wooden steeples. Diamantina was the headquarters of diamond contractor João Fernandes and his slave mistress Xica da Silva. Her stately home is located on **Praça Lobo Mesquita**.

The ornate wood and stone **Igreja do Carmo** church, across the square, was another gift from the diamond czar to his lover. Fernandes ordered the bell tower be moved to the rear of the church when Silva complained its tolling kept her awake. Carmo's ceiling is covered by dark-hued paintings depicting Bible stories, which were favored by 18th-century *mineiro* painters, including José Soares de Araujo, whose work at Carmo and the nearby **Igreja do Amparo** recalls that of Athayde.

Colorful **Nossa Senhora do Rosário**, a block from Carmo, was built entirely by slaves and the woodcarvings of the saints are black. Outside, the roots of a tree nearby have split Rosário's wooden crucifix, leaving only the bar and tip of the cross visible. Folklore says a slave accused of stealing was executed on the spot while protesting his innocence. He told onlookers: "Something extraordinary will occur here to prove my truthfulness." Soon after, buds appeared on the cross, eventually snaking into the ground and producing the sturdy tree.

BELOW: Aleijadinho's Igreja de São Francisco, in São João del Rei.

Across from Diamantina's cathedral is the informative **Museu do Diamante** (Diamond Museum; open Tues–Sat noon–5.30pm; Sun 9am–noon). Period mining equipment, documents and furnishings are displayed. Grisly implements of torture used against the slaves are kept in a back room.

Also near the square is Diamantina's **Public Library**, noted for its delicate trellis and *muxarabiê* (a lattice-work casing covering an entire second-story balcony). A few blocks away, on **Rua Direita**, is the humble birthplace of Juscelino Kubitschek. Nearby is the **Casa da Glória**, a pair of blue and white stone structures linked by a wooden bridge. The site was the headquarters of Diamantina's royal governors.

Sculpture in Congonhas do Campo

Eastern Minas Gerais, more economically developed than the bleak *sertão*, offers artistic treasures of the late *mineiro* baroque. **Congonhas do Campo ❼**, 80 km (48 miles) from Belo Horizonte, is site of Aleijadinho's two greatest masterworks of sculpture: the 12 life-size outdoor carvings of *The Prophets*, located on the esplanade of the **Bom Jesus de Matosinhos Sanctuary**; and the 66 painted woodcarvings of *The Stations of the Cross*, housed in a series of garden chapels

Map on page 204

earby. Carved entirely from soapstone, *The Prophets* are stolid, gray and evere. In their stylized postures and costumes, they possess a mythic quality, s if sculpted entirely from imagination.

While *The Prophets* seem suitably remote, the carved figures of *The Stations f the Cross* are vibrant and filled with emotion. The Christ statue, with its almond yes and half-open mouth, skin pale and veined, and muscles as strained, is as aunting as *The Holy Shroud.* The 12 Apostles, with their worried, working-class aces, probably sculpted after local residents, could well be an 18th-century jury.

A further 80 km (50 miles) to the south is the 1746 birthplace of Joaquim da ilva Xavier. The town, appropriately named **Tiradentes** ❽, preserves the olonial-era feeling better than almost any other in Minas Gerais. Pink slate treets, an occasional horse-drawn cart, lace curtains and brightly painted shutters contribute to a feeling of tranquility. The spacious **Museu Padre Toledo** Rua Padre Toledo; open daily except Tues; 9–11.30am, 1–4.40pm) contains eriod furnishings and sacred art. Nearby is the imposing **Igreja de Santo ntonio** church, with its stone frontispiece carved by Aleijadinho and goldlated decoration. Inside there is an 18th-century organ, a companion piece to he instrument in Mariana.

A decorative shrine in Igreja de Santo Antônio, Tiradentes.

ailroad town

nly 13 km (8 miles) from Tiradentes is bustling **São João del Rei** ❾. The **São oão train station**, on Avenida Hemílio Alves 366, has been turned into a leaming museum, the **Museu Ferroviário** (open Tues–Sat 9–11.30am and –6pm), a fascinating reminder of old-fashioned rail travel. Hulking black and ed Baldwin locomotives, dating as far back as 1880, are lined up in the round-

BELOW: baroque interior in Mariana.

house like oversized toys around a Christmas tree. Wood-paneled excursion cars feature porcelain fixtures and etched windows. The Victorian-style station is clean and authentic, right down to the ear-splitting steam whistle and syncopated huff and puff of the tourist train.

The town has seven churches. **Igreja do Carmo** recalls the baroque masterpieces of Ouro Preto. The nearby cathedral, the **Basílica de Nossa Senhora do Pilar**, presents a blocky facade on the outside, and richly decorated walls and ceilings within. But the pleasing proportions and rounded towers of the **Igreja de São Francisco**, which has been justifiably hailed as Aleijadinho's most mature architectural triumph, is the town's proudest treasure. Double rows of swaying palm trees lead to a graceful esplanade of wide steps and curving balustrades.

TIP

From Tiradentes, the best way to get to São João is by a clattering tourist steam train – a 35 minute ride – on the restored "Smoking Mary," which offers an exhilarating excursion on rolling stock dating from the turn of the 20th century. Trains run Fri–Sun at 1pm and 5pm.

Nature in Espírito Santo

The coastal city of **Vitória** ⑩, capital of the state of **Espírito Santo**, was founded in 1551 and has remained a relatively small town (pop. 313,000) whose heart comprises an island connected to the suburbs by a series of bridges. There are a few buildings recalling its colonial past, and some beaches along the coast north and south of the city that are quite pretty. But this state has not been reached by the tourist boom of its neighbors Bahia and Minas Gerais (and, of course, Rio).

The **Teatro Carlos Gomes** (Praça Costa Pereira) in Vitória was built as a copy of La Scala in Milan. It frequently hosts music festivals as well as putting on plays. The **Catedral Metropolitana** (Praça Dom Luis Scortegagna), built in 1918, has beautiful stained-glass windows.

BELOW: elegant architecture in São João del Rei.

Map on page 204

The lovely alpine-like countryside around the village of **Venda Nova do Imi-rante** (known as Venda Nova) ⓫, 113 km (70 miles) west of Vitória, is pop-lar for walking and mountaineering. About 70 km (44 miles) northwest of itória is the Swiss-founded town of **Santa Leopoldina** ⓬, which offers a leasant day trip from the capital.

Continuing northwards a further 21 km (13 miles), one reaches the charming ill town of **Santa Teresa** ⓭. Just outside it, the **Museu Biológico Professor Mello Leitão** (Avenida José Ruschi 4; open daily except Mondays, 8am–5pm) s a natural history museum founded by Augusto Ruschi, a world-famous hum-ningbird expert who died in 1986. In an area of forests rich in orchids and vildlife, the museum has attached to it a small zoo, a hummingbird and butterfly arden and grounds containing a wide variety of plants and trees.

Close to **Linhares** ⓮, 135 km (84 miles) from Vitória, is the **Reserva Biológ-ca Comboios** (open daily 8am–noon, 1–5pm; tel: 027-984 3788) a nature eserve set up to protect marine turtles. There are a number of hotels and restau-ants in the town. Two other nature reserves near Linhares, the **Linhares Reserve** (tel: 027-371 9797) and the **Sooretama Biological Reserve** (tel. 027 84 1673), protect the rainforest and its incredible variety of plants (including rchids), birds, and other wildlife. Over 370 species of birds have been recorded, ncluding the red-billed curassow. To visit either of these reserves, you will eed special authorization.

Further north, near the border with Bahia state, is **Conceição da Barra**, a mall town from which one reaches **Itaúnas** and its enormous sand dunes and onely beaches. The dunes have buried the old town of Itaúnas, and only the hurch tower can still be seen above the sand. ❑

BELOW: out for a ride in the sun.

THE SPLENDOR OF BRAZILIAN BAROQUE

Brazil's exuberant tradition in baroque art and architecture is one of the most memorable and impressive sights in the east of the country

Unlike the monumental structures that often overwhelm many of the Latin capitals, Brazil's earliest public works of art are fresh, noble and lively.

The baroque movement had three main centers in 18th-century Brazil: Salvador; Rio de Janeiro; and Minas Gerais.

The Jesuits, who sponsored the colonial explosion of baroque in Bahia, were noted for their openness to new ideas and local trends, encouraging what many in Europe regarded as "the secular opulence" of the baroque. Brazilian themes were brought to the decorative arts and great bunches of tropical fruits and wavy palms formed an incongruous background to the traditional Bible stories depicted in paintings and wood carvings. In Rio de Janeiro the baroque experience was less intense, as Rio was then secondary to the vice-regal capital of Salvador. Its best example of the trend is the small, princely Igreja da Glória do Outeiro.

MINEIRO BAROQUE

It was in Minas Gerais that Brazilian baroque reached its apex. Ouro Preto, the former state capital, has been transformed into a delightful museum town. The secret is the substitution of the curve for the line. The purest example, Ouro Preto's Rosário dos Pretos Chapel *(see page 207)*, has a convex facade, ending in two delicate bell-tower curves. Inside, the nave is an oval. Doors and windows are elegantly framed by archways.

◁ **DECORATIVE ART**
Fine attention to detail, such as this 1749 fountain spout, is typical of the preserved colonial town Tiradentes, in Minas Gerais.

△ **COLONIAL SALVADOR**
Baroque architecture and pastel-colored facades are typical blend of European and Brazilian styles found the Pelourinho district.

◁ **PRESERVING HISTORY**
The 16th-century town of Cachoeira has been declared a World Heritage Site by UNESCO because of its fine baroque architecture.

△ **WOOD CARVINGS**
Brazilian themes crept into Bahian decorative arts in the 18th century, such as Indian-faced saints depicted in typically European style.

MULTICULTURAL FAITH
ıurches in Bahia, such as ɔssa Senhora da Conceição ɔ Monte in Cachoeira, had appeal to European, dian and Afro-Brazilian orshipers alike.

PARATI
tuated on the edge of Rio Janeiro state, this pretty 8th-century town is lined ith colonial buildings along e waterfront.

▷ **CHRISTIAN SYMBOLS**
Sculptures and carvings of Christ figures abound, such as this example in Minas Gerais. The Jesuit missionaries who arrived in Brazil in the 18th century were aware that ornate baroque art would attract and awe the religious Brazilians.

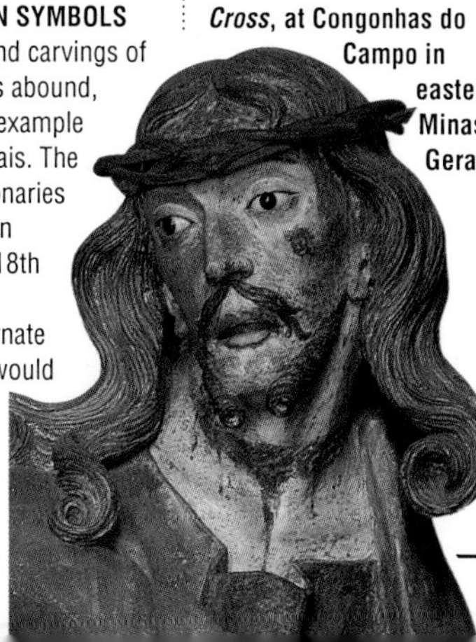

BRAZIL'S BAROQUE GENIUS

One reason for the artistic unity of *mineiro* churches is the dominance of one baroque artisan – Antônio Francisco Lisboa (1730s–1814). The uneducated son of a Portuguese craftsman and a black slave woman, he became an individualistic sculptor and architect.

Struck by a crippling disease that left his hands paralysed, he was known as Aleijadinho – the "little cripple." Undaunted, however, he worked by strapping a hammer and chisel to his wrists.

Lisboa applied the principles of European baroque he learned from books and missionaries. His greatest achievements are in Ouro Preto, plus the 12 soapstone figures of the *Old Testament Prophets* and the 66 wood carvings of the *Stations of the Cross*, at Congonhas do Campo in eastern Minas Gerais.

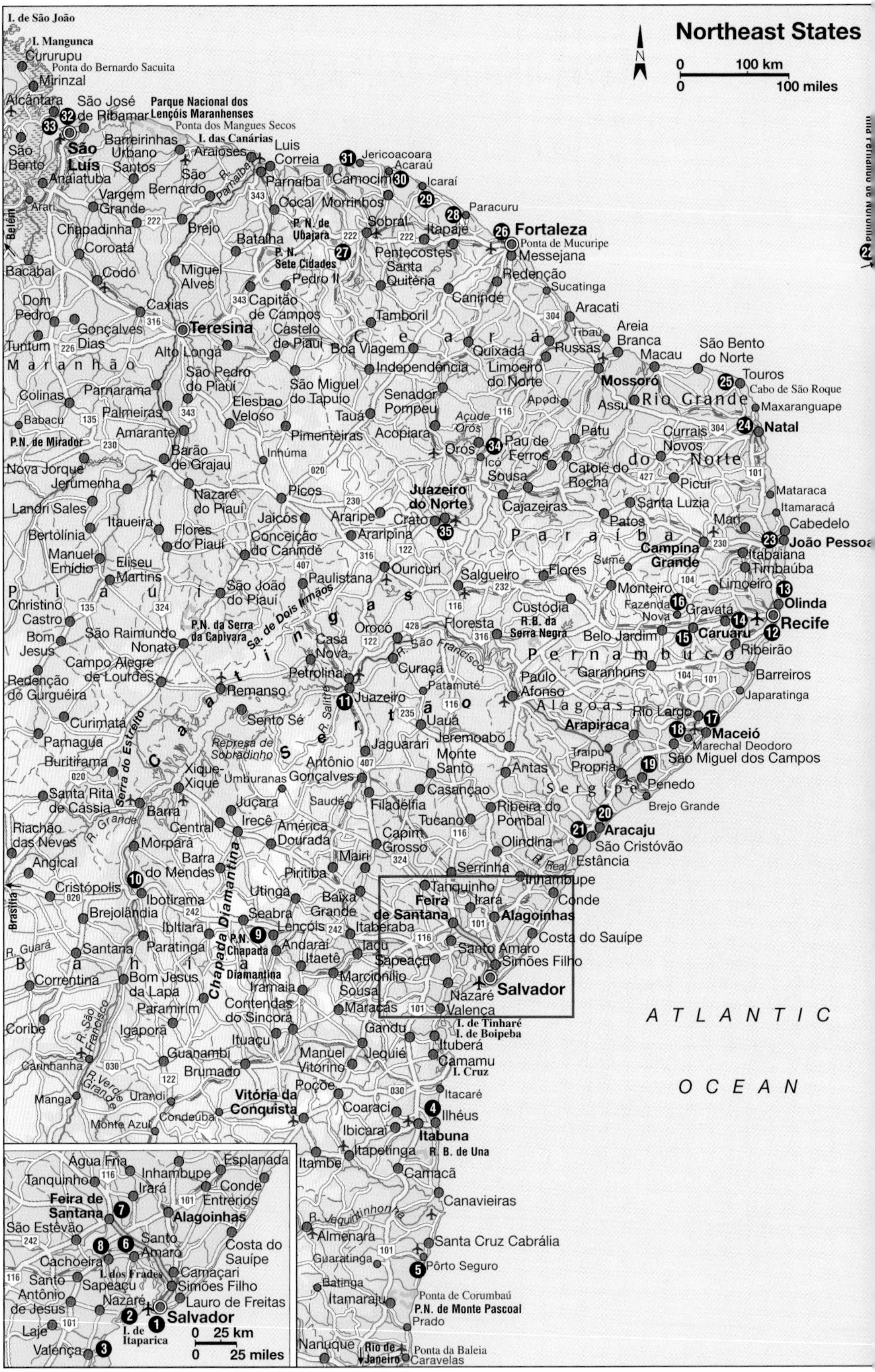
Northeast States
0 100 km
0 100 miles
N
I. de São João
I. Mangunca
Cururupu
Ponta do Bernardo Sacuita
Mirinzal
Alcântara
São José de Ribamar
Parque Nacional dos Lençóis Maranhenses
Ponta dos Mangues Secos
São Bento
São Luís
Barreirinhas
I. das Canárias
Urbano Santos
Araioses
Luis Correia
Jericoacoara
Acaraú
Anajatuba
São Bernardo
R. Parnaíba
Parnaíba
Camocim
Icaraí
Vargem Grande
Arari
Cocal
Morrinhos
Paracuru
Belém
Chapadinha
Brejo
P. N. de Ubajara
Sobral
Itapajé
Fortaleza
Ponta de Mucuripe
Batalha
Coroatá
P. N. Sete Cidades
Pentecostes
Messejana
Bacabal
Codó
Miguel Alves
Pedro II
Santa Quitéria
Redenção
Sucatinga
Dom Pedro
Caxias
Capitão de Campos
Canindé
Aracati
Tamboril
Teresina
Gonçalves Dias
Castelo do Piauí
Tibau
Areia Branca
Tuntum
Alto Longá
Boa Viagem
Quixadá
Russas
Macau
São Bento do Norte
Maranhão
São Pedro do Piauí
Independência
Limoeiro do Norte
Touros
Mossoró
Cabo de São Roque
Colinas
Parnarama
São Miguel do Tapuio
Senador Pompeu
Apodi
Assu
Rio Grande
Maxaranguape
Babacu
Elesbao Veloso
Palmeiras
Tauá
Açude Orós
Patu
Currais Novos
Natal
Amarante
Pimenteiras
Acopiara
P.N. de Mirador
Pau de Ferros
Inhúma
Orós
Barão de Grajau
Icó
Catolé do Rocha
do Norte
Nova Jorque
Sousa
Picuí
Jerumenha
Nazaré do Piauí
Picos
Juazeiro do Norte
Cajazeiras
Santa Luzia
Mataraca
Itamaracá
Landri Sales
Jaicós
Araripe
Crato
Patos
Mari
Cabedelo
Itaueira
Flores do Piauí
Conceição do Canindé
Araripina
Paraíba
Campina Grande
João Pessoa
Bertolínia
Manuel Emídio
Eliseu Martins
Sumé
Itabaiana
Ouricuri
Flores
Timbaúba
Paulistana
Salgueiro
Monteiro
Limoeiro
Piauí
São João do Piauí
Olinda
Christino Castro
Sa. de Dois Irmãos
Custódia
Fazenda Nova
Gravatá
Recife
Bom Jesus
São Raimundo Nonato
P.N. da Serra da Capivara
Orocó
Floresta
R.B. da Serra Negra
Belo Jardim
Caruaru
Casa Nova
R. São Francisco
Pernambuco
Ribeirão
Campo Alegre de Lourdes
Curaçá
Paulo Afonso
Garanhuns
Barreiros
Redenção do Gurguéia
Petrolina
Patamuté
Remanso
Juazeiro
Japaratinga
Caatinga
Sertão
Alagoas
Rio Largo
Curimatá
Sento Sé
Uauá
Maceió
Serra do Estreito
Jeremoabo
Arapiraca
Marechal Deodoro
Parnaguá
Represa de Sobradinho
R. Salitre
Jaguarari
Monte Santo
Traipu
São Miguel dos Campos
Buritirama
Xique-Xique
Antônio Gonçalves
Antas
Propriá
Penedo
Umburanas
Sergipe
Santa Rita de Cássia
Barra
Juçara
Saúde
Filadélfia
Casançao
Ribeira do Pombal
Brejo Grande
R. Grande
Irecê
Tucano
Aracaju
Riachão das Neves
Central
América Dourada
Capim Grosso
São Cristóvão
Morpará
Olindina
Angical
Barra do Mendes
Chapada Diamantina
Mairi
Serrinha
R. Real
Estância
Piritiba
Inhambupe
Brasília
Cristópolis
Ibotirama
Utinga
Baixa Grande
Tanquinho
Irará
Conde
Brejolândia
Seabra
Feira de Santana
Alagoinhas
Lençóis
Itaberaba
Ibitiara
P.N. Chapada Diamantina
R. Guará
Santana
Paratinga
Andaraí
Iaçu
Costa do Sauípe
Itaetê
Santo Amaro
Bahia
Sapeaçu
Simões Filho
Correntina
Bom Jesus da Lapa
Iramaia
Marcionílio Sousa
Salvador
Contendas do Sincorá
Nazaré
Paramirim
Maracás
Valença
ATLANTIC
Coribe
R. São Francisco
Igaporã
Ituaçu
Gandu
I. de Tinharé
I. de Boipeba
Ituberá
Guanambi
Manuel Vitorino
Jequié
Camamu
Carinhanha
Brumado
I. Cruz
OCEAN
R. Verde Grande
Poções
Manga
Urandi
Vitória da Conquista
Itacaré
Coaraci
Condeúba
Ilhéus
Monte Azul
Ibicaraí
Itabuna
Itapetinga
R. B. de Una
Itambé
Camacã
Canavieiras
R. Jequitinhonha
Almenara
Santa Cruz Cabrália
Guaratinga
Pôrto Seguro
Batinga
Ponta de Corumbaú
Itamaraju
P.N. de Monte Pascoal
Prado
Nanuque
Rio de Janeiro
Ponta da Baleia
Caravelas
Água Fria
Esplanada
Tanquinho
Inhambupe
Irará
Conde
Feira de Santana
Entrerios
São Estêvão
Alagoinhas
Santo Amaro
Costa do Sauípe
Cachoeira
I. dos Frades
Camaçari
Santo Antônio de Jesus
Sapeaçu
Simões Filho
Nazaré
Lauro de Freitas
Salvador
Laje
I. de Itaparica
0 25 km
0 25 miles
Valença

THE NORTHEAST

The most economically deprived region of Brazil possesses arguably its most beautiful beaches and richest folk culture

A predominantly desert-like territory of nine states making up 18 percent of Brazil, the northeast had its short-lived glory days at the beginning of the colonial period, when its economy was based on sugarcane and cotton plantations, and Salvador was Brazil's capital.

After competition killed off the sugarcane trade, the northeast went into decline. It has since been neglected due to its general lack of productive potential: the vast, arid *sertão* (scrubland) of the interior is a hard place to eek out a living. Periodic droughts are devastating for the small-scale farmers, who exist barely above subsistence level – and some have starved during famines. Deprivation in parts of the northeast is evidenced also by levels of literacy 20 percent lower than in any other region.

Of course, not all *nordestinos* are poor. The most populous areas are concentrated along the coast, where there is a strip of fertile land, as there is also along the course of the São Francisco River, which runs through Bahia, Pernambuco, Sergipe and Alagoas. The coastal economy benefits not only from more successful agriculture and industry in the cities, but also from wonderful tropical beaches – and, consequently, the income gained from tourism.

The world is waking up to the potential of the northeast as a tourist destination: communications have been improved (you can fly direct to Salvador and Recife from a number of foreign cities) and, especially in Bahia and the city of Recife, new facilities such as hotel complexes have been developed.

The attraction is obvious: quite simply, the northeastern coast is a paradise. It is warm and sunny all year round, the beaches are perhaps the best in Brazil, and certainly the least spoilt, the wilderness areas are magical, and then there is the culture... The colonial towns are the oldest in Brazil, and *nordestinos* are a colorful people whose distinctive Carnival and religious festivals rival Rio's. And Bahia, set apart from the rest of the northeast by its strong African roots, has a uniquely rich heritage, religion and folk traditions.

The hardy and resiliant *sertanejo* farmers gain little from tourism, but the *sertão* has been targeted by numerous state-funded development schemes. Many of these, however, have involved large-scale cultivation that has simply squeezed the smaller farmers. Yet the emphasis is gradually shifting to projects designed to benefit those in greatest need and thus stem the tide of migration. ❑

PRECEDING PAGES: fishermen haul in the nets on one of Bahia's many beaches.

ANARQUIA

SALVADOR

The capital of Bahia has a festive atmosphere and a rich store of sights, from beautiful colonial churches to events such as Carnival afoxé *dance groups and other processions*

Maps:
Area 218
City 222

Salvador was first colonized some 30 years after Brazil was discovered. In 1530, King João III sent a group of colonists to stake claim to this new land and thereby strengthened the Portuguese presence against French and Dutch invaders in the area. Salvador became the first capital of Brazil in 1549, when the Portuguese court sent Tomé de Souza as the country's initial governor-general.

Perched atop cliffs, the tiny settlement was considered an ideal national capital because of its natural protection. Since then, Salvador has lost economic and political importance but increased its fame as the center of Brazilian culture, a mixture of black and white races, descending from the Africans and Europeans. With a population of 2.6 million, Salvador is Brazil's fourth largest city and capital of the state of Bahia. Because life in Bahia revolves around Salvador, Brazilians frequently intermix the two, saying Bahia when they mean Salvador.

The religion and mysticism that are so much a part of Bahian life are reflected in the name Salvador, which means savior. The peninsula where the city was built, first "discovered" by Amerigo Vespucci in 1501, faces **Baía de Todos os Santos** (All Saints' Bay), named in honor of the November 1 "discovery". According to legend, Salvador has 365 churches, one for each day of the year.

What is most striking about Salvador is the way it assaults the senses: the sight of the gold-encrusted altars and panels of its churches; the inviting scent and exotic taste of the African-influenced food; the sounds of the street vendors' cries, the roar of traffic, the chant of soccer game fans or political rally enthusiasts and, most of all, the distinctive sounds and rhythm of Bahian music.

City of music

On almost any street corner in Salvador, and certainly on any beach, weekends are a time of music-making. Though much of it today is commercial, forming the lion's share of Brazilian popular hits, this music has its roots in *candomblé* (Catholic and African syncretist) worship services, where the pulsating, hypnotic rhythm provides a means for contacting the gods. Groups of native Bahians, known as *baianos*, gather at corner bars singing their favorite songs, often just with a box of kitchen matches used as a tambourine.

Other clusters of amateur musicians can be seen playing small drums and other percussion instruments, as well as the occasional guitar or *cavaquinho*, which has four strings and resembles a ukulele. Music and religion are as essential a part of the people's lives here as eating and sleeping. The year is organized around religious holidays. Street processions mark the celebrations. The religious calendar culminates in Carnival, traditionally the one last fling before the 40-day Lenten period of prayer and penance preceding Easter.

LEFT: a Bahian fortune teller in a traditional *Baiana* dress.
BELOW: helping with the laundry.

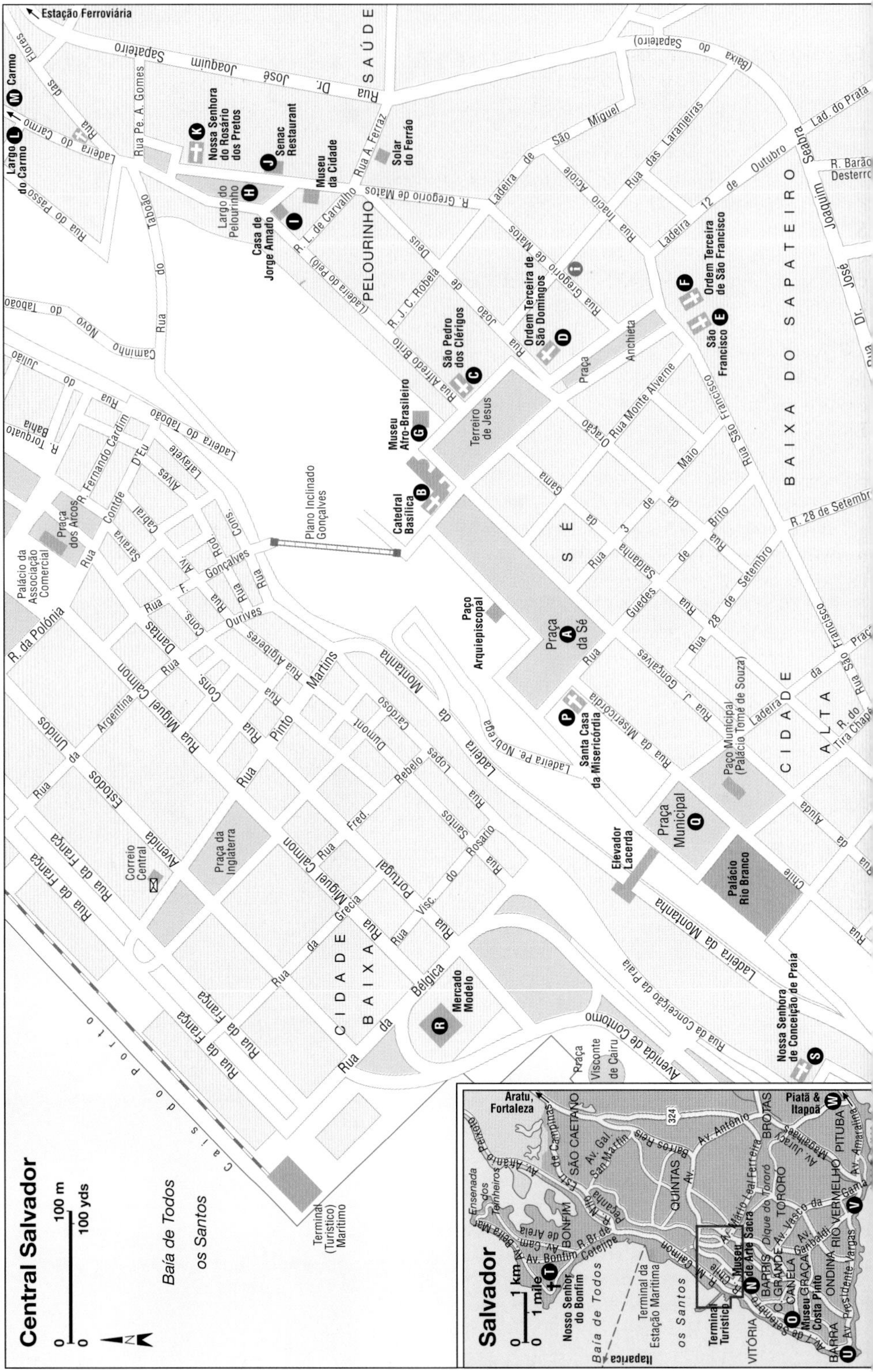
Central Salvador
0 100 m
0 100 yds
N
Baía de Todos os Santos
Cais do Porto
Estação Ferroviária
Praça da Sé
Catedral Basílica
São Francisco
Ordem Terceira de São Francisco
São Pedro dos Clérigos
Ordem Terceira de São Domingos
Museu Afro-Brasileiro
Largo do Pelourinho
Casa de Jorge Amado
Museu da Cidade
Senac Restaurant
Nossa Senhora do Rosário dos Pretos
Largo do Carmo
Carmo
Solar do Ferrão
Terreiro de Jesus
Paço Arquiepiscopal
Santa Casa da Misericórdia
Praça Municipal
Paço Municipal (Palácio Tomé de Souza)
Palácio Rio Branco
Elevador Lacerda
Plano Inclinado Gonçalves
Mercado Modelo
Nossa Senhora de Conceição da Praia
Praça Visconte de Cairu
Terminal (Turístico) Marítimo
Correio Central
Praça da Inglaterra
Praça dos Arcos
Palácio da Associação Comercial
PELOURINHO
SAÚDE
SÉ
BAIXA DO SAPATEIRO
CIDADE ALTA
CIDADE BAIXA
Avenida Estados Unidos
Rua da França
Rua Miguel Calmon
Rua da Bélgica
Rua Portugal
Ladeira da Montanha
Ladeira da Conceição da Praia
Avenida de Contorno
Rua Chile
Rua da Misericórdia
Rua Guedes de Brito
Rua 28 de Setembro
Rua Saldanha da Gama
Rua J. Gonçalves
Rua São Francisco
Rua Alfredo Brito
Rua Gregório de Matos
Rua das Laranjeiras
Ladeira de São Miguel
Rua Dr. José Joaquim Seabra
Ladeira do Carmo
Rua do Passo
Ladeira do Taboão
Salvador
0 1 km
0 1 mile
Aratu, Fortaleza
Piatã & Itapoã
Itaparica
Nosso Senhor do Bonfim
Museu de Arte Sacra
Museu Costa Pinto
Baía de Todos os Santos
Terminal da Estação Marítima
Terminal Turístico
BONFIM
SÃO CAETANO
QUINTAS
BROTAS
TORORÓ
BARRIS
C. GRANDE
CANELA
GRAÇA
ONDINA
RIO VERMELHO
PITUBA
VITÓRIA
BARRA
Av. Bonfim
Av. Presidente Vargas
Barros Reis
Av. Antônio Carlos Magalhães
Av. Juracy Magalhães

Carnival and *candomblé*

Maps: Area 218 City 222

Officially, Carnival lasts four days, from the Saturday to the Tuesday before Ash Wednesday, but in Salvador, Carnival is practically a summer-long event. Clubs host pre-Carnival balls and on weekends the streets fill with pre-Carnival revelers gearing up for the main event.

If you visit during this time, don't expect to get much sleep during the four days; the locals generate enough energy to keep going for 96 hours straight. Salvador's Carnival isn't the organized affair of Rio de Janeiro and São Paulo, there are no samba schools competing for government money and few people dress up. In Salvador, the celebration is pure, wild fun: drinking and dancing and a reasonable amount of promiscuity.

Most characteristic of Carnival in Salvador is the *Trio Elétrico*, a band (not necessarily three-piece) perched on a flatbed truck. The band provides the music for dancing in the streets. Paricipants follow one of three routes. The least crowded is the Pelourinho circuit; the most traditional, Campo Grande; while Barra-Ondina follows the coast and often benefits from a sea breeze.

Candomblé *figurines for sale.*

Though Carnival is an outgrowth of Christian religion, in Bahia, mysticism also has its place. During Salvador's Carnival, *afoxés*, groups of *candomblé* worshippers, take to the streets with banners and images of their patrons, usually African deities to whom they dedicate their songs and offerings. One of the most famous *afoxés*, however, has chosen a different sort of patron. This *afoxé*, based in the center of the historical Pelourinho district, is called *Filhos de Gandhi* (Sons of Gandhi), in honor of the great Indian leader.

It is not only at Carnival time, though, that Salvador is home to joyful religious or para-religious celebrations. There is at least one important holiday per

BELOW: Salvador assaults the senses.

TIP

Not to be missed is Sunday evening in the Largo do Pelourinho, when the internationally renowned drum group Oludum practices (when not on tour), free of charge. They also play at Praça Teresa Batista every Tuesday at 8pm, where there is an entrance fee.

month, and if there is no holiday during your stay, you can still arrange to attend a *candomblé* session or a *capoeira* display *(see below)*. Travel agencies and some hotels can make reservations for folklore shows (including *capoeira*) and those *candomblé* sessions that are open to the public. You may also contact Bahiatursa, the state tourism board (tel: 071-321 2463), where operators with at least one foreign language (usually English) can assist in making reservations.

Candomblé ceremonies are lively, spirited events with much music and dancing but, these are serious religious services and, as such, require respectful behavior and conservative dress. You must be fully clothed – no shorts or halter tops. Also, cameras are strictly forbidden. Ceremonies usually take place at night and can last for up to three hours.

Capoeira, a martial art developed by the slaves, is a foot-fighting technique disguised as a dance. Forbidden by their owners to fight, the slaves were forced to hide this pastime behind the trappings of a gymnastics display. Today, you can see this rhythmic exercise performed on street corners and in the Mercado Modelo in Salvador to the music of the *berimbau*, a one-stringed instrument resembling an archer's bow. The music of *capoeira* is directly related to that of *candomblé*, which paces the ceremony and opens up a channel to the gods.

Saints' days

Another of Salvador's festivals is that of **Procissão do Senhor Bom Jesus dos Navegantes**, a New Year's Day procession in honor of Our Lady of the Seafarers. On this day, a procession of boats escorts the image of Our Lady to the **Boa Viagem beach**, where sailors and their families take over and carry the image to the church of Boa Viagem.

BELOW: many colonial churches remain.

On the third Thursday in January the festival of Bonfim takes place, where *baianas* (Bahian women) in brilliant costumes ritually wash the steps up to the church of **Nosso Senhor do Bonfim** (Our Lord of Good Ending), the most popular house of worship in the city.

Iemanjá, the *candomblé* goddess of the sea, is honored on February 2, when *baianas* in white lace blouses and skirts send offerings, such as combs, mirrors and soaps, out to sea on small handmade boats. This *orixá* (goddess), who is perceived as vain, is placated to guarantee calm waters for the fishermen.

The saints' days celebrated in June (Anthony, John and Peter) are collectively called *festas juninas* (June festivals). On these days, as well as on June weekends, churches sponsor bazaars and neighbors gather together to light bonfires and send up hot-air balloons and fireworks. Street fairs serve corn in every conceivable form and beef chunks on wooden skewers to be washed down with *quentão* (hot spiced *cachaça* or wine). Nossa Senhora da Conceição da Praia (Our Lady of the Beach) is honored on December 8 with a procession to her church.

The best way to orient yourself in Salvador is to think of the town as divided into four: beaches, suburbs, and upper and lower city. Downtown Salvador encompasses both the historical **Cidade Alta** (Upper City) and the newer **Cidade Baixa** (Lower City).

The Upper City

A walking tour of the Cidade Alta starts at the **Praça da Sé** Ⓐ opening on to **Terreiro de Jesus**, home to three of Salvador's most famous churches. The largest, the **Catedral Basílica** Ⓑ, is a 17th-century Jesuit structure largely built of Lioz stone, with beautiful examples of gold-leaf work in its main altar. Next to it are the 18th-century **São Pedro dos Clérigos** Ⓒ (Saint Peter's church) and the 17th-century **Ordem Terceira de São Domingos** Ⓓ (Dominican church). Every Sunday morning, Terreiro de Jesus is the site of a weekly arts-and-crafts fair where it is possible to buy handmade lace and leather goods and lovely primitive paintings.

Map on page 222

Rising majestically from the adjoining square, **Praça Anchieta**, is one of the world's most opulent baroque churches. Rather paradoxically, it is dedicated to a saint who preached the simple, unencumbered life. The church of **São Francisco** Ⓔ (Saint Francis) is an impressive 18th-century structure built of stone imported from Portugal. Its interior is covered from floor to ceiling with highly intricate carvings thickly encrusted with gold leaf. In a side altar is the splendid statue of Saint Peter of Alcântara, which was carved from the single trunk of a jacaranda tree by Manoel Inácio da Costa, one of Brazil's most important and best-known baroque artists. Blue and white hand-painted *azulejos* (tiles), depicting scenes from the life of St Francis, were imported from Portugal in the late 18th century and adorn the church vestibule.

Decorative tiles of São Francisco church.

The Franciscan monastery, annexed to the church, surrounds a delightful courtyard. This monastery can be visited by men only who are accompanied by a church-appointed guide; women must be content to catch a glimpse of the courtyard through a window.

BELOW: Salvador smiles.

Next door, the **Ordem Terceira de São Francisco** Ⓕ (Church of the Third Order of Saint Francis), is noteworthy for its Spanish-style baroque facade.

Returning to the north side of Terreiro de Jesus, the **Museu Afro-Brasileiro** Ⓖ (Afro-Brazilian Museum) in the old medical faculty (open weekdays 9am–5pm) has a fascinating collection of objects that highlight the strong African influence on Bahian culture, including musical instruments, masks, costumes, carvings and other artifacts that are part of the local *candomblé* religion. There are also beautiful wooden panels carved by Carybé, an Argentinian artist who fell in love with Brazil and adopted Salvador as his home.

Largo do Pelourinho

Walk a short distance down **Rua Alfredo Brito**, on your right facing away from Terreiro de Jesus, and you will reach the **Largo do Pelourinho** Ⓗ (Pillory), site of Salvador's best-preserved colonial buildings, whose colorful facades line the steep, meandering cobblestone streets. The name recalls a time when pillories were set up here to punish slaves and criminals.

Today, Pelourinho is considered by UNESCO to be the most important grouping of 17th- and 18th-century colonial architecture in the Americas. Although once a fashionable district of Salvador, the

An icon in the Museu de Arte Sacra.

fortunes of its inhabitants gradually deteriorated. However, Pelourinho is charming, attractive and distinct, well policed, and many of the buildings have been renovated in recent years.

The center of Praça José Alencar square is occupied by the **Casa de Jorge Amado** Ⓘ (open Mon–Sat 9am–6pm), a small museum/library/café replete with books by one of Brazil's most famous novelists (his works have been translated into nearly 50 languages). The collection also includes photographs, memorabilia and a video on the life of Amado, one of Bahia's most beloved sons. Next door is the tiny **Museu da Cidade** (City Museum), with its collection of Afro-Brazilian folklore (open Mon, Wed–Fri 9.30am–6.30pm, Sat 1–5pm, Sun 9.30am–1pm; closed Tues). On the top floor are mannequins dressed as the most important *orixás* (gods) of the *candomblé* faith: they are identified by their African names as well as their equivalent Catholic saint's name.

The self-service **Senac Restaurant** Ⓙ (open Mon–Sat 11.30am–3.30pm and 6.30–11pm; Sun 11.30am–3.30pm) in the square, which is run by a government hotel and restaurant school, is an excellent place to try the local food and see a Bahian folklore show (open Thurs–Sat at 8pm). The restaurant serves lunch and dinner and also offers a Brazilian-style afternoon tea: coffee served with a variety of Bahian pastries and sweets, from 5–8pm.

Just down the street from Pelourinho square is the church of **Nossa Senhora do Rosário dos Pretos** Ⓚ (Our Lady of the Rosary of Black People). Because the slaves were not permitted to go inside their masters' churches, they erected their own places of worship. At the bottom of Pelourinho square is a flight of steps called the Ladeira do Carmo, which leads to the **Largo do Carmo** Ⓛ (Carmelite Square). Scene of the resistance against the Dutch invaders, this block of buildings is the site of the Dutch surrender. The most interesting building is the **Igreja do Carmo** Ⓜ (Carmelite church and convent), dating from 1585. The convent has been partially transformed into a small museum (open Mon–Sat, 9am–1pm and 2–6pm). This area is Santo Antônio, which has enjoyed a renaissance in recent years. Many of the once run-down buildings have been lovingly restored and now house charming European-run hotels.

BELOW: colonial-era home in the old quarter, near Pelourinho.

Art and opulence

Still in the upper city but closer to downtown are two fascinating museums that can be visited in an afternoon. Bahia's **Museu de Arte Sacra** Ⓝ (Museum of Sacred Art) at Rua do Sodré 276, is housed in the 17th-century church and convent of **Santa Teresa**. *Baianos* claim that this is the largest collection of sacred art in Latin America. In any case, it is easily the most impressive of the city's museums, and one of the most fascinating in all of Brazil (open Mon–Fri, 11.30am–5.30pm).

The baroque and rococo art is displayed in large, airy rooms, many of them lined with blue, white and yellow tiles brought from Portugal in the 1600s. Proving that contraband was a part of secular life in the 17th and 18th centuries, many of the larger images of saints, carved from wood, have been

Map on page 222

hollowed out to hide smuggled jewels and gold. Paintings, ivory sculptures, and works in earthenware, silver and gold are also displayed.

Going toward the Barra beach area, at 2490 Avenida Sete de Setembro, one of the city's main thoroughfares, you will find the **Museu Carlos Costa Pinto** O (open Mon and Wed–Fri 2.30–7pm; closed Tues; Sat and Sun 3–6pm), in the **Vitória** district. This museum houses the Costa Pinto family's collection of colonial furnishings, porcelain and jewelry, including crystal, hand-painted porcelain dishes and opulent silver *balagandans*, clusters of charms that were pinned to the blouses of slave women to indicate their owners' personal wealth. Much of the flooring in the main rooms downstairs is pink Carrara marble. At the entrance, employees place cloth slippers over your shoes to protect the floor.

The Lower City

The walking tour of the Lower City also starts off at the Praça da Sé: this time, with your back toward Terreiro de Jesus, walk down Rua da Misericórdia to the **Santa Casa da Misericórdia** P, a late 16th-century church and hospital with 18th century Portuguese tile panels. A short way down the street is the **Praça Municipal** Q, where the town council and city hall are housed in colonial buildings. The square leads you to Salvador's famous **Elevador Lacerda**, a massive blue art deco-inspired structure built in 1930 to link the Upper and Lower cities. The boxcar-like compartment whisks you down to the **Cidade Baixa**.

Straight ahead is the **Mercado Modelo** R, first installed in the old customs house at the city port in 1915. Twice destroyed by fire (the latest in 1984) the market has been completely rebuilt in concrete. In this three-story building you will find stalls selling local handicrafts and souvenirs.

BELOW: a souvenir stall at the Mercado Modelo.

TIP

It helps to know a little Portuguese or to take along a Brazilian friend to bargain with the vendors at the Mercado Modelo. Bartering is part of the market's tradition and you can usually lower the price by 25 percent.

The Mercado Modelo is one of Salvador's not-to-be-missed sights. Although touristy, it is the best place in town to purchase your souvenirs. As you stroll among the stalls, musicians will display their wares by playing them. At one end, you might hear a lively percussion ensemble, at the other, a lone man playing the single-stringed *berimbau*. There are also good displays of *capoiera*, although you will be pressed to give money. For refreshment, try one of the many types of fresh fruit juices.

Turn left from the market, keeping the bay to your right, and walk down the street to the church of **Nossa Senhora de Conceição de Praia** S, which houses the image of Bahia's patron saint. This church, planned and built in Portugal in the early 18th century, was brought over piece by piece. It is the site of the annual religious procession held on December 8, one of the most important feast days in Salvador's Catholic calendar.

About 10 km (6 miles) in the opposite direction stands the famous church of **Nosso Senhor do Bonfim** T (open daily except Mon). On the way to the church, you will pass by the picturesque **São Joaquim Market** (open Mon–Sat 6am–6pm, Sun 6am–noon). The market is fascinating but has been neglected over the years and is now dirty and run-down.

Church of miracles

The Bonfim Church was built in 1745 and is one of the most popular sites for religious pilgrimage in the country. People come from throughout Brazil to pray for jobs or cures, or to give thanks for miracles attributed to Our Lord. As you enter the church, boys and women will try to sell you a colorful ribbon printed with the words "*Lembrança do Senhor do Bonfim da Bahia*" (Souvenir

BELOW: Itapoã beach, outside Salvador.

Map on page 222

of Our Lord of Good Ending). Legend has it that a friend should present you with the ribbon and tie it around your wrist in three knots, representing three wishes: when the ribbon falls off, your wishes will come true.

Lacking the ornateness of Salvador's other churches, Bonfim is still the favorite with both Catholics and *candomblé* practitioners. Don't miss the **Miracle Room**, which is filled with photographs of those who have reached a state of grace, and plaster castings of limbs or organs belonging to devotees cured through divine intervention.

Further down this same road is the church of **Monte Serrat**, a simple 16th-century chapel with Portuguese tiles. Nearby is the **Boa Viagem** church, which marks the destination of Salvador's Our Lady of the Seafarers procession held every New Year's Day.

The beaches

A series of interconnecting streets and roads provide a non-stop promenade along Salvador's beaches, from the near-downtown Barra beach to the distant north coast beaches that are considered among Brazil's most beautiful. The city beach, **Barra** U, is famed less for its beauty than for the conviviality of its bars and sidewalk cafés. Barra is where office workers spend their happy hour, and beyond. It is also good for shopping and is filled with apart-hotels, renting by the week or month and usually much cheaper than hotels. The beach is protected by the gallant old fort **Santo Antônio da Barra**, with its lighthouse and oceanography museum.

The next beach northward from Barra is **Ondina**, home to several top hotels. Inland from the beach, in the same neighborhood, is the **Salvador Zoo** (open

BELOW: *capoeira* fighters.

Map on page 222

daily except Mon, 9.30am–5pm). Next is **Rio Vermelho** ⓥ, an elegant neighborhood where the writer Jorge Amado lived for six months of the year until his death in 2001 (he used to summer in Paris). Coconut groves line the beaches as you travel northward, passing by **Mariquita** and **Amaralina**, where several fine restaurants are located.

At **Pituba**, you can see a host of *jangadas*, primitive sail-driven fishing boats made of split logs roped together. Other beaches along this route include **Jardim de Alá**, **Armação de Iemanjá**, **Boca do Rio**, **Corsário** (which has one of the city's few bicycle paths), **Pituaçu**, and **Patamares** (also with good restaurants).

Piatã and **Itapoã** ⓦ, the last beaches before the airport, are Salvador's best. Itapoã is slightly less crowded than Piatã, especially during the week, but for natural beauty and food and drink, they are equal. The statue of Iemanjá on the border between the two beaches is a meeting point for the city's young people. On weekend afternoons, they both fill up with musicians. One of the most beautiful sights in Salvador is the sunset viewed from Itapoã beach.

After dark

Nightlife in Salvador is concentrated in the cobblestoned streets of Pelourihho, where live music fills the air on most nights of the week, but particularly on Tuesdays, and there are concerts every night in summer – most of them free to enjoy. The majority of nightclubs are in the Barra neighborhood and along the beach drive.

The **Teatro Castro Alves**, located at the **Campo Grande** across from the **Hotel Tropical da Bahia**, is the place for ballet, theater and musical performances and, with seating capacity of 1400, is considered one of the most important venues in Latin America. A huge sign in front of the theater lists the week's events. Occasionally, the Castro Alves is host to a Brazilian or foreign symphony orchestra. More frequently you'll find one of Brazil's top recording artists performing there. Look out for names such as Caetano Veloso, Maria Bethania, Gal Costa or Gilberto Gil – these *baianos* are among Brazil's most popular singers and songwriters.

Soccer is a major form of entertainment in Salvador, as it is throughout Brazil. The local team, Esporte Clube Bahia, play at the city's **Otávio Mangabeira Stadium** (often referred to as Fonte Nova), usually on Wednesday nights and Sunday afternoons. Purchase a seat in the reserved area *(cadeiras especiais)*; it is more expensive but worth it. Tickets are available at the stadium from 8am on the day of the game.

Avoid the port area and the streets surrounding Pelourinho at night.

For the very best in entertainment, day or night, do what the locals do: go to the beach. Pick one of the thatched-roof huts that function as bars on Pituba or Piatã beach, sit on a sawed-off trunk used as a stool, order your *batida* or *caipirinha* (fruit and sugarcane alcohol drinks) and listen to the music played by your neighbors as you watch the waves roll in. ❑

BELOW: image of Christ in the Igreja do Carmo.

Bahian Cuisine

Bahian cooking is a unique Afro-Brazilian cuisine that is delicious and satisfying. Some dishes can be very peppery or rather heavy, so it is worth experimenting.

Though it contains contributions from the Portuguese colonists and the Brazilian native Amerindians, by far the most important influence on Bahian cuisine came from the enslaved Africans, who not only brought their own style of cooking with them, but also modified Portuguese dishes with African herbs and spices.

Bahian cuisine is characterized by the generous use of *malagueta* chile peppers and *dendê* oil extracted from an African palm that grows well in the northeastern climate. Several Bahian dishes also contain seafood (usually shrimp), coconut milk, banana and okra.

Moqueca is one of the region's most popular dishes. It is a mixture of shrimp – perhaps with other seafood – coconut, garlic, onion, parsley, pepper, tomato paste and the ubiquitous *dendê* oil. These ingredients are all sautéed over a low flame and served with rice cooked in coconut milk.

Other traditional stews are *vatapá* – seafood or chicken with *dendê*, coconut, ground peanuts and chopped green peppers – and *carurú de camarão*, containing fresh and dried shrimp, as well as sliced okra.

In the better Bahian restaurants, these dishes are served with a hot *malagueta* sauce. Sometimes this is added directly to the dish in the kitchens and the cook may ask you if you like your food *quente* (spicy hot). Until you get used to the strong flavors of the *dendê* and *malagueta*, it is best to answer no. The hotels are a good place to kick off your culinary adventure, since they tend to go a little easier on the *dendê*.

The women of Bahia, are among the world's great confectioners. They concoct sweets from coconut, eggs, ginger, milk, cinnamon and lemon. *Cocada*, coconut candy boiled in sugar water with a pinch of ginger or lemon, is a favorite. *Ambrosia*, made with egg yolks and vanilla, and *quindim* (little sticky cakes made from eggs and coconut) are other delights. You can buy these from *baianas* in the more sophisticated parts of Salvador, such as Rio Vermelho, and on Piatã and Itapuã beaches.

The colorfully dressed *baianas* set up shop daily in thatched-roof kiosks or at improvised tables where they serve homemade sweets and *acarajé*, a Bahian-style hamburger. Try this typical food at a place that has been recommended to you to be sure of getting a fresh product.

Acarajé is prepared from a batter made of skinned *fradinho* beans (similar to black-eyed peas or navy beans). These are mashed together with ground shrimp and onion and plunged by the spoonful into hot *dendê* oil. Finally, each pattie is filled with a sauce and and you will be asked if you want your *acarajé* served *quente*. *Acarajé* is a wonderful treat between meals. Have it with a beer at one of the beach-front bars.

For a Bahian culinary and cultural experience, go to one of Salvador's restaurants, many of which offer local cuisine together with a folklore show. ❑

RIGHT: a vendor fries *acarajé* bean patties.

MISTURA FINA: AFRO-BRAZILIAN CULTURE

The mix of races in Brazil is mainly European and African, but with Amerindian and many more exotic races, this is a truly multicultural society

Mistura Fina ("exquisite mixture") is a proud term often used to describe Brazil's multiracial origins.

When the Portuguese founded Brazil, they had problems trying to populate an area almost one hundred times larger than the mother country, so they adopted a policy of interbreeding with other races and imported black Africans as slave labor to build the colony. Slavery in Brazil was less rigorous than in the British colonies and Afro-Brazilians were able to preserve much of their culture. The result, many generations later, is that the majority of Brazilians are of mixed blood and in Brazilian culture, African roots are still very much alive.

HIGH DAYS AND HOLIDAYS

Candomblé, *umbanda*, *macumba*, and spiritism all derive from African religions and are often practiced in parallel to Christianity. A follower may go to church on Sunday and to the *terreiro* where the African religions are practiced on Friday.

Carnival was an institution intended to give slaves an annual respite and an opportunity to express their heritage. Today, the whole population gets involved, but it still bears the hallmark of Africa. The rhythms of Brazilian music have strong African roots, transmuted into a distinctly Brazilian sound. The sensual bossa nova and samba, and their derivatives such as lambada are reminiscent of African dances.

Brazil today without its African roots would be unthinkable; its culture would be incomparably poorer for the absence of the African essence, which is now part of every Brazilian soul.

▷ **HOLY ICONS**
The symbol of Oxum, Queen of Freshwater, held and worshiped by a black *candomblé* priestess from the northeast.

△ **RELIGIOUS OFFERINGS**
At the Festival of Iemanjá offerings of flowers and cosmetics are made to the vain goddess of the sea to guarantee calm waters

◁ **AFRICAN BEAT**
Olodum, the world-famous drum group, combine native African rhythms with a typically up-tempo Brazilian interpretation.

△ **LUCKY RIBBONS**
Many Afro-Brazilians have inherited a native faith in superstition, and various objects are deemed to have a good or bad "omen."

FRIDAY PRAYERS
ahian women, dressed in raditional white lace, follow ne *candomblé* ritual, the ost African of all Brazilian eligious followings.

▷ **UMBANDA PRIESTESS**
An example of blended cultures, *umbanda* is a mystic movement that combines worship of African, Brazilian and European figures.

▷ **BLACK EFFIGIES**
This effigy of *Preto Velho* (the "old black man") is typical of the clay figurines reflecting local African heritage, made in the Recife area of northeast Brazil.

AFRO-BRAZILIAN ART AND CRAFTS

A great deal of Brazilian art and local crafts reflect an African heritage and many pieces are derived from the skills and traditions that the slaves brought with them over the centuries. Wooden sculptures from the northeast region, in particular, are strongly reminiscent of African works.

The *carranca* figureheads that traditionally protected the riverboats of the São Francisco River, and that can today be found in the region as souvenirs, come from the figurative art of Africa. Stylized statues in the same area are strongly reminiscent of the masks that proliferate in much of West Africa.

The faithful followers of *candomblé* are usually richly adorned with strings of beads in the colours of the African gods as part of their religious "costume." These are made of seeds or shells, similar to those which can be found in "Mother Africa." The beach-side stalls that sell them, largely in the northeast of the country, also carry a vivid range of T-shirts bearing traditional African designs.

BAHIA

The colorful Bahian lifestyle and culture can be enjoyed in many fascinating and beautiful places beyond its capital, from unspoilt beach resorts to historic towns in the arid interior

Bahia is the soul of Brazil. In this northeastern state more than anywhere else, the country's cultures and races have mixed, producing what is most authentically Brazilian.

It was at **Porto Seguro**, on the southern coast of Bahia, that Pedro Alvares Cabral first "discovered" this land in 1500. A year later, on November 1 – All Saints' Day – the Italian navigator Amerigo Vespucci arrived in what is now **Salvador** ❶, the capital of Bahia and for more than 200 years until 1763 also the capital of Brazil.

Bahia is the site of the country's first medical school, its oldest churches, its most important colonial architecture, and its largest collection of sacred art. Bahia is also the birthplace of many of Brazil's outstanding writers, politicians and composers. Bahia-born novelist Jorge Amado's works have been translated into nearly 50 languages and several of his books have become major films (including *Dona Flor and Her Two Husbands* and *Gabriela*). The music of Bahians João Gilberto, Caetano Veloso, Baden Powell, and Gilberto Gil is enjoyed by aficionados all over the world.

LEFT: Bahian man wears the colors of his *orixá* (African god).
BELOW: tropical Ilha de Itaparica.

There is another side to Bahia, one that appeals to the spirit and the senses. The mysticism of Bahia is so strong, it pervades every aspect of life: it can be perceived in the way people dress, in their speech, their music, their way of relating to each other, even in their food. This mysticism is another reason Brazilians say that in Bahia lies the soul of their country.

The original source of this mysticism was the culture maintained by enslaved Africans. Today, the Pantheist religion of the African Yoruba tribe is still alive and well in Bahia, and many white Bahians who are self-professed Catholics can be seen making their offerings to the deities of the *candomblé* religion.

The phenomenon of syncretism, the blending of Catholicism with African religions, resulted when the slaves were forced to worship their deities masked as Catholic saints. Nowadays, you can see the devout worshipping the African goddess Iemanjá as Our Lady, or the god Oxumaré as Saint Anthony.

Day trips from Salvador

Ilha de Itaparica ❷ is an island set in the Baía de Todos os Santos, a tropical wonderland where Club Med built its first hotel in Brazil. About 19,000 people live on the island, divided mainly between fishermen and wealthy weekenders, whose beachfront mansions often can be reached only by boat. As a popular bolt-hole for middle-class Brazilians, hotels tend to be expensive and the island gets very crowded during weekends and holidays.

Face of Bahia.

There are several ways to reach the island. Ferry boats leave Salvador's port at regular intervals for the 45-minute crossing. You can also drive around to the other side of the bay to the bridge that links Itaparica to the mainland, a three-hour trip that may be extended to include stops at the fascinating historical towns of Santo Amaro and Cachoeira. Or you can take the passenger ferry from the Mercado Modelo in Salvador, which is great fun as long as you are a good sailor. Once on the island, you can rent a bicycle for some exploring along its many beaches. If your time is limited, take the day-long bay cruise sold by the top travel agencies in Salvador. The cruise includes transportation to and from your hotel and free *batidas* (sugarcane alcohol mixed with tropical fruit juice or coconut) and soft drinks. Once aboard the double-masted schooner *(saveiro)*, you're in for a delightful surprise: the guide and crew are also musicians. As the boat gently skims the calm waters of the bay between stops, the crew gathers at the prow to sing and play popular songs. Passengers can join in, and later in the day, after a fair number of *batidas*, nearly everyone is enthusiastically singing along and dancing.

After leaving Salvador, most of these boats make two stops. The first, in the late morning, is at **Ilha dos Frades**, a tiny and all-but-deserted island inhabited by fishermen who have found a second, more lucrative source of revenue: tourists. The boat anchors offshore and visitors are brought ashore ten at a time in rowing boats. Those who are not afraid of the jellyfish ("their sting is just a little nip," the locals say) can swim to the shore. After an hour of exploring, drinking or eating a snack at one of the improvised bars, or purchasing souvenirs, you're taken on to Itaparica Island for lunch and a walking tour. Then it is back to the boat for the return trip to Salvador with a splendid view of the sunset over the city.

BELOW: shade by the shore.

Map on page 218

The Estrada de Coco (Coconut Road) leads northwards away from Salvador's most distant beach, Itapoã. Along this road lined with coconut palms, you will pass by virtually unspoiled tropical beaches, including **Jaua**, **Arembepe**, **Jucuípe**, **Abaí**, and **Itacimirim**.

Located some 85 km (53 miles) from Salvador, at **Praia do Forte**, a hundred thousand coconut palms stand on 12 km (7 miles) of white sandy beach protected against threats to the environment by a private foundation. But the once sand high street has recently been paved, and an increasing number of international tourists visit the village. Praia do Forte is also the site of a major preservation center for sea turtles. The eggs are collected from nests on the beach at night and protected from predators (both human and animal) until the young are old enough to be set free in the sea and fend for themselves.

Continuing along from Praia do Forte, the **Linha Verde** is a coastal road going past spectacular, semi-deserted beaches all the way to the border with the state of **Sergipe**. It passes **Costa do Sauípe**, a purpose-built resort with five luxury international hotels. Completed in 2000, at a cost of a staggering US$600 million, it is Disneyland in Brazil. Fifty more hotels are planned in a series of five more building phases.

Heading south

South from Salvador towards the state of Espírito Santo is the 400-year-old town of **Valença** ❸, where the Una River meets the Atlantic Ocean. The town is the site of Brazil's first textile factory and Bahia's first hydroelectric dam. One of the best beaches in the region, 15 km (9miles) from Valença, is **Guaibim**, with a number of good seafood restaurants and bars.

BELOW: a sculpture at the TAMAR turtle reserve, Praia do Forte.

The statue of Pedro Alvarez Cabral in Porto Seguro.

Morro de São Paulo is a fishing village on the island of Tinharé, situated some 270 km (168 miles) south of Salvador. Once a hippy hangout, the village has become increasingly fashionable with Brazilian and international tourists, although it is still wonderfully relaxed and there are no roads.

Another important city on Bahia's southern coast is **Ilhéus** ❹, the cocoa capital of Brazil and one of its major export ports. Just over 467 km (290 miles) from Salvador, Ilhéus was founded in 1534 and is a modern city that has preserved its historical sites. Beaches abound in the region, and the city's Carnival celebration is one of the liveliest in Bahia. Local travel agents charter schooners that cruise around the islands. The town has reasonably good hotels and campsites on the beach. **Olivença**, a hydromineral spa 20 km (12 miles) from Ilhéus, is an excellent place to camp and "take the waters." Besides Carnival, major festivals in Ilhéus include Saint Sebastian (January 11–20), the city's birthday (June 28), and the cocoa festival (the entire month of October).

Porto Seguro ❺, in the extreme south of Bahia, and the region just south of it – including Arraial d'Ajuda and Trancoso – is a tourist mecca. Porto Seguro has hundreds of hotels and *pousadas*, and inumerable restaurants, bars, and dance halls. Carnival here is especially lively. Pataxo Amerindians still live near Porto Seguro, fishing and fashioning handicrafts to sell to tourists. The area around **Monte Pascoal**, where the Portuguese caught their first sighting of Brazil in 1500, is a densely forested nature reserve of original Atlantic rainforest. Across the bay by ferry is **Arraial d'Ajuda**, with *pousadas* and bars that swing with lively *forró* dancing. Further south by *kombi* or bus is **Trancoso**, with its colorful houses and colonial church (1656) built around a grassy square. The magnificent beaches here attract droves of national and international tourists in the summer.

BELOW: an old church preserves colonial architecture.

The *sertão*

Situated inland, 200 km (120 miles) from the coast, is the northeast's drought-ridden scrubland region. This area has been the setting for a great deal of Brazilian tragedy. Periodic droughts drive local farm laborers from the *sertão* to the coastal cities in search of food and work. When the rains return, so do the *sertanejos*. But often, the rains do as much damage as good: torrential downpours can easily cause massive flooding over this severely parched earth, which is too dry to absorb the rainwater. The *sertanejos* are a hardy people, loyal to their birthplace, and their land holds surprises for those willing to discover them.

A good place to start a trip to the *sertão* is in the Recôncavo da Bahia, the term used for the hot and humid region that surrounds Salvador's Baía de Todos os Santos. The BR-324 Highway takes you to **Santo Amaro ❻**, a colonial town located some 80 km (50 miles) from Salvador and once a center of tobacco and sugar. The town is revered by Brazilian popular music fans as the home of singers and siblings Caetano Veloso and Maria Bethânia.

Along Santo Amaro's cobblestone streets and tiny *praças*, pink and white colonial stucco homes alternate with splendid art deco facades painted in pastel colors and decorated with raised geometric outlines painted in glittering white. These facades, testimony to the area's development in the early part of the 20th century, can be seen in many of the small, interior towns of the northeast.

Map on page 218

Ilhéus is the birthplace of Jorge Amado, and the scene of his most famous novel Gabriela, Cravo e Canela *(Gabriela, Clove and Cinnamon). Many places in the town are named after the book and its characters.*

Fairs and Markets

From Santo Amaro, you can either continue along the same highway to **Feira de Santana ❼**, or take the BR-101 Highway in a southerly direction along the Recôncavo to Cachoeira. Feira de Santana, 115 km (70 miles) from Salvador, is known for its cattle and for its leather goods' fair held every Monday. Food and handicrafts are also sold every day except Sunday (7am–7pm) at the Centro de Abastecimento fair. For a market dedicated to handicrafts alone, pay a visit to the Mercado de Arte Popular (open Mon–Sat 7am–6pm). Feira de Santana also has a handful of small hotels and many restaurants that offer simple but reasonably good fare.

A walking tour through history

Colonial churches and monuments abound in **Cachoeira ❽** (pop. 32,000), which is situated 120 km (72 miles) from Salvador and is a center of tobacco, cashew nut, and orange production. Bahiatursa, the state tourism agency, has created a walking tour that will take you past the most important buildings and historical sites in the town. Just follow the blue and white numbered signs.

The tour leads you to the church of **Nossa Senhora da Conceição do Monte**, an 18th-century structure with a lovely view of the Paraguaçu river and the village of São Félix on the opposite bank. The church is open to the public only in November.

Don't miss the **Correios e Telégrafos**, the post office, which has the best example of an Art Deco facade in town. Cachoeira also has little souvenir

BELOW: transparent ocean pools formed by reefs.

shops, inns, and restaurants. The **Pousada do Convento** is especially interesting: the guest rooms were once nuns' cells and the mausoleum is now a television lounge. Across the bridge, sleepy **São Félix** awakens once a week for the Sunday *samba-de-roda* contests. Both men and women dance the samba in frenetic circles to a beat usually provided by nothing more than hand clapping. The São Félix cultural center, the **Casa da Cultura Américo Simas** (open Tues– Sun 8am–5pm), is located in a restored 19th-century cigar factory. The "culture" taught here ranges from plaster painting to the principles of accounting to weight lifting. The evocative **Centro Cultural Dannemann** (open Tues–Sun 8am–5pm) on the river front has displays of old machinery used for making *charutos* (cigars), as well as art exhibitions, and it sells handmade cigars.

The *recôncavo* is one of the major centers of Bahia's strong agricultural economy. Grains, sugarcane, coconuts and 95 percent of the country's cocoa output are harvested here. The town of **Camaçari** is home to one of Brazil's three petrochemical complexes, and industry in the region is booming.

Once beyond the coastal area, the bleak landscape of the *sertão*, a region of searing heat, cactus and scrubland, fills the horizon. Roads leading west or north from the *recôncavo* head deep into the *sertão*. This is a land that lionizes its folk heroes and also has its own brand of music that is totally different from the samba or *bossa nova* heard in other parts of Brazil. The two-part harmony of *música sertaneja* is simple and linear, the chords rarely numbering more than three. The themes deal with lost love, homesickness, bad weather and death. This music is no longer restricted to the *sertão*: its appeal is universal and popular variety shows on Brazilian television are dedicated to this genre.

BELOW: Pataxo Amerindian children selling tribal artifacts.

Diamond boom town

Situated in the heart of Bahia, 425 km (255 miles) west of Salvador, is one of the state's most distinctive attractions, the town of **Lençóis** ❾. Resting in the foothills of the **Sincorá Mountains**, on the Diamantina Plateau, Lençóis dates back to 1844, when diamonds were discovered in the region. Hoards of fortune seekers descended on the site, improvising shelters out of large cloth sheets, called *lençóis* in Portuguese, a name that has stuck.

The diamond rush turned the little settlement into a boom town. Lençóis society wore the latest Parisian fashions and sent their children to study in France. The French government even opened a consulate in Lençóis. Today, the consular building and the municipal market, an Italian-style structure that once served as the diamond miners' trading post, are the most distinctive constructions.

Though its folklore is unmistakably Bahian, Lençóis has its own peculiarities. Carnival is not a major event, but the Feast of São João in June is. Lençóis also has *Jarê*, its own unique version of *candomblé*. *Jarê* celebrations occur mainly in September, December, and January.

The main attraction of Lençóis is, however, its laid-back atmosphere and the opportunities it provides for exploring the **Chapada Diamantina**. This region is one of the most beautiful in the Bahian countryside. Mountain springs help keep the drought away. The Chapada is a mountain wilderness, best explored with a local guide. Orchids abound near the waterfalls, some of which can only be reached by foot. The **Cachoeira da Fumaça**, 66 km (41 miles) from Lençóis, is 400 meters (1,300 ft) high. It can be reached only after a 7-km (4-mile) walk. The **Gruta das Areias**, a grotto just over 1-km (half a mile)

Map on page 218

A sun-baked street in Maragojipe, near Salvador.

BELOW: a rodeo at Feira de Santana.

Map on page 218

TIP

If you wish to visit the Convento Grotto, it is highly recommended that you hire a guide in nearby Abreus. Only experts should try to explore the cave on their own.

BELOW: northeastern beaches have fine white sand.
RIGHT: colored sand from the Grutas das Areias makes a picture in a bottle.

long, is lined with colored sands used by artisans to fill glass bottles, creating delightful patterns. A stunning view of the region can be seen from on top of the **Pai Inácio Mountain**, where a host of exotic plants thrive.

Local handicrafts include lace, crochet, and earthenware. Lençóis has two good campsites and a number of hotels and inns, such as the Pousada de Lençóis, Canto dos Aguas, and the five-star Portal Lençóis.

Due west of Lençóis, 252 km (157 miles) further along Highway 242, is the city of **Ibotirama** ⑩, on the legendary São Francisco River. A fisherman's paradise, its 24,000 inhabitants raise cattle and plant cassava, corn, beans, and rice but when the drought comes, they depend on the river for food. Dozens of fish species, including the piranha (seen as a delicacy), are here for the taking. Boats and canoes can be rented at the wharf.

Keen photographers can take a canoe out at the end of the day to photograph the spectacular sunset over the river's left bank. From March to October the dry season, the water level drops, exposing sandy beaches on the river islands of **Gado Bravo** (40 minutes upstream) and **Ilha Grande** (25 minutes downstream).

Sobradinho Lake

From Ibotirama, the São Francisco flows northeast to the **Sobradinho Dam** (tel: 612-2511) and its massive reservoir, one of the largest artificial lakes in the world, four times the size of Salvador's All Saints' Bay. Call ahead a week in advance if you want to visit. Close to the northern edge of the lake is the city of **Juazeiro** ⑪, 566 km (352 miles) northwest of Salvador.

During the colonial period, Juazeiro was a stopover for travelers and pioneers on their way to Salvador from the states north of Bahia. A township was officially founded in 1706 when Franciscan monks built a mission, complete with a chapel and a monastery, in a Cariri Amerindian village. By the end of the 18th century, Juazeiro had become the region's most important commercial and social center.

Local fish, caught in the São Francisco River, is served in the restaurants here. Try surubion with coconut milk at Maria.

The folk art of the Juazeiro region is dominated by the *carranca*, the half-man, half-dragon wooden figurehead placed on boats to keep the devil at bay. The *carrancas*, with their teeth bared in a silent roar, are carved from tree trunks and painted in bright colors. You may buy miniature versions of them as souvenirs.

One hundred km (60 miles) from Juazeiro is the **Convento Grotto**, hidden away in the valley of the Salitre River, one of the São Francisco's most beautiful tributaries. The grotto is over 5 km (3 miles) long and contains two mineral water lakes.

For dedicated spelunkers, there is the **Caverna do Padre**, over 15 km (9 miles) in extension and considered the largest in South America. The cave, only recently explored, is located near the town of Santana on the far side of the São Francisco River, deep in the Bahian *sertão,* some 200 km (120 miles) southwest of Ibotirama. ☐

RECIFE AND PERNAMBUCO

Bustling Recife and charming, baroque Olinda nearby are the main focuses of a state whose other attractions include art and handicrafts centers, plus typical northeastern tropical beaches

Maps:
Area 218
City 246

When sugar was king in the late 16th and early 17th centuries, Pernambuco was the richest state in Brazil. Sugar plantations and mills, or *engenhos*, were centered in the region around Olinda, and Recife quickly developed as the ideal port for the export of the produce. Slave labor was easy to come by and political power came with economic dominance. As the economic importance of sugar dwindled, it was largely replaced by cotton, but by the mid-17th century, gold and precious metal finds in Minas Gerais were getting all the attention. The capital of the country was moved south, from Salvador near the sugar plantations to Rio de Janeiro, nearer the rich gold mining areas, and Pernambuco and its capital Recife never regained their former glory.

But while political and economic power have moved south, Recife is again becoming a booming center, this time for the fast-growing tourism industry in the region. Good hotels and restaurants are attracting growing numbers of Brazilian and international tourists looking for beautiful beaches, colonial gems like Olinda and a year-round warm climate.

LEFT: a coconut-milk vendor on the beach.
BELOW: Recife architecture.

Coral reef city

Recife ⓬, capital of the state of Pernambuco, is a metropolis of 1.4 million. Its name comes from the Arabic word for "fortified wall," which in Portuguese has acquired the meaning of "reef." Recife's coastline, like much of the northeast, is characterized by barnacle and coral reefs running parallel to the mainland between 90 meters (100 yards) and 1 km (half a mile) from the shore. The waves break on the far side of the reefs making the shoal water on the near side a shallow saltwater swimming pool for bathers. On **Boa Viagem Beach** in Recife, you can wade out to the reefs at low tide and barely wet your knees.

In 1537, the Portuguese settled the coastal area of Pernambuco. A Dutch invasion a century later, under Prince Maurice of Nassau, brought a new era of art, culture and urbanization to the town. Recife was once a maze of swamps and isles that Prince Maurice made habitable through the construction of canals. Now there are 39 bridges spanning the canals and rivers that separate the three main islands of Recife.

A walking tour of Recife's historical district begins at the **Praça da República** Ⓐ with the **Teatro Santa Isabel** Ⓑ (open weekdays, 1–5pm), a neoclassical building (1850), and one of the most beautiful in the city. Other 19th-century buildings on this square include the governor's mansion, the palace of justice and the law courts, which double as the Catholic University's law school (the oldest in Brazil).

Ornate Recife architecture.

Across the street from the palace of justice is the **Capela Dourada** **C** (Golden Chapel). According to legend, it contains more gold than any church in Brazil except Salvador's Church of São Francisco. Built in the late 17th century by laymen of the Franciscan order, this baroque church is one of the most important examples of religious architecture in Brazil (chapel and adjoining sacred art museum open weekdays 8–11.30am and 2–5pm, Sat 8–11.30am).

Eight blocks from the Santa Isabel Theater down Rua do Sol is the **Casa da Cultura** **D** (open Mon–Sat 9am–7pm, Sun 10am–2pm), a three-story structure that served as a penitentiary for over 100 years. In 1975, it was remodeled to become Recife's largest handicraft center. The prison cells have been turned into booths displaying articles ranging from leather and straw accessories to clay figurines, silk-screened T-shirts and fruit liqueurs. On Praça Visconde de Mauá, opposite the Casa da Cultura and next to the **Estação Central** **E**, built in 1888, is the **Museu do Trem** (open Tues–Sat 9am–noon and 2–5pm, Sun 2–5pm), which traces the history of the railroad in Brazil.

Four hundred meters (440 yards) away, southeast along Rua T. Barreto, is **Patio de São Pedro** **F**, the artists' corner in Recife, with music and folklore performances on the weekends. It is a good place to buy local crafts. The **Igreja de São Pedro** is an interesting example of baroque architecture. Continuing southeast, across Praça Dom Vital, you come to the **Mercado de São José** **G**, a busy market (open Mon–Sat 6am–5.30pm, Sun 6am–noon) in a 19th-century building.

At the southern end of downtown, the massive, star-shaped **Forte das Cinco Pontas** **H**, built by the Dutch in 1630, houses the **Museu da Cidade** (Largo das Cinco Pontas; open Mon–Fri 9am–6pm, Sat and Sun 1–5pm), with displays on the history of Recife.

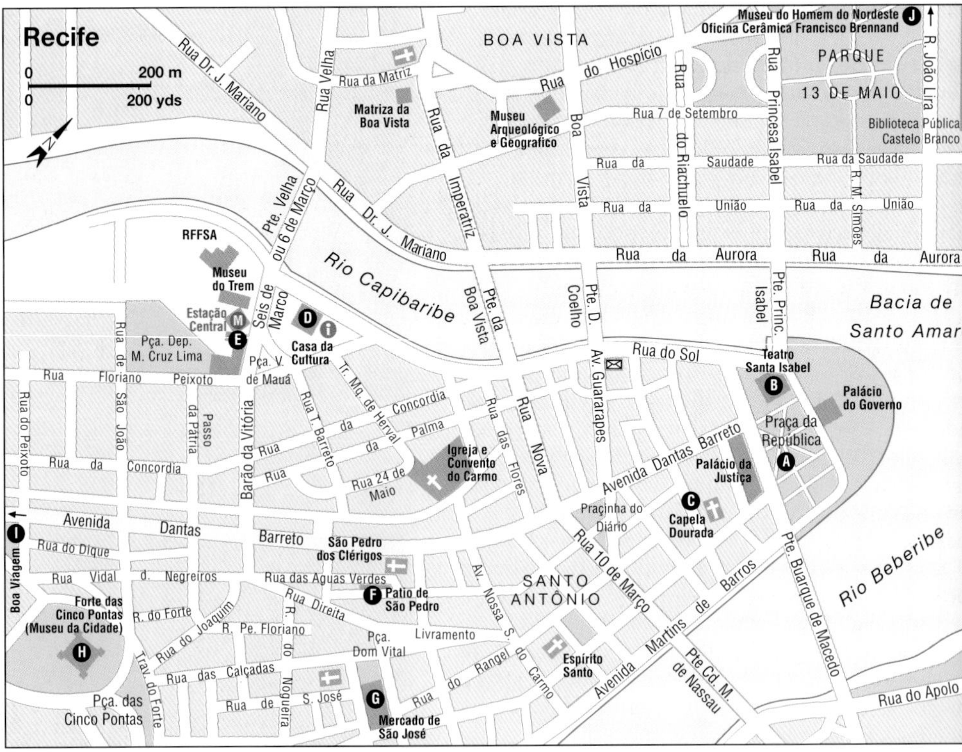

See map opposite

Walking southwest from the Museu da Cidade along Avenida Dantas Barreto, you will eventually come to **Boa Viagem**. Most of the better restaurants and bars and nearly all the city's fine hotels are located on or near the beach here. It is Recife's most beautiful beach and also the center of its social life.

In the evening, the action is concentrated along the beach and on Avenida Conselheiro Aguiar, one block inland. The street is home to a number of small bars and sidewalk cafés offering inexpensive drinks, nibbles, and live music.

There are a dozen museums in Recife but one stands out: the **Museu do Homem do Nordeste** (Museum of Northeastern Man) on Avenida 17 de Agosto 2187. Founded by the late Gilberto Freyre (1900–87), Brazil's most famed anthropologist, the museum is a tribute to the cultural history of this unique region. It has bilingual guides and is located in the **Casa Forte** district, 5 km (3 miles) from downtown (open Tues, Wed and Fri 11am–5pm, Thurs 8am–5pm; weekends and holidays 1–5pm).

Another fascinating stop in the same part of town is the **Oficina Cerâmica Francisco Brennand** (open weekdays 8am–5pm), the workshop and studio of one of the northeast's best-known artisans. Located in the working-class district of **Várzea**, this immense atelier was once a brick and tile factory until Francisco Brennand took it over to use as his workshop. Brennand is famed in Recife for his beautiful hand-painted tiles, pottery, and vaguely erotic statuary, all eagerly bought by locals and tourists. You can visit the workshop, and if you call ahead for a tour you may be escorted by Mr Brennand himself (tel: 081-3271-2466).

Coastal beaches

Apart from Boa Viagem, good city beaches include **Pina**, **Piedade**, and **Candeias**. Outside Recife, the most beautiful beaches lie to the south. One of the best is **Porto de Galinhas**, next to the town of **Ipojuca**, 50 km (30 miles) from downtown Recife. Surfing competitions abound in the summer months and the beach's excellent campsite, run by the state tourism board, Empetur, is shaded by coconut palms and cashew trees. The Pernambuco state governor has his summer retreat here.

To the north, the best beaches are found on **Ilha Itamaracá**, 53 km (33 miles) from Recife, where the locals spend their weekends. On the way, along highway BR-101, is the historical town of **Igarassu**, home of the second-oldest church in Brazil (1535), dedicated to the twin saints of Cosme and Damião. The adjoining Franciscan monastery has the largest collection of baroque religious paintings in the country – more than 200. There are a number of colonial houses, and Brazil's first Masonic hall; much of the town has been declared a National Monument.

Halfway across the bridge to Itamaracá sits a police checkpoint, a reminder that part of the island serves as an open prison for model inmates serving time at a nearby penitentiary. Married prisoners are allowed to live with their families, and all the inmates are engaged in some form of commerce. As you start down the island road, you will see lines of

BELOW: Igreja de São Pedro, Recife.

booths and small shops run by prisoners selling postcards and crafts. Each man is identified by a number stencilled on to his T-shirt.

Before you reach Forte Orange, which was built by the Dutch in 1631, take the side road to **Vila Velha**, the island's first settlement, founded in 1534. This isolated village is tucked away in a coconut grove on the southern coast.

A number of colonial buildings, crowned by the 17th-century Nossa Senhora da Conceição church, line the square. If you're after a midday break, there are several regional and seafood restaurants. Splendid beaches line most of the island's shore.

Downtown Itamaracá and the historical Forte Orange district have good hotels and restaurants. Forte Orange also offers an organized campsite. Next to the fort, there is a visitor center with displays on the work of the Manatee Project, which looks after injured manatees before returning them to the open sea.

TIP

Sítio Histórico is a map with details of historic sites in Olinda, available for free from the tourist office.

A cultural wonder

Time has stood still in **Olinda** ⓭, which stretches like an open-air museum across the hills overlooking Recife. The town is a treasure trove of baroque art and architecture and, as such, was declared a World Heritage Site by UNESCO in 1982. However, many of the buildings are still awaiting restoration.

Legend has it that the first Portuguese emissary sent to govern the region was so enthralled by the beauty of these hills that he uttered, "*O linda situação para uma vila*" (What a beautiful site for a settlement). Hence, Olinda's name. By far the best way to explore Olinda is on foot. Narrow streets lined with brightly colored colonial homes, serenely beautiful churches, sidewalk cafés and shops displaying ornate signs wind through the 17th-century setting of Olinda's hills.

BELOW: Boa Viagem, Recife's most beautiful beach and social center.

Starting off at the **Praça do Carmo**, site of Brazil's oldest Carmelite church (built in 1580), continue up Rua São Francisco to the **São Roque chapel and convent**, with its baroque frescoes depicting the life of the Virgin Mary. Turn left on Rua Bispo Coutinho to visit the **Seminário de Olinda** (seminary) and the **Nossa Senhora da Graça** church – both are well-preserved examples of 16th-century Brazilian baroque architecture. This street opens out on to Alto da Sé, a hilltop square overlooking the ocean and Recife, 6 km (4 miles) in the distance.

The **Igreja da Sé**, the first parish church in the northeast, was built at the time of Olinda's founding in 1537 and is today the cathedral of the archdiocese. The sacred art museum (open weekdays 9am–12.45pm), across from the cathedral, is housed in the **Palácio Episcopal** (1676) and contains a collection of panels portraying the history of Olinda. On weekend evenings, the Alto da Sé comes alive with outdoor cafés and bars.

As you turn down the Ladeira da Misericórdia, on your right is the **Misericórdia** church, dating from 1549. Its richly detailed wood and gold engravings are reminiscent of the French Boucher school. It is only open 11.45am–12.30pm and 6–6.30pm, daily. The **Mercado da Ribeira** on Rua Bernardo Vieira de Melo is an excellent place to buy art, and on the corner of Rua 13 de Maio you'll find the **Museu de Arte Contemporânea** (open daily except Fri; pm only weekends), an 18th-century structure originally designed to house prisoners of the Inquisition.

Most of Olinda's historical buildings are open daily to visits, with a two-hour lunch break, generally noon–2pm. The town has luxury hotels and small inns, many of them housed in historic mansions.

Map on page 218

Coconuts of Pernambuco.

BELOW: Porto de Galinhas, outside Recife.

Mountain resort

The twice-weekly Caruaru handicrafts fair and the backwoods town of **Fazenda Nova** (190 km or 118 miles from Recife) are the final destinations of an excellent day trip out of Recife along the BR-232 highway that winds up the coastal mountain range to the resort town of Gravatá and beyond.

Graffiti art has official approval in Olinda, in view of its status as a World Cultural Monument. The town council commissions local artists to decorate open-air sites in the old city.

Halfway to Gravatá, near **Vitória de Santo Antão**, looming on the left, is an enormous bottle with a crayfish on the label: the symbol of the Pitú *cachaça* distillery. The distillery hardly needs its bottle sign: its product, Brazil's distinctive sugarcane brandy, can be smelled long before the bottle appears. Tours of the plant are available and there's free tasting of the most famous brand of *cachaça* in the northeast.

From here to Gravatá it's 32 km (20 miles) of tortuous mountain road. The air becomes noticeably cooler and the vegetation sparser. **Gravatá** ⓮ is where Recife's wealthy have summer homes and its fresh mountain air attracts visitors to its hotels and inns for the weekend. This is practically the last you'll see of anything green except for scrubland plants and lizards until you return to the coast.

Eclectic trading post

Ideally, a visit to Fazenda Nova should be made either on a Wednesday or a Saturday. On these two days the next-door city of **Caruaru** ⓯ turns into one great trading post, with rich and poor rubbing shoulders at the stalls. At one stand, a wealthy Recife matron will be choosing her hand-painted earthenware tea set, while at another, a toothless old man from the *sertão* will try to exchange a scraggly goat for a few sacks of rice, beans and sugar. People from outlying villages pay the equivalent of a few cents apiece for a place in a truck or a jeep to come to Caruaru just to do their weekly shopping. Others travel from distant states or foreign countries to purchase some of Brazil's most beautiful and artistic handicrafts.

BELOW: a mural in Olinda.

The gaily painted figurines, first created by the late Mestre (master) Vitalino, are among the most popular items for sale, but beware of vendors who try to charge high prices alleging that their figurines were made by the Mestre himself. Vitalino wasn't that prolific. What's on display here and in Recife's Casa da Cultura (where many of the same items are sold, but with less variety) was made by students of Vitalino. Caruaru's fair opens at about 9am and goes on until 5pm and is considered the best of its kind in South America.

Fazenda Nova ⓰, a sleepy village that survived for years on what it could scratch out of the parched earth, took its place on the map in 1968 when the Pacheco family, with support from the state government, inaugurated **Nova Jerusalem**. This open-air theater, which is designed to resemble the Jerusalem of AD33, comes to life once a year, during Holy Week, when the Passion of Christ is re-enacted before tens of thousands of spectators.

The setting is perfect: huge stages, each depicting a station of the cross, rise out of the sandy soil, looming

Map on page 218

over actors and spectators. The audience follows the players (500 in all, most of them village residents) from scene to scene and becomes part of the Passion Play. Audience participation is at its height when Pontius Pilate asks the crowd, "Who shall it be – the King of the Jews or Barabbas?" The actors do not speak. Instead, they mouth the recorded dialogue.

Giant statues

Just a short walk from the theater is the no-less impressive **Parque das Esculturas** (open daily 7am–5pm), a mammoth tribute to the northeast. In the park you'll find immense stone statues, weighing up to 20 metric tons (19.7 tons), representing both folk heroes and the everyday people of the northeast. In one section, there is the washerwoman, the cotton picker, the sugarcane cutter, the lace maker – each of them 3–4 meters (10–13 ft) tall. In another section, Lampião, the legendary Robin Hood of the northeast, and his beloved, Maria Bonita, stand tall. There is also a collection of figures taken from Pernambuco's unique folk dances and celebrations, including the immense sea horse and his rider; the *jaraguá*, half-man, half-monster; and the *frevo* dancer.

Frevo is the centerpiece of Pernambuco's Carnival. In this festival there are no samba schools as are found in the south and no electric instruments as found in Salvador. People dance in the streets holding up parasols to help keep their balance. Groups portray *maracatu*, a typical northeastern legend that tells the history of the *candomblé* religion and its roots in the times of slavery.

The center of northeast Carnival is Olinda, whose narrow streets become packed with delirious celebrants throughout the four-day blow out. ❑

BELOW: Olinda, world cultural monument.

SERGIPE AND ALAGOAS

The northeast's two smallest states are best known for their beaches, but they also have their share of well-preserved historic towns and recommended festival centers

Map on page 218

Sergipe and Alagoas were part of the rich sugarcane cycle in Brazilian history. As in neighboring Bahia and Pernambuco, the population was divided between landlords and slaves, who arrived in growing numbers to work in the sugar mills and plantations. But there were many rebellions; runaway slaves hid in the forests and formed independent communities, or *quilombos*, some of which flourished and lasted for decades.

The most famous, and largest, of these *quilombos* was the Republic of Palmares in the state of Alagoas, which lasted for 65 years and had at one time almost 30,000 inhabitants. In 1695, the *quilombo* was destroyed and its inhabitants killed or taken back into slavery. The site of the Republic has become a pilgrimage center.

Vestiges of the state's colonial past can also be seen in the sugar mills and once grand farmhouses in the region, and the historical buildings and towns. These vie for tourists' attention with stunning palm tree-ringed beaches and the deep blue sea that lure increasing numbers of visitors to the area each year.

LEFT: graceful palms are a typical feature of the northeast coast
BELOW: a homemade surfboard in Maceió.

Maceió

Between Recife and Salvador, the two most important cities in the northeast, are 840 km (500 miles) of beautiful coastline. Bordering Pernambuco to the south is the state of Alagoas, whose capital, **Maceió** ⓱, has a total population of 880,000. The city, founded in 1815, grew out of a sugar plantation established there in the 18th century.

Maceió beaches are famous for the transparent bright emerald green of the water, especially at low tide on downtown **Praia Pajuçara**. Trapped between the beach and offshore sand bars, the water becomes an enormous wading pool. Local fishermen will take you out to the sand bars in their *jangadas* (outrigger fishing boats) for a small price.

The city is struggling to keep up with the flow of tourists who descend upon it every year in summer. December is an especially busy month, when Maceió holds its Festival do Mar (Festival of the Sea) at Pajuçara. It is celebrated with a giant street and beach party that includes sporting events, folk dancing and booths selling native handicrafts.

Maceió is mostly modern, but a few interesting old buildings survive, including the Pierre Chalita sacred art museum (open weekdays 8am–noon and 2–6pm), in the Palácio do Governo; the church of Bom Jesus dos Martirios (1870); and the Catedral de Nossa Senhora dos Prazeres (1840) on Praça Dom Pedro II.

One of the most popular beaches outside the city limits is **Praia do Francês**, which is situated near the historical town of **Marechal Deodoro** ⓲, the first ital of Alagoas. The town itself is home to some lovely examples of colonial Brazilian architecture, among which are the 1684 Convento de São Francisco (Monastery of St Francis) and the church of Nossa Senhora da Conceição (1755). Originally called Alagoas, the town was renamed after its most famous son, Field Marshall Manuel Deodoro da Fonseca, the first (non-elected) president of Brazil (1891).

Disgraced president Fernando Collor de Mello was mayor of Maceió before he rose to the top of the greasy pole. Collor's presidency ended in 1992, when he was forced to resign following a corruption scandal (see page 40).

Moving south along the BR-101 highway from Maceió is the state border between Alagoas and Sergipe, delineated by the immense São Francisco River. Here, the town of **Penedo** ⓳, built in the 17th and 18th centuries, is a good place to stop on your way to the beaches of Aracaju, capital of the state of Sergipe, Brazil's smallest state. The town's baroque and rococo churches are its main attractions, in particular, Nossa Senhora dos Anjos (1759) and Nossa Senhora da Corrente (1764). River trips downstream to the mouth of the São Francisco at **Brejo Grande** can be arranged at the town's port. Or take the ferry across the river to **Carrapicho** to buy handmade earthenware and porcelain goods. Food and lodging in this region are very simple.

Festivals galore

Aracaju ⓴, 140 km (87 miles) from the border with Bahia, lies in the middle of the Sergipe coastline. Founded in 1855, Aracaju (pop. 490,000) is noted for the beauty of its beaches and the hospitality of its people, whose festival calendar is one of the fullest in the northeast.

These festivals, nearly always based on religious holidays (though they may often appear more secular then sacred), include: Bom Jesus dos Navegantes, a maritime procession of gaily decorated boats (January 1); St Benedict, folk

BELOW: a cool regard.
BELOW RIGHT: fresh coconut milk for sale on the beach.

dances and mock battles (the first weekend in January); Festas Juninas – harvest festivals in honor of three saints: John, Anthony and Peter (throughout the month of June); Expoarte, a handicraft fair (the month of July); and Iemanjá, a religious procession in honor of the *candomblé* goddess (December 8).

Delicious seafood abounds here but Aracaju's main claim to fame is its freshwater shrimp (similar to crayfish in appearance), caught in the Sergipe River. Crab is another of this city's specialties, and for dessert, breadfruit compote or stewed coconut. The obligatory appetite-opener is the *batida*, made from sugarcane liquor *(cachaça)* and any of a variety of local fruits (the best are mango, cashew, coconut and mangaba).

Map on page 218

Panoramic view

The **Morro de Santo Antônio**, site of the city's founding, offers an excellent view of the region, including the Sergipe River and Atalaia Beach. Motorboats take visitors to **Ilha de Santa Luzia**, a tropical paradise of coconut palms and sand dunes. Other good beach areas include Abaís, Caueira and Pirambu.

A few miles to the south of the Santo Antônio is the historical town of **Sao Cristóvão** ㉑, founded in 1590. One of the oldest cities in Brazil, it has a number of well-preserved colonial structures, including the Convento de São Francisco (1693), the Igreja e Convento do Carmo (1743–66), and the Nossa Senhora da Vitória church (late 17th century), as well as museums, the Museu de Arte Sacra, in the São Francisco convent and, next door, the Museu Histórico de Sergipe (both open Tues–Sun 1–6pm).

Nearby **Laranjeiras** is another town that has preserved its heritage, notably the churches of Sant'Aninha (1875) and Comendaroba (1734). ❑

BELOW: shrimp for sale at a market.

Map on page 218

FERNANDO DE NORONHA

For years, a military outpost off-limits to visitors, this unspoiled island reserve is now on the tourist trail, but remains sufficiently undisturbed to safeguard turtles and other sea life

With crystal-clear waters and an exuberance of corals, dolphins, lobsters and colorful tropical fish, as well as wonderfully preserved beaches and virtually no pollution, **Fernando de Noronha** ㉒ is a paradise for divers, surfers and all nature lovers, and a reminder that the world can still be a beautiful and peaceful place.

The island is formed from the tip of a mountain whose base is 4,000 meters (13,125 ft) below sea level, and is part of a volcanic archipelago of 21 islands covering an area of 26 sq km (10 sq miles). It was discovered in 1503 by the Portuguese explorer Amérigo Vespucci, and given to the nobleman Fernando de Loronha in 1504 by the Portuguese king, hence its name (with one letter changed). The nobleman, however, never set foot on the island, which, because of its strategic position, was invaded in turn by the French, the Dutch and the French again, before returning to Portuguese domination. In 1938, already Brazilian territory, it was turned into a prison, and during the World War II Fernando de Noronha served as an American base. The army barracks from that period have been converted into the island's only classified hotel.

BELOW: some come to the island purely to relax.

In 1988 Fernando de Noronha became part of a Marine National Park covering an area of 112 sq km (43 sq miles) around the archipelago, protected by IBAMA, the Brazilian Institute for the Environment. To preserve the unspoiled environment, only 480 tourists are allowed on the island at any one time, and an environment tax of $R24 (US$8) is charged. Check www.noronha.com for latest details.

Thousands of migratory birds stop off at the island on their way south. On a boat trip to the **Enseada dos Golfinhos**, hundreds of playful dolphins can be seen out at sea. Swimming is allowed only at the entrance to the bay so as not to disturb them, but lucky divers sometimes encounter the dolphins as they enter or leave the bay in the early mornings or late afternoons. Between January and June, tourists can observe marine turtles laying their eggs in the sand at night at **Praia do Leão**, and – with permission from the Tamar Project (for turtle protection) on the island – they can even help monitor the baby turtles going out to sea.

But the greatest marvels are underwater, so it is unsurprising that scuba diving and snorkeling are the most popular activities among visitors. The sight of a myriad of multi-colored fish and corals, sponges and plants is unforgettable, and there are also wrecks of sunken ships to visit. For the more adventurous, there is the possibility of meeting sharks on a night dive.

Riding, mountain-biking or trekking to some of the remoter beaches is also popular. There are interesting natural rock sculptures at the **Baía dos Porcos** beach, a waterfall at **Praia do Sancho** during the rainy season and a heavenly natural swimming pool among the rocks at **Praia do Atalaia**.

The Igreja Nossa Senhora dos Remédios, built in 1772, in the village of Vila dos Remédios, the Forte de Nossa Senhora dos Remédios nearby, built in 1737, and a few scattered ruins are the only remains of the island's chequered history. The **Morro do Pico** is the highest point on the island at 321 meters (1,053 ft); it offers a splendid view of the archipelago, especially at sunset. Warm and pleasant temperatures of around of 26°C (79°F) year-round, with a refreshing rainy season from February to July, complete the idyll.

Many of the island's inhabitants are descended from soldiers and prisoners sent here when it was a correctional institute and war-time prison.

Most of Fernando de Noronha's 2,000 inhabitants are employed in local tourism, as guides, boatmen, drivers, or looking after one of the nearly 100 *pousadas*. The island's one hotel, the Esmeralda do Atlântico (tel: 081-3619 1255), is expensive and often fully booked. Most of the *pousadas* are slightly cheaper, such as the Solar dos Ventos (tel: 081-3619 1347), with a stunning view over the bay. The Pousada Monsieur Rocha (tel: 081-3619 1252) is also very comfortable. In the evenings, there is *forró* dancing at the Mirante do Boldró bar. The Bar do Cachorro serves delicious fried shark *(tubarão)* appetizers.

There are two daily flights to Fernando de Noronha from Natal and Recife with local Nordeste or Trip airlines. The flight takes one and a half hours from Recife, about an hour from Natal. You can travel independently, or book your trip through a travel agency or tour operator who may secure discounts on lodgings. The island has to import food and water from the mainland, so IBAMA discourages lingerers by charging an environmental preservation tax, the price of which depends on how many days you stay. ❑

BELOW: turtles keeping their heads down.

THE FAR NORTHEAST

Fishing villages, lunar dune-scapes, mestiço *culture, fossil sites, and a place of pilgrimage are typical images of the communities north of Pernambuco state*

Map on page 218

The northern coastline stretches along beautiful semi-deserted beaches from dry Rio Grande do Norte all the way to the borders of the Amazon and the *babaçu* palm groves of Maranhão state. Rio Grande do Norte and the small state of Paraíba just south of it were part of the sugarcane boom of the early years of Portuguese colonization, and they declined with the demise of the *engenhos* (sugar mills).

Colonization in Ceará and Piauí came with the cattle ranchers in the late 17th century, though it is Ceará's beaches and fishermen that have made its fame. Maranhão was first colonized by the French, then the Dutch, and only after they were expelled in the mid-17th century did the Portuguese show any interest in the state, developing sugar and cotton plantations. Maranhão's economy now centers on the multi-use *babaçu* plant, parts of which are made into food products (especially cooking oil), or are added to fertilizers, cellulose, timber and roofing materials.

While these northeast states remain among the poorest in Brazil, tourism and an incipient industry, mostly in Ceará, bring hopes of a brighter future. The natural beauties of the region are unparalleled.

LEFT: local girls head for the kitchen.
BELOW: *Maternity* wood carving in Fortaleza's Museu de Arte e Cultura Populares.

A 16th-century city

Just over 100 km (60 miles) north of Recife on the Atlantic coast lies **João Pessoa** ㉓ (pop. 625,000), the easternmost point of the Americas. The dozens of beaches in this region share two fortunate characteristics: they are protected from the pounding surf by rows of reefs and from the tropical sun by lines of coconut palms.

Capital of the state of **Paraíba**, João Pessoa is the third oldest city in Brazil. It celebrated its 400th anniversary in 1985. Tropical greenery is abundant in the city, especially palm trees, bougainvilleas, flamboyants and other flowering trees. The lake in **Parque Solon de Lucena** downtown is ringed with majestic royal palms.

The lovely baroque architecture exemplified by the **São Francisco** church contrasts with the futuristic design of the Tropical Tambaú Hotel, which looks like an immense flying saucer set halfway into the Atlantic Ocean. All guest rooms look out on to the sea. At high tide, the waves nearly reach the windowsills.

If you make a pre-dawn trek out to **Cabo Branco** (White Cape), 14 km (8 miles) from the city, you can enjoy the knowledge that you are the first person in the Americas to see the sun rise.

One of the best beaches in the region is **Praia do Poço**, just 10 km (6 miles) north of the Tropical Tambaú Hotel. Go there at low tide, when the ocean

Sporting a local-style straw hat.

recedes to reveal the island of **Areia Vermelha** (Red Sand). Rows of *jangadas*, the fishermen's primitive rafts that are an integral part of the coastal scenery, take out visitors to the island. Sea algae and schools of colorful fish glitter in the transparent water.

Around Calcanhar Cape

Rio Grande do Norte, which borders Paraíba to the north, lies on the northeastern curve of the continent. **Natal** ㉔, its capital, 185 km (110 miles) from João Pessoa, is another of the region's popular beach resorts. The enormous sand dunes at Natal (pop. 750,000), especially those at **Genipabu Beach**, 30 km (18 miles) north, attract visitors from all over the country, who rent buggies to do their beach exploring. The name Natal is Portuguese for Christmas, the day in 1599 when the city was officially founded. Its most famous monument, the star-shaped **Forte dos Reis Magos** (Three Kings' Fort) was so named because construction on it began on the Epiphany, January 6, 1600. Natal's **Museu Câmara Cascudo** (Avda Hermes da Fonseca 1398; open Tues–Fri and Sun 8–10.30am and 2–4.30pm), has displays ranging from Amazonian Indian artifacts to objects used in *candomblé* rites.

Ribeira, on the riverfront, forms the oldest part of the city. Here, some of the buildings, including Teatro Alberto Maranhão, have been restored.

Some 20 km (12 miles) south of Natal is the town of **Eduardo Gomes**, home to Barreira do Inferno, the country's rocket launching center. It is open to the public (reservations needed, Mon noon–4pm, Tues–Thurs 9–11am and 1–5pm, Fri 8.30–11am). A view of Barreira can be had from nearby **Cotovelo Beach**, one of the most beautiful on the state's southern coast.

BELOW: harvesting sugarcane.

The 100-km (60-mile) drive from Natal northwards to Touros Beach is an adventure, following a succession of semi-deserted beaches marked by sand dunes and coconut palms. You'll pass by Genipabu, Maxaranguape, and Ponta Gorda, the site of Cabo de São Roque, where, on August 16, 1501, the first Portuguese expedition arrived, one year after the discovery of Brazil. Other beaches discovered include Caraúbas, Maracajaú, Pititinga, Zumbi, Rio do Fogo, Peroba and Carnaubinha. Fishermen's huts dot the landscape.

Touros ㉕, a town of 28,000, gets its name from the bulls that once wandered freely here. There are a handful of small inns, bars and restaurants (the locals recommend Castelo) where you can enjoy shrimp roasted in garlic butter or fresh broiled lobster. At night, go to Calcanhar Cape, 8 km (5 miles), to watch the sun go down and the Touros lighthouse come on. The island of Fernando de Noronha, a wildlife preserve, lies 290 km (180 miles) northeast off the cape *(see pages 256–257)*.

The state of Ceará's coastline has 560 km (350 miles) of exuberant beaches backed by palms, sand dunes and freshwater lagoons, where the favored sons of state capital **Fortaleza** ㉖ spend strenuous weekends drinking beer, and cracking open crabs and lobsters while watching the *jangadas* bring the day's catch through the rollers.

In the coastal villages, where offshore breezes blow constantly, lace makers and embroiderers still ply their trade. But tourism and the weekend homes of city dwellers are rapidly changing the coastal area. Even **Jericoacoara**, once a paradisaical fishing village cut off behind the dunes, is now linked by a four-wheel-drive service to the city. Declared a national park in 2002, it is still a beautiful – even magical – spot.

In gritty contrast, the hinterland of **Ceará** is periodically wracked by drought. When the crops are ruined, and the landlords dismiss their *vaqueiros* or cowboys, these *flagelados* or "whipped ones" pack their belongings and head for the swollen cities in order to survive. Those who remain keep alive a strong oral culture derived from the troubadours. Village poets or *repentistas* duel for hours to cap each other's rhymes with more extravagant verbal conceits. Traditions are also recorded in the *cordel* pamphlets (chapbooks) illustrated with woodcuts, whose humorous rhymes recount deeds of the anarchic *cangaceiros* or cowboy-warriors, of local politics and religious miracles. The toughness of existence has produced a succession of religious movements rejecting outside control, and thousands of pilgrims still pay homage to Padre Cícero (*see page 266*), who, if not yet officially a saint, is certainly the northeast's patron.

The first attempt to colonize the arid *sertão* of Ceará, which separated the Rio Grande and Maranhão, was in 1603. The Amerindian fighter Pero Coelho de Souza led a mob of Portuguese soldiers and Amerindian warriors on a raid for slaves. He returned in 1606 but was driven off by a terrible drought.

Fortaleza's founder

Martim Soares Moreno was on the first expedition and was ordered by the governor-general of Brazil to open up the region by befriending the Amerindians. By 1611, he was promoted to captain of Ceará and founded Fortaleza by building the first fortress of São Paulo and a chapel by the Ceará River's mouth.

The fortress stood Moreno in good stead when the French attacked that year – as did the Tapuia and Tupinambá tribes whom he had befriended. Fighting alongside the Amerindians stark naked, his body smeared with vegetable dye, he drove off the French, but then succumbed to the charms of Iracema, a seductive Amerindian princess who is still the city's muse and patron saint. Brazilian literati, led by José Alencar, rediscovered Amerindian history in a romantic movement that flowered a century ago with the novel *O Guaraní*, and a short story retelling Iracema's story.

Dutch invaders in 1649 built the foundations to the **Schoonenborch Fort** in what is now the center of Fortaleza. The fort is still used today as a garrison. By 1654, the Dutch were driven out by the Portuguese, who rechristened the fort Nossa Senhora de Assunção. Fortaleza consolidated itself as a trading center for the arid cattle country of the interior.

Many of the Amerindian-fighting *bandeirantes* from São Paulo stayed behind, to establish immense cattle ranches that still exist today. In contrast to the sugar plantations of Pernambuco, Ceará's ranches

Map on page 218

TIP

As there is no vegetation on Areia Vermelha, you should be aware of the twin dangers of sunburn and sunstroke. It's essential to bring along a hat and sunscreen as, reflected off the sand, the sun can burn your skin in a matter of minutes.

BELOW: regional flora in a hotel garden.

Selling bottles filled with local, artificially-colored red sand.

used almost no African slave labor, and the region's culture is more influenced by its Amerindian-Portuguese *mestiço* past than African roots.

Ceará's southeastern beaches

The southeastern coast of the state has a selection of attractive beaches, starting with **Canoa Quebrada**, some 60 km (37 miles) from the border with Rio Grande do Norte and 10 km (6 miles) from the town of Aracati.

During the 1970s, the lunar dunes scape of Canoa Quebrada attracted a lingering generation of hippies from Brazil and abroad. They settled down in the fishermen's primitive houses, blending natural fruit juices, *forró* and free love with a village lifestyle that had changed little in 300 years. Development and its accompanying ills have inevitably followed the influx. Fortunately, Canoa Quebrada's broad expanse of beach, the dunes behind and its crumbling red sandstone cliffs still retain something of the original magic.

The eroded sandstone cliffs of **Morro Branco**, 70 km (43 miles) north of Aracati and 85 km (53 miles) south of Fortaleza, provide the raw material for craftsmen while the less-crowded beach here provides a welcome relief from Fortaleza's urban sprawl. **Iguape**, 50 km (30 miles) from Fortaleza, is famous for its lacemakers (ask to look at the Renaissance pattern) and the artificially colored sands from Morro Branco packed into bottles to depict landscapes.

Just a 34-km (21-mile) drive from Fortaleza is **Aquiraz**, which in the 17th century was Ceará's first capital, and contains the ruins of a Jesuit mission. It is home to an 18th-century church with the image of São José do Ribamar, the state's patron saint. The historic church ruins may be reached by way of a rum distillery.

BELOW: sliding down a dune in Natal.

Map on page 218

Of those beaches still closer to the city, **Prainha** is the most authentic. There are several seafood restaurants and bars stretching across the sand. The local fishermen here will take tourists for *jangada* rides. The flat rafts with lateen sails are covered in advertising as if they were racing cars because in July, professionals compete in the Dragon of the Sea regatta. The still-urban and sophisticated resort of **Porto das Dunas** is also worth checking out, as is the Beach Park Hotel, close to the water park of the same name.

The city seafront

Today, nothing remains of the original fortress that gave Fortaleza its name. With a population of 2.2 million, the ungraceful city instead looks forward, as the aptly named **Praia do Futuro** indicates. Here, beachfront condominiums and bars have sprouted up, pushing visitors in search of unspoiled coastline away to beaches outside the sprawling city. Fortaleza's real strength is its selection of out-of-town beaches. Praia do Futuro is a lively spot on Thursday evenings.

The city's seafront hotels are situated on Avenida President Kennedy, which runs along the **Praia do Meireles**, the main meeting place. At night, the noisy bars and the broad sidewalks below the Imperial Othon Palace Hotel are packed with strollers drawn by the handicraft market, offering lace, ceramics, leather goods, colored sand packed into bottles, and a wide variety of general souvenirs.

Fortaleza is a major exporter of lobster. Seafood restaurants along the ocean front, such as Cemoara, offer crab, shrimp, lobster or *peixada* – the local seafood specialty. Northeasterners round off the night at hot, crowded dance halls like Clube do Vaqueiro (Wednesday evenings) and Parque do Vaqueiro (Friday evenings), where couples clinch for the *forró*, a lively but seductive jig accompanied by accordion music. The restaurants and bars in restored historic buildings around the Centro Cultural Dragão do Mar often host live music. The Planetarium and contemporary art museum here are worth a visit during the day.

The **Meireles beach** stretches from Mucuripe near the docks, where there's an 1840 lighthouse, to the breakwater at Volta de Jurema. The central section, **Praia de Iracema**, is marked by a modern sculpture designed by Fortaleza's Morena and his native princess, but the beach is too polluted for discerning swimmers. At night, however, its variety of bars and restaurants make it a must-see.

Handicrafts are best purchased at the Tourist Center (Rua Senador Pompeu 350), the tastefully converted old city jail or sometimes at a lower price at the Mercado Central, which has over 1,000 close-packed booths. The Ceart Center (Avenue Santos Dumont 1589, Aldeota) provides a third alternative.

Another attraction is the Teatro José de Alencar, a cast-iron structure imported from Britain in 1910. You can also take a sunset cruise across the harbor.

West of Fortaleza, in the Ibiapaba hills, is the **Parque Nacional de Ubajara** ㉗, with caves that contain interesting stalagmite formations and a cable car that takes visitors up to waterfalls and lush green vegetation.

BELOW: enjoying leisure time on the beach.

TIP

At Cumbuco, dune-buggy owners offer exhilarating rides up to Parnamirim lagoon. There, for a small tip, village kids teach visitors to slither on sand "skateboards" down the dunes and into the cool water.

Ceará's northwestern beaches

To the northwest of Forteleza, a series of beaches begins again at **Barra do Ceará** – the river's mouth where the city was established – but **Cumbuco** is the first port of call, 33 km (20 miles) from the city. The attractions are its surfing beach and the dunes stretching inland as far back as the black surface of the **Parnamirim** freshwater lagoon. At the beach bars, rides are available on the sailing rafts that set out through the surf.

There is no coastal road running north, but 85 km (53 miles) from Fortaleza is **Paracuru** ㉘, reached from inland on the BR-222 federal highway. A lively community that enjoys a week-long Carnival and regular surf or sailing regattas, the town is a favorite weekend beach spot. A few miles further on is the less sophisticated **Lagoinha**, where rooms are available to rent in local village houses. An intersection on the highway leading from BR-222 to Paracuru goes to Trairi, with access to the beaches of **Freixeiras, Guajiru**, and **Mundaú**.

Icarai ㉙ is 140 km (87 miles) from Fortaleza, via the BR-222 intersection leading past Itapipoca, behind the Mundaú dunes and across the Trairi River. Beaches here include the Pesqueiro, Inferno and Baleia. **Acaraú** ㉚, a further 90 km (57 miles) from Fortaleza, is one of the most popular beach centers. The adjacent fishing village of **Almofala** also has a fine unspoilt beach and an early 18th-century church, which for years was covered by shifting sands.

The finest of Ceará's beaches is **Jericoacoara** ㉛, which is the picture postcard of Brazil's northeast. Although remote, it is a very popular place with Brazilian tourists and international backpackers. The pure horizontals of sea, dunes, and sky are cut by coconut palms, and the fishing village has no electric lights or motorcars. A preservation effort means that rare and endangered species

BELOW: salt being extracted from seawater near Fortaleza.

Map on page 218

are protected in the dunes and lagoons. Sea turtles come up the beach to lay their eggs, and the village has taken on much of the mystique that Canoa Quebrada enjoyed a decade ago, its simplicity attracting foreigners and Brazilians alike.

Reaching Jericoacoara, about 320 km (200 miles) from Fortaleza, is difficult because it is still cut off by the dunes. The trip can be made by bus and then four-wheel drive jeep. There are tour agencies which organise short excursions to Jericoacoara, for example Matusa (tel: 085-246 9894) and Hippopotamus (tel: 085-242 9191).

Colonial-style restaurant sign, Sao Luis.

Ancient sites in Piauí

The state of Piauí has impressive geological monuments formed by erosion over millions of years. These can be visited at the Parque Nacional Sete Cidades, 180 km (112 miles) from the capital, **Teresina**.

The **Parque Nacional da Serra da Capivara**, in the southwest of the state, is the oldest archeological site in the Americas – over 50,000 years old, and was declared a World Heritage Site by UNESCO in 1991. Besides fossils of mastodonts and giant ground sloths, it has the largest set of rock art in the world. The **Museu do Homem Americano** has interesting specimens of fossils and prehistoric tools (open by authorization only, tel: 086-582 1567).

At the top of Brazil's northeast region, between the Amazon basin and the *sertão*, is **São Luís** ㉜, capital of the state of Maranhão and another World Heritage Site. Perched on the bayside of São Luís Island (pop. 890,000), the city was founded in 1612 by French colonists, who were driven out by the Portuguese three years later. In 1641, the Dutch invaded the island but, like the French, were able to maintain their dominion for only three years.

BELOW: pilgrims touch an image of Padre Cícero in Juazeiro do Norte.

Map on page 218

The city's most striking feature is the colorful sight of brightly tiled two story homes that line its narrow, sloping streets. These blue, yellow, white and green *azulejos* were originally imported from Portugal and today have become the city's trademark. Major points of interest include the **Catedral** (1763), **Praça Remédios** (1860), **Capela de Santo Antônio** (1624), and the **Museu Histórico e Artístico do Estado** (Maranhão Art and History Museum, open Tues–Fri 9am–7pm, weekends 2–7pm), housed in an early 19th-century villa.

The best beaches are **Ponta d'Areia**, with its Santo Antônio fort (1691) to the north and Calhau to the east. The undercurrent can be strong at these and other beaches; swimmers should inquire first before diving in.

Across **São Marcos Bay**, 53 km (33 miles) from São Luís, is the historical town of **Alcântara** ㉝, originally a Tupinambá Amerindian village, which in the 17th century became the favored retreat for the landed gentry of Maranhão. A walking tour begins at the Praça da Matriz, and includes the **Alcântara Museum** (open daily 9am–1.45pm except Mon), the Nossa Senhora do Carmo church (1663) and the ruins of the São Sebastião fort. The boat trip to Alcântara takes 60 minutes over choppy waters. Air taxis are also available.

The arid interior

Heading southward into the northeast's *sertão*, back in the state of Ceará, **Icó** ㉞, 362 km (226 miles) south of Fortaleza on the BR-116 Highway, is an interesting historical monument. It is also the turnoff for **Orós**, the northeast's biggest reservoir, built in the 1950s, and has a hotel and local handicraft center. Icó's town hall and several other buildings date from the 18th century.

Juazeiro do Norte ㉟, 521 km (323 miles) south of Fortaleza and reachable by plane, is a religious center where pilgrims come to make their promises to Padre Cícero Romão Batista, who in 1889 wrought a miracle that earned him excommunication from the Catholic Church in 1894. Padre Cícero then consolidated his temporal powers and in 1911 became a political leader whose rabble army of *cangaceiros* defeated federal troops sent to arrest him.

Pilgrims or *romeiros* visit a 25-meter (75-ft) statue of the austere Padre Cícero with his characteristic hat and stick. The devotional tour begins in the **Capela de Socorro** where he is buried, and passes through churches and the House of Miracles. High points in Juazeiro's devotional year are March 24, July 20 and November 1.

The Cariri Valley's other townships are **Crato**, noted for its university, museums and active cultural life, and **Barbalho**, whose hot springs offer more corporeal pleasures. The hilly **Chapada do Araripe**, due west of Juazeiro, 700 meters (2,200 ft) above sea level, provides welcome relief, with waterfalls and natural pools inside a national park.

East of Juazeiro, across the border in Paraíba, 5 km (3 miles) from the town of **Souza**, is the Vale dos Dinossauros (Dinosaur Valley, open daily 8am–6pm), which has the largest grouping of dinosaur footprints in the world. There is a visitor center here where you can hire a guide. ☐

BELOW: colorful São Luís.

São Francisco River

The São Francisco, Brazil's third-largest river, has served as one of the most important catalysts in helping to shape the country's economic and cultural development. In the 19th century, the 3,000-km (1,800-mile) river played a vital role in the development of the northeast, through which its reddish-brown waters flow. It served as virtually the only major thoroughfare in the region, which lacked roads and railways.

The river's role as primary mover of the northeast's people and products has given the São Francisco a place in Brazilian history and legend equivalent to that of the Mississippi river in the United States. In the 19th century and well into modern times, riverboats plied the São Francisco, carrying supplies to backwoods towns.

Born from a spring in the hills of Minas Gerais, the São Francisco runs through four other states: Bahia, Pernambuco, Alagoas and Sergipe. It is between these last two states that it empties into the Atlantic Ocean.

The villages and settlements that sprung up along the riverbanks during the colonial period had become important trading centers and commercial outposts by the mid-19th century. Today, the river valley still serves as a farming oasis in an otherwise arid terrain.

One of Brazil's most curious native art forms has its origins in the São Francisco. Known as *Velho Chico* (Old Chico) to the local inhabitants, the river is both admired and feared as the home of evil spirits. In order to protect themselves from these spirits, boatmen in the 19th-century made wooden figureheads for their vessels of fierce, ugly beasts. These figureheads, called *carrancas* (half-man, half-animal), are unique to Brazil.

Today, only the older boatmen still believe in the powers of *carrancas*, which are also attributed with the ability to warn the boat's crew of danger by emitting three low moans. However, the figures are still attached to modern boats as curios.

Two of the best places to purchase authentic *carrancas*, carved from cedar wood, are Petrolina, Pernambuco (750 km/466 miles from Recife) and Juazeiro, Bahia (566 km/351 miles from Salvador). Smaller versions, in the form of table decorations or key chains, can be found in all the main handicraft fairs around the country.

Many of the boatmen who live in the towns along the river offer day-long cruises. Towns from which tourists can take boat rides include Penedo, Alagoas; Paulo Afonso, Bahia; Juazeiro, Bahia and directly across the river, Petrolina, Pernambuco (these two towns lie at the spot where the river widens into lake-like proportions); Ibotirama, Bahia; Januária and Pirapora, both in Minas Gerais.

One gallant old steamboat, built in the United States in 1913 for use on the Mississippi river, makes regular jaunts down the São Francisco. For many years, it made the 1,370-km (820-mile) trip from Pirapora to Juazeiro, serving both tourists and the people who live along the route. Today, the boat is used exclusively for tourists and goes only as far as Januária. Reservations can be made with the tour operator Unitour in Belo Horizonte (tel: 031-3201 7144). ❑

RIGHT: the São Francisco at Itacarambi.

THE AMAZON

Map on page 272

In the north of Brazil, humanity is dwarfed by the continent's great river and its magnificent forested basin. Ecotours and river cruises from Belém and Manaus ply the Amazon and its tributaries

Though it is not the longest river in the world, there can be no doubt that the **Amazon** is the world's *greatest* river. At the end of a 6,570-km (4,080-mile) journey that begins in the Peruvian Andes, the river's massive mouth discharges a fifth of all the world's freshwater into the Atlantic, permeating the saltwater over 100 km (60 miles) from the shore. And Amazonia is a vast, open-air greenhouse of global evolution, where a tenth of the world's 10 million living species make their homes. The River Amazon dominates Brazil, yet Brazilians are only just beginning to discover it.

Amerigo Vespucci, an engaging Italian adventurer much given to exaggeration, and after whom the American continents were named, claimed to have sailed up the Amazon in 1499. He was followed a year later by the Spaniard Vicente Pinzon, but the credit for the first voyage of discovery down the river goes to Francisco de Orellana. He set out by boat in 1542 on a short reconnaissance during an expedition in search of the legendary gold of El Dorado, for which he had joined forces with Gonzalo Pizarro, younger brother Francisco, one of the conquistadors of Peru.

For six months, his boat was swept down river through "the excellent land and dominion of the Amazons," where his scribe Friar Carvajal was amazed by sightings of a matriarchal tribe, with bare-breasted women "doing as much fighting as ten indian men." It was these remarkable warriors who later inspired the name "Amazons," after the women of Greek mythology who removed their right breasts to facilitate using a bow and arrow.

Amazonia began to excite scientific interest all over the world a century after its "discovery", when in 1641 Spanish Jesuit Cristóbal de Acuña published *A New Discovery of the Great River of the Amazons,* carefully recording Amerindian customs, farming methods and herbal medicine, and concluding that – mosquitoes notwithstanding – it was "one vast paradise."

Botanical research

Bedrock scientific research about the Amazon was carried out by a trio of long-suffering English collectors led by Alfred Russell Wallace, whose work on the diversity of Amazonian flora and fauna influenced Darwin's *Origin of the Species*. Together with Henry Walter Bates and Richard Spruce, he set out in 1848 and discovered over 15,000 species new to science.

Another Englishman used his botanical skills to provoke the region's economic undoing when he broke Brazil's extravagant rubber monopoly. For a modest fee of £1,000, the adventurer Henry Wickham in 1876 loaded 70,000 seeds of *hevea brasiliensis* aboard a chartered steamer and slipped them past

PRECEDING PAGES: flooded rainforest on the River Negro. **LEFT:** outside a *caboclo* home near the River Ariau. **BELOW:** Manaus docks.

Amazonia
0 200 km
0 200 miles
ATLANTIC OCEAN
Equator
VENEZUELA
GUYANA
SURINAME
French Guiana
COLOMBIA
PERU
BOLIVIA
BRAZIL
Amapá
Roraima
Amazonas
Pará
Maranhão
Piauí
Tocantins
Mato Grosso
Rondônia
Acre
Bahia
Bogotá
Paramaribo
Cayenne
Macapá
Belém
São Luís
Santarém
Manaus
Boa Vista
Marabá
Imperatriz
Porto Velho
Rio Branco
Iquitos
Cuzco
Leticia
Tabatinga
Benjamin Constant
Tefé
Altamira
Óbidos
Alenquer
Monte Alegre
Parintins
Humaitá
Tucuruí
Rio Negro
Rio Amazonas
R. Solimões
R. Purus
Rio Madeira
Rio Xingu
Rio Aripuanã
Rio Juruena
R. Tapajós
Ilha de Marajó
Serra do Cachimbo
Serra dos Carajás
Serra Formosa
Serra do Roncador
Serra do Tombador
Serra dos Apiacás
Sa. do Tumucumaque
Sa. Parima
Serra Cuntamana
Parque Nacional da Amazônia
Parque Nacional do Jaú
Parque Nacional do Pico da Neblina
Arquipélago das Anavilhanas

Brazilian customs in Belém, pretending they were rare plant samples for Queen Victoria. The seedlings sprouted under glass in London's Kew Gardens, and by 1912, they had grown into Malaya's ordered, disease-free rubber plantations.

Map on facing page

Rubber riches

The properties of rubber, which had been discovered by the Omagua Amerindians, fascinated French travelers in the 18th century. Then Charles Goodyear's 1844 discovery of vulcanization followed by Dunlop's 1888 invention of the pneumatic tire caused a commercial explosion. As the price of rubber soared, production rose from 156 metric tons in 1830 to 21,000 metric tons in 1897. The cities were emptied of labor and thousands migrated from the northeast to become rubber tappers or *seringueiros.*

During the first decade of the 19th century, Brazil sold 88 percent of all exported rubber in the world, and for 25 years, around the turn of the 20th century, rubber made the Amazon port of Manaus, 1,600 km (1,000 miles) from the Atlantic, one of the richest cities in the world. A system of debt slavery was used to harvest Brazil's "black gold" over a vast area of Amazon jungle. The hundred or so rubber barons who controlled Manaus sent their laundry to Lisbon and their wives and children to Paris.

However, British-controlled plantations in Asia undercut Amazon rubber prices just before World War I, and within a decade Manaus was a jungle backwater again. The American industrialist Henry Ford, attempted to compete with the British by organizing his own Amazon rubber plantation in 1927, but was unsuccessful. Ford's two plantation sites, Fordlandia and Belterra, near the Amazon River 825 km (500 miles) from Belém, can still be seen.

LEFT: a watchful caiman.
BELOW: a toothy piranha grin.

Amazonian children with their friendly parrot and caiman.

Elegant Belém

With its public parks, wrought-iron bandstands, beaux-arts buildings and mango-tree-lined avenues, **Belém ❶** retains more elegance of the bygone rubber era than its rival Manaus. During its *belle époque*, French visitors to this city compared it favorably with Marseilles or Bordeaux. A city of 1.4 million set on the river's southern bank just one degree south of the Equator and 145 km (90 miles) from the open sea, Belém is the gateway to the Amazon.

Between the months of November and April it rains almost every day, but a breeze generally makes the humid climate tolerable. Belém is the capital of the state of Pará, which covers an area twice the size of France. It was properly linked to southern Brazil by the Belém–Brasília Highway only in 1960, and is still chiefly a port city for export of tropical hardwoods, Brazil nuts, jute and other primary products.

A tour of the old city, whose narrow streets still contain old houses fronted with Portuguese tiles, begins at the **Forte do Castelo Ⓐ**, the nucleus of the original settlement of Santa Maria do Belém do Grão Pará and now sadly rundown. Adjacent is the 18th-century **Santo Alexandre church Ⓑ**, now a museum of religious art (open daily 1–6pm, except Mon). The cathedral church, **Catedral de Nossa Senhora da Graça Ⓒ**, opposite the fort, contains artworks in Carrara marble and paintings by the Italian de Angelis.

One block away, on the south side of Praça Dom Pedro II, is the **Palácio Lauro Sodré Ⓓ**, the former seat of government, which now houses the Museu do Estado do Pará (State of Pará Museum) (open Tues–Sat, 10am–6pm, Sun 10am–2pm). It was built in the 18th century by the Italian architect Landi, and contains many examples of fine 19th-century furniture. Also on Praça Dom

BELOW: rubber tapping.

AMAZON FACTS

- The official source of the Amazon, found in 1953, is on Mount Huagra in the Peruvian Andes.
- The river is 6,570 km (4,080 miles) long (only the Nile is longer) and its mouth is 330 km (200 miles) wide.
- The Amazon has 1,100 tributaries, including 17 that are more than 1,600 km (1,000 miles) long.
- In places, the Amazon is 110 km (68 miles) wide, and its lower course has depths of over 60 meters (297 ft). Ocean-going freighters can travel 3,720 km (2,310 miles) inland from the Atlantic to Iquitos, Peru.
- The river system is the globe's largest body of fresh water. Its total water flow is 160,000 to 200,000 cubic meters (42–53 million US gallons) per second – five times that of the Congo and 12 times that of the Mississippi.
- The Amazon basin is larger than that of any other river, and it contains the world's largest – but rapidly diminishing – rainforest. This spreads over nine countries, but most of it lies within the national boundaries of Brazil.
- Amazonia supports 30 percent of all known plant and animal species, including 2,500 fish species, 50,000 higher plant species and untold millions of insects.
- The average annual rainfall is over 2,000mm (79 inches), making the Amazon basin the wettest region in the world.

Maps:
Area 272
City 276

Pedro II is the current local government building, **Palácio Antônio Lemos** Ⓔ. Dating from the late 19th century, the height of the rubber boom, it was built in the Portuguese imperial style and houses an art museum (open Tues–Thur 9am–5pm, Fri 9–11am, Sat and Sun 9am–5pm), with many fine paintings and furnishings.

The **Ver-O-Peso** Ⓕ, Belém's vast dockside market at the northern end of Avenida Portugal, is a store window of Amazonia's prodigious variety of fish and tropical fruit. Fishing boats bring in their catches, which may include 90-kg (200-lb) monsters. The **Feira do Açaí** at the end of the market is the exclusive purveyor of the small açaí coconut that is the basis of much of Belém's cooking.

There are few souvenirs to buy inside the two food pavilions, but alongside is a fascinating covered area of booths selling herbal medicines and charms used in African-Brazilian *umbanda* rituals. Sea horses, armadillos' tails, tortoise shells and tiny pineapples used for birth control are piled up beside herbs that locals swear will cure rheumatism and heart problems. Also on sale are perfumes said to be guaranteed to attract men, women, money and good fortune. Pickpockets can be a problem, and the area is best avoided after dark.

The east side

Continuing along the dockside, you will come to **Estação das Docas**. Here, the dilapidated warehouses have been transformed into an impressive cultural space with restaurants, bars, and a theater. Close to the customs house on **Praça Waldemar Henrique** Ⓖ, the state tourism authority Paratur operates a visitor center and a **Feira do Artesanato** (Handicraft Fair) that is useful for souvenirs.

LEFT: the rare blue hyacinth macaw.
BELOW: a golden sunset.

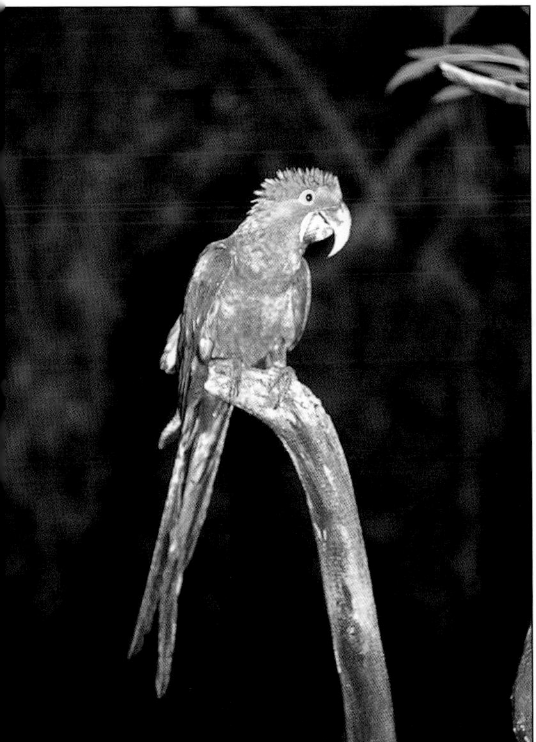

A basketware store in Belém.

Icoaraci H, about half an hour from the city (the bus stop is two blocks from the visitor center), is a center for modern ceramic ware that follows the pre-Columbian Amerindian maroajara pottery tradition whose elaborate motifs are believed to have been borrowed from Inca culture.

Continuing along Avenida Presidente Vargas – the main shopping street – away from the port, you will come to the **Praça da República I**, then Belém's theater, the **Teatro da Paz J**. This recently restored theater, built in 1874, is set in a green area complete with bandstand and the Bar do Parque – an agreeable place to sit and drink a *Cerpa*, the city's local beer.

About fifteen minutes walk inland from the Praça da República, along Avenida Nazaré, is Belém's most important church, the **Basílica Nazaré K**, built in 1909, with impressive marble work and stained glass. It is the center of the Cirio de Nazaré religious procession that was instituted by the Jesuits as a means of catechizing Amerindians and still draws over a million faithful on the second Sunday of every October – a period for which visitors need to make advance hotel reservations. The venerated image of the Virgin was found in the forest near Belém in 1700.

Continuing on, you will come to the **Museu Emílio Goeldi L**, on Rua Magalhães Barata 376 (open Tues–Thur 9–noon and 2–5pm, Fri am only, weekends 9am–5pm), which incorporates a fine zoological garden with many tropical species. The museum, founded in 1866, has a superb anthropological collection and often has excellent temporary exhibitions about Amazon life. Further from the center but also worth a visit are the Bosque Gardens (open daily except Mon 8am–5pm), which enclose an area of almost natural forest and a small zoo.

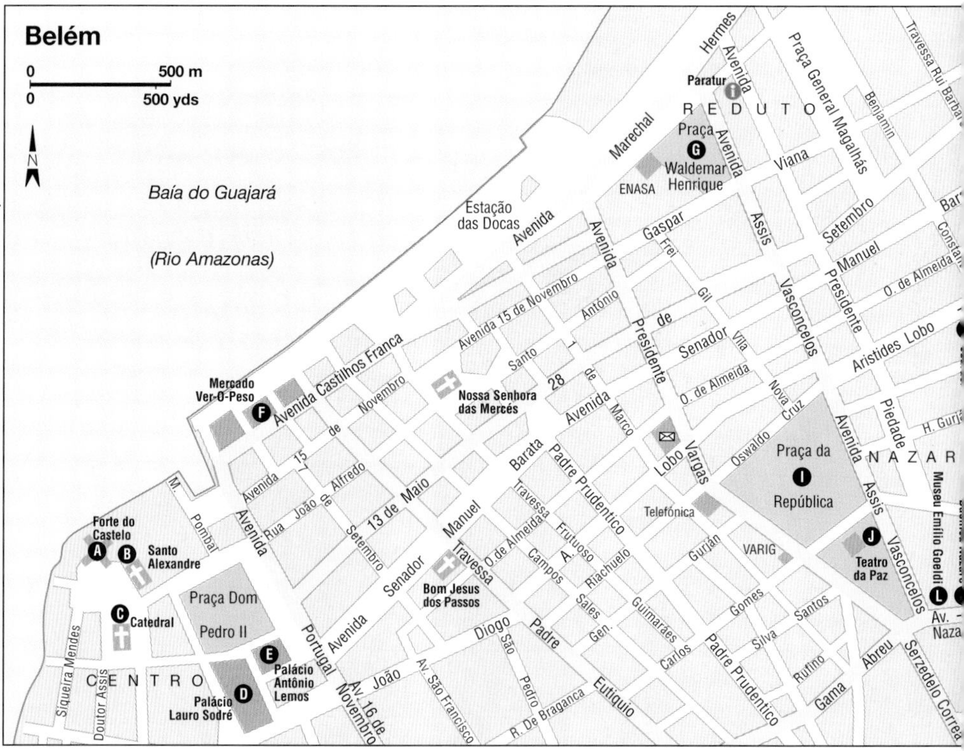

Trips from Belém

Maps:
Area 272
City 276

Several tour agencies, including Ceotur, operate one-day trips up-river, but they usually simply go up the Guajará River and visit some well-prepared *caboclo* dwellings. A better option is the Acará Lodge, which is two hours up the river and offers two-day stays in very modest accommodation.

One of the world's largest river island's (48,000 sq km/18,535 sq miles), **Ilha de Marajó ❷** (Marajó Island), at the river's mouth, is larger than Switzerland yet has a population of just 250,000 people. They are far outnumbered by the herds of water buffalo that wallow in the flat, swampy northern part. The island is an ecological haven with its fine unspoiled beaches and abundance of flora and fauna. There are at least 361 species of birds: the rare red ibis can be seen in many places on the island. Also, there have been finds of Pre-Columbian ceramics.

A government-owned ENASA ferryboat makes the five-hour trip to **Soure ❸** on the island's eastern tip (tel: 091-257 4972 or 091-212 2479). Air taxis from Belém Aeroclub do the trip in about 30 minutes. The best place to stay in Soure is the Hotel Ilha do Marajó. The Marajoara Hotel can arrange trips to the Praia do Pesqueiro and Praia Araruna, which are beaches washed by water that is part-river, part-ocean, or the Santa Caterina buffalo ranch. A ferry crosses the river to Salvaterra, where a battered taxi continues to Joanes (where you can stay at the comfortable Pousada dos Guarás).

First called the Ilha Grande do Joanes, Marajó was settled in 1617 by Franciscan monks who built a stone church here in 1665, the ruins of which survive by the lighthouse. At nearby **Monserrat** there is another stone-built church containing baroque images.

LEFT: unloading river fish at the docks, Belém. **BELOW:** *pupunha* palm fruit on display.

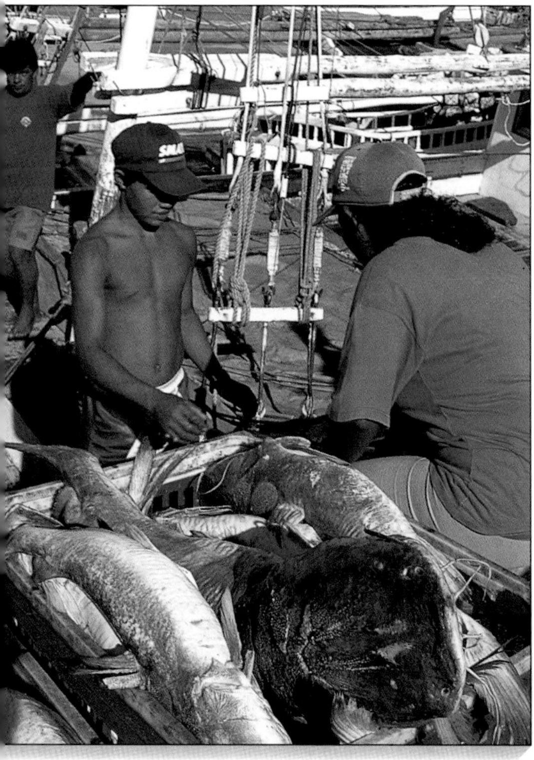

Map on page 272

From Soure, day trips can be arranged to the **Providencia buffalo farm**. But buffalo ranches in the island's interior, reachable only by boat, horse, or tractor, have much more wildlife than the populated coastal region. **Fazendas Laranjeira** and **Tapeira** both have private museums containing archeological relics from ancient Amerindian sites.

Macapá ❹, at the Amazon's northern mouth, stands on the Equator, where you can straddle the marker line or *marco zero*. It has a large fort built of Lisbon brick by the Portuguese in 1782 and a thriving economy based on shrimp fishing and manganese mining. Planes leave Macapá for **Monte Dourado ❺** and the Jari Project, US billionaire Daniel K Ludwig's ill-fated attempt to substitute the natural forest with plantations to mass-produce pulp and paper.

The Carajás project

The southeastern Amazon occupies a special place in the perennial dreams of economic greatness that have haunted Brasília's government planners – dreams that have become nightmares for conservationists. Development mega-projects that have consumed billions of dollars sprout across the region under the umbrella of the Carajás project.

Conceived around an 18-billion ton iron-ore mine in the hills around **Carajás ❻**, 880 km (547 miles) south of Belém, Brazil's "moonshot" in the Amazon includes the Tucuruí hydroelectric dam, an 890-km (560-mile) railroad through the forest, and an immense complex supporting an aluminum smelting plant and a deepwater port. This highly controversial project has caused immense social and environmental damage, having flooded 2,400 sq km (927 sq miles) of Amazon rainforest and expelled 30,000 people from their home.

BELOW: The Ilha de Marajó, at the mouth of the Amazon.

The Lost City of El Dorado

The search for cities paved with gold is integral to the romance associated with the conquest and exploration of South America. *El Dorado*, the Golden Man, was the name given by Spanish explorers to a fabled Amazon king, who ruled over the fantastically wealthy Kingdom of Manoa deep in the jungle. The king himself was rumored to encrust his large naked body daily in gold dust, which he regularly washed off in a sacred lake.

Such tales of limitless riches spread abroad soon after Brazil's discovery. In the early 20th century, Colonel Percy Fawcett, whose lifelong obsession was to prove the existence of lost Amazonian civilizations, came across records indicating that a 16th-century shipwrecked adventurer, Diego Alvarez, found numerous mines of gold, silver and precious stones.

So it was that explorers such as Francisco de Orellana, the first European to traverse the entire Amazon Basin, were less interested in national glory or the conversion of souls than in the gold of *El Dorado*. Spaniard Orellana, who had won his spurs fighting alongside Francisco Pizarro in Peru – where the *conquistadores* had helped themselves to copious Inca gold – became second-in-command on Gonzalcs Pizarro's 1540 expedition in search of new territories, gold and cinnamon.

Pizarro was eventually forced, in the face of starvation and hostile Amerindians, to return ignominiously to his base in Ecuador. But Orellana became separated from his patron, and with a smaller band of men, found favor with some Amazon tribes and glimpsed both tall, white Amazons and female warriors who, according to a captured male, lived in all-women villages and once a year invited men from surrounding tribes to a mating festival. Their leader, Orellana was told, ate with gold and silver utensils, and the villages were littered with golden female idols. However, Orellana never uncovered the vast quantities of gold he heard about.

Portuguese explorer Francisco Raposo may have discovered the remains of *El Dorado*'s kingdom, apparently devastated by an earthquake. His 1754 report describes relics of a great city, with stone-paved streets, elaborate plazas and stately architecture, beautiful statues, hieroglyphics and colorful frescoes – and a handful of gold coins.

This fascinating city has never been rediscovered, yet the eccentric Briton, Fawcett – described by colleagues as both a dreamer and a rascal – wrote in 1925, "It is certain that amazing ruins of ancient cities, ruins incomparably older than those of Egypt, exist in the far interior of Mato Grosso." Fawcett obtained a 10-inch black stone image allegedly taken from the ruined city by Raposo, and his irresistible fascination with the stone led him to venture several times into Brazil's deep interior, where he was eventually lost.

Dreams of *El Dorado* continue. In the early 1980s and again in 1996, gold was discovered in the Serra Pelada mountains in the Amazon. Each discovery drew thousands of prospectors – sparking a new rush to become rich from the same yellow metal that first brought the white man to the Amazon. ❑

RIGHT: artistic view of the idyllic Amerindian life.

Those interested in Brazil's development and the bravura of the entrepreneurs can reach both Tucuruí and the Carajás mine at **Serra Norte** by plane from Belém. The treacherous terraces of the Serra Pelada gold mine, made infamous in the late 1980s, no longer exists. The mine is mechanized, and the *garimpeiros* (gold prospectors) are long gone.

TIP

Most visitors breeze in and out of Manaus, stopping only to arrange a jungle tour. But Manaus has a surprisingly rich history, and an increasingly lively performing arts scene, making it worthwhile to spend time in the city itself.

Toward Manaus

Along the river from Belém, en route to Manaus, lies **Monte Alegre** ❼, a small village that became famous when American archaeologist Anna Roosevelt discovered pictographs and artifacts in caves in the area, which significantly altered existing ideas on human colonization in South America and the Amazon.

About 160 km (100 miles) further upstream, **Santarém** ❽ stands exactly halfway between Belém and Manaus, at the junction of the Tapajós and Amazonas rivers. Founded in 1661 as a fort to keep foreign interests out of the mid-Amazon before the arrival of the Portuguese, Santarém was the center of a thriving Amerindian culture. Nearby lie the rubber plantations of **Belterra** and **Fordlandia**, which were expensive failures set up by the Ford Motor Company in the 1930s.

This mid-Amazon town, has the comfortable Amazon Park Hotel and riverboats that bring produce for the busy daily market along the waterfront. Most one-day boat tours travel up the Tapajós as far as **Alter do Chão**, site of the original settlement and a superb beach some 38 km (23 miles) from Santarém. The white sand beach forms a long curving spit that almost closes off the **Lago Verde** lagoon from the river. Also reachable by car, the village has a simple fish restaurant, a *pousada* and a number of weekend homes for Santarém's wealthy.

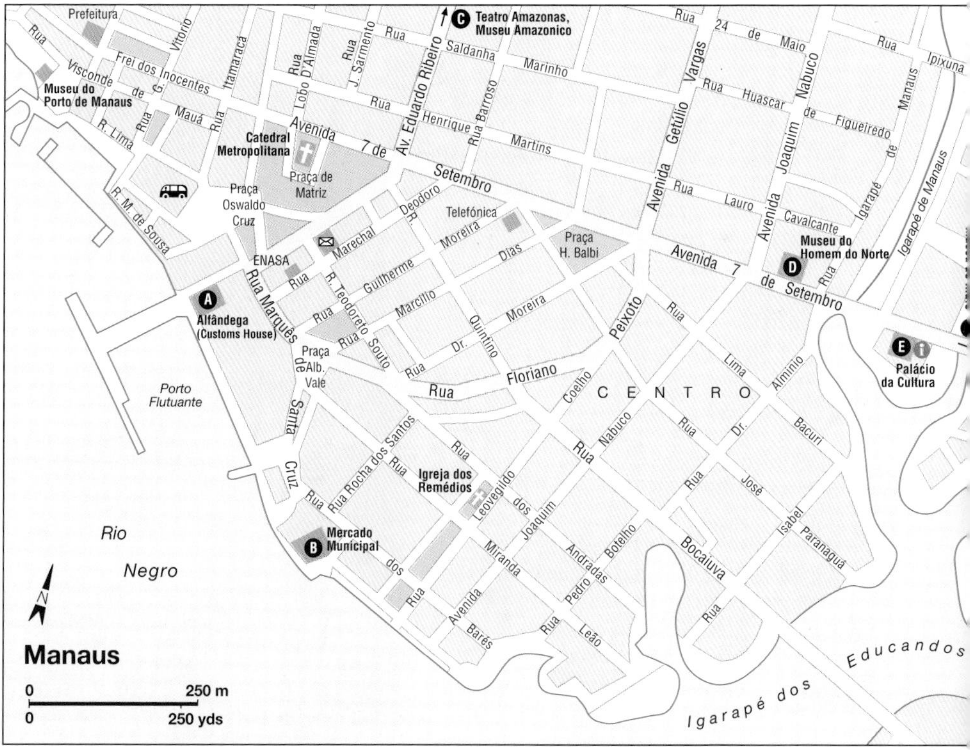

In Alter do Chão, the **Centro do Preservação de Arte Indígena** (Center for the Preservation of Indigenous Art) exhibits art and crafts made by a number of Amazon tribes (open daily). Most hotels organize trips to the **Floresta Nacional do Tapajós** (National Forest Reserve), a well-preserved area of original forest.

Maps:
Area 272
City 280

The port city

The city of **Manaus** ❾ is an oddity, an urban extravagance that turns its back on the rich surrounding forest and survives instead on federal subsidies, its exotic past and, increasingly, on tourism. Its moving spirit has always been quick riches. Once it had Art Nouveau grandeur; then, in the latter half of the 20th century it acquired an image of a tawdry electronics bazaar justified only by its status as a free port. Now, an ambitious restoration program is breathing new life into the city's architectural and cultural aspects. The port city's strategic position, close to the point where the three greatest tributaries form the Amazon river, means that it has long been the collecting point for forest produce from a vast area, and today is an important base for jungle tours.

Manaus still has reminders of its rubber wealth at the turn of the 20th century. British engineers in 1906 built the **Alfândega** Ⓐ (Customs House) out of Scottish bricks in an imperial style; and to accommodate the river's 14-meter (40-ft) rise and fall, they assembled foreign-made sections of the floating dock.

The **Mercado Municipal** Ⓑ, on Rua dos Barés, southward along the dockside, is a busy market filled with regional produce, from exotic fruit to magic herbs to cure all ills. Handicrafts can also be bought there. The market is housed in an interesting cast-iron building, imported from Europe in 1882, which is a replica of the old Les Halles market in Paris (open daily 8am–6pm).

Busy dockside in Manaus.

BELOW: the floating port of Manaus.

The **Teatro Amazonas** **C** (Amazon Opera House; open for tours Mon–Sat 9am–4pm), located in the northern part of downtown, was begun in 1881, after complaints from European touring companies who had been forced to play in smaller halls. Arriving there to sing during a cholera scare, the Italian tenor Enrico Caruso returned to Europe without disembarking. After the inaugural performance of *La Gioconda* there were scant records of other operas before the boom collapsed. The theater has been restored four times since it was constructed. The columns and banisters are of English cast-iron, with stage curtains, chandeliers and mirrors supplied by France. The marble came from Italy and the porcelain from Venice. Decorative motifs show the meeting of the Amazon waters and scenes from romantic literature about the Amerindians. The Teatro is the venue for ballet, opera, and theater performances during the evening, while the **Teatro da Instalação** on Rua Frei José dos Inocentes hosts free music and dance performances (open May–Dec Mon–Fri 6pm) in a newly restored historic building.

The **Museu do Homem do Norte** **D** (Northern Man Museum), on Avenida Sete de Setembro 1385, gives a good idea of traditional lifestyles (open Mon–Fri 9am–noon and 1–5pm). Also worth a look is the nearby wedding cake-like **Palácio da Cultura** **E**, a former palace, then seat of the state government and now the venue for cultural events.

Though its rubber industry enjoyed a brief wartime recovery, Manaus was not rescued from lingering decay until 1967, when it was declared a free trade zone. To take advantage of tax breaks, hundreds of factories have installed themselves in the industrial zone. A Zona Franca selling electronic consumer goods has also sprung up in the city center. Prices will hardly excite foreigners.

BELOW: the famous Teatro Amazonas, Manaus.

The narrow streets of the port district are lined with stores selling goods to those who live on outlying tributaries. There is busy trade in some of the 1,500 different varieties of river fish and, in a separate section, Amerindian artifacts, basketware, *umbanda* items and *guaraná* – a popular ginseng-like herbal energy preparation. More Amerindian relics can be seen at the **Salesian Museu do Indio** **F** (Rua Duque de Caxias 296; open Mon–Fri and Sat am).

Maps: Area 272 City 280

Outside the center

A 20-minute ride out of the city along the Estrada Ponta Negra leads to **CIGS**, the army's training school for jungle warfare. There is an excellent zoo (open daily except Mon 9.30am–4.30pm) stocked with hundreds of Amazonian animals.

The **National Amazonian Research Institute** (INPA) carries out advanced studies with the help of many top foreign scientists. The aquatic mammals division has a collection of manatees, freshwater dolphins and other species (about 25 minutes by taxi along the Estrada do Aleixo; open Mon–Fri 9am–noon and 2–4pm, Sat am).

The **Tropical Hotel** (tel: 658 5000), situated on the Praia da Ponta Negra, 20 km (12 miles) outside the city, has become the social center of Manaus. Its modern architecture is hardly tropical, but the gardens, circular swimming pool and, above all, the excellent swimming in the **Rio Negro** during the low-water season, make it a major attraction. The hotel operates daily boat tours 9 km (5 miles) up the Rio Negro to **Lago Salvador** and the **Guedes Igarapé**. Visitors may fish, swim, walk the forest paths and eat at a floating restaurant. An overnight stay at the lake allows time to travel up the *igarapé* (a forest backwater or creek) by motorized canoe and go flashlighting for alligators.

Grains, cereals and spices on sale at the Mercado Municipal in Manaus.

BELOW: the bustling *Zona Franca*, duty-free zone, in Manaus.

Day trips from Manaus

Several tour companies operate day-long river trips that follow a well-beaten track toward the **Lago de Janauary** ecological park to examine the Victoria Regia giant waterlilies (best from April to September). The boats then turn toward the "meeting of the waters". The warm, clear waters of the Rio Negro collide with the silty Rio Solimões and run parallel without mixing for 20 km (12 miles) in a great churning pattern through which tour boats pass. Some trips pause on **Terra Nova** island, where river dwellers show their rubber-tapping skills and sell souvenirs. The leading operator is Paradise (tel: 092-633 8301); Swallows and Amazons (tel: 622 1246) is another.

Jungle Lodges

A three-day trip allows visitors to fish for piranha, watch birds leaving their roosts at sunrise and, during the March–August high-water season, explore the *igapos* or flooded woodland by canoe. Guides may want to catch a caiman, but this is detrimental in the long term. Among jungle lodges, the most popular is the Ariaú Amazon Towers on the banks of the Rio Negro (tel: 622 5000), reached after a three-hour boat ride or by helicopter from Manaus.

The luxurious Pousada dos Guanavenas (tel: 656 1500; www.guanavenas.com.br) on Silves island – reached by a combination of boat and bus – has a panoramic view over Lago Canacari, near **Itacoatiara** ❿. The Amazon Lodge (tel: 656 3878), some 80 km (50 miles) south of Manaus on the Mamori River, near the town of **Careiro**, offers the visitor something more modest. Also to the south of the Solimões is the Janauaca Jungle Lodge, set on the banks of a placid lake.

BELOW: life along the River Amazon.

River cruises

The **Anavilhanas Arquipelago** on the Rio Negro is one of the best options for a longer river cruise. Various operators organize trips to the archipelago, usually of about a week's duration; or a trip for Portuguese speakers can be arranged with the IBDF forestry institute in Manaus a trip to the **Parque Nacional do Jaú** ⓫, close to Nova Airão. Due north of São Gabriel da Cachoeira, reachable by boat or plane from Manaus, is the **Pico da Neblina** ⓬, at 3,014 meters (6,630 ft) Brazil's highest mountain.

Map on page 272

TIP

On any trip to the jungle, bring insect repellent, and wear long sleeves and long trousers to protect yourself.

Traveling by boat

Although a growing number of roads are being built in the Amazon, rivers remain by far the most practical form of transport for most people. Locals, and a few intrepid tourists, use the picturesque, cheap and, in many ways, practical *gaiolas* that ply the waters of the Amazon River system. There is no better way to appreciate the character of the rural people of the Amazon than by travelling aboard a *gaiola*.

Although accommodation on board these riverboats is extremely basic, the open-sided decks festooned with hammocks are a logical solution to the slow, pitching gait of the boats and the sultry, humid climate. The movement of the boat keeps insects away, and many more passengers can be accommodated than by more conventional use of the space.

The trip from Manaus to Belém takes a little over a week – as long as there are no breakdowns. However, there are shorter trips that will give much the same flavor – one or two days is usually enough for most people – for example **Santarém** to **Obidos**. On any *gaiola* it is advisable to take your own food, hammock, and

BELOW: giant *Victoria Amazónica* water lilies.

Map on page 272

bottled water. The food served on board is usually basic, often badly cooked, and occasionally inedible. Toilet facilities are extremely limited, and by the end of the journey they can be unpleasantly smelly. To offset these hardships, you will experience the closeness of the river and the forest at their most magical.

You will also be forced to come to terms with the pace of life in Amazonia, which is somewhere between very slow and stationary. Generally speaking, it is better to travel upstream because the boats keep closer to the edge of the river, where the current is slower. Travelling downstream, you may find yourself several hundred yards from either shore, with only a distant view of the vegetation. Bear in mind, however, that these trips are essentially a way of getting from A to B, and you will be lucky to see much wildlife.

For the less intrepid, there are better equipped vessels with cabins and regular bunks. The boats are run by the government ENASA line, principally for tourists. These are luxurious by comparison with the *gaiolas*, with a bar, restaurant and observation deck. They even make stops to allow passengers to soak up the Amazon experience.

Whichever vessel you choose, a voyage on the river is an experience that will never be forgotten. But unless you want your trip to include many frustrations and hours, or even days, spent waiting, you would be advised to book and pay for it in advance on one of the tourist vessels.

Those with time to spare can travel up the Solimões as far as **Benjamin Constant** and **Letícia** (in Colombia) on the Peruvian-Columbian border, where it becomes the Marañón River. Launches from Manaus – subject to frequent delays – usually take about eight days. The riverbanks are lined with small homesteads, where *caboclos* scratch a living from a few cultivated acres, fish and sell palm-hearts, or turtles to passing boats.

The traditional Amazon riverboat is called a "gaiola," meaning "birdcage." This refers to the cage-like sides of the open decks, but the image of the songbird is also pertinent to the long, intricate ballads that the local passengers sing to while away the hours.

BELOW: a Serra Pelada gold prospector. **RIGHT:** the lush rainforest.

Roraima

The Rio Branco drains Brazil's northernmost state, Roraima, whose dense forests and unmapped borders divide the Amazon and Orinoco river basins. Until a highway was built in 1977 from Manaus, with considerable loss of life due to clashes with Amerindian tribes, its capital **Boa Vista** ⓭ was isolated from the rest of Brazil.

As well as it being the last truly undiscovered fragment of Latin America, Roraima is according to legend the location of the mythical El Dorado. The mysterious, flat-topped **Mount Roraima** ⓮ is believed to have inspired Sir Arthur Conan Doyle's novel *The Lost World*.

The 27,000-strong Yanomami Amerindian tribe – the continent's largest and least acculturated indigenous group – occupy a region straddling the Brazil-Venezuela border in the **Parima** mountain range – a region of jagged, forested peaks and chasms.

The rare minerals on the Yanomami's land have attracted the ruthless interests of businessmen and *garimpeiros*. Invasions in the 1990s wiped out 20 percent of the population owing to attacks or disease. In 1992 Yanomami land was finally demarcated, but Brazil continues to refuse to recognize tribal land ownership. ❑

THE RICHES OF THE RIVER AMAZON

The world's greatest river and largest rainforest is estimated to contain one-tenth of the plant, animal and insect species to be found on earth

The River Amazon is one of the greatest symbols of Brazil. It rises in the snows of the Peruvian Andes just a short distance from the Pacific Ocean. It then travels across the heart of South America – a distance of 6,570 km (4,080 miles) – before it flows out into the Atlantic Ocean at the equator. It has about 15,000 tributaries, some of which, like the Araguaia and the Madeira, are mighty rivers in themselves. Just past Manaus, one of the most spectacular river sights is the meeting of the "black waters" of the River Negro with the "white waters" of the River Solimões, two other Amazon tributaries. The Amazon has a greater flow than any other river, depositing in the ocean each year about one-fifth of the world's freshwater.

At its mouth the Amazon is 300 km (185 miles) wide, a labyrinth of channels and islands, one of which has a greater land mass than Switzerland. The water flows with such force that it still tastes fresh 180 km (110 miles) out into the ocean.

RAINFOREST AND AMERINDIANS

The Amazon's network of dark, dense jungles has often been referred to as The Great Green Hell. In the west of the Amazon basin, it is still possible to fly for several hours and see nothing below but a carpet of tropical forest, broken only by rivers snaking their way through the trees. The Amazon has remained virtually unchanged for the past 100 million years, for it did not pass through the same ice ages that altered other parts of the world's landscapes. Some areas are still inhabited by Amerindian groups who have never had contact with the world outside their own jungle.

△ **AMAZON CRUISES**
A boat safari along an Amazonian side-creek, taking in the sights, sounds and smells of the jungle, is one of the highlights for many visitors to the region.

▷ **BLACK SPIDER MONKEY**
This delightful animal uses its tail to swing from branch to branch in the forest.

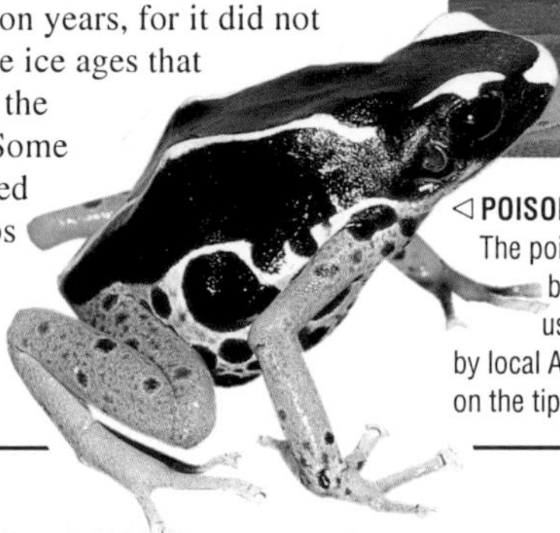

◁ **POISON ARROW FROG**
The poison from this brightly colored frog used to be extracted by local Amerindians to use on the tip of arrows.

△ **RIO MADEIRA**
Though just a tributary of the Amazon, the River Madeira itself flows over a distance of more than 1,60 km (1,000 miles).

◁ **URUCU BERRIES**
Amerindians treasure the Urucu tree for its berries. They contain a red-colored dye the indians use to paint their faces and bodies.

JUNGLE LODGING
t the Ariau Amazon Towers otel guests can hear the ewitching sounds of the opical forest at night.

▽ **VICTORIA REGIS**
This water lily has enormous, circular leaves that can be up to 2 metres (6½ feet) across.

△ **RUBBER TAPPING**
Thousands of families, living deep in the rainforest, still tap rubber trees for the latex.

▷ **TOUCAN**
This striking-looking bird, a recognizable image of the Amazon forest, uses its huge yellow bill to crush the seeds it feeds on.

DEFORESTATION IN THE AMAZON

About 16 percent of the Amazon forest – an area the size of France or twice the size of Colorado – has already been cut down, almost all over the past 40 years. Most of the destruction has taken place in the east of the basin, "opened up" in the 1960s and 1970s when the military government built a vast network of roads. Cattle companies then moved in, slashing and burning the forest to sow pasture. "Avança Brasil" was announced in 2001. The US$40-billion program will include the building of 10,000 km (6,215 miles) of highways, electric dams, and power lines. Some 30 percent of the Trans-Amazon and 40 percent of the Cuiabá-Santarém paving has been completed. The program has been halted pending reviews by the government.

THE CENTER-WEST

The capital region, a territory of vast plains and pockets of wildlife-rich wetland, is still in the process of colonization

Setting aside the federal district, this region is truly Brazil's "Wild West," whose parallels with North America's eponymous land in centuries past are manifold. *Bandeirantes* first traveled west to push back the frontiers of discovered territory, seeking gold but, for the most part, surviving by hacking down swathes of jungle so they could run cattle on the land.

The vast *cerrado* (savanna plains, the terrain of most of the region) is still sparsely populated, and many modern-day fortune hunters still claim their prize from the land and then move on, while others stay to run huge isolated cattle ranches. Dusty frontier towns, like the set of a Western film, are spread thinly. There are even still a few Amerindians.

Since 1960, the region has been host to Brazil's capital city, and has experienced rapid development over the past three decades. Intensive soybean cultivation is now the center-west's principal source of income, with cattle-raising a close second. Today, a staggering 85 percent of the population of 14 million live in urban areas. Most visitors, however, still come for adventure in an untamed land.

The chief attraction, especially for bird watchers and fishing enthusiasts, is the Pantanal, an enormous seasonally flooded swamp with a unique population of water birds. Tourists might otherwise come to see spectacular canyons and waterfalls; to ride horseback through cowboy country; to view the high plains from a hot-air balloon; to witness pioneering history; or to learn about Amerindian culture.

While in the center-west, you might wish to see Brasília. Modern, orderly Brasília – so incongruous in the middle of the empty *cerrado* – was conceived as a symbol of national unity, located physically in the center of the country.

It was intended to provide the impetus to populate the west, but Brasília today has few links with the wild country surrounding ❑

PRECEDING PAGES: a statue of former president Juscelino Kubitschek before the Palácio da Justiça, Brasília.
LEFT: land clearance in Mato Grosso.

THE WILD WEST

The rapidly developing backland states of Rondônia, Mato Grosso, and Mato Grosso do Sul offer visitors a glimpse of cowboy and Amerindian culture and the natural paradise of the Pantanal marshland

Map on page 296

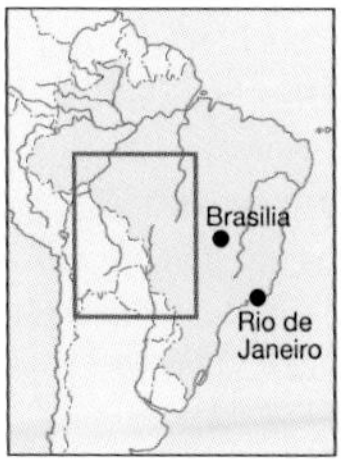

Soldier-president Emilio Medici described Brazil's wild western frontier territory in the early 1970s as "a land without men for men without land." It was an area inhabited by rural migrants from the overpopulated south, and wild it was until well into the 20th century. Overland travel between the western states and the Atlantic coast was one of Brazil's great adventures.

Brazil's western states stand on an immense elevated plateau three times the size of France, from which spring the northern-flowing tributaries of the Amazon, and those draining southward into the rivers Paraná and Paraguay, and thence to the River Plate. Only in the past 20 years have paved roads penetrated the region, bringing with them adventurers and dreamers who have quickly introduced modern civilization to Brazil's backlands.

The states of Mato Grosso, Mato Grosso do Sul, and Rondônia still embody the elusive myth of the last frontier, where virgin land is free and quick riches await the strong and the brave. In truth, however, this romance has long since moved onward and thousands of new arrivals a year find the best land settled, and often protected against squatters by *pistoleiros*, or hired gunmen, although migration has decreased sharply over the past 20 years. Brash, brawling new towns, their unruly main streets choked with red dust sprouted up almost overnight. The frontier has its share of losers, who filter back to the shantytowns of São Paulo, defeated by malaria and the labor of hacking down the forest barrier. Notwithstanding this, the region is currently experiencing an economic boom, triggered partly by the growth of tourism, but also by cattle ranching and agricultural successes.

This was never a land without men. The first gold-seeking *bandeirantes* who forced their way up the rivers to Cuiabá, the capital of Mato Grosso, in the 1720s, discovered a forest filled with often hostile Amerindian tribes. Today, the tribes of Mato Grosso and Rondônia form an important part of Brazil's few surviving Amerindians. There are still occasional clashes between settlers and the Amerindian tribes that have been driven deep into the forest, where one or two groups untouched by Westernization still exist.

Rondon's mission

In 1890, Cândido Mariano da Silva Rondon began a military mission to link Cuiabá to the coast by telegraph, a Herculean effort that was to revolutionize popular awareness of the forest and its Amerindian inhabitants. In 1907, he agreed to link Cuiabá with Porto Velho, capital of Rondônia, to the north, by cutting across unmapped Amerindian territory, on condition that his men would also compile a complete ethnographic, plant, and animal survey during the course of the eight-year mission.

LEFT: Aquidauana River in the Caiman Ecological Reserve, Pantanal.
BELOW: *capivara* in the Pantanal.

The land rights of the oppressed Terena Amerindians, in valleys to the west of Campo Grande, were supported by Lieutenant Rondon. Today, they are regarded as one of the most successfully integrated in Brazil, owing to their astuteness in adapting to capitalism.

Rondon's saddle, riddled with Amerindian arrows, survives as evidence of his first contact with Amerindians. His idealism won over hostile Amerindian tribes and bloodthirsty white woodsmen alike. The telegraph, operated by some of these Amerindians, became obsolete almost immediately after it was built. But Rondon's thrilling lectures about the forest and the prestige he was later to gain by escorting former US president Theodore Roosevelt on an Amazon expedition, helped him set up the first Amerindian protection service in 1910, which he developed into a highly humane organization. He was made a marshal in 1955.

The state of Rondônia was named after Rondon, himself the grandson of Amerindians and one of the most striking figures in modern Brazilian history.

In 1935 the French anthropologist Claude Lévi-Strauss followed the remains of Rondon's line, establishing camp in tiny settlements like Pimenta Bueno and Vilhena, where abandoned telegraphists had received no supplies for eight years.

The Wild West

Map on facing page

Today, these are bustling cities astride the BR 364 Highway – which is also the backbone of the new frontier. Before it was asphalted in 1984 with World Bank financing, buses and trucks sometimes took months to travel the 1,460 km (907 miles) between Cuiabá and Porto Velho.

Porto Velho

Porto Velho ❶, Rondônia's capital on the River Madeira, is within striking distance by bus or boat of Manaus and the river Amazon itself. Like Rondônia – which became a state only in 1981, after many years as an unclassified and largely unsettled region – Porto Velho has grown too fast for its own good. In the 1950s, Rondônia's population was just 37,000, mostly leftovers from the rubber-tapping era. Today, the state has over a million residents. They were attracted by colonization programs that promised them patches of fertile soil that gave high yields of coffee and cocoa.

Porto Velho was born over a century ago from one of man's tragic attempts to tame the Amazon: the Madeira–Mamoré Railway. A restored steam locomotive still cheerfully plies a tiny section of track on occasional Sundays, its engineer the last custodian of the territory's dramatic history.

In the 1860s, American and British engineers began building a railway that was intended to link landlocked Bolivia and its rubber forests to the River Amazon and the Atlantic Ocean. The railway would bypass treacherous rapids on the River Madeira. But for every rail laid, legend held that a man died of fever or malaria. Of the 900 American laborers sent to the Amazon in 1879, 80 drowned, and 141 died of fever, as did 400 Brazilians and 200 Bolivians – all for just 7 km (4 miles) of track.

BELOW: a cattle-drive slows highway traffic.

Helping out in the timber yard.

Bankruptcies, mutiny, and death dogged the railway – nicknamed the Devil's Railroad by laborers. In 1903, Brazil bought rubber-rich Acre from Bolivia in exchange for completing the railway. Ten years and 30,000 diseased workers later, 370 km (230 miles) of track was laid, just in time for the collapse of the Amazon rubber trade. A visit to the cemetery a few kilometers from the station is interesting, but take a guide.

There are short trips from Porto Velho down the Madeira River on one of the lively two-story floating bars, during which impromptu music is often played. Porto Velho itself has the Museu Ferroviário in one of the old station sheds as railway memorabilia and Casa do Artesão (Praça Madeira-Mamoré; open Thur–Sun), where Amerindian handicrafts are on sale.

Gold, diamonds and feathers

Cuiabá ❷, in the center of Mato Grosso, was the west's first settlement, founded in 1719 by a group of slave-hunters from São Paulo who struck shallow gold and diamond deposits. The resulting rush of prospectors made Cuiabá the third most important city in colonial Brazil. Then, a century ago, the city found a new resource and acquired fame as a major supplier of exotic bird feathers to the milliners of Paris.

Today, this prosperous, hot city is a major starting point for trips into the Pantanal as well as the capital of an immense logging, farming, and mining state. Unfortunately, little of colonial Cuiabá survives. The city's cathedral church of Bom Jesus de Lapa has a small adjoining museum of religious artifacts. The square, Praça da República, is the location of Sedtur, the state tourism authority, with a very helpful visitor center.

BELOW: Véu de Noiva (Bride's Veil) waterfall at Chapada dos Guimarães. **BELOW RIGHT:** the red-necked tuiuiú.

Map on page 296

The excellent **Museu do Indio Marechal Rondon** (at the university entrance, 10 minutes by bus from downtown; open Mon–Fri 7.30–11.30am and 1.30–5.30pm, weekends 7.30–11.30am) shows the artifacts and lifestyle of the Xingu tribes. Some of the items are on sale at a handicrafts shop run by FUNAI, the government Amerindian affairs bureau. Other landmarks are the Governor's Residence and the **Fundação Cultural de Mato Grosso** (Praça da República 151; open weekdays pm only) in an historic mansion, which houses three interesting museums: Antropológica, História Natural and Cultura Popular.

Fish is Cuiabá's culinary forte. Piranha may be deadly in the water, but legend has it that in soup they possess aphrodisiac powers – try the *caldo de piranha* (piranha broth). Another regional specialty not to be missed is *peixada* – fish chargrilled on a spit.

After the lowland heat, relief is close at hand 70 km (45 miles) from Cuiabá. The **Chapada dos Guimarães National Park** is a rocky outcrop overlooking the flat plain of the Paraguay River and the Pantanal, 800 meters (2,600 ft) above sea level. In the misty cool of the Chapada's folded hills and jutting, monolithic rock formations are caves and stunning waterfalls. Local residents attest to the region's mystical qualities and confirm frequent UFO sightings. These uplands provide one of the many water sources for the Pantanal marshlands below.

Later, the road curves through the **Portão de Inferno** (Gates of Hell) – a vertical drop that marks the edge of the sandstone escarpment. Overhead tower pencil-like rock formations. Further on, visitors can admire the 86-meter (280-ft) **Véu da Noiva** (Bride's Veil) waterfall from above, or walk for half an hour down the thickly wooded canyon to reach its base. Further into the Chapada is the **Casa de Pedra** – a natural cave-house capped by an immense stone shelf – and the **Caverna Aroe Jari**, on whose walls there are primitive paintings. Guides, lamps and equipment are needed to enter these caves.

Chapada dos Guimarães ❸ is a historical town, with its 200-year-old church of Santana, which grew up to provide Cuiabá's hungry miners with food. It is a good base for many excursions into the lovely, surrounding countryside and the national park of the same name. Just outside the town is a monument to mark the geodesic center of South America.

Wildlife preserve

The highlight of any visit to western Brazil is the **Pantanal ❹**, a vast natural paradise that is one of Brazil's major ecological attractions. Because it does not feature the dense vegetation of the Amazon, wildlife is much easier to spot here. The Pantanal comprises 230,000 sq km (89,000 sq miles) of seasonally flooded swampland offering a density of tropical wildlife unknown outside of Africa, and the world's largest concentration of great wading birds: storks, egrets, ibises, the elegant roseate spoonbill, and the stately tuiuiú or jabirú storks that stand as tall as a human child. Basking caiman, deer, otters, emus, boa constrictors, and monkeys are also to be found in abundance. The area contains a number of globally threatened species

BELOW: Pantanal caimans.

Giant otter in the Pantanal.

Jeep tours, with accommodation in lodges, are offered by travel agents in Cuiabá, Campo Grande, and Corumbá. A two-day trip is a good option, and may involve visiting the woodstorks' treetop nesting sites, fishing for *dourado* or waiting in a hideout for the elusive *onça pintada,* or jaguar.

Though the Pantanal offers sanctuary for migratory geese and ducks moving between Argentina and Central America, most of the 600 species of water birds found here are residents that follow the changing water levels inside the huge swamp, in pursuit of the 250 species of fish that support them in the food chain.

Seasonal precipitation

Rainfall cycles are the key to the Pantanal: from October to April (January and February are months to avoid) the rains flow into the northern part of the Pantanal from the hilly regions, at a time when the southern part is drier. The rivers rise by more than 3 meters (10 ft), flooding their banks and spreading into huge *baias* or closed lakes where fish have been breeding. The waters activate ground vegetation and enable the overhanging trees to produce fruit on which the fish gorge themselves, before swimming through open canals to spawn in the rivers.

Because the altitude varies little throughout the 600-km (375-mile) extension of the Pantanal, waters drain very slowly, producing a tremendous surge in fertility. During high water in the northern part, the southern Pantanal has shallow water, which attracts the wading birds. After April, the situation is reversed and the birds fly northward to nest between June and September. Here the lakes are once again cut off from the rivers and their fish become captives for predators.

BELOW: sunset over the Pantanal's still waters.

The northern Pantanal

The northern edge of the Pantanal may be reached on a tour from Cuiabá. All of the better travel agencies in the city operate or are associated with *fazendas* (lodges) in the swamp. These hotels supply boats, ground transportation, and sometimes even hot-air balloons to visit the nesting-sites and lakes where the wildlife concentrate – but visitors must be prepared to wake before sunrise and endure the mosquitoes. Care must be taken to choose the right region in the Pantanal, and a hotel and guide supplied by a reputable travel agency. A recommended agency is Anaconda (Rua Mal Deodaro 2142; tel: 624-4142; anaconda@ anacondapantanal.com.br). There are also a number of simpler *Portos de Pesca* – campsites and facilities for sport fishermen.

Santo Antônio de Leverger marks the edge of the swamp, and is just 28 km (17 miles) south of Cuiabá on state highway 040. Here, light aircraft take off for the hotels and *fazendas*. Boats may also be hired as far as **Barão de Melgaço** ❺, which was once the region's sugar mill center.

Close by is the **Baia Chacororé**, an immense shallow lake that is filled with caiman and has flocks of pink spoonbills and larger mammals, which gather in numbers around its shore, particularly at dusk (also the mosquitoes' favorite feeding time) and dawn.

River tours

The sleepy town here is the starting point for the Pantanal's most luxurious option: 10- or 17-day river tours extending as far south as the city of Corumbá down the Cuiabá, São Lourenço and Paraguay rivers. Barco Cidade Barão de Melgaço, a floating hotel with eight double cabins, good cooking and air conditioning, is operated by the Pérola do Pantanal agency. Pérola do Pantanal also has two big boats for fishing and a smaller one for day trips in the Corumbá area, so there is plenty of opportunity for birdwatching from the decks, or venturing into the lakes.

The boat takes seven days to descend the river and 10 days to return to Cuiabá again. Shorter trips are also much favored by the European visitors. During the low-water season, the floating hotel operates in the Southern Pantanal only.

Pérola do Pantanal also operates in conjunction with the highly recommended Passargada Pousada, reachable only by boat and situated on a small tributary of the Cuiabá river. This 10-apartment hotel is run by Marival Sigeault, who takes his visitors out on treks and willingly imparts Pantanal lore.

Due south of Cuiabá on state highway 060 is **Poconé** ❻, where the Trans-Pantaneira Highway begins. Poconé itself is a dry area given over to farming and the swamps nearby have all been disturbed by gold-mining, wildlife poaching and excessive fishing. But it is the jumping-off point for some of the best parts of the Pantanal.

Porto Cercado, 200 km (125 miles) from Cuiabá, has a few hotels that provide good access to wildlife, with large lakes and a superb nesting-site for woodstorks, ibises, and spoonbills nearby. Well-situated beside the river, Pousada Porto Cercado has 34 rooms in reasonable comfort. Hotel Cabanas do

Map on page 296

BELOW: at home in the Caiman Ecological Reserve, Pantanal.

Pantanal on the River Piraim has 18 rooms. Both hotels cost upwards of US$50 per night, plus stiff ground transfer charges. Hiring boats is expensive, too: a canoe with a 25 horsepower outboard engine may be about US$20 an hour. Upstream is the much simpler lodging, the Baias do Pantanal.

From Poconé the Trans-Pantaneira Highway runs 145 km (90 miles) southward to **Porto Jofre** ❼ over 126 bridges. Begun in the 1970s, the highway was originally intended to link Cuiabá with Corumbá, but local political wrangles and ecologists' pressure cut it short. Because the road runs parallel to the rivers, huge bodies of water collect beside it, ensuring views of alligators and bird life even for those unwilling to get out of their cars. The highway is in a poor state of conservation, but it does permit forest guards to control part of the Pantanal and give visitors access.

There are also irregular cargo boats, usually transporting cattle, which sail 185 km (115 miles) down the River São Lourenço to Corumbá, and which may take passengers, by negotiation with the captain (bring your own hammock and food; facilities are likely to be very basic.)

Beside the highway are two hotels, the comfortable Pousada das Araras and the much simpler Pousada Pixaim. At the highway's end is the Hotel Porto Jofre (tel: 065-623 0236), specializing in fishing and ecological safari trips, as well as the hotels Beira-Rio and Piuval. On the São Lourenço, in the heart of the swamp and accessible only by aeroplane, is the Hotel Pirigara.

Other hotel-*fazendas* include the Pantanal Rios, 40 km (25 miles) south of the town of **Cáceres** ❽ on the Paraguay River. From this town the BR 364 goes northward to Porto Velho, and there are daily buses to San Matias on the Bolivian border and on to the city of Santa Cruz de la Sierra.

TIP

The place to buy cowboy accessories in Campo Grande is Rua 14 de Julho, where there is a row of shops selling everything from cowboy boots to gunbelts and western-style saddles.

BELOW: Pantanal fisherman in a dug-out canoe.

The southern Pantanal

For the southern Pantanal in Mato Grosso do Sul, the entry points are Campo Grande and Corumbá. Mato Grosso do Sul's state capital, **Campo Grande** ❾ began life in 1889 and is still an overgrown cowboy town that has borrowed some habits from Paraguay's Chaco. The **Museu Dom Bosco** (Rua Barão do Rio Branco 1843; open daily) has interesting Amerindian exhibits and a large insect collection.

Corumbá ❿, situated on the Bolivian border opposite **Puerto Suarez**, was founded in 1778. From here, there is access to the Pantanal by both road and river – it laps right into the city and even a brief boat tour gives a vivid impression. The more intrepid may be able to arrange rides on slow cement barges, small trading vessels, or cattle barges going as far as Porto Cercado or Barão de Melgaço. A selection of leatherwork, ceramics, Amerindian artifacts and other handicrafts are available at the Casa do Artesão, once the city's jail. A short drive along the Pantaneira highway back to Campo Grande offers interesting views of the swamps.

Nearby hotel-*fazendas* are Rio Vermelho (tel: 067-721 4373), Agua-Pé (tel: 067-241 2889); and Passo do Lontra Pantanal Parque (tel: 067-231 6569). The best option in the southern Pantanal is the huge Caiman Ecological Reserve (tel: 067-687 2102 or tel: 011-3079 6622 in São Paolo, fax: 067-687 2103), incorporating four luxury *pousadas* in an area of 53,00 hectares (130,000 acres) which even has its own airstrip close to **Miranda** on the Campo Grande–Corumbá highway. The owner, Roberto Klabin, has established his own wildlife reserve, the Réfugio Ecológico Caiman. Students and professors carrying out research mix with tourists. At the *fazenda* visitors can explore the Pantanal by foot, on horseback, by boat or by truck. ❑

Map on page 296

BELOW: a gold prospector sifts his precious booty.

BRASILIA AND GOIAS

The capital of Brazil represents the realization of a dream and is an impressive architectural monument, located at the edge of a formerly remote state cut by major river systems

Map on page 296

For over two centuries, it had been the aim of Brazilian visionaries to fill the vacuum in the center of their country with a new city. In 1891, Brazil's first republican government sent a scientific team to survey possible sites ı Goiás, where the three great rivers of the country rise – the Amazon, the 'araná and the São Francisco. For this purpose, too, a commission was sent ıter, in 1946, to conduct an aerial survey of the region. Yet until the election f president Juscelino Kubitschek in 1955, Brasília remained as an idea only.

Kubitschek made the development of Brasília the centerpiece of his camaign to modernize the country. The pace of the project was determined by polics; Kubitschek knew that if the city was ever to be completed, it had to be one by the end of his five-year term. He selected as his architect Oscar Jiemeyer, a communist and a student of Le Corbusier. Niemeyer decided to onfine himself to designing the major public buildings. An international jury elected the city plan, which was submitted by a friend of Niemeyer's.

LEFT: Giorgi's *The Warriors* honors the laborers who built Brasília.
BELOW: the Congresso Nacional building.

ìroundbreaking construction

'he work began in September 1956 on the highest and flattest of the five sites lentified by the aerial survey. The first task was to build a runway, which was sed to bring in the initial building materials and eavy equipment. **Brasília** ⓫ thus became the 'orld's first major city conceived in terms of air ccess. Only after construction had begun was a road ushed through from Belo Horizonte, 740 km (460 ailes) to the southeast. A dam followed and Lake aranoá began to emerge. By April 1960, the city oused 100,000 people and was ready for its inaugution as capital. In 1987 it was declared a World Herage Site by UNESCO, and in 2002 an elegant iple-span steel bridge was built over Lake Paranoá – ıscelino Kubitschek Bridge.

Most visitors will come to Brasília the way Kubschek first came – by plane. After flying over the :mi-arid and sparsely inhabited Central Plateau, the ty suddenly emerges as a row of white building ocks set along a gentle rise above the artificial lake.

Overland, the most spectacular approach is by road om the northeast. After driving through miles of red ıst and gnarled scrub, known as *cerrado,* you reach eucalyptus-lined ridge just beyond **Planaltina**, the dest town in this region. Brasília is laid out in a eaming arc in the valley below.

Like the United Nations Secretariat in New York, e present-day city is trapped in a 1950s vision of e future. Built around the automobile, its urban core a complex of superhighways, which creates a hose environment for pedestrians.

TIP

Brazilía's streets were not made for walking. To see the city, take a city-tour which includes all the main sights.

While under construction, Brasília captured the world's imagination. Soon after, the world lost interest and Brasília became synonymous with technocracy run wild. Yet to this day, the building of Brasília remains a point of great pride among Brazilians. It was the only postwar project intended to serve the people, not industry; and it was entirely financed and built at the behest of an elected president, in a time of democracy. For all the flaws that are now evident, Costa speaks for the majority of Brazilians when he asserts, "The only important thing for me is that Brasília exists."

The first recommended stop in Brasília is the **Torre de Televisão** Ⓐ (Television Tower; open Tues–Sun 9am–6pm, Mon 2–8pm) at the highest point of the **Eixo Monumental** (Monumental Axis) that runs through the center of the city. A good map at the foot of the tower explains how the streets are laid out. An elevator to the top of the tower gives a bird's-eye view of Costa's plan: two gently curving arcs indicating the residential areas of the city, bisected by the Eixo Monument containing the buildings of government.

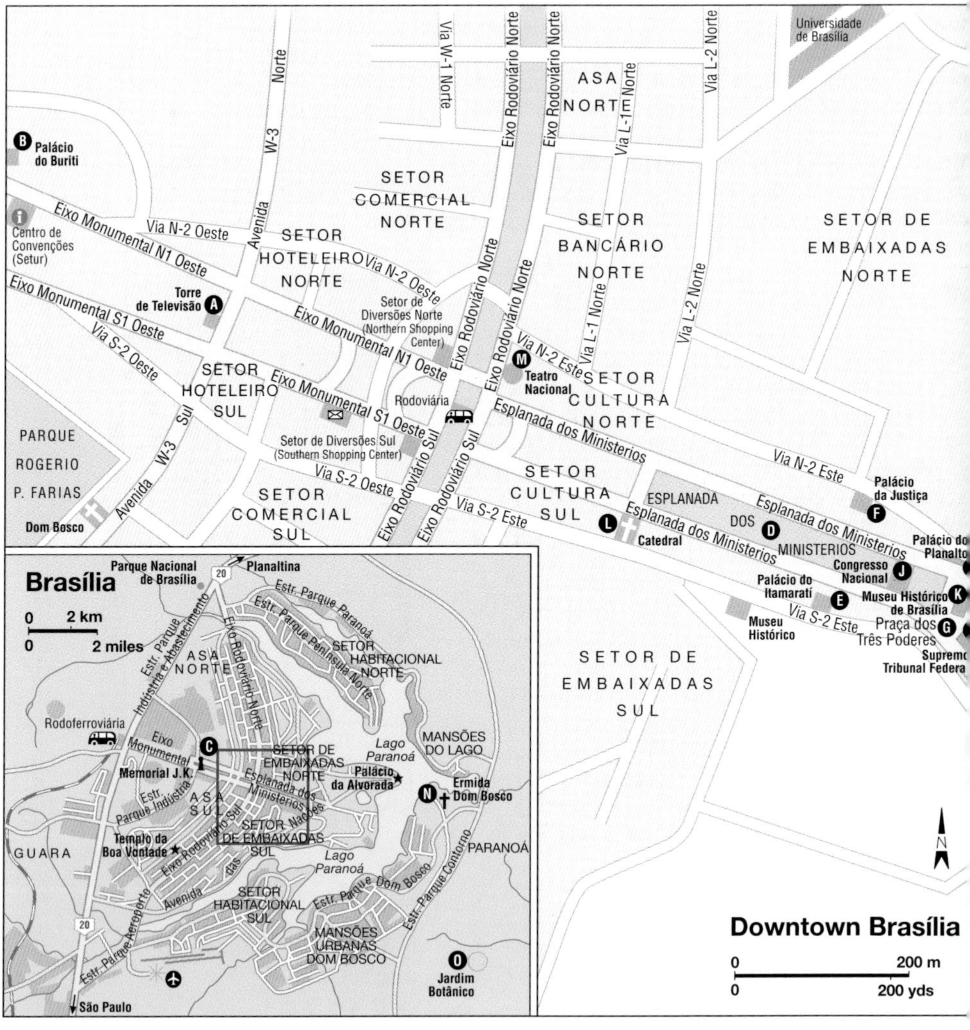

Costa's plan has been variously described as a cross, a bow and arrow, or an air-
lane. Costa accepts all these interpretations but claims he did not design Brasília
fit a preconceived symbol. Instead, he chose its shape to accommodate the
urvature of the terrain above the lake, while emphasizing the civic buildings at
ie center of the city. Costa's design was selected because of its simplicity and suit-
bility for a national capital.

he government sector

leading west from the center along the Eixo Monument, you next come to the
dministrative seat of the Federal District in **Palácio do Buriti B**, in pretty Praça
Municipal. Continuing westward you come to the **Memorial JK C** (open
'ues–Sun 9am–5.40pm, closed Mon), the memorial to Kubitschek. It was the first
uilding in Brasília that the military allowed Niemeyer to design after their takeover
1964. The curious sickle-shaped structure on top of the monument in which the
atue of Kubitschek stands seems more like a political gesture by Niemeyer than
symbol of Kubitschek's beliefs. Inside the monument is Kubitschek's tomb and
collection of memorabilia about his life and the construction of Brasília. One
iowcase contains a summary of the unsuccessful entries in the competition to
esign the city, including a proposal to house most of its population in 18 enormous
ower blocks over 300 meters (1,000 ft) high, housing 16,000 people.

Heading in the other direction from the Television Tower, down the hill past
ie main bus terminal, the Eixo Monument opens on to the **Esplanada dos
Iinistérios D** (Esplanade of the Ministries). A row of 16 pale green identical
ox-shaped buildings runs down both sides of the vast open boulevard. Each
uilding houses a different government department whose name is emblazoned

Map on facing page

TIP

The bustling downtown shopping malls – the northern and southern *conjuntos* either side of the *Rodoviária* provide relief from the antiseptic artificiality of most of the center.

BELOW: patterns of Brazil's artificial city.

in gold letters on the front. Since every ministry has long since outgrown it original quarters, they have sprouted additions out the back, connected in midai by concrete tubes to their mother ship. In the late 1960s, several buildings wer subject to arson attacks, reportedly by disgruntled civil servants protestin against their forced move from Rio.

Brasília's population is renowned for its sexual permissiveness. The city has the highest divorce rate in Brazil, and has been described as "a town where people are in bed by ten and home by six o'clock in the morning."

Niemeyer's best

Flanking the end of the Esplanade are Niemeyer's two finest buildings: th **Palácio do Itamaratí** Ⓔ, housing the Foreign Ministry, which floats in splen did isolation in the midst of a reflecting pool; and the **Palácio da Justiça** (Min istry of Justice; open Mon–Fri 10am–noon, 3–5pm) Ⓕ, whose six curtains o falling water on the exterior echo the natural waterfalls around Brasília.

Beyond the end of the Eixo Monument is the **Praça dos Três Poderes** Ⓖ (Plaza of the Three Powers) – a dense forest of political symbols. Name after the three divisions of powers under the Brazilian Constitution, the exec utive is represented by the **Palácio do Planalto** Ⓗ on the left, housing th president's offices, while the judiciary is represented by the **Suprem Tribunal Federal** Ⓘ (Supreme Court) on the right. Overshadowing both, ar chitecturally if not politically, are the twin towers and offset domes of th **Congresso Nacional** Ⓙ – the building whose silhouette is the signature o Brasília. Even the former monarchy has a place in the plaza. The rows of im perial palms behind the congress building were transplanted from Dom Joã VI's Botanical Garden in Rio.

On the plaza proper are a number of notable sculptures. The basaltic hea of Kubitschek protrudes from the marble walls of the small **Museu Históric de Brasília** Ⓚ (open Sun–Fri 9am–6pm), which i actually just a series of panels outlining the histor of Brasília and the most memorable sayings o Kubitschek, whose powers of hyperbole must hav rivaled his talent for construction.

BELOW: soldier guards a government building

In front of the supreme court is a blindfolded fig ure of Justice, sculpted by Alfredo Ceschiatti. Facin the Palácio do Planalto are the figures of *The War riors* by Bruno Giorgi, a tribute to the thousands o workers who built Brasília. A note of whimsy i added to the plaza by Niemeyer's pigeon house, th **Pombal**.

The most recent addition to the plaza is the **Pan theon Tancredo Neves** – a tribute to the foundin father of the New Republic, who died in April 198 before he could be sworn in as president. Inside th darkened interior is Brasília's most extraordinar and disturbing artwork. The mural, by João Camara depicts the story of an uprising in the 18th centur led by Brazil's best known revolutionary, Tiradente (Joaquim José da Silva Xavier). Painted in sever black and white panels (rather like Picasso's *Guer nica*), it is heavy with masonic symbolism.

The **Catedral Metropolitana da Nossa Senhor Aparecida** Ⓛ (open daily 8am–8pm) at the wester end of the Esplanada dos Ministérios is a uniqu concrete building with a spectacular stained-glas domed roof. Three hundred meters (330 yards) away n the northern side of the Eixo Monument near the Rodoviária, is the pyra-ıid-shaped **Teatro Nacional** Ⓜ (open daily 9am–6pm), where art shows and ther exhibitions are held.

Map on page 306

ıesidential Brasília

'o appreciate Brasília as a living city, it is necessary to leave the center and visit ıe areas where people actually live – the purpose-built *quadras* that are arrayed long the city's north and south wings. Each *quadra* is made up of six to eight ɔw-rise residential blocks, grouped around well-landscaped lawns and court-ards. Short commercial streets, which provide a range of basic services for the ɜsidents, are evenly interspersed between them. The *quadras* provide an essen-ally uniform standard of living across the city, which for many residents is a ʌelcome respite from the urban jungles of Brazil's coastal cities.

Lucío Costa's original pilot plan for Brasília gives the city a rigid shape.)nce all the *quadras* planned for the north wing are built, the city proper can row no further. The great surprise in the evolution of Brasília has been the xplosive growth of the "satellite cities" beyond its green belt. These cities ʌere originally settled by construction workers from the northeast, who ɜmained after their contracted work in the city was finished. Their numbers ave since swelled with new migrants and lower-middle-class residents, who ave sold the free apartments they were awarded in the pilot plan.

Today, Brasília proper accounts for only 22 percent of the population of the 'ederal District. Despite the egalitarian architecture of the pilot plan, the class arriers in the Federal District are even more rigid than in the rest of the coun-ʼy. The population is zoned by income into completely separate cities.

Congresso Nacional at sunset.

BELOW: the setting sun gilds the Catedral Metropolitana.

Dawn Valley sect worshiper.

Visitors staying in the hotel sector in the center of Brasília often get the mistaken impression that the city is completely dead at night. But there is a lively scene in the bars, restaurants and clubs concentrated along certain commercial streets in the residential wings: notably 109/110 South, 405/406 South and 303/304 North. Brasília's very fluid and casual social life is defined by the fact that it is a relatively affluent city with no established upper class. Many young professionals have moved here from other parts of Brazil.

Unconventional spiritualism

Brasília's spiritual life is as unusual as its social mores. Niemeyer's concrete cathedral along the Eixo Monument represents the official faith. Closer to the city's true faith is the cult of Dom Bosco, an Italian priest and educator who prophesied in 1883 that a new civilization would arise in a land of milk and honey on the site of present day Brasília.

The first structure built on the city site, overlooking Lake Paranoá, was a small marble pyramid commemorating Bosco's vision. Brasília's most striking church, the **Ermida Dom Bosco** Ⓝ (Sanctuary of Dom Bosco; open daily 7am–7pm) in 702 South, is also named after him. It is a cubical chapel whose walls are made entirely of blue and violet stained-glass. In effect, Dom Bosco's prophecy provided spiritual legitimacy for Kubitschek's secular dream of a new capital.

Brasília also enjoys a reputation as "The Capital of the Third Millennium," by virtue of the 400-plus contemporary cults that flourish here. Further south, at 915, is the extraordinary **Templo da Boa Vontade** (Temple of Goodwill; open daily, 24 hours). Built in the form of seven (said to be the number of perfection) pyramids in 1989, it is crowned with one of the world's largest crystals.

BELOW: the regimented ministry buildings.

Maps:
City 306
Area 296

Several "new age" communities have been founded on the outskirts of rasília. The most accessible is **The Valley of the Dawn**, south of **Planaltina**. very Sunday, several hundred worshipers come to the valley to be initiated to the commune established by a retired woman truckdriver. The weekly arade of initiates, dressed in multicolored cloaks and veils, around a pond lorned with astrological symbols, is undoubtedly Brasília's eeriest sight.

A short drive away from the Dom Bosco church, to the southeast of the city, the **Jardim Botânico** ⓾ (Botanic Garden; Setor de Mansões D. Bosco, conj. 2, Lago Sul; open daily 9am–5pm, except Mon), a pleasant place to look at the ora of the *cerrado*. To the north of the city is a 30,000-hectare (74,000-acre) ature reserve operated by the botanical gardens, the **Parque Nacional de rasília** (open daily 8am–4pm). This is an area of savanna *(cerrado)* and low orest where birds, wolves, monkeys and armadillos, and many other local una, find refuge. There are forest trails, natural swimming pools and a visitor's enter.

ioiás state

he state of **Goiás** is an area of savanna and large rivers that attract growing umbers of keen fishermen and ecotourists. The riverbanks are densely orested and rich in wildlife. Much savanna land is being taken over by plantions of soybeans and the state is now the center of a campaign to protect the *errado*.

The principal attractions of the state are its colonial towns and its national arks. **Pirenópolis** ⓬, a picturesque town 137 km (85 miles) from Brasilía in e Pireneus mountain range, was founded in the 18th century to house gold

BELOW: the empty back roads of Goiás seem far removed from the capital.

Map on page 296

miners. Its cobbled streets and fine baroque houses are well worth a visi The surrounding area is particularly rich in wildlife and flowers, with man private nature reserves, some of which can be visited.

About 265 km (165 miles) north of Brasilía is the **Parque Nacional d Chapada dos Veadeiros** ⓭, a nature reserve with many beautiful waterfall rock formations and natural swimming pools.

Goiás Velho ⓮ (often just called Goiás), 340 km (212 miles) from Brasili is the former capital of the state, interesting for its colonial architecture wit many well-preserved 18th-century churches and houses.

Forming Goiás' western border is part of a river whose valley is described b Durval Rosa Borges, author of *Araguaia, Heart and Soul,* as "the Garden c Eden." The Araguaia River is, in fact, 2,630 km (1,634 miles) long, cuttin Brazil in two, from the wetlands of the Pantanal across the *cerrado* or centr plains to the Atlantic Ocean at Belém. When the muddy floodwaters shrink i August to reveal immense white sand beaches, 200,000 vacationing Brazilian descend on the river at **Aruanã** ⓯, 530 km (330 miles) west of Brasília, an **Barra do Garças** ⓰, both in western Goiás state, to establish lavish campsite and sound systems for all-night parties. Yet their presence, is dwarfed by th **Araguaia's** vast scale.

The river's source in southern Goiás is in the **Parque Nacional das Emas** ⓱ from which it flows northward forming a barrier between the states of Mat Grosso, Goiás, Tocantins and Pará, dividing to form the **Ilha do Bananal** ⓲ the world's largest fluvial island. To the north of the island is the **Parqu Nacional do Araguaia** ⓳. During the low-water season, floating hotels oper ate on the river's tributaries. The river is also a favorite of sport fishermen.

BELOW: farmer from central Brazil

Wild Bus Rides

Imagine going on a week-long, buttock-numbing 5,000-km (3,000-mile) bus ride from the borders of Argentina right through to Venezuela, almost from the pampas to the Caribbean.

Brazil's longest bus line stretches – with a few breaks – from **Cascavel** in Paraná state in southern Brazil to Sta Helena in Venezuela, as far as Los Angeles to St. Louis – and back. The **BR 364 Highway**, built by more than a million migrants seeking a new start in the wild west, cuts through five states and the heartland of Amazonia. Less daunting sections of the line offer an interesting way of glimpsing the western Amazon.

The 1,400-km (875-mile) **Cuiabá–Porto Velho** journey once took weeks; it now takes 24 hours but is over rough terrain.

The Transamazonia Highway, or BR 230, was built in the 1970s with World Bank aid. The original intention was to create a road stretching as far east as Marabá near Belém, but only parts of it have been successfully opened for traffic. The 820-km (500-mile) trip from **Manaus** to Venezuela via Roraima's capital, **Boa Vista**, is a pleasant journey on an asphalt road, passing a number of Amerindian reserves and areas of unspoilt forest. The small town of **Presidente Figueiredo** en route is surrounded by many beautiful waterfalls. A pause there provides welcome relief from the cramped buses and long roads

Unscheduled stops on these routes, caused by blowouts, engine failures, cattleherds or tropical storms, often provide more intriguing glimpses of Amazon life than the scheduled halts at gas stations or small-town bus stations *(rodoviárias)*, where passengers gulp down sandwiches at a *lanchonete* (snack counter). The succession of bus stations, each crowded with bundle-clutching migrants, reveals Brazil as a nation in motion, and buses are the means by which millions filter into the unoccupied spaces of the wild west.

Traveling by bus is the cultural icebreaker, the quintessential Brazilian experience. Cramped into the same hot space for days on end, no foreign aloofness can resist the unfolding, mobile drama of escaping chickens, family rows or intimate friendships forged around impromptu English lessons that can result in weary travelers being invited into Brazilian homes for a much-needed bath or bed at journey's end.

Medianeira, an Eucatur affiliate, operates on the **Cuiabá–Santarém** BR 163 Highway. This route takes you through the pioneer towns in the heart of the Amazon forest and bisects Brazil from north to south.

The **BR 153 Highway**, running through Goiás and Tocantins, and Pará's **BR 010** give a grandstand view of the climatic transition from dry *cerrado* flatlands around Brasília to the humid density of the Amazon. However, the dreary uniformity of slash-and-burn cattle ranching has forced back the forest, now only a green line on the horizon.

Although dusty and suffocatingly hot, the Belém–Brasília route is in many ways typical of the country's highways, but stark evidence of the devastation of the rain forest – the view being mostly of parched land – means it can also be a depressing experience. ❑

RIGHT: sun-baked dirt road in Pernambuco.

THE SOUTHERN STATES

This subtropical, prosperous region of Brazil has spectacular natural attractions and a distinctive European and gaucho *heritage*

Map on page 318

The south of Brazil is different. Here, palm trees give way to pines, forested mountains are split by tranquil valleys, nature in general is more rugged, with roaring waterfalls and monumental canyons, and the temperate climate provides four seasons with cold weather and even snow in the winter. The people, too, are different. Blue-eyed blonds replace the dark-featured types of the north and northeast, reflecting the deep European roots of the south.

The traditional breadbasket of Brazil, the south is a region of bounty. The farms and ranches of the states of **Paraná**, **Santa Catarina** and **Rio Grande do Sul** are the country's leading grain producers. Paraná is home to coffee plantations as well as the country's most extensive pine forests. Across the flat pampas of Rio Grande do Sul wander Brazil's largest cattle herds. In recent years, the south has drawn from its agricultural wealth to invest in industry and, today, the region is the center of Brazil's booming textile and footwear industries. Together, the south's rich earth and surging industrial power have given the inhabitants of its three states a standard of living second only to that of those in the state of São Paulo.

PRECEDING PAGES: the magnificent Iguaçu Falls.
LEFT: rock formations at Vila Velha, Paraná.
BELOW: the Paranaguá railroad.

Natural wonder

A combination of unleashed nature and pleasing urbanity are the trademarks of Paraná. Here, you will find the wildly beautiful **Cataratas do Iguaçu** ❶ (Iguaçu Falls).

They are undoubtedly one of the greatest natural wonders of the world, and were declared a World Heritage Site by UNESCO in 1986. A mammoth series of waterfalls plunge through a gorge on the **Iguaçu River** some 650 km (390 miles) from Curitiba on the border with Paraguay and Argentina. A total of 275 falls cascade over a precipice 3 km (1.8 miles) wide, sending up an unending wall of spray that keeps the sky decorated by rainbows.

At the heart of this unforgettable scene is the **Devil's Throat**, where 14 separate falls join forces, pounding down the 90-meter (350-ft) cliffs in a deafening crescendo of sound and spray. A catwalk runs to the base of the first level of the falls where you are surrounded by the roaring water, the mist and white foam that is boiling up all around the green of the jungle, uprooted trees and a 180-degree rainbow. It is an overwhelming sensation.

Iguaçu is part of a national park of the same name that is divided between Brazil and Argentina. Over the past few years, new facilities have been built on both sides, which some cynics see as the playing out of the rivalry between the two countries. Visas are not required for a visit to the Argentine side, which can

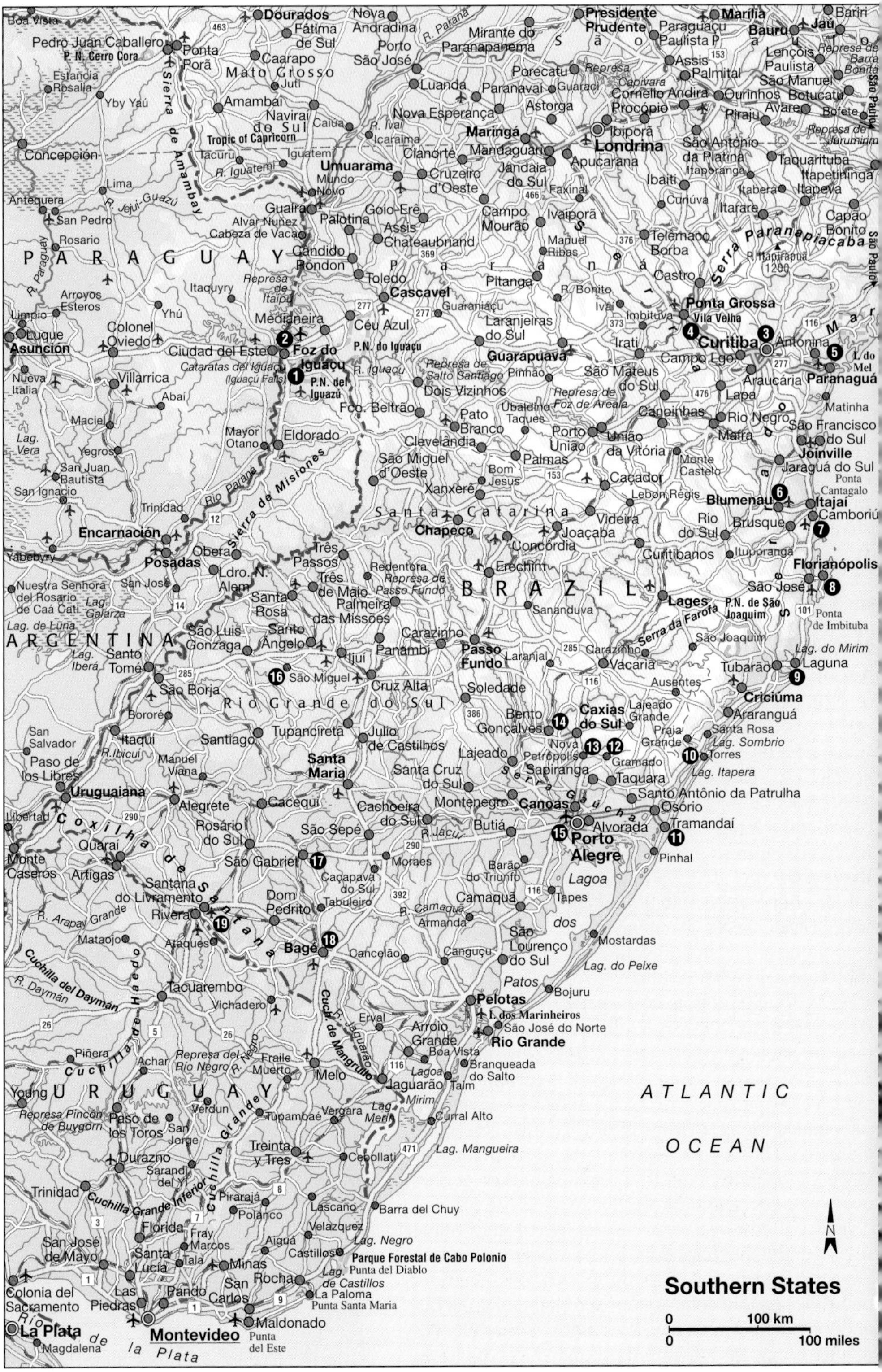
Southern States
0 100 km
0 100 miles
ATLANTIC
OCEAN
PARAGUAY
ARGENTINA
URUGUAY
BRAZIL
Paraná
Santa Catarina
Rio Grande do Sul
Mato Grosso do Sul
São Paulo
Tropic of Capricorn
Asunción
Concepción
Encarnación
Posadas
Ciudad del Este
Foz do Iguaçu
Cataratas del Iguaçu (Iguaçu Falls)
P.N. del Iguazú
P.N. do Iguaçu
Cascavel
Guarapuava
Ponta Grossa
Vila Velha
Curitiba
Antonina
Paranaguá
Joinville
Blumenau
Itajaí
Camboriú
Florianópolis
São José
Lages
P.N. de São Joaquim
Laguna
Tubarão
Criciúma
Torres
Caxias do Sul
Bento Gonçalves
Nova Petrópolis
Gramado
Canoas
Porto Alegre
Tramandaí
Osório
Pelotas
Rio Grande
Santa Maria
Passo Fundo
Chapecó
Uruguaiana
Santana do Livramento
Rivera
Bagé
Jaguarão
Melo
Chuy
Barra del Chuy
Parque Forestal de Cabo Polonio
Punta del Diablo
La Paloma
Maldonado
Punta del Este
Montevideo
Colonia del Sacramento
La Plata
Río de la Plata
Lagoa dos Patos
Lag. Mirim
Lag. Mangueira
Londrina
Maringá
Dourados
Presidente Prudente
Marília
Bauru
Jaú
Serra Paranapiacaba
Serra Geral
Serra Gaúcha
Serra da Farofa
Sierra de Misiones
Sierra de Amambay
Coxilha de Santana
Cuchilla Grande
Cuchilla Grande Inferior
Cuchilla de Haedo
Cuchilla del Daymán
Cuch. de Mangrullo
Tacuarembó
Durazno
Florida
Minas
Rocha
Treinta y Tres
Salto Santiago
Represa de Itaipú
Represa de Passo Fundo
Represa del Río Negro
Represa de Foz de Areala
Represa de Salto Santiago
Represa Pincón de Buygorri
Umuarama
Apucarana
Pedro Juan Caballero
Ponta Porã
Villarrica
Santo Ângelo
São Miguel
Cruz Alta
Erechim
Concórdia
Joaçaba
Vacaria
São Joaquim
Jaraguá do Sul
São Francisco do Sul
Rio Negro
Mafra
Porto União
União da Vitória
Lapa
Araucária
Campo Lgo.
Santa Cruz do Sul
Cachoeira do Sul
São Gabriel
Alegrete
Quaraí
Artigas
Santo Tomé
São Borja
Paso de los Libres
Rosário do Sul
Camaquã
São Lourenço do Sul
Mostardas
Tapes
Taquara
Santo Antônio da Patrulha
Alvorada
Pinhal
Arroio Grande
Santa Vitória do Palmar
I. dos Marinheiros
São José do Norte
Canguçu
Dom Pedrito
Caçapava do Sul
Santiago
Tupanciretã
Júlio de Castilhos
Lajeado
Montenegro
Sapiranga
1
2
3
4
5
6
7
8
9
10
11
12
13
14
15
16
17
18
19

easily be done in a half-day trip. To see the full force of the falls, go to the park in January and February when the river is high. However, this is also when the humidity and heat are nearly unbearable and the park is packed with tourists. From September to October, the water level is down but the temperature is pleasant and there are far fewer people. A new shuttle bus service runs from the visitor center to various points of interest.

On the Brazilian side, the catwalk leading to the falls can be reached either by a winding trail or an elevator. For another view of the scene, you may take a helicopter ride, but this option is ecologically unsound as the noise disturbs the park animals. An even better look at the falls and forest is offered by the **Macuco Boat Safari**. The one-and-a-half hour journey starts with a trip through the jungle in open wagons pulled by a jeep, slowly descending to the floor of the canyon. A boat trip then takes you to the edge of the crashing water where you have an unmatched view of the water falling from the cliffs above.

A different view can be had on the Argentine side. In 2001 a train service was established between the visitors' center and the start of the walkways. A lower circuit leads to the canyon floor, where a short boat trip (included in the entrance fee) takes you to the island of **San Martín**, looking directly at the falling water. While beautiful, this option is only for the physically fit. A less strenuous walk can be had along an upper cat walk that stretches for over a mile at the top of the falls, affording an excellent view of the water plunging over the top. Another walkway leads to the Devil's Throat, allowing you to see it in dramatic close-up.

Map on facing page

TIP

If you take your photography seriously, bear in mind that light conditions over the Iguaçu Falls favor views taken from the Brazilian side in the morning and the Argentine side in the afternoon.

Itaipú hydroelectric plant

The neighboring city of **Foz do Iguaçu** ❷ underwent a population and economic boom between 1975 and 1984 due to the construction in recent years of the nearby Itaipú hydroelectric plant, which currently stands as the world's largest. But the costs were high: the US$18 billion project has caused dramatic environmental damage. Free tours of the dam are given between 8am and 4pm from Mon–Sat. Only one hotel, the **Hotel das Cataratas**, is located inside the Brazilian side of the park, with an unobstructed view of the falls. It is advisable to book well in advance.

BELOW: Foz do Ignaçu.

Relaxed capital

Five hundred and fifty kilometers (340 miles) east of Foz do Iguaçu, **Curitiba** ❸ is an urban planner's dream, with ample green space, wide avenues, flower-decked pedestrian malls, and a relaxed and comfortable pace of life.

Founded by gold-seekers in the 17th century, Curitiba today is a bustling metropolis with a population of 1.7 million, located atop an elevated plateau at 900 meters (2,800 ft). In the latter half of the 19th century and the beginning of this century, Curitiba, together with the state as a whole, received an infusion of immigrants from Europe (Italians, Poles, Germans and Russians), which transformed the city into a European outpost in the heart of South America. The profusion of blonds on the city's streets, plus

The Itaipu dam, a joint Brazilian and Paraguayan project, was built between 1975 and 1984, and has been listed as one of the Seven Wonders of the Modern World. Its 18 turbines generate about 75 billion kilowatts annually.

Curitiba's annual ethnic festivals, are proof of the mixed origins of its citizens. The city's best-known ethnic neighborhood is **Santa Felicidade**, founded in 1878 by Italian immigrants and today home to Curitiba's finest *cantinas*.

Aside from its deserved reputation as Brazil's cleanest city, Curitiba is also a pedestrian's delight. A walking tour should begin at the city center, **Rua das Flores**, an extensive pedestrian mall named after its beautiful flower baskets and flanked by stores and boutiques as well as inviting cafés, restaurants and pastry shops. Along the way is the **Boca Maldita**, where in the morning and late afternoon, Curitiba's would-be philosophers, politicians and economists discourse at will on the country's latest crises, a Brazilian version of Speakers' Corner in London's Hyde Park.

Nearby is the historical center of Curitiba, concentrated in the blocks around the **Largo da Ordem**, a cobblestoned square dominated by the **Igreja da Ordem Terceira de São Francisco das Chagas** (1737). This is the city's oldest church, known popularly as the Ordem Church.

Up the hill from the church is the **Garibaldi Mini Shopping**, replete with handicrafts from throughout Brazil, including wood-carvings, pottery, leather and straw goods. At night, the Ordem square comes alive with musicians and outdoor cafés.

Back down the hill towards the Rua das Flores is the **Praça Tiradentes**, where Curitiba's neo-Gothic cathedral stands, not far from the state historical museum (open Tues–Fri 9.30am–5.30pm, weekends 10am–4pm; admission free) at **Praça Generoso Marques**. Close to the latter is a walkway (with a glass roof) known as "Rua 24-horas," where the shops, cafés, and bars stay open round the clock.

BELOW: Curitiba's botanical garden.

Rock formations

Some 80 km (50 miles) west of Curitiba is the area's second great natural attraction, the **Vila Velha State Park** ❹ (open daily 8am–6pm). Sitting majestically atop the plateau, with the wind whipping around them, are a series of fantastical rock formations carved over an incredible 400 million years by the wind and rain. There are 23 separate formations, each identified by the object, animal, or human form that it appears to represent. Nearby are the 50-meter (164-ft) deep Furnas Craters (the deepest has an elevator) and forest-fringed Dourada Lagoon.

A mini-train hustles back and forth among the formations, but most visitors will find it hard to resist a long, contemplative walk through the near-mystical site with its haunting mixture of shadows, rocks and the sound of the wind.

Close by is another mystery left by nature, two enormous holes sliced into the rocky ground to a depth of nearly 100 meters (400 ft), half-filled with water. In one of these natural wells an elevator has been installed for visitors to descend to the level of the water.

Map on page 318

Paranaguá train ride

Although Paraná is not known for its beaches, the trip to them is one of the most breathtaking in Brazil. From Tuesday to Sunday at 8am, the train leaves Curitiba's station for the winding trip down the coastal mountains to the sea port of **Paranaguá** ❺, the state's oldest city. Completed in 1885, the railroad clings to the side of the mountains, at times threatening to march off into space as it passes over viaducts and through tunnels during the long, slow three-hour descent to the coastal plain (for the best views sit on the left

BELOW: visiting Vila Velha.

Smile of a southern Brazilian.

side of the train when going down). The trip offers an unmatched tour through the best preserved section of Brazil's Atlantic rainforest, a richly green tangle of trees and undergrowth broken occasionally by waterfalls.

Founded in 1648, Paranaguá is today one of Brazil's leading ports but, unfortunately, has preserved little of its historical past. What remains is located along **Rua XV de Novembro**, where an archeological museum (open daily except Mon, noon–5pm; admission charge) is housed in the town's grandest building (completed 1755), formerly a Jesuit college. The museum contains indian artifacts and items from colonial life.

The area's primary attraction is the **Ilha do Mel**, an island paradise that is reached by a 20-minute boat ride from the town of **Pontal do Sul**, an hour's drive from Paranaguá (boats from Paranaguá also make the trip but it takes two hours). The island is a nature reserve with natural pools, grottos and deserted beaches. It is also home to the ruins of an 18th-century fort and a 19th-century lighthouse. There are no cars on the island and transportation is either by foot along the many paths or by fisherman's boat. Its primitive, unspoiled nature has made the Ilha do Mel a popular spot for campers. Visitors may also stay in one of the pousadas on the island. For overnight campers, a flashlight and insect repellent are essential.

The best option for the return trip to Curitiba is the **Graciosa Highway**, a wind-ing road that cuts through the verdant forest with explosions of wildflowers along the route. From the viewpoints, you can catch glimpses of the old mule trail used by the original Portuguese settlers to climb the mountainside to Curitiba. Real adventurers may still make this trip.

BELOW: Alpine-style building in Blumenau.

Beaches of Santa Catarina

Or you can continue down the coast from Paranaguá into Santa Catarina. The smallest of the southern states, Santa Catarina is also the most boisterous. Its German heritage is apparent in the Bavarian architecture in inland **Blumenau** ❻, home to South America's liveliest Oktoberfest, a three-week blowout that attracts over a million visitors, making it Brazil's second-largest festival after Rio's Carnival.

But the state's real treasure is its coastline, with miles of unspoiled white sand beaches. The northern coastal resort of **Camboriú** ❼ has a long crescent beach that is a near carbon copy of Rio's Copacabana.

The coastal capital, **Florianópolis** ❽, is an island city with 42 beaches, ranging from quiet coves to roaring surf. **Praia Joaquina** is a world-famed surfing center holding international competitions each year. A few minutes away is the **Conceição Lagoon**, a beautiful freshwater lake wedged in between the island's mountain spine and the sea, with jet-ski and windsurfing facilities. This central area is the most hotly disputed by residents and tourists. Restaurants and bars abound, some of them exceptional, such as the unpretentious **Martin Pescador**, which serves world-class gourmet seafood.

The island's southern beaches are its most unspoiled. Many of them can be reached only by dirt roads. Here are the huts of fishermen whose wives

Map on page 318

spend the days making lace. **Campeche** and **Armação** beaches are good choices for a day trip. Nearby is the colorful village of **Ribeirão da Ilha**, site of one of the first Portuguese settlements on the island. To the north are the upscale beaches of **Ingleses**, **Canasvieiras**, and **Jurerê**, where hotels and condominiums are rapidly filling up the empty space.

Florianópolis is a laid-back city where life centers around basic and simple pleasures: swimming, sunbathing, eating, and drinking. It is a measure of the relaxed lifestyle of the island's inhabitants that hitchhiking is young residents favorite mode of transport.

On Santa Catarina's southern coast, the principal beaches are **Garopaba**, **Laguna ❾**, and **Morro dos Conventos**. Of these, the acknowledged champion is the beach at the fishing port of Laguna, a 17th-century colonial city that has preserved many of its historical structures together with the beauty of its nearby beaches.

Considered a jewel of Brazil's southern coast, Laguna is popular among Argentine tourists and the wealthy of São Paulo. Like the major cities and tourism centers of the south, Laguna is affluent, clean, and efficient, a far cry from the often depressing poverty and urban decay that has gripped the beach cities of the northeast. The main beach of Mar Grosso is built-up, but Farol de Santa Marta 18 km (11 miles) out of town is a beautiful spot.

Gaucho state

The southernmost state of Brazil, Rio Grande do Sul is also the most distinct. Bordering Uruguay and Argentina, it has developed a culture of its own, a mixture of Portuguese and Spanish together with Italian and German. The unique

Below: the island city of Florianópolis.

gaucho culture is the trademark of Rio Grande do Sul, where swarthy cowboys roam the southern pampas with their distinctive flat hats and chin straps, their baggy pantaloon trousers, red neckerchiefs and leather boots, and the symbol of *gaucho*-land, the *chimarrão*, a gourd of hot *mate* tea.

Here, machismo runs strong and a man is definitely a *man*, a heritage of the state's violent history. More than any other in Brazil, Rio Grande do Sul has seen the ravages of war. In the 18th and 19th centuries, it served as a battleground for warring armies, revolutionaries, adventurers and indians who marched back and forth across its grasslands, leaving a bloody stamp that has been transformed into legend.

Proud and boastful, today's *gauchos* have rechanneled their warrior fury. Rio Grande is Brazil's leading manufacturer of leather footwear and has recently been producing the country's finest wines. In addition, vast herds of cattle and sheep today graze on it's former battlefields, providing the state and the rest of Brazil with beef for the succulent *churrasco* barbecues, a *gaucho* tradition, and wool for the south's textile factories.

The landscape of Rio Grande do Sul is as rugged and uncompromising as its inhabitants. The state's 450-km (280-mile) coastline is marked by pounding surf and rocky promontories, the best known of which are located in the resort city of **Torres** ❿. Although the water is colder here, the sun is still warm and the bikinis just as brief as in Rio. **Tramandaí** ⓫ and **Capão da Canoa** are other top beach resorts, while stretching southward between the bulk of the mainland and the ocean is the **Lagoa dos Patos**, the largest freshwater lagoon in South America, whose banks offer beaches and camping sites from **Tapes** to **Laranjal**.

BELOW: folk dancing in traditional *gaucho* costume.

The Serra Gaúcha

A few miles inland is the **Serra Gaúcha**, a coastal mountain range that has become the prime attraction for visitors to the state. Pine trees, lush green valleys, waterfalls, shimmering rivers and awesome canyons distract the eyes of visitors as they wind their way through the *serra*. It was to this idyllic setting that thousands of German and Italian immigrants flocked in the late 19th century, establishing their homesteads along the valley floors. Today, many of the original stone and wood houses of these homesteaders still stand as testimony to the hardy nature of the transplanted *gauchos*.

The crown jewels of the Serra Gaúcha are the twin cities of **Gramado** ⓬ and **Canela**. Gramado hosts a Brazilian and Latin American film festival every August. It is a tranquil, slow-moving mountain resort where the harried residents of Brazil's non-stop cities escape the rush and indulge in the rare activity of doing absolutely nothing. Because of this trend, Gramado and its sister city Canela, which are separated only by a sign, offer dozens of small hotels, inns and chalets, all of them tucked away beneath the pines.

Some 30 minutes away from Gramado and Canela is the small town of **Nova Petrópolis** ⓭, where the area's German heritage is prominent. In addition to the Bavarian architecture in the community's homes and buildings, Nova Petrópolis' roots are visible in the Immigration Park, highlighted by a reproduction of a German colonial settlement of the 19th century.

The park also contains a bandstand and *biergarten* that are the center of festivities in January, February and July. During these traditional Brazilian vacation periods, the small hotels and inns of Nova Petrópolis, as well as Gramado and Canela, fill up with tourists. The German influence is apparent both in names and architecture and in the carefully landscaped parks and avenues.

Bento Gonçalves ⓮, 48 km (30 miles) to the north, was founded in 1875 by Italian immigrants. The **Museu do Imigrante** (Rua Erny Dreher 127; open Tues–Fri 8–11.30am and 1.30–5.30pm, Sat 9am–5pm, Sun 8am–noon; admission charge) documents its history. This town of 92,000 is at the heart of Rio Grande do Sul's wine-producing area, and tours and tastings are available at a number of *adegas* (vineyards) in and around Bento Gonçalves. There is an annual wine festival in February and March in the nearby city of **Caxias do Sul.**

Brazil's "Grand Canyon"

On the outskirts of Canela is the **Caracol State Park**, where the **Caracol Falls** plunge 130 meters (400 ft). The area's premier natural attraction, however, is three hours away, at the end of a potholed road, in the **Aparados da Serra National Park**, about 120 km (75 miles) from Canela. The view is well worth the effort, for suddenly, in the midst of pasture and forest, the earth seems to open up, revealing the enormous **Itaimbézinho Canyon**. Some 700 meters (2,200 ft) deep, 7 km (4 miles) long and in places over 2 km (1 mile) wide, the canyon is the largest in Latin America. There are walking trails and horseback rides through the beautiful national park.

Map on page 318

TIP

For information about traditional *gaucho* meals, music and dance performances in Porto Alegre, contact the Movimento Tradicionalista Gaúcho at Rua Guilherne Schell 60 (tel: 51-217 4325. Website: www.mtg.org.br).

BELOW: performers at the Blumenau Octoberfest.

Map on page 318

Unlike North America's Grand Canyon, located in the dry southwest, Itaimbézinho impresses not simply because of its extraordinary size but also because of the varied shadings of green that mark it out, from the light green pasture to the deep green of its forested cliffs. Waterfalls cascade down the canyon's sides.

The capital city of this southernmost state is **Porto Alegre** (15), a modern, commercial conurbation with a population of 1.4 million – the largest city of the south. Located near the coast at the northern end of the Lagoa dos Patos, the city is the ideal jumping off point for sojourns into the state's other areas. Gramado and Canela, the wine country and Rio Grande do Sul's beaches can all be visited in day trips from the capital city. Trips to the mission region and the pampas, however, require two days at least. Porto Alegre is also a stopover on the land route from Brazil to Argentina and Uruguay.

As befits its status as the capital of a beef producing state, Porto Alegre offers excellent leather goods sold in downtown boutiques, plus steak houses where you will be treated to the real mouthwatering Brazilian *churrasco.* Although far removed from the *gaucho* lifestyle, Porto Alegre provides visitors with a close-up look at their traditional music and dances at a number of popular nightspots.

The missions

The area known as the mission region lies due west of the Serra Gaúcha. Here, in the 17th century, Jesuit priests organized members of the Guaraní tribe into a series of settlements built around missions. The Jesuit fathers controlled the region for nearly a century, overseeing the construction of Amerindian cities that reached up to 5,000 inhabitants. But in 1756, the missions were attacked in force and overwhelmed, the Jesuits were expelled, and almost all of the Amerindians were killed.

Today, the ruins of the missions, most notably **São Miguel** (16), stand in dramatic solitude on the plain, all that is left of a once-thriving Amerindian community. Visitors to the mission region should stay at the city of **Santo Angelo**, from where day trips may be made to the ruins. The São Miguel mission offers an audio-visual show at night, portraying the history of the area. Other mission ruins may also be visited across the border in Argentina and further north, near the Iguaçu Falls.

BELOW: a southern macho and his gun. **PAGE 328:** a packed trolley bus on the Lapa aqueduct, Rio de Janeiro.

Cowboy country

For *gauchos*, the soul of their state resides in the **Campanha**, the region on the border with Uruguay and Argentina. Across these windswept prairies, the pampas of legend, the *gaucho* cowboy still rides herd over the cattle and sheep that first brought wealth to Rio Grande do Sul.

The far southern cities of **São Gabriel** (17), **Rosário do Sul, Bagé** (18), **Lavras do Sul, Santana do Livramento** (19), and **Uruguaiana** still seem to ring with the sound of musketry and cannon fire from the battles of the past. *Gaucho* tradition and culture are best preserved in these cities and on the surrounding *estancias* (ranches) of the Campanha, where Portuguese and Spanish intermix in the colloquial language of the frontier. ❑

Wine Country

Although it came comparatively late to Brazil, wine production has taken a firm hold in the country. Brazil's wine industry is concentrated in the coastal mountains of Rio Grande do Sul, which is responsible for 90 percent of national production.

The grapes and resulting wines were first brought to Rio Grande by Italian immigrants who arrived in the 1880s. Since then, their descendants have carried on the tradition. Today, the cities and small farms of this area still retain an air of Italy about them. Cheeses and salamis hang from the ceilings of the prized wine cellars of the region's small farmers, many of whom make their own wine, cheese and pasta. This culinary combination is also found in the area's restaurants, which are heavily dominated by Italian cuisine.

The starting point for a visit to Brazil's wine country is **Caxias do Sul**, a booming industrial city tucked away in the mountains. Caxias is home to the region's Grape Festival held every other year in February/March, a long party during which the wine flows freely. The leading vineyard in Caxias is the **Château Lacave**, with headquarters in a mock European castle complete with drawbridge. In the city proper is the *cantina* of the **Granja União** vineyard. The *cantinas* are in effect tasting rooms for the wineries and are found scattered throughout the region's principal cities.

More wine country tasting treats are to be found in and around **Garibaldi** and **Bento Gonçalves**, the recognized capitals of the wine-growing region. On the main road, just outside Garibaldi, is the **Maison Forestier**, which today is Brazil's leading producer of quality table wines.

Forestier and other leading vineyards began to invest in quality in the mid-1970s because of the growing local demand for good wines. Using imported varieties of grapes, over the next 10 years Forestier and the others began to turn out increasingly high-quality products. While the process isn't yet complete, Brazilian wines, especially the whites, have made a major leap in quality. Several brands are now exported, mainly to the United States, and it is expected that Brazil's wines will soon be challenging those of Chile and Argentina for pre-eminence in South America.

Guided tours are offered at Forestier and the other large wineries. Most of the wine makers still adhere to the old tradition of oaken barrels, but some are stepping into the high-technology world of stainless-steel vats and tight quality controls.

The *pièce de résistance* of any vineyard tour is the generous tasting session at the end. For a full-scale introduction to Brazilian wines, begin at Forestier then continue on to Bento Gonçalves for a visit to the **Aurora Cooperative**. Bento is also home to several smaller producers, including **Salton**, **Monaco**, **Riograndense** and **Embrapa**.

If you have managed to stay on your feet, head back to Garibaldi for a sampling of the best in Brazilian champagnes. The most respected of the champagne producers are **Peterlongo**, the French-owned **Moët-Chandon**, **Georges Aubert**, **Château d'Argent** and **Vinícola Garibaldi**. ❑

RIGHT: harvesting the grapes in Rio Grandedo Sul.

INSIGHT GUIDES

TRAVEL TIPS

CONTENTS

Getting Acquainted

The Place

Area: The largest country in South America, occupying almost half of the continent (8,511,965 sq km/3,286,500 sq miles).
Capital: Brasília.
Highest Mountain/Longest River: Pico da Neblina (3,014 meters/9,888 ft); most of the Amazon (6,570 km/4,080 miles) flows through Brazil.
Population: 176 million.
Language: The official language is Portuguese.
Religion: More than 90 percent Roman Catholic. Brazil is the largest Catholic country in the world.
Time Zones: Over half of Brazil and most of its major cities are three hours behind GMT. *See box for further details.*
Currency The *real* (plural, *reais*), which is made up of 100 centavos. For exchange, US$1 is about R$3 and £1 about R$5.7, but this is subject to a great deal of fluctuation. *(See Money section on page 336 for more details.)*
Weights and Measures: The metric system is used throughout Brazil and temperature is measured on the centigrade or Celsius scale (°C). Other measuring units are used in rural areas, but people are familiar with the metric system.
Electricity: Voltage is not standard throughout Brazil, but most cities use 127V electricity; Brasília, Florianópolis, Fortaleza, Recife and São Luis use 220V electricity; Manaus uses 110V electricity.

If you can't do without your electric shaver, hair dryer or personal computer, enquire about the voltage when making hotel reservations. If you plug an appliance into a lower voltage than it was made for, it will function poorly, but if you plug it into a much stronger current it can overheat and short-circuit. Many appliances have a switch so they can be used with either a 110- or 220-volt current (110-volt appliances work normally on a 127-volt current). Many hotels have adapters and some even have more than one voltage available.
International Dialing Code: To call Brazil from overseas, dial the relevant code to get an international line, then dial 55 for Brazil. Do not dial the zero at the beginning of the Brazilian number.

To call overseas from Brazil, dial 00 to get an international line, dial the international code for the country you are calling, then dial the telephone number, omitting any initial zero. *(See the Telecommunications section on page 340 for more details.)*

Climate

Almost all of Brazil's 8.5 million sq km (3.2 million sq miles) of territory lie between the equator and the Tropic of Capricorn. Within this tropical zone, temperatures and rainfall vary from north to south, from coastal to inland areas, and from low areas (Amazon River basin and Pantanal, as well as along the coast) to higher altitudes. If you're coming from the Northern Hemisphere, remember that seasons are inverted, although at this latitude, seasons are less distinct than in temperate zones.

THE NORTH

In the Amazon River basin jungle region, the climate is humid equatorial, characterized by high temperatures and humidity, with heavy rainfall all year round. Although some areas have no dry season, most places have a short respite between July and November so that the rivers are highest from December through June. Average temperature is 24–27°C (75–80°F).

Time Zones

There are four time zones in Brazil.
Two hours behind GMT: The archipelago of Fernando de Noronha, 350 km (220 miles) off the Atlantic coast.
Three hours behind GMT: The western extension of Brazil's main time zone – in which 50 percent of the country lies – is a north–south line from the mouth of the Amazon River, going west to include the northern state of Amapá and the entire southern region. Rio de Janeiro, São Paulo, Belém and Brasília are all located in this zone.
Four hours behind GMT: Another large zone encompassing the Pantanal states and most of the north.
Five hours behind GMT: The far western state of Acre and the westernmost part of Amazonas.
Daylight-saving time has been used in recent years, with clocks being set ahead in October and back to standard time in March. This, confusingly, means that time differences do not remain the same. Daylight saving is only used in certain parts of Brazil, and takes place in the other half of the year in the Northern Hemisphere. Therefore, the time in Rio de Janeiro, for example, is often only two hours behind GMT.

THE EAST COAST

The Atlantic coast from Rio Grande do Norte to the state of São Paulo has a humid tropical climate, also hot, but with slightly less rainfall than in the north and with summer and winter seasons. The north-eastern coast, nearer to the equator, experiences little difference in summer/winter temperatures, but more rainfall in winter, especially April–June. The coastal southeast receives more rain in summer (December–March). Average temperature is 21–24°C (70–75°F), being consistently warm in the northeast, but fluctuating in

Rio de Janeiro from summer highs of more than 40°C (104°F) down to 18°C (65°F), with winter temperatures usually around the 21°C (70°F) mark.

THE INTERIOR

Most of Brazil's interior has a semi-humid tropical climate, with a hot, rainy summer (December–March) and a drier, cooler winter (June–August). Year-round average temperature is 20–28°C (68–82°F). São Paulo, at an altitude of 800 meters (2,600 ft) above sea level, and Brasília, over 1,000 meters (3,300 ft) above sea-level on the central plateau, as well as mountainous Minas Gerais, can get quite cool: although the thermometer may read a mild 10°C (50°F), it will not feel so balmy indoors if there is no heating.

The mountainous areas in the southeast have a high-altitude tropical climate, similar to the semi-humid tropical climate, but rainy and dry seasons are more pronounced and temperatures are cooler, averaging from 18–23°C (64–73°F).

Part of the interior of the northeast has a tropical, semi-arid climate – hot with sparse rainfall. Most of the rain falls during three months, usually March–May, but sometimes the season is shorter and in some years there is no rain-fall at all. The average temperature is 24–27°C (75–80°F).

THE SOUTH

Brazil's south, below the Tropic of Capricorn, has a humid, subtropical climate. Rainfall is distributed regularly throughout the year and temperatures vary from 0–10°C (32–50°F) in winter, with occasional frosts and a rare snowfall, to 21–32°C (70–90°F) in summer.

Government

Brazil's transition to full democracy was completed at the end of 1989 with its first direct presidential elections in almost three decades.

Brazil is a federal republic with 27 states and one federal district. Each state has its own legislature. The overwhelming majority of government tax receipts are collected by the federal government, then distributed to the states and cities.

The head of government is the president, who has extensive powers and exercises more control over the nation than the American president does over the United States. The legislative branch of the federal government is composed of a Congress divided into a lower house, the Chamber of Deputies (with 513 seats), and an upper house, the Federal Senate (with 81 seats).

Economy

Despite past political problems, Brazil has shown excellent economic growth rates for most of the past 30 years. Although growth faltered with the high inflation of the 1980s, and the 1990 austerity package took the country into recession, Brazil has held on to its position as the economic leader among developing nations.

The government has privatized many of the giant, state-owned companies that once controlled much of the economy. Gone are the days of 30 percent per month inflation and heady dealing on the *paralelo*, the black market, in dollars that used to offer up to twice the official rate.

Road Safety

While they are at all other times a polite, decent people, something happens when Brazilians get behind the steering wheel, especially in Rio. Be cautious when driving or crossing streets and be prepared to make a dash. Despite recent tightening of traffic regulations, most drivers expect pedestrians to watch out for themselves and move out of the way.

Brazil's most recent president, Luiz Inácio Lula da Silva, a former lathe operator and union activist, won a landslide victory in October 2002 and took office in January 2003. He continues to comply with IMF demands resulting from a $30 billion agreement made in August 2002, which has meant there is less money for his social program. Although the economy shrank in the first half of 2003 and unemployment has risen (in São Paulo it is currently 20 percent), growth of 3 percent is predicted for 2004. "Lula" remains popular and his government has already achieved some legislative goals as well as increased confidence from foreign investors.

For the tourist, the stabilized economy means that a visit to Brazil is now much easier to budget and, since the devaluation, much cheaper for those earning foreign currencies. Brazil now offers the traveler great value for money.

Etiquette

Generally speaking, social customs in Brazil are not vastly different from those you will find in "western" countries, but Brazilians can be both awkwardly formal and disarmingly informal.

Surnames are little used. People start out on a first-name basis, but titles of respect – *senhor* for men and most frequently *dona* for women – are used not only to be polite to strangers but also to show respect to someone of a different age group or social class. In some families, children even address their parents as *o senhor* and *a senhora* instead of the equivalent of "you."

While handshaking is a common practice at introductions, it is also customary to greet friends, relatives and even complete strangers to whom you are being introduced with hugs and kisses. The "social" form of kissing consists usually of a kiss on each cheek. However, in most circles men do not kiss each other, rather shaking hands while giving a pat on the shoulder with the other hand. If they are more intimate, men will embrace, thumping each other on the back. Although this is the general custom in Brazil, there are subtleties about who kisses whom that are governed by factors such as social position. Brazilians are incredibly kind people in general. You will encounter offers of help wherever you go. Ask for directions and you are likely to be taken there in person.

Brazilians are also generous hosts, ensuring that guests' glasses, plates or coffee cups are never empty. Besides the genuine pleasure of being a gracious host, there is the question of honor. Even poor people like to put on a good party.

Although Brazil is definitely a male-dominated society, machismo takes a milder and more subtle form than is generally found in neighboring Hispanic America.

Expect schedules to be more flexible than you may be used to. It's not considered rude to show up half an hour late for a social engagement. Except in the larger cities, even business appointments are often leisurely when compared with the US or Europe. Don't try to include too many in one day, as you may well find your schedule badly disrupted by unexpected delays.

Planning the Trip

What to Bring

Brazilians are very fashion conscious, but are casual dressers. What you bring will depend on where you will be visiting and your holiday schedule. São Paulo tends to be more dressy, while in small inland towns people are more conservative. If you are going to a jungle lodge, you will want sturdy clothing and perhaps boots. If you are in Brazil on business, however, a suit and tie for men, and suits, skirts or dresses for women are the office standard.

Although some restaurants in the downtown business districts of the larger cities require a tie at lunch, other restaurants have no such regulations. Generally speaking, suits and ties are used less the further north you go in Brazil, even by businessmen, and the opposite holds true as you go south. Bring a summer-weight suit for office calls: linen is smart and cool.

If you like to dress up, there are plenty of places to go to in the evening in the big cities. But avoid ostentation and expensive or flashy jewelry. There are many desperately poor people in Brazil and unwitting foreign tourists make attractive targets for both pickpockets and purse snatchers.

Shorts are acceptable for men and women in most areas, especially near the beach or in resort towns, but they are not usually worn downtown. Most churches and some museums do not admit visitors dressed in shorts, and the traditional gafieira dance halls will not admit those dressed in shorts, especially men. Jeans are acceptable and often worn, but can be too hot.

If you come during Carnival, remember that it will be very hot and you will probably be in a crowd and dancing nonstop. Anything colorful is appropriate. If you plan to go to any of the balls, you will find plenty of costumes in the shops – you might want to buy just a feathered hair ornament, flowered *lei* (garland) or sequined accessory to complete your outfit. Many women wear no more than a bikini and makeup, and sometimes even less. Most men wear shorts – with or without a shirt – or sometimes a sarong. There are fancy-dress balls with themes such as "Hawaii" or "Arabian Nights."

If you are traveling in the south or in the mountains or to São Paulo in winter, it can be quite chilly. Even in the areas where it is hot all year

Bikini Rules

Don't forget to pack your swimsuit! Or buy a tiny local version of the string bikini, called a *tanga*, for yourself or someone back home – there are stores that sell nothing but beachwear. New styles emerge each year, in different fabrics and colors, exposing this part or that. The tiniest are called *fio dental*, or dental floss.

Topless sunbathing on Brazil's beaches has never really caught on. Women should avoid exposing their breasts on the beach; for most Brazilians, this is offensive behavior. Despite their open attitude towards sex, it is worth remembering that Brazilians are a deeply Catholic, and often conservative people.

Decently dressed women get ogled, too. Brazilian men don't go in for catcalls, but they draw their breath in sharply between clenched teeth and murmur comments as the women pass by. Brazilian women certainly don't let this cramp their style.

round, you may need a light sweater, jacket or sweatshirt, if not for the cooler evenings, then for the chilly airconditioning in hotels, restaurants, and offices.

Rain gear is always handy to take along – Brazilians tend to use umbrellas more than raincoats. Seaside hotels will provide you with sun umbrellas and beach towels.

As on any trip, it is sensible to bring a pair of comfortable walking shoes – there is no better way to explore than on foot. Sandals and beach thongs are comfortable in the heat and even if you don't plan to wear them for walking around the streets, they're very convenient for getting across the hot sand from your hotel to the water's edge. If there's one thing that gives Brazilians the giggles, it's the sight of a *gringo* going to the beach in shoes and socks.

There is nothing better for the summer heat than cotton, and since Brazil produces linen and exports cotton you might want to pack the bare essentials and acquire a new wardrobe. When buying clothes, remember that some natural fabrics will shrink. *Pequeno* = Small; *Médio* = Medium; and *Grande* = Large (often marked "P," "M" and "G"). *Maior* means larger; *menor* means smaller.

Entry Regulations

VISAS

Tourist visas used to be issued routinely to all visitors upon arrival, but Brazil now has a reciprocity policy: if Brazilians need a visa in advance to visit your country, you will need a visa in advance to visit Brazil. US citizens need to apply for a visa in advance; European Union citizens do not. Your airline or travel agent should be able to tell you if you need a visa; or contact a Brazilian consulate or embassy.

If you do not need a visa in advance, your passport will be stamped with a tourist visa upon entry. This permits you to remain in the country for 90 consecutive days. If you apply for a visa in advance, you have up to 90 days after the issue date to enter Brazil. Upon entry, you will get a tourist visa allowing you to stay in Brazil for up to 90 days.

If you are traveling to several countries and not going straight to Brazil, the entry visa needn't be issued in your home country. But it's still a good idea to allow for enough time so as to avoid surprises and hassles. The 90-day tourist visa can be renewed once only for another 90 days. To get an extension, go to the immigration section of the federal police.

Temporary visas for foreigners who will be working or doing business in Brazil allow a longer stay than a tourist visa. If you are a student, journalist or researcher, or employed by a multinational company, contact the Brazilian consulate or embassy in your country well before you plan to travel. It is usually difficult or even impossible to change the status of your visa once you are in the country. If you come with a tourist visa, you will probably have to leave the country to return on another type of visa.

Permanent work and residency visas are very difficult for foreigners to obtain, without giving up their own nationality.

CUSTOMS

You will be given a declaration form to fill out in the airplane before arrival. Customs officials spot-check some incoming "nothing to declare" travelers. If you are coming as a tourist and bringing articles obviously for your personal use, you will have no problem. As with most countries, food products of animal origin, plants, fruit and seeds may be confiscated.

You can bring in $500-worth of anything bought at the airport duty-free shop on arrival and $500-worth of anything brought from abroad, except liquor, which is limited to one bottle (each) of wine and spirits.

If you are coming on business, it's best to check with the consulate as to what limitations or obligations you are subject to.

Electronic devices worth no more than $500 can be brought in on a tourist visa and need not leave the country with you. You do not need to deal such items while visiting as a tourist and they can be left in the country as gifts. Professional samples may be brought in as long as the quantity does not lead customs inspectors to suspect that they are, in fact, for sale.

Baggage of outgoing travelers is not usually checked, except for a security check of hand luggage.

Protected Species

Do not attempt to buy or bring out wild animal skins, including alligator, as hunting of these species is strictly prohibited. It's a good idea to find out what you can or cannot bring back into your own country.

Health

A yellow fever certificate may be required if you are arriving from certain South American and African countries. This is subject to change, so check with the Brazilian embassy. If you plan to travel in areas outside of cities in the Amazon region or in the Pantanal in Mato Grosso, however, it is recommended that you have a yellow fever shot. This protects you for 10 years, but is effective only after 10 days, so plan ahead. It is also a good idea to protect yourself against malaria in these same jungle areas: there are drugs that will provide immunity. Consult your local public health service and be sure to get a certificate for any vaccination.

Don't drink tap water in Brazil. The water in the cities is treated and is sometimes quite heavily chlorinated, but people filter water in their homes. Any hotel or restaurant will have inexpensive bottled mineral water, both carbonated *(com gas)* and uncarbonated *(sem gas)*. If you are out in the hot sun, make an effort to drink extra fluids. Coconut and other fruit juice or mineral water are good for replacing lost fluids.

Don't underestimate the tropical sun. There is often a pleasant sea breeze, and you may not be aware of how the sun is baking you until it's too late. Use an appropriate sunscreen or *filtro solar* – there are several brands on sale in Brazil.

Prescription drugs are available in abundance – frequently without a prescription – and you may even find old favorites that have been banned for years in your country. Bring a supply of any prescription drugs that you take regularly but simple things like aspirin, antacids, plasters, sunscreen, and such, are easy to obtain. However, there have been cases of falsification of medicines, so it's best to buy drugs in larger chain stores or in the big cities. Drug-stores also sell cosmetics; sanitary protection can be purchased in any drugstore or supermarket.

Some health insurance plans cover any medical service you may require while abroad. Check with the company before traveling.

Money

For exchange, US$1 is about R$3.5 *(reais)* and £1 about R$5.7, but it will change over time.

The use of commas and decimal points in Portuguese is the opposite of what you may be used to. In Portuguese, one thousand *reais* is written R$ 1.000,00.

ATM machines are found throughout Brazil, including airports, and major shopping areas usually accept Visa and MasterCard/Cirrus cards. The two major banks who provide this service are HSBC and Banco do Brasil. There will usually only be one international machine at a branch. Using ATMs is the easiest way to obtain foreign currency. You can exchange dollars, yen, pounds and other currencies at accredited banks, hotels and tourist agencies. If you can't find one of these, some travel agencies will exchange your currency, although this is, strictly speaking, an illegal transaction. The few hotels that exchange travelers' checks give a poor rate.

Banks will not exchange *reais* or travelers' checks into foreign currency. The only exception is the Banco do Brasil, with branches at international airports. As you leave the country, they will exchange back, at the official rate, 30 percent of the currency you exchanged at a similar airport branch bank on your way into Brazil, if you show the receipt for the initial exchange. You cannot get travelers' checks cashed into dollars.

Most hotels will accept payment in travelers' checks or most major credit cards. Many restaurants and shops take credit cards; the most frequently accepted are American Express, Diners Club, MasterCard and Visa, which all have offices in Brazil. You can also pay with dollars. Hotels, restaurants, stores, taxis, and so on, will usually quote an exchange rate.

Public Holidays

Besides national holidays such as Carnival, Easter and Christmas, many religious or historical events are commemorated locally. Each city celebrates the date on which it was founded and the day of its patron saint. Some regional folk celebrations are movable, with each village and neighborhood staging their own party – usually festivals with music, dancing (sometimes in costumes) and stalls hawking the food and drinks traditionally prepared for the event. There are too many to mention here. The following calendar includes a few of the most important local festivals.

January

1 – New Year's Day
National holiday. Bom Jesus dos Navegantes. A four-day celebration in Salvador starts with a spectacular boat parade.

6 – Epiphany
Regional celebrations, mostly in the northeast.

3rd Sunday – Festa do Bonfim
One of the largest in Salvador.

February

2 – Iemanjá
Festival in Salvador. The Afro-Brazilian goddess of the sea corresponds, in syncretism with Catholicism, with the Virgin Mary.

February/March

Carnival
National holiday celebrated all over Brazil on the four days leading up to and including Ash Wednesday. Dates change every year, but are either in February or March. Most spectacular in Rio, Salvador and Recife/Olinda.

March/April

Good Friday
National holiday. Colonial Ouro Preto puts on a procession; passion play staged at Nova Jerusalem.

April

21 – Tiradentes Day
National holiday in honor of the martyred hero of independence. Celebrations in his native Minas Gerais, especially Ouro Preto.

May

1 – Labor Day
National holiday.

May/June

Corpus Christi
National holiday.

June

15–30 – Amazon Folk Festival
Held in Manaus.

June/July

Bumba-Meu-Boi
Processions and street dancing in Maranhão are held in the second half of June and beginning of July.

Festas Juninas
Street festivals in June and early July in honor of saints John, Peter and Anthony, featuring bonfires, dancing and mock marriages.

August

Festa do Peão Boiadeiro
In Barretos, São Paulo state. The

world's largest annual rodeo, also country music.

September

7 – Independence Day
National holiday.

October

Oktoberfest
In Blumenau, staged by descendants of German immigrants.
Ciriô
Religious procession in Belém.
12 – Nossa Senhora de Aparecida
National holiday honoring Brazil's patron saint.

November

2 – All Souls' Day
National holiday.
15 – Proclamation of the Republic
National holiday; also election day.

December

25 – Christmas Day
National holiday.
31 – New Year's Eve
Millions gather on Rio de Janeiro beaches to watch fireworks and to offer gifts to Iemanjá.

Getting There

BY AIR

Many airlines offer international services to and from Brazil with a variety of routes *(see Getting Around section, page 343)*. Most incoming flights head for São Paulo, and then stop at Rio de Janeiro, Brasília, Salvador, Forauleza and Recife on the northeastern coast, and the northern cities of Belém and Manaus on the Amazon River. Direct international flights link Brazil with both the east and west coasts of the United States, as well as with Florida and Canada, major cities in Europe, South America, and Japan and several African cities.

Flight time from the US is nine hours from New York, slightly less from Miami, and 12 hours from Los Angeles. Flights from Europe take 11–12 hours. Almost all international flights are overnight, so you arrive in the early morning.

There is a variety of special low cost package deals, some of them real bargains. A travel agent will tell you what is available and make arrangements at no extra cost to you. See *Getting Around, page 343* for details on Brazilian air passes, which must be purchased outside Brazil.

Upon arrival, the airports have ATMs, currency exchange facilities and information posts to help you find transportation or make a connecting flight.

Airlines

Tam
www.tam.com.br
Varig
www.varig.com.br
Vasp
www.vasp.com.br

BY SHIP

There is no regular ocean passenger service to Brazil, but it is possible to arrive by boat. *Linea C* operates cruises up and down the Atlantic coast of South America during the European winter and will take on transatlantic passengers when the ships return. Several round-the-world cruise ships call at Brazilian ports and reservations can be made for the trip to Brazil only. Special cruises travel up the Amazon River or visit Rio at Carnival time. *The Blue Star Line*, headquartered in London, carries a limited number of passengers on its cargo boats. Passenger trips with cargo operators can be booked through Strand Travel Centre, London. Tel: 020-7836 6363; fax: 020-7497 0078, or visit: www.strandtravel.co.uk

BY BUS

Long-distance bus services run between a few of the larger Brazilian cities and major cities in neighboring South American countries, including Asunción (Paraguay), Buenos Aires (Argentina), Montevideo (Uruguay) and Santiago (Chile). While undoubtedly a good way to take in the landscape, remember that the distances are great and you may find youself on a bus for several days and nights at a time. They are usually of a high standard, though, in many cases providing toilets, food, and even almost fully reclining seats.

Contacting Varig

Varig Brazilian Airlines, which is part of the Star Alliance, can be contacted through the Alliance at www.varig.com.br, or directly in the following countries:
Canada: 06-926 9945
Mexico: 280-9027
United Kingdom: 020-8321 7170
USA: 1-800 468 2744

SPECIALIST TOURS

A variety of individual and group tours to Brazil is available. Some are all-inclusive packages with transportation, food and lodgings, excursions, and entertainment all arranged for you; some include only air transportation and hotel accommodation. There are also special interest tours that include international travel to and from Brazil. These include boat trips on the Amazon River, fishing, and wildlife (including bird watching) tours to the Pantanal, Mato Grosso in the center–west, and Carnival tours to Rio, Salvador or Recife.

If you aren't on a tour where everything is planned, you might want to go on one of the readily available city sightseeing tours, boat outings to nearby islands, day trips to mountain and beach resort areas, and evening entertainment tour groups that take in a show. If you ask your hotel reception to arrange a tour (best avoided) they will take a hefty commission and often not give impartial advice.

Longer excursions can also be easily arranged once you are in Brazil – from Rio or São Paulo, for example, it is easy to get on a tour to the

Amazon or Pantanal, take a day trip by plane to Brasília or the Iguaçu Falls, or join a tour of the northeast or the colonial towns of Minas Gerais. However, in the peak season there may be a wait, as these excursions do get fully booked. Ocean cruises along the coast need to be booked well in advance and this is best done through your travel agent back home.

RIVER AND SEA TRIPS

Local boat tours and excursions are available in coastal and riverside cities. There are also longer trips. Amazon River boat trips may last a day or two or a week or more. These range from luxury floating hotels to more rustic lodgings. Boat trips can also be taken on the São Francisco River in the northeast and in the Pantanal marshlands of Mato Grosso, popular for the incomparable birds and wildlife.

A lot of towns have local ferry services across bays and rivers and to islands. Schooners and yachts, complete with crew, may be rented for an outing.

Travel Agents

Rio de Janeiro

Just Fly
Tel/Fax: 2268 0565
Cellphone: 9985 7540
E-mail: justfly@justfly.com.br
www. justfly.com.br
Hang gliding over Rio, jeep tours of Tijuca National Park and bicycle hire.

Brazilian Incentive & Tourism
Barao de Ipanema 56, 5th floor, Copacabana
Tel: 21-2256 5657
www.bitourism.com
Comprehensive program of tours which cover the whole of Brazil.

São Paulo

Freeway
Rua Cap. Cavalcanti 322, Tel: 011-5088 0999
www.freeway.tur.br
E-mail: freeway.adventures.com.br
Trips to Fernando de Noronha, Bahia and the Amazon. Ecotourism, trekking, climbing, and diving expeditions.

Salvador

Kontik Operadora
Avenida Tancredo Neves 969, 10th Floor, Sala 1004/1005
Tel: 071-838686
www.kontik.com.br
Specialized tours in the state of Bahia, including climbing, trekking and sailing; folklore and city tours.

Natal

Manary Ecotours
Rua Francisco Gurgel 9067, Praia de Ponta Negra
Tel: 084-219 2900
www.manary.cam.br
Cultural and ecological trips in the northeast and to Fernando de Noronha. Soft adventure and archaeology.

Cuiabá (Pantanal)

Anaconda,
Rua Marachal Deodoro 2142
Tel: 065-624 4142
www.anacondapantanal.com.br
Trips in the northern Pantanal.

Manaus (Amazon)

Swallows and Amazons
Rua Quintino Bocaiuva 189, Suite 13
Tel/Fax: 622-1246
www.swallowsandamazonstours.com
American/Brazilian company offering good Amazon tours.

Brazilian Embassies and Consulates

Australia:
19 Forster Crescent, Yarralumla, Canberra, ACT 2600
Tel: 612-6273 2372
Fax: 612-6273 2375
www.brazil.org.au

Canada:
77 Bloor Street West, 1109 and 1105, Toronto, Ontario, M5S 1M2
Tel: 416-922 2503
Fax: 416-922 1832
www.consbrastoronto.org

Italy:
Piazza Navona, 14, 00186 - Rome
Tel: 06-683 981
Fax: 06-686 7858

Republic of Ireland:
Harcourt Centre, Europa House, Block 9, Harcourt Street, Dublin 2
Tel: 1-475 6000
Fax: 1-475 1341

United Kingdom:
32 Green Street, London W1Y 4AT
Tel: 020-7499 0877
Fax: 020-7399 9100
www.brazil.org.uk

United States:
Washington DC:
3006 Massachusetts Avenue NW, DC 20008
Tel: 202-238 2700
Fax: 202-238 2827
www.brasilemb.org
Houston:
1700 West Loop South 1450A, TX 77027-3006
Tel: 713-961 3063
Fax: 713-961 3070
Los Angeles:
8484 Wilshire Blvd., Suites 730–711, Beverly Hills, CA 90211
Tel: 213-651 2664
Fax: 213-651 1274
Miami:
2601 Bayshore Drive
Suite 800,
FL 33131
Tel: 305-285 6200
Fax: 305-285 6232
www.brazilmiami.org
New York:
1185 Avenue of the Americas, 21st Floor, New York, NY 10036
Tel: 917-777 7777
Fax: 212-827 0225
www.brasilny.org

There are Brazilian consulates in Boston, Chicago, and San Francisco. American citizens must contact one of these to obtain a visa before traveling to Brazil.

Practical Tips

Business Hours

Business hours for offices in most cities Mon–Fri 9am–6pm. The lunch hour may last hours. Banks open Mon–Fri 10am–4pm. *Casas de câmbio* currency exchanges usually operate 9am–5pm.

Most stores are open Mon–Fri 9am–6.30pm or 9am–7pm, and Saturday until 12.30 or 1pm. They may stay open much later depending on their location. The shopping centers are open Mon–Sat 10am–10pm as a rule (many are also open Sunday), although not all the shops inside keep the same hours. Large department stores are usually open Mon–Fri 9am–10pm and 9am–6.30pm on Saturday. Most supermarkets are open 8am–8pm. Some stay open 24 hours, 7 days per week.

Service station hours vary, but they now have the option of staying open 24 hours a day, seven days a week. Post offices are open Mon–Fri 9am–5pm and 9am–1pm on Saturday. Some of the larger cities have one branch that stays open 24 hours a day. Many pharmacies stay open until 10pm and larger cities will have 24-hour drugstores.

The 24-hour and 12-hour clocks are both in common usage.

Religious Services

Catholicism is the official and dominant religion in Brazil, but many people follow religions of African origin. Of these, candomblé is the purer form, with deities (the *orixás*), rituals, music, dance and even language very similar to those practiced in the parts of Africa from which it was brought. Umbanda involves a syncretism with Catholicism in which each *orixá* has a corresponding Catholic saint. Spiritualism, also widely practiced in Brazil, contains both African and European influences. Many Brazilians who are nominally Catholic attend both Afro-Brazilian and/or spiritual and Christian rites.

Candomblé is practiced most in Bahia, while Umbanda and spiritualism seem to have more mass appeal. You can arrange through your hotel to see a ceremony – visitors are welcome so long as they show respect for the belief of others. Ask permission before taking any photographs.

If you wish to attend a service at a church of your faith while in Brazil, many religious groups can be found in the larger cities and, besides the ever-present Catholic churches, there are many Protestant churches throughout Brazil. In recent years, evangelical churches have expanded their presence dramatically. Because of the diplomatic personnel in Brasília, there is a large variety of churches and temples. Rio de Janeiro and São Paulo both have several synagogues, as well as churches with services in foreign languages, including English.

Your hotel or your country's consulate should be able to help you find a suitable place of worship.

Media

NEWSPAPERS AND MAGAZINES

The *Miami Herald*, the Latin America edition of the *International Herald Tribune* and the *Wall Street Journal* are available on many newsstands in the big cities, as are news magazines like *Time* and *Newsweek*.

At larger newsstands and airport bookshops you will find other foreign newspapers and a large selection of international publications, including German, French, and English magazines.

You may want to buy a local paper to find out what's on in town.

Security & Crime

Personal crime, in the form of pick-pocketing and theft from hotel rooms, is sadly common in parts of Brazil, particularly in bigger cities. But, with a little caution and common sense, most visitors manage to avoid trouble.

When traveling, always carry valuables and money in a money-belt, worn out of sight underneath clothing, and don't wear a flashy watch or expensive jewelry. Be especially alert in crowded places, such as rush-hour subway stations, city buses, beaches, and markets. Seek advice from your hotel about local areas to avoid at night. A good, general if not golden rule is to avoid the beach after dark.

Thieves often operate in teams and are masters at diversionary tricks. If carrying expensive camera equipment, never let it out of sight, and be wary of strangers telling you, for instance, that you have stepped in something smelly, and offering to assist you.

Leave valuables in your hotel safe if available, but check to see that they are actually put away, and ask for a list of items deposited. Make sure that you can get access to them at all hours, if checking out very early or late.

Take photocopies of your passport and important documents and, if traveling with a friend, keep copies of each other's documents.

Always report any losses or injuries to the police and ask for a written report of the incident for insurance purposes. Tourist police *(delegacia de proteção ao turista)* can be contacted in the following cities:

- **Rio de Janeiro**, tel: 3399 7564
- **Salvador**, tel: 071-242 2885
- **Santos**, tel: 0800-173887
- **São Paulo**, tel: 3107 5642
- **Aeroporto de São Paulo**, Congonhas, tel: 011-5090 9032
- **Aeroporto Internacional de São Paulo**, Guarulhos, tel: 011-6445 2221 or 6445 2214.

Besides the musical shows, there are always many foreign movies showing in the original language with Portuguese subtitles. Entertainment listings appear under the headings of *cinema*, *show*, *dança*, *música*, *teatro*, *televisão*, *exposicões*, etc. Crianças means "children."

If you do know some Portuguese and want to read the Brazilian newspapers, the most authoritative and respected include: São Paulo's *Folha de São Paulo*, *Estado de São Paulo* and *Gazeta Mercantil*, and Rio's *Jornal do Brasil* and *O Globo*. There is no nationwide paper, but these wide-circulation dailies reach a good part of the country. The colorful weekly magazine *Epoca*, along with *Veja* and *Isto E*, are also good sources of information.

TELEVISION AND RADIO

Brazilian television mostly features light entertainment programs, like quiz shows, comedies, and soaps. It is big business – with Brazil exporting programs around the world. There are a staggering 170 million viewers in the country.

There are six national and several hundred local networks, which bring television to nearly all parts of Brazil. Only one network, for educational television, is government controlled. Brazil's giant *TV Globo* is the fourth largest commercial network in the world. With over 40 stations in a country with a high illiteracy rate, it has great influence over the information many people have access to *(see the TV feature on page 117)*.

Only about a third of all television programs in Brazil are imports and these are mostly from the United States. Foreign series, specials, sports coverage and movies are dubbed in Portuguese, except for some of the late-night movies and musical shows.

Most hotels and many middle- and upper-class homes in the cities receive cable television offering close to 100 channels, including most of the global favorites such as CNN, BBC World and ESPN. It is even possible to watch American breakfast television while in Brazil. At present, cable television is the fastest growing media industry in the country.

There are several thousand radio stations around Brazil which play international and Brazilian pop hits, as well as a variety of Brazilian music reflecting regional tastes. A good deal of American and British music is played; classical music programs are also popular, including Sunday afternoon operas in some areas.

The Culture Ministry station often has some interesting musical programs. All Brazilian broadcasts are in Portuguese.

Tipping

Hotels and more expensive restaurants will add a 10 percent service charge to your bill, but this doesn't necessarily go to the individuals who were helpful to you. Don't be afraid of overtipping – employees earn a pittance and rely on the generosity of tourists.

Tipping taxi drivers is optional; most Brazilians don't. Again, if your driver has been especially helpful or waited for you, reward him appropriately. At the airport, tip the last porter to help you – what you pay goes into a pool.

A 10–20 percent tip is expected in barbershops and beauty salons. Shoeshine boys, gas station attendants, etc. should be paid about a third to half of what you would expect to tip at home.

If you are a house guest, leave a tip for any household help (who cooked or laundered for you while you were there). Ask your hosts how much would be appropriate to give them. A tip in dollars will be especially appreciated. A small gift brought from home may be even better.

Post

Post offices are generally open 9am–5pm Monday–Friday, 9am–1pm on Saturday, and are closed on Sunday and holidays. In large cities, some branch offices stay open until later. The post office in the Rio de Janeiro International Airport is open every day 7am–8pm. Post offices are usually designated with a sign reading *Correios* or sometimes ECT (for Empresa de Correios e Telégrafos – Postal and Telegraph Company).

An airmail letter to or from the United States takes about a week to arrive. In the more densely populated areas, domestic post is usually delivered a day or two after it is mailed. National and international rapid mail service is available, as well as registered post and parcel services (the post office has special boxes for these). Stamps for collectors can be also be purchased at the post office.

You can have mail sent to you at your hotel. Although some consulates will hold mail for citizens of their country, they tend to discourage this practice.

Telecommunications

TELEPHONE

The good news is that Brazil's overstretched telecommunications structure has been given a complete overhaul since privatization of the sector.

The bad news is that all standard telephone numbers in the country are changing from seven to eight digits. This process has already been completed in Rio, but will continue in the rest of the country until 2005.

Consumers have to choose which long-distance service to use when calling between cities by dialing a three number access code, something that was complicated unnecessarily by the ruling body allowing Embratel to choose 021 as its access code, the same as the city of Rio. Hence, to call São Paulo from Rio using Embratel you have to dial 21 11+phone number. This is not the case with every phone, however, as some companies and hotels have already built the long-distance code into their system so you would dial as before, 011+phone number.

The access code for Embratel's rival, Intelig, is 23. For Telemar dial 31; for Telefônica, 15.

So, accepting that the obvious is not always obvious, if you have to call long distance within Brazil ask staff hotel or the owner of the phone what the best – and cheapest – long distance server is.

Pay phones in Brazil use phone cards, which are sold at newsstands, bars or shops, usually located near the phones. The phone card, *cartão de telefone*, comes in several values. The most common is a 30-unit card, but 90-unit cards can also be bought.

The sidewalk *telefone público* is also called an *orelhão* (big ear) because of the protective shell which takes the place of a booth – yellow for local or collect calls, blue for direct-dial, long-distance calls within Brazil. You can also call from a *posto telefônico*, a telephone company station (at most bus stations and airports), where you can either use a phone card, or make a credit card or collect call.

For international calls, country codes are listed at the front of telephone directories. For long-distance domestic calls, area codes within Brazil are listed on the first few pages of directories.

Domestic long-distance rates go down 75 percent 8pm–6am and are half price weekdays 6–8am and 8–11pm, Saturday 2–11pm and Sunday and holidays 6am–11pm.

If you need a cell phone to use in Brazil you can rent from the duty free shop in the arrivals hall or from city outlets. The main service is operated by Gradiente Cellular Travel, tel: 0800-167167; www.gradiente.com.br.

Useful Telephone Numbers

International calling and enquiries:
Direct dialing – **00**+country code +area code+phone number.
000333 or 0800-703 2100 – information regarding long-distance calls (area codes, directory assistance and complaints).
0800-703 2111 – international operator, to place person-to-person, collect and credit-card calls. Operators and interpreters who speak several languages are available.
000334 or 0800-703 2100 – information regarding rates. International rates go down 20 percent 8pm–5am (Brasília time) Monday–Saturday and all day Sunday.
To access your US phone company: Connect: **000-8012**; Sprint: **000-8016**; AT&T: **1-800 437 0966 ext 60330** (English); **1-800 541 5281 ext 59859** (Spanish).

Domestic calling and enquiries:
Direct dialing (IDD) – **0**+operator code+area code+phone number. (Embratel's code is 21, Intelig's is 23).
Direct-dial collect call – **90**+operator code+area code+phone number. A recorded message will tell you to identify yourself and the city from which you are calling after the beep. If the party you are calling does not accept your call, you will be cut off.
107 – operator-assisted collect calls from pay phones (no token needed).
Other service numbers:
102 – local directory assistance.
area code+102 – directory assistance in that area.
108 – information regarding rates.
0800-55135 – telegrams (local, national and international).
138 – wake-up service.
130 – correct time.

TELEX AND FAX

A telex or fax can be sent from some post offices, and most hotels have telex and fax services for their in-house guests. Fax services are also widely available at travel agents, office-services bureaux and many other outlets. The prices charged for sending and receiving faxes vary widely.

Internet

Brazil is now one of the most web-savvy countries on the planet and has helped make Portuguese the second most used language on the Internet after English. 20 million people in Brazil use the internet. Internet cafés are found throughout the country, although service can be slow in smaller beach areas. Many larger hotels offer internet facilities free to their guests. It also means it is easy to stay in touch via email.

The importance and size of the Brazilian Internet market is reflected by Yahoo! setting up its own special Portuguese language search engine for Brazil.

While a lot of the web content on Brazil is in Portuguese, major websites tend to offer pages in English.

Below is a list of some Brazilian web sites likely to be useful for travelers and if you are looking for the obvious in Brazil, remember to try ".com.br" rather than ".com":

Brazilian Government
www.brazil.gov.br
Brazilian Embassy
(Washington)
www.brasil.emb.nw.dc.us
Embratur
(Brazilian Tourist Board)
www.embratur.gov.br
Estado de São Paulo
(Newspaper/links)
www.estado.com.br
Google
(Search engine)
www.google.com.br
O Globo
(Newspaper/links)
www.oglobo.com.br

Rio Tourist Board
www.rio.rj.gov.br/riotur
Salvador Tourist Board
www.emtursa.com.br
São Paulo Tourist Board
www.spguia.com.br
Veja
(News magazine)
www.uol.com.br/veja

Tourist Offices

Each state has its own tourism bureau, as do the major cities like Rio and São Paulo. Addresses for some of these offices in the main cities are listed below.

If you would like the address for a tourism board in an area not listed here, you can obtain it through the national tourist board, Embratur, who will also send information abroad on request.

Embratur
Rua Uruguaiana 174, 8th Floor, 20050-092,
Rio de Janeiro
Tel: 021-2509 6017
Fax: 021-2509 7381
www.embratur.gov.br
Belém
Paratur, Praça Waldemar Henrique
Tel: 091-223-2130
Fax: 091-223 6198
Belo Horizonte
Belotur, Praça Rio Branco 56, Centro Belo Horizonte, M6
Tel: 031-3272 8545
Fax: 031-3272 5619
Brasília
Setur, Setor de Divulgação Cultural, Centro de Convenções, Cetur, 3rd Floor
Tel: 061-321 3318
Information Center: Airport
Florianópolis
Mercado Público 3rd booth from Rua Arcipreste
Paivawww.guiafloripa.com.br
Tel: 048-224 5822
Fortaleza
Setur, Centro Adm. Governador Viríglio Távora, Cambeba, Ed. Seplan, 60839-900 CE
Tel: 085-488 7411
Manaus
Emamtur, Avenida 7 de Setembro 1546, 69005-141, AM
Tel: 092-633 2850
www.visitamazonas.com.br
Information Center: Airport
Porto Alegre
Sindetur, Rua Vigário, José Inacio 368, 90020-110, RS
Tel: 051-224 9228
www.turismo.rs.gov.br
Information Center: Airport.
Recife
Empetur, Complexo Rodoviário de Salgadinho, s/n, 53111-970
Tel: 081-3463 3621
www.empetur.pe.gov.br
Information Centers: Airport, Bus Station, Casa da Cultura
Rio de Janeiro
Rio Convention and Visitors Bureau
Rua Visconde de Pirajá
547 Salas 610-617
Tel 21-2259 6165
www.rioconventionbureau.com.br
Information Centers:
International airport, Bus Station, Corcovado, Sugar Loaf, Cinelândia Subway Station, Marina da Glória.
Salvador
Bahiatursa, Rua das Laranjeiras 12, Historical Centre, BA
Tel: 071-3212133
www.bahiatursa.ba.gov.br
Information Centers: Airport, Bus Station, Mercado Modelo, Porto da Barra.
São Paulo
Setur, Praça Antonio Prado 9–6th Floor, 01010-904
Tel: 011-239 5822
Fax: 011-3107 8767
www.spcvb.com.br
Information Centers:
Praça da República, Praça da Liberdade, Praça da Sé, Praça Ramos de Azevedo, Av. Paulista in front of Top Center and at the corner of Rua Augusta, Shopping Morumbi, Shopping Ibirapuera

Foreign Embassies

In Brazil

Embassies are found in Brasília, where consulates are located. Also in Rio and Sao Paulo and sometimes other cities. Many countries also have diplomatic missions in several cities. Call before visiting because they frequently keep unusual business hours. If you're coming to Brazil on business, remember that your consulate's commercial sector can be of great help.

Australia
Brasília:
SHIS, QI 09, cj. 16,Casa 1
Tel: 061-248 5569
Fax: 061-248 1066
São Paulo:
Rua Tenente Negrão 140/12 (Itaim Bibi)
Tel: 061-384 96281
Canada
Brasília:
SES, Av. das Nações, Q 803, lote 16, s1. 130
Tel: 061-321 2171
Fax: 061-321 4529
São Paulo:
Av. Nações Unidas 12901, 16th Floor, Torre Norte
Tel: 011-550 94321
Ireland
São Paulo:
Av. Paulista 2006, sl. 514 (Cerqueira Cesar)
Tel: 011-287 6362
United Kingdom
Brasília:
SES, Av. das Nações, Q 801, cj. K, Lote 8
Tel: 061-225 2710
Fax: 061-225 1777
Rio de Janeiro:
Praia do Flamengo 284, 2nd Floor (Flamengo)
Tel: 021-2555 9600
Fax: 021-553 5976
São Paulo:
Rua Ferreira de Araújo 741, 2nd Floor
Tel: 011-3816 2303
Fax: 011-3811 9981
United States
Brasília:
SES, Av. das Nações Unidas, Q 801, Lote 3
Tel: 061-321 7272
Fax: 061-225 9136
Rio de Janeiro:
Av. Pres. Wilson 147 (Centro),
Tel: 024-2292 7117
São Paulo:
Rua Padre João Manoel 933 (Jardim America)
Tel: 011-3081 6511

Other Embassies and Consulates in São Paulo

Argentina
Av. Paulista 1106,
9th Floor
Tel: 011-3171-1596

Mexico
Rua Holanda 274
Tel: 011-3081 4144

New Zealand
Alameda Campinas 579,
15th Floor
Tel: 011-288 0307

Paraguay
Rua Bandeira Paulista 600,
15th Floor
Tel: 011-3167-7793

Peru
Rua Votuverava 350
Tel: 011-381 91793

South Africa
Av. Paulista 1754
Tel: 011-3285 0433

Uruguay
Rua Estados Unidos, 1284
Tel: 011-3085 6492

Venezuela
Rua Veneza 878
Tel: 011-388 74583

Photography Tips

Both Kodakcolor and Fujicolor film for color prints can be bought and developed in Brazil, as well as Ektachrome, Kodachrome and Fujichrome slide film. Hotel shops will have film and specialty shops carry equipment and accessories, and handle film processing.

Developing is quick and of good quality. In the larger cities you will find 24-hour finishing and many one-hour services. Reliable labs include Kodak, Fuji, Multicolor and Fotoptika

Revelar = to develop
Revelação = developing
Filme = film

Although it is often easier to wait and have your pictures developed when you return home, if you are going to be traveling around a great deal, remember that exposure to heat and multiple x-ray security checks at airports could ruin your film.

Avoid taking pictures during the middle of the day when the sun is strongest and tends to wash out colors. Light in the tropics is very white and bright and you may want to use an appropriate filter. 9–11am is the best time for photography, or wait until the sun has set a little in the afternoon.

Don't walk around with your camera hanging around your neck or over your shoulder; it is an easy target for a snatcher. Carry it discreetly and never leave it unattended on the beach. If you have expensive equipment, it's a good idea to have it insured.

Medical Emergencies

Should you need a doctor while in Brazil, your hotel should be able to recommend reliable professionals who often speak several languages. Many of the better hotels have a doctor on duty. Your consulate will also be able to supply you with a list of physicians who speak your language.

Getting Around

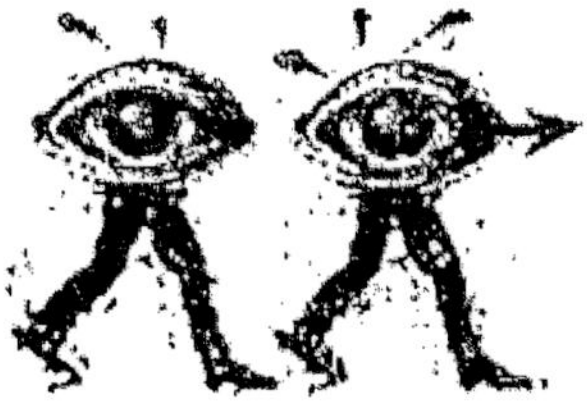

On Arrival

At the airport, take a special taxi, for which you pay in advance at a fixed rate and can use credit cards. There are fewer communication problems, no misunderstanding about the fare, and if the driver takes you the "scenic route" you won't be charged extra. If you take a regular taxi, check out the fares posted for the official taxis so that you will have an idea of what is a normal rate.

An efficient special airport bus service will also take you into town. The route includes stops at the larger hotels. Inquire at the airport information desk.

Some of the top-class hotels will send a driver to pick you up – it's best to arrange for this service when you are making your room reservation.

Domestic Flights

Because Brazil is such an enormous country, it has a good network of domestic flights. Recent deregulation means that as well as established companies such as Varig, TAM and Rio-Sul, there are also budget airlines such as Gol, BRA and Trip. Rio-Sul and Nordeste are both part of Varig. All of the larger lines fly extensive routes throughout the country and have ticket counters at the airports and ticket offices in most cities. At smaller airports in the more remote cities, these may only be manned shortly before a flight.

Tickets can also be purchased at travel agencies and often at hotels, and reservations can be made by phone or on the airline's websites.

Information is usually provided in English as well as Portuguese. Airlines used to offer a toll-free service, but most now charge a premium rate. When planning your route, you will find that it may be easier to travel in one direction than the other. In the case of Varig, most internal flights go clockwise around the country, especially in the Amazon. If you try to plan your itinerary anti-clockwise, you may find yourself having to use some very indirect routes, or being severely limited as to when you can travel.

Deregulation means that on some routes, flying is cheaper than traveling by bus. Discounts of up to 60 percent can be obtained for most internal flights. Travel agents in Brazil can give you details. Varig and VASP offer a variety of air passes, which must be purchased outside Brazil. The cost depends on the number of flights, the season, and the region they cover. They are valid for 21 days and allow you to visit four or five cities (not including your starting point in Brazil). Each pass is only available for the flights of the issuing airline. Extra stops can be purchased. Because bargain flights can be bought from the "no-frills" airlines now, air passes represent less good value than they used to.

The large airlines also operate shuttle services between Rio and São Paulo (with flights every half hour), Rio and Brasília (flights every hour) and Rio and Belo Horizonte (usually about 10 flights per day). The Rio to São Paulo shuttle between the city airports of Santos Dumont (Rio) and Congonhas (São Paulo) is not available on the air pass.

On domestic flights checked baggage is limited to 20 kg (44 lb) and internationally accepted norms apply for hand luggage.

Brazilian Airlines

Three major Brazilian airlines currently operate both domestic and international flights: TAM, Varig and Vasp. These, plus their subsidiaries and several budget airlines, are listed bleow.

Flight Reconfirmation

You must *always* reconfirm your domestic and international flights by telephone, or in person at an airline office, at least 48 hours beforehand. If you don't, you risk being "bounced" onto a later flight.

You do not have to reconfirm with the major international carriers, but it is as well to arrive early at the airport for your flight during high season as they have been known to be overbooked.

Gol
www.voegol.com.br
Tel: 0300-789 2121 ($R.30 per min)
Tam
www.tam.com.br
Tel: 0300-123 2000 ($R.30 per min)
Varig
www.varig.com.br
Tel: 0300-788 7000 ($R.30 per min)
Vasp
www.vasp.com.br
Tel: 0300-789 1010 ($R.30 per min)
Nordeste
www.nordeste.com
Tel: 0800-992 004
Rio-Sul
www.rio-sul.com
Trip
www.voetrip.com.
Tel: 0800-701 8747

International Airlines

Most of the major international airlines have headquarters in São Paulo. Main contact numbers are:

Aerolíneas Argentinas
Rua Araújo 216, 6th Floor
tel: 6445-3806
www.aerolineas.com.ar
Aeroperu
Rua da Consolação 293, 1st Floor – Centro
tel: 011-257 4866
Air Canada
Avenida Paulista, 949, 13th Floor 01311-100
tel: 011-3254 6600
Air France
Avenida Dr Cardoso de Mello 1955, 2nd Floor
tel: 011-3049 0909 or 0800-551 407
Aeroporto de Guarulhos
tel: 011-6445 2211
Alitália
Avenida São Luís 50, 29th Floor/ conj. 291
tel: 011-257 1922
Aeroporto de Guarulhos,
tel: 011-6445 3791
www.alitalia.com.it
American Airlines
Rua Araújo 216, 9th–10th Floors
tel: 011-3214 4000
www.avianca.com
Avianca
Rua da Consolação 293, 10th Floor
tel: 011-257 6511;
Aeroporto de Guarulhos
tel: 011-6445 3798
www.aerolineas.com.ar
British Airways
Alameda Santos 745, 7th Floor
tel: 011-3145 9700 or 0800-176 144
www.britishairways.com
Canadian
Avenida Araújo 216, 2nd Floor
tel: 011-259 9066
Aeroporto de Guarulhos
tel: 011-6445 2462
Continental Airlines
Rua da Consolação 247, 13th Floor
tel: 0800-554 777
Aeroporto
tel: 011-6445 4188.
Delta Airlines
Rua Marquês de Itu 61, 12th Floor
tel: 011-3225 9120 or 0800-221 121
Aeroporto de Guarulhos
tel: 011-6445 3282
Ibéria
Rua Araújo 216, 3rd Floor
tel: 011-6445 2060
Aeroporto Internacional de Guarulhos
tel: 011-6445 2060
Japan Airlines
Avenida Paulista 542
3rd Floor – Paraíso
tel: 011-2288 6121
Aeroporto de Guarulhos
tel: 011-6445 2040

KLM
Aeroporto de Guarulhos,
tel: 011-6445 2011
Avenida São Luís 86, 13th Floor
tel: 0800-231 818
Korean Airlines
Avenida Paulista 1842, 5th Floor/ cj. 58 – Ed. Cetenco Plaza Torre Norte
tel: 011-283 2399
Aeroporto de Guarulhos
tel: 011-6445 2840
Lan Chile
Rua da Consolação 247, 12th Floor
tel: 011-257 8844
Aeroporto de Guarulhos
tel: 011-6445 2824
Lloyd Aéreo Boliviano
Avenida São Luís 72, Centro
tel: 011-258 8111
Aeroporto de Guarulhos
tel: 011-6445 2425
Lufthansa
Rua Gomes de Carvalho 1356, 2nd Floor – Itaim Bibi
tel: 011-3048 5800
Aeroporto de Guarulhos
tel: 011-6445 2499
Tap
Aeroporto de Guarulhos
tel: 011-6445 2150
United Airlines
Avenida Paulista 777, 9th/10th Floor
tel: 011-253 2323 or 0800-162 323
Aeroporto de Guarulhos
tel: 011-6445 3283

Air Taxis

The air taxi service is available to fly anywhere in the world. Inquire at the airport or make arrangements through a travel agent or your hotel.

Be sure to verify from which airport your flight leaves, if the city has more than one. Your hotel will be able to help you with such arrangements and provide transportation to the airport.

Trains

Except for crowded urban commuter railways, trains are not a major form of transportation in Brazil and rail links are minimal. There are a few train trips, however, which are tourist attractions in themselves, either because they are so scenic or because they run on antique steam-powered equipment. Their schedules can be rather erratic, so check carefully before going to catch one of these trains.

In the southern state of Paraná, the 110-km (66-mile) Curitiba–Paranaguá railroad is famous for spectacular mountain scenery *(see page 321).*

A return trip can be done in a day. Bear in mind that you may not see much on a cloudy day.

In the state of Minas Gerais, antique steam locomotives haul passengers the 12 km (7 miles) between São João del Rei and Tiradentes on Friday, weekends and holidays *(see pages 211–12).*

In the state of Rio de Janeiro, the Mountain Steam Train runs 28 km (17 miles) between Miguel Pereira and Conrado every Sunday.

Long-distance Buses

Comfortable, on-schedule bus services are available between all major cities, and even to several other South American countries. Remember that distances are great and bus rides can be long – in other words, several days. But you could break up a long journey with a stop along the way.

On most routes there are three classes available. You can take a regular bus, with upholstered, reclining seats; an executive bus, with more comfortable seats; or the top-rate sleeper *(leito)* bus, which has wider and fully reclining seats with foot rests, as well as coffee and soft drinks on board.

On some routes, there may be just one bus per day (such as the Rio–Belém route, a 52-hour trip) or just one or two per week. Try to buy your ticket in advance through a travel agent or at the bus station.

There is a local bus service to the smaller, more isolated towns. This is quite a different experience and will leave you with no doubts that you are in a still-developing country. Almost always over-crowded, buses bump along dirt roads, picking up passengers who wait along the roadside, often with large bundles they are taking to market. Those who travel standing up – often for three to four hours or more – are charged the same as those who paid for a numbered seat. For the visitor, it may be a new experience, but you certainly have to admire the endurance and patience of the people for whom this precarious system is the only form of getting around.

South American Experience is a new service that allows visitors to arrange bus trips in advance or as part of a fly-drive package. A flexible pass allows you to get on or off at stops within Rio state. English-speaking staff will arrange accommodations and act as guides en-route. The two main routes are "Costa Verde", taking in the islands of Angra do Reis and historic Parati before heading inland, and "Route Sol", which takes in the same sites, but with extra stops at Buzios and the surfing spot of Saquarema. Contact South American Experience, Rua Raimundo Correa 36A, Copacabana. Tel 21-2548 8813; www.southamericaexperience.com

Travel Translated

Entrada = Entrance
Saída = Exit
Unitário = Single
Ida e volta = Return/Round-trip

City Buses

Since just a small percentage of Brazilians can afford cars, public transport is used a great deal. The larger cities have special air-conditioned buses connecting residential areas to the central business district, including routes from airports and bus stations that swing by many of the larger hotels. You will be handed a ticket as you board. Take a seat and an attendant will come around to collect your fare, which will be extremely modest by North American and most European standards.

Daylight Robbery

Be on guard against robberies on crowded buses, which occur frequently, even in broad daylight. If you are bent on riding the regular city buses, try at least to avoid the rush hour when passengers on certain lines are packed tighter than the proverbial sardines in a can.

Don't carry valuables, keep your shoulder bag in front of you and your camera inside a bag. Avoid calling attention to yourself by speaking loudly in a foreign language. In other words, be discreet.

Your hotel may be helpful in providing information about bus routes, but most hotels discourage tourists from riding anything but the special buses.

The regular city buses are very cheap. Get on (often quite a high step up) and after paying the "*cobrador*", who will give you change, move through the turnstile. It's a good idea to have your fare handy – several people may board at your stop and all have to get through the turnstile before they can sit down. This is also a favorite bottleneck for pick-pockets who can jump out the back door as the bus takes off, so be alert to what's going on around you.

If you travel standing up, be sure to hold on tight. Some bus drivers (especially in Rio) can be very inconsiderate, jamming on the brakes suddenly, careening around corners at full tilt, etc. Signal when you want to get off by pulling the cord (some buses have buttons).

The Metrô

Rio de Janeiro and São Paulo have excellent, though not extensive, subway services, with bright, clean, air-conditioned cars. Maps in the stations and in each car help you find your way without needing to communicate in Portuguese.

Lines radiate from the city center and the service is further extended by bus links, often with train-bus combination tickets. Subway extension bus lines are marked *integração*.

São Paulo has three lines, two of them crossing underneath the Praça da Sé at the city's heart. The north–south line connects Tucuruvi and Jabaquara, and the east–west line runs from Barra Funda to Itaquera. They run from 5am–midnight and there are stops at the inter-city bus stations and bus link-ups to the Guarulhos International Airport. The other line is the Paolista, connecting Ana Rosa and Vila Mariana.

Rio's two lines reach out from downtown as far south as Copacabana, to the station at Arcoverde. On the northern side they run as far as Irajá, with stops near the Sambadrome and Maracanã soccer stadium.

The Rio subway is closed on Sunday and operates 6am–11pm Monday–Saturday and holidays.

Taxis

Taxis are probably the best way for visitors to get around in the cities. Of course, it's easy to get "taken for a ride" in a strange city. Whenever possible, take a taxi from your hotel where a member of staff can inform the driver where you want to go.

Radio taxis are slightly more expensive, but safer and more comfortable. Although the drivers of the yellow cabs you flag down on the street won't rob you, some occasionally try to overcharge or take you the long way around. Try to find out the normal fare for a given destination – most trips will be just a few dollars. Airport taxis charge high rates by Brazilian terms, but you will still probably find fares relatively low compared to North America or Europe.

Radio taxis calculate a certain percentage above the meter rate (about 50 percent). If you hail a taxi at the curbside, be sure the tarrif shows no. 1 on the computerized display when the driver resets the meter for your run. The no. 2 tarrif indicates that the meter is set at a 20 percent higher rate – chargeable after 8pm and on Sundays and holidays, when going beyond certain specified city bounds or up steep areas. Cab drivers can also use the no. 2 rate during the month of December to earn the "13th month salary" that Brazilian workers receive each year as a sort of a Christmas bonus.

Private Transportation

RENTAL CAR SERVICES

Car rental facilities are available in the larger cities. Both **Avis** and **Hertz** operate in Brazil; www.avis.com, tel: 0800-198456 (with a large number of outlets across Brazil) or www.hertz.com, tel: 0800-701 7300 toll free; fax: 011-4332 7158, São Paulo office open Mon–Fri 6am–11.45pm.

The two largest Brazilian national chains are: **Localiza** (www.localiza.com.br) and **Nobre** (www.nobre.com.br). Note that both these websites are in Portuguese only. There are also good local companies. Rates vary depending on the type of car. Some companies bill a flat daily rate, while others bill by mileage. Major international credit cards are accepted by these rental companies. Some will charge extra if you rent a car in one city and hand it back in another.

Arrangements can be made at the airport as you arrive, through your hotel or at the agencies. An international driving license is helpful, but you can also rent a car with your own country's driving license. For a relatively modest additional fee you can hire a driver with the car.

DRIVING

Motoring in Brazil may seem chaotic compared to the rest of the world. Rio drivers are especially notorious for their erratic lane-changing, in-town speeding and disregard for pedestrians and other drivers on the road. Be on the defensive and expect the unexpected. Speeding fines can be huge (several hundred dollars) even for going slightly over the limit, which can change erratically. There are speed cameras on many roads.

In the big cities, parking can be a difficult business downtown. A good solution in Rio is to park your car near the Botafogo subway station and take the underground into town. Wherever you park in Brazil, always lock your car. Never leave anything visible inside; even if you don't think of it as valuable, someone else might.

It seems wherever you park in the cities, within seconds a freelance car "guard" will appear, either offering to keep an eye on your car in the hopes of receiving a tip or even demanding that you pay him in advance for his (dubious) vigilance. The fee is quite modest; a few coins will usually be enough. It's best to pay up or you risk finding some slight damage to the car upon your return.

In recent years licensed guards have been introduced in Rio and São Paulo and they will supply a receipt which covers a certain period of parking time.

The highways, especially the interstates, are generally quite good but are crowded with more trucks than you will have ever seen. These huge vehicles bog down traffic on winding, climbing stretches of road in the mountains. Be aware that there are different rules of the road. It is polite to beep your horn when overtaking and flashing your lights is a warning, for example.

If you plan to drive a lot in Brazil, buy the excellent Quatro Rodas (Four Wheels) *Guia Brasil* road guide, complete with road maps, city and regional itineraries, and hotel and restaurant listings (in Portuguese), which is available at most newsstands.

Tourist Bus – Rio

City Rio has three bus routes aimed specifically to help visitors to the city. The drivers have even been taught a rudimentary form of English.

Color coded – Blue, Orange and Lilac – the air-conditioned tourist buses run daily at half hourly intervals from 8am to 6pm, with 64 stops covering most of the city's main attractions and points of interest; tourists can get on and off the bus as many times as they like. A ticket valid for 24 hours costs R$16; for 48 hours it is R$30; and for 72 hours, R$40. Another ticket, valid for 72 hours with free entrance to Sugarloaf and Corcovado, costs R$49.

The **Blue Route** covers the city center, including the historic parts of the city and the main museums and uses Sugarloaf as its starting and ending point.

The **Orange Route** also leaves from Sugarloaf and stops at the station for Corcovado, circum-navigates the Lagoa, and passes the Botanical Garden before heading out to São Conrado (where it links with the Lilac Route). From there it returns to Sugarloaf along the coast taking in Leblon, Ipanema and Copacabana.

The **Lilac Route** opens up Barra da Tijuca to visitors. From São Conrado it takes the beach route along to Barra Shopping, the largest shopping center in Latin America.

Where to Stay

Hotels

There is no shortage of excellent hotels in Brazil. The larger cities and resort areas especially have international-standard hotels, with multilingual staff. Many have their own travel agencies. At all grades, rooms are usually clean and staff are polite. However, it's a good idea to see the room before deciding to take it. A continental breakfast is usually included in the price.

It is always best to book well in advance, especially if you are visiting during Carnival or a major holiday. Hotels then are full of Brazilian tourists as well as visiting foreigners. Travelers from colder climates often come to get away from the northern hemisphere winter and Brazilians also travel more during the school holidays in the summer months of January and February, and in July. Even if you are traveling to an area that you think is off the usual tourist route, local facilities may be saturated with Brazilian vacationers during these peak months. Hotels can be unexpectedly full because of local festivals or events at various times of the year.

If traveling by car, you should be aware that motels may not be what you're used to at home: rooms, often garishly decorated and outfitted with mirrors, private pools and round beds are rented out by the hour for amorous trysts.

Budget Accommodation

CAMPGROUNDS

If you are interested in camping, contact the Camping Clube do

Brasil. Their national headquarters is located at Rua Senador Dantas 75, 29th Floor, Rio de Janeiro, RJ. Tel: 021-2210 3298 or 0800-227 050; www.campingclube.com.br.

HOSTELS

The Casa do Estudante do Brasil, located at Praça Ana Amelia, 9, 8th Floor, Castelo, Rio de Janeiro, RJ, tel: 021-2220 7223, has a list of hostels in 10 Brazilian states that are registered with the International Youth Hostel Federation and charge just a few dollars. Despite the name, there is no age restriction.

Price Guide

Approximate price per person per night in *reais* (R$). Breakfast is usually included, except in some top-notch city hotels.

$$$$	over R$190
$$$	R$100–190
$$	R$50–99
$	under R$50

Hotel & *Pousada* Listings

The following list includes just a few of the best accommodations in the major tourism areas. *Pousadas* (inns) may be cheaper and simpler than hotels. Note that since room rates fluctuate greatly according to demand, our price guide is only a general approximation.

(For the meaning of abbreviations used in addresses, see page 371.)

RIO DE JANEIRO

Rio de Janeriro

Arpoador Inn
Rua Francisco Otaviano 177
Ipanema
Tel: 021-2523 0060
Fax: 021-2511 5094
www.ipanema.com/hotel/arpoador_inn.htm
A small, simple hotel, but great value because it is situated in one of the most beautiful spots in Rio, right by the sea. Try and get a beach-front room as they are much quieter. **$$**

Caesar Park
Avenida Vieira Souto 460
Ipanema
Tel: 021-2525 2525
Fax: 021-2521 6000
www.caesarpark-rio.com
Of international standard, this hotel is well situated on Ipanema beach overlooking the sea, and has excellent restaurants and business facilities. One of Rio's top-five hotels. **$$$$**

Copacabana Palace
Avenida Atlântica 1702
Copacabana
Tel: 021-2548 7070
Fax: 021-2235 7330
www.copacabanapalace.com.br
An oasis of calm with superb restaurants and an excellent swimming pool. Good business facilities. Best afternoon tea in Brazil. Classic luxury at the heart of Copacabana beach. **$$$$**

Excelsior Copacabana
Avenida Atlântica 1800
Copacabana
Tel: 021-2257 1950
Fax: 021-2257 1850
www.windsorhoteis.com.br
This once traditional hotel has been totally refurbished offering excellent value as a beach-front executive hotel. Same block as the Copacabana Palace. **$$$$**

Glória
Rua do Russel 632, Gloria
Tel: 021-2555 7272
Fax: 021-2555 7282
E-mail: hotel@hotelgloriario.com.br
www.hotelgloriario.com.br
Beautiful old building, with a convention center. Its downtown location makes it very convenient for those doing business in the city center. **$$$**

Hostel Ipanema
Rua Barão da Torre 175, Casa 14
Tel: 021-2247 7269
Ipanema
www.justfly.com.br
Friendly house with dorm beds just two blocks from the beach. Lovely staff; tours offered. **$**

Inter-Continental Rio
Rua Prefeito Mendes de Morais 222, São Conrado
Tel: 021-3323 2200
Fax: 021-3322 5500
A good Inter-Continental hotel with full resort facilities. The nearest of the city's top ranking hotels to Barra. **$$$$**

Ipanema Inn
Rua Maria Quitéria 27
Ipanema
Tel: 021-2523 6092
Fax: 021-2511 5092
www.ipanema.com/hotel/ipanema_inn.htm
A good low-priced hotel; well located for sightseeing. The rooms are small but comfortable. Just round the corner from the beach.**$$**

Leme Othon Palace
Avenida Atlântica 656
Leme
Tel/Fax: 021-2543 8080
Reservations, tel: 0800-210 799
E-mail: leme@othon.com.br
Traditional beach-front hotel. Located at the Leme end of Copacabana makes it convenient for the city. **$$$**

Luxor Regente
Avenida Atlântica 3716
Copacabana
Tel: 021-2525 2070
Fax: 021-2267 7693
www.luxor-hotels.com/regente
A good hotel well situated for the beach. **$$$$**

Marina Palace
Avenida Delfim Moreira 630
Leblon
Tel: 021-2540 5212
Fax: 021-2294 1644
E-mail: hotelmarina@callnet.com.br
www.hotelmarina.com.br
Well situated on Leblon beach close to many restaurants. **$$$$**

Meridien
Avenida Atlântica 1020, Leme
Tel: 021-12546 0866
Fax: 021-541 6447
www.meridien-br.com
One of Rio's top hotels; excellent French restaurant, the Saint Honoré, with great views. **$$$$**

Praia Ipanema
Avenida Vieira Souto 706
Ipanema
Tel: 021-2540 4949
Fax: 021-2239 6889
www.praiaipanema.com/

Well located beachfront hotel on the border of Ipanema and Leblon. **$$$$**

Sheraton Rio Hotel & Towers
Avenida Niemeyer 121, Vidigal
Tel: 021-2274 1122
Reservations, tel: 0800-111 345
Fax: 021-2239 5643
Top resort hotel close to Leblon and Ipanema – offers top-flight accommodation and facilities. **$$$$**

Sofitel Rio Palace
Avenida Atlântica 4240
Copacabana
Tel: 021-2525 1232
Fax: 021-2522 1232
www.accorhotelsbrasil.com.br
Good conference and business hotel, with beautiful views. **$$$$**

Angra dos Reis

The hotels below are set in beautiful locations with sports facilities.

Hotel do Frade Golf Resort
BR-101 Sul km 123
Tel: 024-3369 2244
Fax: 024-3369 2254
www.frade.com
Features an 18-hole golf course and hosts international competitions in June and November. **$$$$**

Portogalo Suite
BR-101 Norte km 71
Tel: 024-3361 1434
Fax: 024-3361 1461
www.redeprotel.com.br
Comfortable, with wide range of water sports facilities. **$$$**

Club Med Village Rio das Pedras
BR-101 Norte km 445
Tel: 021-2688 9191
Reservations, tel: 0800-2213 782
Fax: 021-2688 3333
www.clubmed.com
At the top of the range is this Club Med located in its own spectacular valley and on its own beach. **$$$**

Búzios

Pousada Hibiscus Beach
Rua 1, 22 Quadra C, Praia de Joáo Fernandes
Tel: 024-2623 6221
www.hibiscusbeach.com.br.
Beautifully laid-out and designed rooms. Very relaxing. British-run. **$$$**

Pousada La Chimère
Praça Eugenio Honold 36
Praia dos Ossos
Tel: 024-2623 1460
Fax: 024-2623 1108
www.lachimere.com.br
Has its own pool and bar. **$$$**

Villagio Valtur Nas Rocas
Ilha Rasa, Marina Porto Buzios
Tel: 024-2629 1303
Fax: 024-2629 1333
Exclusive accommodation: a resort on its own tropical island – you can arrange to be met by a hotel boat for the 15-minute crossing. **$$$$**

Cabo Frio

La Plage
Rua dos Badejos 40, Peró
Tel/Fax: 022-2647 1746
www.redebela.com.br
Cabo Frio's top beachfront property. **$$$**

Pousada Ponta de Areia
Avenida Espadarte 184
Caminho Verde, Ogiva
Tel/fax: 024-2643 2053
Out of town, with pool and sauna. **$$**

Pousada Porto Peró
Avenida dos Pescadores 2002
Tel/fax: 024-2643 6565
A fairly basic inn. **$$**

Pousada Portoveleiro
Avenida dos Espardartes 129
Caminho Verde, Ogiva
Tel/fax: 024-2647 3081
Comfortable hotel; facilities include pool and sauna. **$$$**

Itacuruçá

Elias C
Ilha de Itacuruçá
Tel: 021-2680 7089
Fax: 021-2680 7017
Forty minutes by boat. Two restaurants and very good sports facilities. **$$$**

Hotel do Pierre
Ilha de Itacuruçá
Tel: 021-2253 4102
www.hotelpierre.com.br
Twenty minutes by boat from the mainland. Restaurant, bars, sporting facilities. **$$$**

Itatiaia National Park

Hotel do Ypê
Parque Nacional km 14
Tel/fax: 024-3352 1453
www.hoteldoype.com.br
Located on the park road, with good meals included in the room rate. **$$$**

Hotel Simon
Parque Nacional km 13
Tel: 024-3352 1122
Fax: 024-3352 1230
www.hotelsimon.com.br
In a beautiful setting, with an orchid garden attached. Helpful advice given on getting around the park. **$$$**

Nova Friburgo

Bucsky
Estrada Niteroi–Nova Friburgo
Km 76.5, Mury
Tel: 024-2522 5052
Fax: 024-2522 9769
www.hotelbucsky.com
A short distance from town. Meals included. **$$$**

Fazenda Garlipp
Estrada Niteroi–Nova Friburgo
km 71.5, Mury
Tel/fax: 024-2542 1330
German-run chalets, with meals included in the price. **$$$**

Parati

Casa do Rio
Rua Antônio Vidal 120
Tel: 024-3371 2223
A youth hostel in a gorgeous house with a courtyard and hammocks next to the river. Boat and four-wheel-drive trips. A real home-from-home. **$**

Pousada do Corsário
Beco do Lapeiro 26
Tel: 024-3371 1866
Peaceful spot with riverside garden and pool. **$$**

Pousada do Ouro
Rua Dr Pereira 145
Tel: 024-3371 2221
For reservations in São Paolo, tel: 011-3813 3433.
Fax: 024-3371 1311
www.pousadaouro.com.br
Centrally located, discreetly luxurious accommodation. **$$$**

Pousada do Sandi
Largo do Rosario 1
Tel: 024-3371 2100
Reservations, tel: 0800-232 100
Fax: 024-3371 2038
www.paraty.com.br/sandi.htm
Considered by many to be Parati's top *pousada*. Good restaurant.

Petrópolis

Casa do Sol
Estrada Rio–Petrópolis
km 115, Quitandinha
Tel/fax: 024-2243 5062
Comfortable, with a wide range of facilities. **$$**

Locanda Della Mimosa
Alameda das Mimosas 30
Vale Florido
Tel/fax: 024-2233 5405
www.locanda.com.br
Luxury *pousada* situated on the outskirts of Petrópolis (en route to Teresópolis) which has one of the region's great restaurants. **$$$$**

Pousada da Alcobaça
Rua Agostinho Goulão 298
Tel: 024-2221 1240
Fax: 024-2222 3162
One of the best in town, housed in an old building in lovely gardens, with swimming pool, sauna, and tennis court. **$$$**

Teresópolis

Rosa dos Ventos
Estrada Teresópolis–Nova Friburgo km 22.6
Tel: 021-2642 8833
Fax: 021-2642 8174
www.roteirosdecharme.com.br
Interesting mix of alpine and *fazenda*-style buildings. The best – large grounds, lake, good sports facilities. **$$$$**

SAO PAULO

São Paulo

Caesar Park
Rua Augusta 1508
Cerqueira Cesar
Tel: 011-3371 3000
Reservations, tel: 0800-111 164
Fax: 011-3287 1123
www.caesarpark.com.br
Top-ranking executive hotel. **$$$$**

Eldorado Higienópolis
Rua Marquês de Itu 836
Higienópolis
Tel: 011-3361 6888
Reservations, tel: 0800-171 888
Fax: 011- 3338 0633
www.hoteiseldorado.com.br
Well-equipped, international-standard hotel, good for business visitors. **$$$$**

Excelsior
Avenida Ipiranga 770
Tel: 011-3220 0377
Fax: 011-3221 6653
Simple but very reasonable hotel near the town center. **$$$**

George V
Rua José Maria Lisboa 1000
Tel: 011-3088 3088
Fax: 011-3082 3082
The best apart-hotel in town, with swimming pool and sauna. Small; executive service. **$$$$**

Inter-Continental São Paulo
Avenida Santos 1123
Tel: 011-3179 2669
Reservations, tel: 0800-118 003
Fax: 011-3179 2666
Best executive hotel in São Paulo. Elegant with good service but very expensive. **$$$$**

Maksoud Plaza
Alameda Campinas 150
Bela Vista
Tel: 011-3145 8000
Fax: 011-3145 8001
E-mail: maksoud@maksoud.com.br
One of the best (and most expensive) hotels in São Paulo. Offers catering facilities and night-life to suit everyone, as long as the wallet can stand the shock. **$$$$**

Meliá São Paulo & WTC Convention Center
Avenida das Nações Unidas 12.559
Broklin Novo
Tel: 011-3043 8000
Reservations, tel: 0800-155 555
Fax: 011-3043 8052
Popular conference venue and a favorite those who need a hotel to the south of the city. **$$$$**

Othon Palace São Paolo
Rua Líbero Badaró 190, Centro
Tel: 011-3232 6000
Fax: 011-3107 7203
www.hoteis-othon.com.br
Right in the city center, close to the main sights. **$$$$**

Parthenon Golden Tower
Avenida Cidade Jardim 411
Tel: 011-3081 6333
Fax: 011-3088 3351
An apart-hotel; very comfortable and good value. **$$$**

Renaissance
Alameda Santos 2233
Tel: 011-3069 2233
Fax: 011-3064 3344
A large business hotel in a great location with all facilities. **$$$$**

San Michel
Largo do Arouche 200
Tel: 011-3223 4433
Fax: 011-3221 5131
Recommended budget hotel. **$**

Sofitel São Paulo
Sena Madureira 1355
Bloco 1, Ibirapuera
Tel: 011-5574 1100
Fax: 011-5575 4544
E-mail: sofitel@dialdata.com.br
Modern executive hotel overlooking Ibirapuera Park. **$$$$**

Transamérica
Avenida Nações Unidas 18.591, Santo Amaro
Tel: 011-5693 4511
Fax: 011-5693 4990
www.transamerica.com.br
São Paulo's top resort property for those who prefer to be further south rather than in the city center. Center of activities for Formula One Grand Prix, plus there's a nine-hole golf course. **$$$$**

Price Guide

Price per person per night in *reais* (R$). Breakfast is usually included, except in some top-notch city hotels.

$$$$	over R$190
$$$	R$100–190
$$	R$50–99
$	under R$50

Top Touring Guide

If you are venturing away from tourist spots to places where no hotels are included in our listing, you will find the Quatro Rodas ***Guia Brasil*** road guide useful. Available at newsstands, it has road maps and lists hotels, restaurants, and local attractions for more than 800 Brazilian towns and cities. It has a system of symbols with explanations in English and Portuguese.

Aguas da Prata

Ideal
Rua Gabriel Rabelo de Andrade 79
Tel: 019-642 1206
Fax: 019-642 1906
A fairly simple hotel, but with its own pool. **$$**

Panorama Prata
Rua Dr Hernani G Correa 45
Tel/fax: 019-642 1511
www.panoramaprata.com.br
As its name implies, well situated with panoramic views. **$$**

Aguas de Lindóia

Hotel das Fontes
Rua Rio de Janeiro 267
Tel: 019-3824 1511
Fax: 019-3824 1972
Fairly simple medium-sized hotel. **$$**

Hotel Vacance
Avenida Nações Unidas 1374
Tel/fax: 019-3824 1191
www.vacancehotel.com.br
This hotel within a park has many sports facilities. **$$$$**

Atibaia

Park Hotel Atibaia
Rod. Fernão Dias km 37
Tel: 011-3864-5299
www.parkhotelatibaia.com.br
Comfortable; in a lovely setting. **$$$**

Recanto da Paz
Avenida Jerônimo de Camargo km 14
Tel: 011-4415 1369
A small hotel with good views. **$$$**

Village Eldorado
Rod. Dom Pedro I km 75.5
Tel: 011-4411 0533
Fax: 011-4411 0300
www.hoteiseldorado.com.br
Well-equipped holiday hotel. **$$$$**

Campos do Jordão

Mont Blanc Othon
Rua Adolfo Torresin 500
Tel: 012-260 2000
Fax: 012-260 2030
www.interhotel.com/brazil
Beautiful setting in park. Campos do Jordão's best. **$$$$**

Orotour Garden Hotel
Rua Eng Gustavo Kaiser 165
Jaguaribe 4
Tel: 012-262 2833
Fax: 012-262 4416
www.orotour.com.br
Well equipped and nicely situated holiday hotel. **$$$$**

Toriba
Avenida Ernesto Diederichsen 2962
Tel: 012-3668 5005
www.toriba.com.br
Good holiday hotel with panoramic views. **$$$$**

Caraguatatuba

Pousada da Tabatinga
Estr. Caraguatatuba–Ubatuba
Praia Tabatinga.
Tel: 012-3884 6010
www.pousadadaportaldatabinga.com.br
Situated near the beach, and well-equipped. **$$$$**

Guarujá

Casa Grande
Avenida Miguel Stefano 1087
Praia da Enseada
Tel/fax: 013-3389 4000
www.casagrandehotel.com.br
A well equipped, colonial-style hotel with spa facilities, set on one of the best beaches in Guarujá. Excellent restaurant. **$$$$**

Delphin Hotel
Avenida Miguel Stefano 1295
Praia da Enseada
Tel: 013-3386 2112
Fax: 013-2286 6844
www.delphinhotel.com.br
Also on the beach but more modest than the Casa Grande. **$$$**

Ilhabela

Ilhabela
Avenida Pedro Paula de Morais 151
Saco da Capela
Tel/fax: 012-3896 1083
www.hotelilhabela.com.br
Good sports facilities available here. **$$**

Mercedes
Avenida Leonardo Reale, Mercedes
Tel: 012-3896 1071
Fax: 012-3896 1074
www.hotelmercedes.com.br
Own grounds; beach access. **$$$**

Porto Pousada Saco da Capela
Rua Itapema 167
Tel: 012-3896 2255
Fax: 012-3896 1052
www.sacodacapela.com.br
Situated in a park, next to the beach. Beautiful panorama over the surrounding area. **$$$**

Santos

Avenida Palace
Avenida Presidente Wilson 10
Gonzaga
Tel: 013-3289 3555
Fax: 013-3289 5961
www.avenidapalace.com.br
A modest hotel situated on the beachfront. **$$**

Mendes Plaza
Avenida Floriano
Peixoto 42
Tel: 013-3289 4243
Fax: 013-3284 8253
Upmarket option with full range of facilities. Serves afternoon tea.

Charming Hotels

The Roteiros de Charme is a small group of hotels and *pousadas*. They are of a very high standard and usually in historical buildings.

Charming, intimate, and with good food, these establishments are likely to be the most memorable of your trip. For more information consult www.roteirosdecharme.com.br.

Ubatuba

Recanto das Toninhas
Praia das Toninhas km 56.5
Tel: 012-3842 1410
Reservations, tel: 0800-177 557
www.toninhas.com.br
Luxury resort. **$$$$**

Sol e Vida
Praia da Enseada, Rua Domingo Della Monica Barbosa 93
Tel: 012-3842 0188
Fax: 012-3842 0488
www.solevida.com.br
Situated on the beach, with watersports facilities. **$$$**

Solar das Aguas Cantantes
Praia do Lázaro
Tel: 012-3842 0178
Fax: 012-3842 1288
With pool and restaurant. **$$$**

Wembley Inn
Estrada Ubatuba–Caraguatatuba
Praia das Toninhas
Tel: 012-3842 0198
Fax: 012-3842 0484
www.wembleyinn.com.br
Good facilities. **$$$**

MINAS GERAIS

Araxá

Hotel Colombo
Estância do Barreiro
Tel: 034-3662 4016
www.hotelcolombo.com.br
Hotel in its own grounds with swimming pool and sauna. **$$**

Price Guide

Price per person per night in *reais* (R$). Breakfast is usually included, except in some top-notch city hotels.

$$$$	over R$190
$$$	R$100–190
$$	R$50–99
$	under R$50

Belo Horizonte

Belo Horizonte Othon Palace
Avenida Afonso Pena 1050
Centro
Tel: 031-3273 3844
Fax: 031-3212 2318
One of the best in town, and located. **$$$$**

Comodoro Tourist
Rua dos Carijós 508, Centro
Tel: 031-3201 5522
Fax; 031-3201 5843
Very simple and good value for money. **$$**

Ouro Minas Palace
Avenida Cristiano Machado 4001
Tel: 031-3429 4001
Fax; 031-3429 4002
www.ourominas.com.br
The best hotel in town, with a modern business complex. Located outside the city center. **$$$$**

Wembley Palace
Rua Espírito Santo 201
Centro
Tel: 031-3273 6866
Fax: 031-3273 1601
Expensive but with a conveniently central location. **$$$**

Caxambu

Glória
Avenida Camilo Soares 590
Tel/fax: 035-3341 3000
The best hotel in town, with many facilities. **$$$$**

Grande Hotel
Rua Dr Viotti 438
Tel: 035-3341 3377
www.grandehotelltda.com.br
Comfortable, with pool and sports facilities. **$$**

Diamantina

Diamante Palace
Avenida Sílvio Félicio dos Santos 1050
Tel/fax: 038-3531 1561
www.diamantinanet.com.br
Comfortable hotel, with restaurant and bar. **$**

Pousada do Garimpo
Avenida da Saudade 265
Consolação
Tel/fax: 038-3531 2523
Probably the area's best equipped *pousada*. **$$**

Ouro Preto

Estalagem das Minas Gerais
Rod. Dos Inconfidentes km 87
Tel: 031-3551 2122
Fax: 031-3551 2709
In its own grounds with panoramic views. Good facilities. **$$$**

Grande Hotel de Ouro Preto
Rua Senador Rocha Lagoa 164
Tel: 031-3551 1488
Fax: 031-3551 5028
Modern building in a colonial town. Central, good service. **$$**

Luxor Pousada
Rua Dr Alfredo Baeta 16
Tel/fax: 031-3551 2244
Reservations, tel: 0800-165 322
Converted colonial mansion from the 18th century. **$$$$**

Poços de Caldas

Minas Gerais
Rua Pernambuco 615
Tel: 035-3722 1686
Fax: 035-3722 1559
www.hotelminasgerais.com.br
Superb value. Two pools, sauna, children's playground. **$$**

Palace
Praça Pedro Sanches
Tel: 035-3722 1392
Fax: 035-3722 1922
www.palacehotelpocos.com.br
Traditional, well-run establishment with sulphur baths. **$$$**

São Lourenço

Brasil
Praça João Lage 87
Tel: 035-3332 1313
Reservations, tel: 0800-351 313
Fax: 035-3331 1536
www.hotelbrasil.com.br
Luxury hotel with excellent spa facilities. **$$$**

Primus
Rua Colonel José Justino 681
Tel: 035-3332 3232
Reservations, tel: 0800-350 006
Fax: 035-3332 4100
www.hotelprimus-mg.com.br
Large, comfortable hotel with pool, sauna, restaurant and bar. **$$$**

BAHIA

Salvador

Bahia Othon Palace
Avenida Oceânica 2456, Ondina
Tel: 071-203 2000
Fax: 071-245 4877
www.othon.com.br.
All rooms overlook the ocean. **$$$$**

Club Mediterranée
Estrada Itaparica–Nazaré km. 13
Tel: 071-880 7141
Reservations: tel: 0800-213 782
Fax: 071-880 7165
www.clubmed.com.br
On the magical island of Itaparica. Allow plenty of time to get there from the airport. All facilities. Closed in June. **$$$$**

Hotel Palace
Rua Chile 20
Tel: 071-322 1155
Fax: 071-243 1109
Comfortable and good value. **$$**

Hotel Tropical da Bahia
Praça 2 de Julho 2, Campo Grande
Tel: 071-374 8000
Fax: 071-374 4749
www.tropicalhotel.com.br
Close to the city center, good location for Carnival. **$$$$**

Paris
Rua Rui Barbosa 13
Tel: 071-321 3922
Good budget option with air conditioning and restaurant. **$**

Pousada Arco Iris
Estrada de Rodagem 102
Ilha de Itaparica
Tel/fax: 071-833 1130

A small *pousada* in an idyllic setting. Offers excellent food, and is 30 minutes by passenger ferry from the Mercado Modelo. **$$**

Pousada do Boqueirão
Rua Direita do Santo Antônio 48
Tel/fax: 071-241 2262
www.pousadaboqueirao.com.br
Family-run house overlooking the bay; recommended. **$$**

Pousada Redfish
Rua Direita do Santo Antônio
Tel/Fax: 071 243-8473
www.hotelredfish.com
English-owned and beautifully designed hotel in historic mansion. **$$$**

Transamérica
Morro do Conselho 505
Rio Vermelho
Tel: 071-330 2233
Fax: 071-330 2200
www.transamerica.com.br
Top-class resort property with spectacular views over the ocean and city. **$$$$**

Ilhéus

Cana Brava Resort
Rod. Ilhéus–Canavieiras km 24, Praia de Canabrava
Tel/fax: 073-269 8000
www.canabravaresort.com.br
Many sports facilities, private beach, swimming pool, sauna, and lake for kayaking. **$$$**

Pontal Praia
Avenida Lomanto Jr 1358
Pontal
Tel/fax: 073-231 3033
Situated outside center but with a good bus service. Swimming pool, and many other facilities. **$$**

Transamérica Ilha de Comandatuba
Estrada P/Canavieiras km 77, Una
Tel: 073-686 1122
Fax: 073-686 1457
www.transamerica.com.br
A top-class luxury resort hotel offering every amenity. Excellent location. **$$$$**

Lençóis

Pousada de Lençóis
Rua Altina Alves 747
Tel: 075-334 1102
Reservations Salvador,
Tel: 071-450 9100
Fax: 075-334 1201
Set in its own grounds, with a swimming pool. **$$**

Pousada Casa de Helia
Rua da Muritiba
Tel: 75 334-1173
www.casadehelia.hpg.ig.com.br
Two-, three- and four-bedroom apartments in a charming setting.**$$**

Porto Seguro

Pousada Casa Azul
Rua 15 de Novembro 11, Pacatá
Tel/fax: 073-288 2180
A beautiful but simple colonial building, set in a quiet location. **$$**

Porto Seguro Praia
BR-367, km 65, Praia de Curuipe
Tel: 073-288 9393
Fax: 073-288 2069
www.portoseguropraiahotel.com.br
Set just 3½ km (2 miles) from Porto with excellent facilities. **$$$**

PERNAMBUCO

Olinda

Pousado do Amparo
Rua do Amparo 199
Tel: 081-3439 1749
www.pousadoamparo.com.br
Fine historic house with garden. The best hotel in Olinda. **$$$$**

Pousada dos Quatro Cantos
Rua Prudente de Morais 441
Tel: 081-3429 0220
Fax: 081-3429 1845
Beautiful old building; lovely rooms and good restaurant; occasional live music. **$$**

Recife

Hotel do Sol
Avenida Boa Viagem 978
Boa Viagem
Tel: 081-3091 0991
www.hsol.com.br
Reasonable prices; on the beach. **$$**

Recife Monte
Rua dos Navegantes 363
Boa Viagem
Tel: 081-3465 7422
Fax: 081-3465 8406
www.recifemontehotel.com.br
All mod cons. Business hotel. **$$$**

Recife Palace Lucsim
Avenida Boa Viagem 4070
Boa Viagem
Tel: 081-3465 6688
Fax: 081-3465 6767
www.lucsimhoteis.com.br
Luxurious, with pool, sauna, and great views of the beach. **$$$**

ALAGOAS

Maceió

Jatiúca
Rua Lagoa da Anta 220
Lagoa da Anta
Tel: 082-355 2020
Fax: 082-355 2121
www.hoteljatiuca.com.br
Luxury hotel on the beach with swimming pool. **$$$$**

Pajuçara Othon
Rua Jangadeiros Alagoanos 1292
Pajuçara
Tel: 082-217-6400
Reservations, tel: 0300-789 8087
Fax: 082-231 5499
www.hoteis-othon.com.br
Comfortable hotel with pool. **$$$**

Ponta Verde Praia
Avenida Alvaro Otacílio 2933
Praia Ponta Verde
Tel: 082-231 4040
Fax: 082-231 8080
www.hotelpontaverde.com.br
On the seafront, with restaurant, bar, and pool. **$$$**

PARAIBA

João Pessoa

Tropical Tambaú
Avenida Almirante Tamandaré 229
Tambau
Tel: 083-247 3660
Reservations, tel: 0800-991 511
Fax: 083-247 1070
www.tropicalhotel.com.br
Landmark Modernist building, situated on the beach, with excellent facilities. **$$$$**

RIO GRANDE DO NORTE

Natal

Manary Praia Hotel
Rua Francisco Gurgel 9067

Praia de Ponta Negra
Tel/fax: 084-219 2900
www.manary.com.br
Luxury, beachfront hotel. Safes in rooms, air conditioning, swimming pool. **$$$**
Ocean Paláce
via Costeira, km 11
Tel: 084-219 4144
Fax: 084-219 3081
Luxury beachfront hotel. The best in town. **$$$$**

CEARA

Fortaleza

Beira Mar
Avenida Beira Mar 3130
Praia de Meireles
Tel: 085-242 5000
Fax: 085-242 5659
www.hotelbeiramar.com.br
Very comfortable hotel situated on the beach, with pool. **$$$**
Caesar Park
Avenida Beira Mar 3980
Praia do Mucuripe
Tel: 085-466 5000
Fax: 085-466 5111
www.caesarpark-for.com.br
An excellent, luxury hotel located on the beach with several restaurants. **$$$$**
Imperial Othon Palace
Avenida Beira Mar 2500
Praia de Meireles
Tel: 085-242 9177
Fax: 085-242 7777
www.hoteis-othon.com.br
On the beach with stunning ocean views; good restaurant. **$$$$**
Holiday Inn
Avenida Historiador Raimundo Girão 800, Iracema
Tel: 455-5000.
New, almost faultless hotel opposite the beach. **$$$**

MARANHAO

São Luis

São Francisco
Rua Dr Luís Serson 77
São Francisco
Tel: 098-235 5544
Fax: 098-235 2128
By the river with good views. **$$$**
Sofitel São Luis
Avenida Avicênia
Praia do Calhau
Tel: 098-235 4545
Well located with good views. **$$$$**
Vila Rica
Praça Dom Pedro II 299
Centro
Tel: 098-232 3535
Fax: 098-232 7245
www.hotelvilarica.com.br
A luxury hotel offering many amenities. **$$$$**

PARA

Belém

Beira-Rio
Avenida Bernardo Sayão 4804
Guamá
Tel: 091-249 7111
Fax: 091-249 7808
Outside town center, with a pool and air conditioning. **$$$**
Equatorial Palace
Avenida Braz de Aguiar 612
Nazaré
Tel: 091-241 2000
Fax: 091-223 5222
Gym and swimming pool. **$$$**
Hilton International Belém
Avenida Presidente Vargas 882
Praça da República
Tel: 091-217 7000
Fax: 091-225 2942
Rather run down, but still one of the best in town. **$$$$**
Regente
Avenida Governador José Malcher 485, Centro
Tel: 091-241 1222
Fax: 091-242 0343
Modest but comfortable. **$$**

Santarém

Santarém Palace
Avenida Rui Barbosa 726
Tel: 091-523 2820
Fax: 091-522 1779
Offers good rates and is close to center. Runs river tours. **$**

AMAZONAS

Manaus

Ana Cássia Palace
Rua dos Andradas 14, Centro
Tel: 092-622 3637
Fax: 092-234-4163
Swimming pool and sauna. **$$$**
Best Western Lord Manaus
Rua Marcílio Dias 217,
Centro
Tel: 092-622 7700
Reservations, tel: 0800-110 098
Fax: 092-622 2576
www.bestwestern.com.br
Well located for city center. **$$$**
Manaós
Avenida Eduardo Ribeiro 881,
Centro
Tel: 092-633 5744
Fax: 092-232 4443
Next to the Teatro Amazonas, 39 rooms with airconditioning. **$$**
Holiday Inn Taj Mahal
Avenida Getúlio Vargas 741,
Centro
Tel: 092-633 1010
Fax: 092-233 0068
Reservations, tel: 0800-925 333
Probably the best hotel in the city center. **$$$$**
Tropical
Praia da Ponta Negra
Tel: 092-658 5000
Reservations, tel: 0800-150 006
Fax: 092-658 5026
Fabulously situated in its own park 12 km (7 miles) from the center, on the banks of the Amazon. **$$$$**

Amazon Jungle Lodges

Manaus is the gateway for most visitors wishing to explore the Amazon proper and there is little point in going there without spending at least one or two nights at a lodge on the river. The price of packages usually includes food, canoeing, piranha fishing, etc.

Among the best lodges close to Manaus – on which travel agents can find details – are:

Amazon Ecopark Lodge
Igarapé do Tarumã-Açu
Tel: 092-234 0939
20 km (13 miles) – 30 minutes by boat – from Manaus. **$$$$**
Amazon Lodge
Lagoa Juma
Tel: 092-656 6033
www.naturesafaris.com
80 km (50 miles) – 4 hours by boat and car – from Manaus. **$$$**

Amazon Village
Rio Amazonas,
Lago do Puraquequara
Tel: 092-633 1444
Fax: 092-633 3217
45 km (28 miles) – 2 hours by boat – from Manaus **$$$**

Ariaú Towers
Rio Negro
Tel: 092-622 5000
Fax: 092-233 5615
www.ariautowers.com
55 km (34 miles) – 3 hours by boat – from Manaus. The most upmarket lodge. **$$$$**

Laga Salvador Lodge
Rio Negro
Tel: 092-658 4221
8 km (5 miles) from Manaus

Price Guide

Price per person per night in *reais* (R$). Breakfast is usually included, except in some top-notch city hotels.

$$$$	over R$190
$$$	R$100–190
$$	R$50–99
$	under R$50

AMAPA

Macapá

Macapá
Avenida Eng. Azarias Neto 17
Centro
Tel: 096-217 1350
Fax: 096-217 1351
Good range of facilities and pool; on the riverside. **$$$**

Pousada Ekinox
Rua Jovino Dinoá 1693
Tel: 096-223 0086
www.ekinox.com.br
Very popular, friendly, with excellent restaurant. In the center. **$$$**

MATO GROSSO/PANTANAL

Corumbá

Nacional Palace
Rua América 936
Tel: 067-231 6868
Fax: 067-231 6202
www.hnacional.com.br
Air conditioning, fridges in rooms, swimming pool, parking. **$$**

Pousada do Cachimbo
Rua Alan Kardec 4
Dom Bosco
Tel/fax: 067-231 3910
Situated on the riverside with good views. **$$**

Santa Mônica Palace
Rua Antônio Maria Coelho 345
Tel: 067-231 3001
Fax: 067-231 7880
Air conditioning, good restaurant, swimming pool. **$$**

Cuiabá

Áurea Palace
Avenida General Mello 63,
Centro
Tel: 065-623 5008
Fax: 065-623 7390
Nice rooms, restaurant, swimming pool, and sauna. **$$**

Jaguar Palace
Avenida Getúlio Vargas 600
Tel: 065-624 4404
Restaurant and pool. Good value for money. **$$**

Pousada Ecoverde
Rua Pedro Celestino 391
Tel: 065-6241 386.
Rooms around courtyard in intimate colonial building. **$**

Pantanal

The following establishments offer all-inclusive packages.

Botel Amazonas/Botel Corumbá (boat hotels)
Information in Corumbá
Tel: 067-231 2871
Fax: 067-231 1025

Cabana do Lontra
Estrada Miranda–Corumbá
Information in Aquidauana
Tel: 067-383 4532
Specializes in fishing tours.

Cabanas do Pantanal
Rio Cuiabá, Estrada para Porto Cercado, km 42
Tel: 065-345 1887
Reservations, tel: 065-9972 6755
On the northern edge of Pantanal. Chalet rooms with meals included. Boat trips, horse-riding, and fishing are also available. **$$**

Caiman Ecological Reserve
Aquidauana
Tel: 067-687 2102
Reservations, tel: 011-3079 6622
www.caiman.com.br
Air-conditioned rooms; swimming pool, lake. The reserve offers 25 different tours of the area. **$$$$**

Fazenda Barranquinho
Rio Jauru, Caceres
Information in Cuiabá
Tel: 065-221 2641

FEDERAL DISTRICT

Brasília

Carlton
Setor Hoteleiro Sul
Quadra 5, Bloco G
Tel: 061-224 8819
Fax: 061-226 8109
www.carltonhotelbrasilia.com.br
Good business hotel with all the usual facilities. **$$$$**

Eron Brasília
Setor Hoteleiro Norte
Quadra 5, Lote A
Tel: 061-329 4118
Reservations, tel: 0800-610 999
Fax: 061-326 2698
www.eronhotel.com.br
Large and comfortable, with restaurant and bar. **$$$**

Hotel Diplomat
Setor Hoteleiro Norte
Quadra 2, Bloco L
Tel/fax: 061-326 2010
Good value. **$$**

Nacional
Setor Hoteleiro Sul
Quadra 1, Bloco A
Tel: 061-321 7575
Reservations, tel: 0800-644 7070
Fax: 061-223 9213
www.hotelnacional.com.br
Old-fashioned but excellent. Discounts at weekends. **$$$$**

PARANA

Curitiba

Bourbon & Tower
Rua Cândido Lopes 102
Tel: 041-322 4001
Wonderfully traditional, enormous and swish. **$$$$**

Curitiba Palace
Rua Ermelino de Leão
Tel: 041-322 8081
Fax: 041-322 3356.
Spacious and very comfortable. Pool and good facilities. **$$$**

Del Rey
Rua Ermelino de Leão 18, Centro
Tel/fax: 041-322 3242
Reservations, tel: 0800-413 242
www.hoteldelrey.com.br
Luxurious hotel with good restaurants. **$$$**

FOZ DO IGUAÇU

Carimã
Rod. das Cataratas km 10
Tel: 045-523 1818
Fax: 045-574 3531
Good value. Air conditioning, pool, bars, restaurant. **$$$**

Hotel das Cataratas
Rod. das Cataratas km 25
Tel: 045-521 4100
Reservations, tel: 0800-150 006
Fax: 045-522 1717
www.tropicalhotel.com.br
A real experience; a luxury, colonial-style hotel situated amidst immaculate grounds right in front of the falls. Also known as the Tropical. **$$$$**

Internacional Foz
Rua Almirante Barroso 2006
Tel: 045-521 4100
Reservations, tel: 0800-454 100
Fax: 045-521 4101
www.internacionalfoz.com.br
Good location in the city center, with all facilities. **$$$$**

Nadai
Avenida República Argentina 1332
Tel/fax: 045-523 5251
www.hotelnadai.clm.br
In town, with air conditioning, swimming pool, and sauna. **$$**

Panorama
Rod. das Cataratas km. 12
Tel: 045-523 1200
Reservations, tel: 0800-451 221
Fax: 045-574 1456.
Located halfway between the town and the falls. **$$$**

Rafain Centro
Marachal Deodoro 984
Tel: 045-523 1213.
In center, with nice pool area. **$$**

SANTA CATARINA

Blumenau

Garden Terrace
Rua Padre Jacobs 45
Tel: 047-326 3544
Fax: 047-326 0366
Large hotel, with restaurant, bar, and travel agency. **$$**

Grande Hotel Blumenau
Alameda Rio Branco 21
Tel: 047-326 0145
Fax: 047-326 1280
www.hoteisbrasil.com/garden
With restaurant, bar and pool. **$$$**

Plaza Blumenau
Rua 7 de Setembro 818
Tel: 047-231 7000
Fax: 047-231 7001
www.plazahoteis.com.br
A luxury hotel, the best in town, with business facilities. **$$$**

Ilha de Santa Catarina

Costão do Santinho Resort
Rodovia Vereador Onildo Lemos 2505, Praia do Santinho
Tel: 048-261 1000
Fax: 048-261 1200
www.costao.com.br
The best in the region (38 km/24 miles from the city). Sports facilities include tennis, canoeing, swimming, and soccer. **$$$$**

Praia Mole Park Hotel & Spa
Estrada Geral de Barra da Lagoa 2001, Praia Mole
Tel: 048-232 5231
Reservations, tel: 0800-480 008
Fax: 048-232 5482
Beach hotel with good watersports facilities. **$$$$**

Jurerê Praia
Alameda César Nascimento 200
Praia de Jurerê
Tel: 048-261 5100
Fax: 048-282 1644
www.jurere.com.br
Good watersports facilities. It is possible to rent chalets with one or two rooms; good for families. **$$$$**

Florianópolis

Faial
Rua Felipe Schmidt 603, Centro
Tel: 048-225 2766
Reservations, tel: 0800-480 099
Fax: 048-225 0435
www.hotelfaial.com.br
Old-style comfort, with good food. **$$**

Florianópolis Palace
Rua Artista Bittencourt 14
Centro
Tel: 048-224 9633
Fax: 048-222 0300
www.floph.com.br
One of the best hotels in the downtown area. **$$$**

Joinville

Anthurium Parque
Rua São José 226
Tel/fax: 047-433 6299
www.anthurium.com.br
A good value, colonial-style hotel. English spoken. **$$**

Tannenhof Othon
Rua Visconde de Taunay 340
Tel/fax: 047-47433 8011
Quality hotel with swimming pool, gym, restaurant. **$$$**

Laguna

Taperoá
Praia de Itapirubá
BR-101 Norte
Tel: 048-356 0222
Fax: 048-646 0294
Located on the beach. Good sports facilities. **$$**

Lagoa
Trevo BR-101 Sul km 313
Cabeçudas
Tel: 048-446 0844
Lower price than the Taperoá, with a restaurant. **$**

Laguna Tourist
Praia do Gi
Tel: 048-647 0022
Fax: 048-647 0123
www.lagunatourist.com.br
Well located on the beach with good views and great facilities. **$$$**

Price Guide

Price per person per night in *reais* (R$). Breakfast is usually included, except in some top-notch city hotels.

$$$$	over R$190
$$$	R$100–190
$$	R$50–99
$	under R$50

RIO GRANDE DO SUL

Caxias do Sul

Alfred Palace
Rua Sinimbu 2302
Tel/fax: 054-221 8655
With good restaurant and bar. **$$$**

Cosmos
Rua 20 de Setembro 1563
Tel/fax: 054-223 7688
www.cosmoshotel.com.br
Reasonable value, with health club on site. **$$**

Canela

Grande Hotel
Rua Getulio Vargas 300
Tel/fax: 054-282 1285
www.grandehotel.com.br
Modest hotel with a restaurant, a beautiful garden, and lake for fishing. **$$**

Laje de Pedra
Avenida Presidente Kennedy
Tel: 054-282 4300
Fax: 054-282 4400
Excellent hotel, situated in its own grounds with spectacular views of the Rio Caí in valley below. **$$$**

Gramado

Pequeno Bosque
Rua Piratini 486
Tel: 054-286 1527
Fax: 054-286 1771
Located in wood close to Véu da Noiva waterfall. **$$**

Hotel Serrano
Avenida das Hortênsias 1480
Tel: 054-286 1332
Fax: 054-286 1639
www.hotelserrano.com.br
Situated in a private park. **$$$$**

Nova Petrópolis

Recanto Suiço
Avenida 15 de Novembro 2195
Tel/fax: 054-281 1229
15 rooms with airconditioning. Bar, restaurant, swimming pool. **$$**

Porto Alegre

Alfred Porto Alegre
Rua Senhor dos Passos 105
Centro
Tel: 051-3226 2555
Fax: 051-3226 2221
With restaurant and bar, swimming pool and sauna. **$$**

Embaixador
Rua Jerônimo Coelho 354
Centro
Tel: 051-3215 6600
Fax: 051-3228 5050
www.embaixador.com.br
Very comfortable. **$$$**

Plaza São Rafael
Avenida Alberto Bins 514
Centro
Tel: 051-3220 7000
Reservations, tel: 0800-512 244
Fax: 051-3220 7001
www.plazahoteis.com.br
A luxury hotel, the best in Porto Alegre, it also has the best convention center in the city. Some rooms overlook the river. **$$$$**

Metropolitan Centro
Rua Andrade Neves 59
Tel: 051-226 1800
Fairly basic but clean. **$**

Santo Angelo

Avenida II
Avenida Venâncio Aires 1671
Tel/fax: 055-313 3011
Small, simple hotel. **$$**

Where to Eat

What to Eat

Many Brazilians live on simple staples: rice, beans and manioc. However, there is a wonderful variety of foods, reflecting Brazil's size and the influence of its many immigrant groups. Seafood, sushi, barbecued meat, Italian dishes and delicious salads are widely available *(see also pages 64–5)* Some of the most traditional Brazilian dishes are adaptations of Portuguese or (especially in Bahia) African foods.

Brazilian food tends to be tastily seasoned, but is not usually peppery – with the exception of some very spicy dishes from Bahia. Notwithstanding this, hot peppers *(pimenta)* and the local *malagueta* chilis, which can be infernally fiery or pleasantly nippy, are popular. Brazilian pepper sauce (most restaurants prepare their own, sometimes jealously guarding the recipe) is almost always available at the table.

In restaurants a portion is usually for two people. It is perfectly acceptable to ask for a doggy bag.

BAHIAN COOKING

The African-influenced, spicy Bahian food is the most unusual and exciting in Brazil *(see the feature on Bahian Cuisine on page 231)*.

Feijoada, consisting of black beans simmered with a variety of dried, salted and smoked meats (and often also the tail, ears, feet, etc. of a pig) was developed as slave food, but is now considered Brazil's national dish (although it is not found in every part of the country). *Feijoada* for lunch on Saturday has become something of an institution in Rio de Janeiro, enjoyed both at home and in the better restaurants, where it is served complete with white rice, finely shredded kale *(couve)*, *farofa* (manioc root meal toasted with butter) and sliced oranges.

PORTUGUESE COOKING

Two Portuguese dishes that are popular in Brazil are *bacalhau* (imported dried, salted codfish) and *cozido*, a glorified "boiled dinner" of meats and vegetables (usually several root vegetables, squash, cabbage and/or kale) served with *pirão* made out of broth. Also try the delicate *palmito*, palm heart, served with either a salad, a soup or as a pastry filling.

SNACKS

Salgadinhos (usually small pastries stuffed with cheese, meat, *palmito*, etc.) are a Brazilian style of finger food, served as appetizers and canapés, ordered with a round of drinks or as a quick snack at a lunch counter – a native alternative to the US-style fast-food counters that are also evident throughout the country. Other tasty snack foods include *pão de queijo* (a cheesy bread), and *pastel* (two layers of a thinly rolled, deep-fried, pasta-like dough with a filling sealed inside). Instead of French-fries, try *aipim frito* (deep-fried manioc root).

DESSERTS

The wonderful tropical fruit is the basis of many Brazilian desserts, also made with coconut, egg yolk or milk. Compotes and thick jams, often served with mild cheese, are made out of many fruits and also out of squash and sweet potatoes. Coconut appears in both desserts and candies – sidewalk vendors sell molasses and *cocadas*. Portuguese-style egg yolk desserts are delicious, especially *quindim* (a rich, sweet egg yolk and coconut custard). Special sweet shops sell *docinhos* (homemade bon-bons) and a variety of sweet snacks.

REGIONAL SPECIALTIES

These include seafood dishes in the northeast and all along the coast. Try *peixe a Brasileiro*, a delicious fish stew served with *pirão* (manioc root meal cooked with broth from the stew to the consistency of porridge). In the inland areas of the northeast, tasty specialties include *carne seca* or *carne de sol* (dried salted beef, often served with squash) and roast kid.

In the Amazon region, there are many varieties of fruit that are found nowhere else, and the rivers produce a great range of fish, including piranha and the giant pirarucu. The *churrasco* or barbecue – popular throughout Brazil – originated with the southern gaucho cowboys who roasted meat over an open fire. Most *churrascarias* offer a *rodizio* option: for a set price diners eat all they can of a variety of meats selected from the spit. In Minas Gerais, try the tasty pork sausage called *linguiça*.

In some parts of the south, the cuisine reflects a German influence; Italian and Japanese immigrants brought their cooking skills to São Paulo *(see the feature on the Japanese quarter on page 200)*.

Where to Eat

Lunchtime is usually noon–3pm. For locals, this is the heaviest meal of the day. Dinner is 7pm–midnight (locals eat late), but some restaurants stay open all afternoon and until 1 or 2am. Many restaurants in Brazil are closed on Sunday evening and/or Monday, so check before setting out. At the more expensive restaurants, it is advisable to make reservations. *Comida a kilo* restaurants (literally meaning food by weight) are great, cheap places to get a wide choice of usually good quality dishes. Because you help yourself you can sample foods you would not otherwise order and you are not limited by your level of Portugese. *Lanchonetes* are snack bars.

The following is a selection of places to eat, including restaurants, bistros, cafés and ice cream parlors, in the main cities.

RIO DE JANEIRO

Albamar Praça Marechal
Âncora 184 Praça XV, Centro
Tel: 021-2240 8378
This is one of the city's oldest restaurants, in a historic building. Seafood and Brazilian dishes. **$$$**

Casa da Feijoada
Rua Prudente de Morais 10
loja B, Ipanema
Tel: 021-2247 2776
Open daily
Specializes in this favorite Brazilian dish made with black beans and various cuts of pork. **$$**

Celeiro
Rua Dias Ferreira 199
Leblon
Tel: 021-2274 7843
Open daily except Sun, lunch only Mon and Tues
A paradise for vegetarians and salad lovers. Original and delightful salads made with organic vegetables plus quiches, and pies, and good desserts, sold by weight. **$**

Cipriani
Copacabana Palace
Avenida Atlântica 1702
Tel: 021-2545 8747
Open daily
Even if you aren't staying at the legendary Copacabana Palace, you can experience the mystique and glamour enjoyed by Hollywood greats and royalty in this elegant Italian restaurant overlooking the pool. **$$$**

Claude Troisgros
Rua Custódio Serrão 62
Jardim Botânico
Tel: 021-2537 8582
Open daily except Sun
According to many, this restaurant serves the best food in Rio. The friendly owner and chef Troisgros is

Price Guide

Price in *reais* (R$) for a three-course meal for one, without wine but including the 10 percent service charge.

$$$	over R$50
$$	R$25–50
$	up to R$25

heir to a distinguished lineage of and his creative French cuisine is superb. He also creates special personalized menus for every desire or taste. **$$$**

Colombo Tearooms
Confeitaria Colombo
Rua Goncalves Dias 32
Centro
Tel: 021-2232 2300
An institution. Serves afternoon tea, Mon–Fri at 5pm. **$$$**

Confeitaria Colombo
Rua Goncalves Dias 32
Centro
Tel: 021-2232 2300
Open daily, closed Sun noon–4pm
Worth a visit for the fantastic art nouveau decor with mirrored walls and huge chandeliers. Pies, snacks, light meals. Afternoon teas a specialty. **$**

Garcia & Rodrigues
Avenida Ataulfo de Paiva 1251
Leblon
Tel: 021-2512 8188
Open daily, lunch only Sun, dinner only Mon
A French restaurant, bakery, wine cellar, delicatessen, coffee house and snack bar, all in one, and all of the finest quality. **$$**

Grottamare
Rua Gomes Carneiro 132
Ipanema
Tel: 021-2523 1596
Open weekdays dinner only, weekdays dinner only, weekends lunch and dinner. Popular and busy seafood restaurant.

Le Saint Honoré
Hotel Le Méridien, 37th F loor
Avendia Atlântica 1020
Tel: 021-2546 0880
Open daily except Sun dinner
Serves superior French and international cuisine with a beautiful view over Copacabana below. **$$$**

Margutta
Avenida Henrique Dumont 62
Ipanema
Tel: 021-2259 3887
Open weekdays dinner only, weekends lunch and dinner
Come to this cozy restaurant for beautifully prepared lobster, shrimps and a variety of other seafood. **$$$**

Marius
Rua Francisco Otaviano 96
Tel: 021-2521 0500; and
Avenida Atlântica 290
Tel: 021-2542 2393
Open daily
Adjoining restaurants serve superb all-you-can-eat seafood and *rodizo* respectively in elegant surroundings. Definitely not to be missed. Be sure to book, and even then be prepared to wait up to an hour for your table. **$$$**

Milfrutas
Rua J.J. Seabra (Jardim Botânico)
Tel: 021-2511 2550; and
Rua Garcia Dávila, corner of Barão da Torre, Ipanema.
Open daily
Drop in for unforgettable ice creams in the flavored by a thousand exotic fruits or spices, or mixed with chocolate or nuts. **$**

Porcão
Avenida Infante Dom Henrique
Aterro do Flamengo
Tel: 021-2554 8535
Open daily
If you have to choose one barbecue house to go to, the Porcão is it. Located bay side in the middle of Flamengo Park, it offers glorious views over the bay to Sugarloaf and back across to Corcovado from the other side. The food is equally good. Branches in Ipanema and Copacabana. **$$$**

Quadrifoglio
Rua J.J. Seabra 19
Jardim Botânico
Tel: 021-2294 1433
Open daily, Sat dinner only
Excellent, light, aromatic Italian cooking in comfortable and friendly surroundings. **$$$**

Quinta do Bacalhau
Rua do Teatro 5
Largo de São Francisco
Tel: 021-242 8205
Right in the center of historic Rio. Simple but extremely good Portuguese restaurant specializing in *bacalhau* (Portuguese cod). **$**

Siri Mole
Rua Francisco Otaviano 50
Copacabana
Tel: 021-2267 0894
Open daily, Mon dinner only
Considered the city's best for genuine Brazilian cooking. Many Bahian specialties. **$$**

SAO PAULO

Arabia
Rua Haddock Lobo 1397
Jardim Paulista
Tel: 011-3061 2203
Open daily
Spacious, comfortable restaurant that serves wonderful Lebanese food. **$$**

Baby Beef Rubaiyat
Alameda Santos 86, Paraíso
Tel: 011-289 6366
Avenida Brigadeiro Faria Lima 2954
Itaim Bibi
Tel: 011-3849 9488
Open daily
Elegant *churrascarias* that are generally considered among the city's best. **$$**

Capim Santo
Rua Arapiraca 152
Vila Madalena
Tel: 011-3813 9103
Open daily
In a beautiful rustic setting among trees. Particularly good value is the lunchtime buffet with seafood, salad, and meat. On Sundays the buffet includes shrimp or lobster. Evenings à la carte. **$$**

Cheiro Verde
Rua Peixoto Gomide 1413
Jardim Paulista
Tel: 011-289 6853
Open daily
Vegetarians can have a tough time in meat-loving Brazil. Here they are well catered for in a simple but friendly restaurant. **$**

Fasano
Rua Haddock Lobo 1644
Jardim Paulista
Tel: 011-852 4000
Open daily for dinner except Sun

If you can afford it, go to one of the most luxurious restaurant in São Paulo. Finest Italian cooking in grandiose black marble and mahogany high-ceilinged rooms. **$$$**

Gero
Across the street at Rua Haddock Lobo 1629
Tel: 011-3064 0005
Open daily
A bistro version of the Fasano, across the street, offering the same quality for a lower price, in a younger, more informal setting. **$$$**
There is also the shopping center version, Gero Caffé, which can be found in the Iguatemi shopping centre. **$**

Jardim de Napoli
Rua Dr Martinico Prado 463
Higienópolis
Tel: 011-3666 3022
Open daily
Typical Italian *cantina* serving good pasta and pizzas. **$**

Koyama
Rua 13 de Maio 1050
Bela Vista
Tel: 011-283 1833
Open daily except Sun
Exceptionally good Japanese food served in traditional surroundings. **$$**

Laurent
Alameda Jaú 1606
Cerqueira César
Tel: 011-853 5573
Open daily except Sun
Brazilian ingredients transmuted by French cooking into original delights. The lunchtime executive menu offers a cheaper deal. **$$$**

Maria Zanchi de Zan
Rua Barão de Capanema 568
Jardim Paulista
Tel: 011-3085 1047
Open daily, Sat dinner only, Sun lunch only
A delightful restaurant serving exquisite, delicately flavored Italian food. **$$**

Massimo
Alameda Santos 1826
Cerqueira César
Tel: 011-284 0311
Open daily
Top-class Italian and international cuisine in spacious, elegant surroundings; excellent wines. A favorite with top executives and politicians. **$$$**

Panino Giusto
Rua Augusta 2963
Tel: 011-3064 9992
Open daily
Deliciously elaborate sandwiches and light meals. **$**

Portucale
Rua Nova Cidade 418
Vila Olímpia
Tel: 011-3845 8929
Open daily except Mon
Traditional Portuguese specialties nicely presented. **$$**

Roanne
Rua Henrique Martins 631
Jardim Paulista
Tel: 011-3887 4516
Open daily, Sat dinner only, Sun lunch only
Superb French cuisine. Trust the chef with the menu and your meal will be transformed into an ambrosial delight. **$$$$**

Price Guide

Price in *reais* (R$) for a three-course meal for one, without wine but including the 10 percent service charge.

$$$	over R$50
$$	R$25–50
$	up to R$25

SALVADOR

Alfredo di Roma
Avenida Oceânica 1545, Ondina
Tel: 071-331 7775
Open daily
Branch of the Rome original, in the Caesar Towers Hotel. **$$$**

Barbacoa
Avenida Tancredo Neves 909, Pituba
Tel: 071-342 4666
Open daily
One of the best barbecue houses in Salvador. **$$**

Bargaço
Rua P, Quadra 43
Lotes 18 e 19
Jardim Armação
Tel: 071-231 5141
Open daily
Regional cooking. **$$**

Bernard
Rua Gamboa de Cima 11
Aflitos
Tel: 011-329 5403
Open Mon–Sat except Sat lunch
Excellent French bistro serving traditional food. **$$$**

Jardim das Delícias
Rua João de Deus 12
Pelourinho
Tel: 011-3211 449
Open daily
Tasty regional cooking, Bahian cuisine, seafood, and pasta served in an exquisite garden setting. **$$**

Maria Mata Mouro
Rua Inácio Acioly 8
Pelourinho
Tel: 011-321 3929
Open daily
Eclectic menu reflecting a wide range of culinary inspiration. **$$**

Senac
Largo do Pelourinho
This is the city's catering school, so a wide variety of dishes is offered. Open 11.30am–3.30pm and 6.30–9.30pm. Live music Thurs–Sat evenings, US$5 cover charge. **$$**

Trapiche Adelaide
Praça dos Tupinambas 2
Avenida do Contorno
Tel: 011-326 2211
Open daily, Sun lunch only
Serves international cuisine in a wonderful location right by the Baía de Todos os Santos. The pier doubles as a bar. **$$$**

RECIFE

Bargaço
Avenida Boa Viagem 670
Boa Viagem
Tel: 081-3465 1847
Open daily
Privileged beachfront location on Boa Viagem. Part of an upmarket chain. Menu specializes in seafood dishes. **$$**

Chez George
Rua Manoel Borba 350
Praça do Jacaré
Carmo, Olinda
Tel: 081-3439 5858

Open daily for dinner
This well-known beachfront restaurant in Olinda offers an exquisite culinary mix of French, Swiss and Brazilian styles. **$$$**

Famiglia Giuliano
Avenida Engenheiro Domingos Ferreira 3980
Boa Viagem
Tel: 081-3465 9922
Open daily
Located in a replica of a medieval castle, a good international and Italian menu has the added attraction on Saturday of Recife's best *feijoada*. **$$**

Oficina do Sabor
Rua do Amparo 355
Tel: 3429-3331
Award-winning restaurant. **$$$**

Pescatore
Avenida Boa Viagem 97
Pina
Tel: 081-3466 6304
Open daily
Comfortable seafood restaurant on the seafront at Pina in the historic Cassino Americano. **$$$**

Porcão
Avenida Engenheiro Domingos Ferreira 4215
Boa Viagem
Tel: 081-3465 3999
Open daily
Branch of one of Brazil's top barbecue houses that uses the *rodizio* system of paying one price for all you can eat. **$$**

BELEM

Circulo Militar
Praça Frei Caetano Brandão
Bafa de Guajará
Tel: 081-223 4374
Open daily
Occupying a huge barrack room in the old fort, here is a feast not to be missed. A good menu with plenty of choice, served with humor at long tables. Overlooking the Amazon River. **$$**

Curupira
Avenida Tavares Bastos 1400
Tel: 081-243 1549
Open daily; lunch only Sun–Mon.
Restaurant with typical *paraense* musicians during the week and a folklore show on Thursday and Friday. **$**

Lá em Casa/O Outro
Rua Governador José Malcher 247
Nazaré
Tel: 081-223 1212
Open daily
One of the best restaurants for delicious Amazonian specialties, including ice cream flavored with from various exotic fruits. **$$**

MANAUS

Canto da Peixada
Rua Emilio Moreira 1677
(Praça 14 de Janeiro)
Tel: 092-234 3021
Open daily except Sun
Serves fresh Amazon fish and regional dishes. **$**

Fiorentina
Rua José Pararegua 44
Traditional Italian restaurant. Standard cuisine but a good option in this area. **$$**

Himawari
Rua 10 de Julho 618
Tel: 233 2208
Upmarket Japanese food, including sushi. Near Teatro Amazonas. **$$$**

Paramazon
Rua Santa Isabel 1176
Cachoeirinha
Tel: 092-233 7768
Open daily
Typical Amazonian recipes. **$$**

BRASÍLIA

Antigamente
Setor de Clubes Esportivos Sul
Trecho 4, Conjunto 5
Tel: 061-316 6967
Open daily for lunch except Mon
Typical Brazilian food in a beautiful building that is also a cultural and antiques center. **$$**

Vila Borghese
Comércio Local Sul
Quadra. 201, bl. A lj.33
Tel: 061-226 5650
Open daily
Serves good Italian food with delicious homemade pasta. **$$$**

PORTO ALEGRE

Barranco
Avenida Protásio Alves 1578
Petrópolis
Tel: 051-331 6172
Open daily
Excellent, well-known barbecue house with a charming outdoor area situated under the trees. **$$**

Le Bon Gourmet
Avenida Alberto Bins 514, Centro
Tel: 051-3211 5767
Located in the Hotel Plaza São Rafael, Le Bon Gourmet is one of the city's best and most stylish restaurants. **$$$**

Il Gattopardo
Rua 24 de Outubro 1585
Auxiliadora
Tel: 051-3325 1972
Open daily except Sun
Unquestionably one of Porto Alegre's best, offering a full international menu with Italian specialties. Also has the city's best wine list and a fine selection of Cuban cigars. **$$$$**

Pampulhinha
Avenida Benjamin Constant 1641
Floresta
Tel: 051-3342 2503
Open daily except Sun (closed Feb)
Top seafood choice with the *bacalhau* being a particular favorite of local residents. **$$**

Steinhaus
Rua Coronel Paulino Teixeira 415, Rio Branco
Tel: 051-3330 8661
Open daily for dinner except Sun
Considered by the immigrant German population to be the city's best German restaurant . Local and Brazilian dishes are also available. **$$**

BELO HORIZONTE

Parrilla del Mercado
Rua Ouro Fino 452
Mercado do Cruzeiro
Tel: 031-3225 5507
Inspired by the Mercado del Puerto in Montevideo, Parrilla del Mercado offers diners three different settings to enjoy the city's best barbecued meats. **$$**

Sagarana
Rua Coelho de Souza 20
Santo Agostinho
Tel: 031-3275 2684
Open daily
On Saturday Sagarana serves the town's best feijoada; the rest of the week the specialties are dishes typical of Minas Gerais. **$$**

Taste Vin
Rua Curitiba 2105
Lourdes
Tel: 031-3292 5423
Open daily for dinner except Sun
The city's leading French restaurant also has a fine wine cellar with over 8,000 bottles and 500 different brands on offer. **$$$**

Vecchio Sogno Ristorante
Rua Martim de Carvalho 75
Praça da Assembléia
Santo Agostinho
Tel: 031-3292 5251
Open daily
Specializing in modern dishes from central northern Italy, Vecchio Sogno is generally considered to be the best restaurant in Belo Horizonte. Located in the basement of the Legislative Assembly. **$$**

Price Guide

Price in *reais* (R$) for a three-course meal for one, without wine but including the 10 percent service charge.

$$$	over R$50
$$	R$25–50
$	up to R$25

CURITIBA

Boulevard
Rua Voluntários da Pátria 539
Centro
Tel: 041-224 8244
Open daily except Sun; Sat for dinner only
Boulevard is one of the city's top restaurants offering a varied menu of international and Brazilian favorites. **$$$**

Famiglia Caliceti Ristorante Bologna
Alameda Doutor Carlos de Carvalho 1367, Batel
Tel: 041-223 7102
Open daily except Tues, for lunch only on Sun
In a pretty house with a fire and winter garden and respected for its pasta dishes. **$$$**

Maccheroni
Rua Manuel Eufrásio 1124
Tel: 041-3532 2131
Open daily for dinner except Mon, also for lunch Sat–Sun
Good meats, pasta, and wines. **$$**

Madalosso
Avenida Manoel Ribas 5875
Santa Felicidade
Tel: 041-273 1014
Open daily except Mon, lunch only on Sun
This claims to be the largest restaurant in Brazil and is a popular stop with visitors. Not surprisingly, given it can seat 4,800 and has 52 chefs. It offers a wide-ranging set menu with pasta, salads, chicken, liver, risotto and fried polenta. **$**

Marinheiro
Rua Bispo Dom José 2315
Batel
Tel: 041-243 3828
Open daily except Mon, for lunch only on Sun
Set up by an Italian sailor who first came to Brazil in 1986, Marinheiro is one of the city's most reliable for seafood. **$$$**

99 Brasserie Café
Rua Cândido Lopes 102
Bourbon and Tower Hotel
See Where to Stay, page 355
Tel: 041-322 4001
Brazilian and international cuisine. **$$**

FORTALEZA

Café Matisse
Rua Silva Jatahy 942
Meireles
Tel: 085-242 1377
Open daily, for lunch only on Sun
Attractive French restaurant. **$$$**

Cemoara
Avenida Abolição 3340
Meireles
Tel: 085-263 5001
Open daily
The best seafood restaurant in town. Pleasant surroundings for a menu of Brazilian favorites. **$$$$**

Le Dinner
Rua Afonso Celso 1020
Aldeota
Tel: 085-224 2627
Open daily for dinner, except Sun. The city's best restaurant offers a fascinating mix of French and Chinese with a Brazilian touch. **$$$**

Paulinho da Maraponga
Avenida Godofredo Maciel 3884
Maraponga
Tel: 085-296 1526
For more than three decades the choice in Fortaleza for regional dishes. **$$**

Pulcinella
Rua Osvaldo Cruz 640
Aldeota
Tel: 085-261 3411
Open daily
Run by an ex-Bologna goalkeeper, Pulcinella is one of the best Italian restaurants in Fortaleza. **$$$**

Drinking Notes

Brazilians are great social drinkers and love to sit for hours talking and often singing with friends over a few (or more) drinks.

BEER

During the hottest months, socializing usually takes place in open-air restaurants, where most people will be ordering *chope*, draft beer, drunk ice-cold. Take note that although *cerveja* means beer, the word usually refers specifically to bottled beer.

The regional beers of Pará and Maranhão – Cerma and Cerpa – are generally acknowledged to be the best, while the most popular brands throughout Brazil are Brahma and Antarctica.

DRINKS OF BRAZIL

Brazil's own unique brew is *cachaça*, a strong liquor distilled from sugar cane – a type of rum with a distinct flavor. Although usually colorless, it can also be amber.

Restaurant Tipping

Most restaurants will add a 10 percent service charge to your bill. If you're in doubt as to whether it has been included, it's best to ask *(O serviço está incluido?)*. Give the waiter a bigger tip if you feel the service was above average.

Tipping at a lunch counter is optional, but people often leave the change from their bill.

MIXED DRINKS

Delightful mixed drinks are concocted out of *cachaça*, including the popular *caipirinha* – the national drink – which is a simple mixture of crushed lime (with peel) and sugar topped with plenty of ice. *Caipirinhas* may be mixed sweeter than you prefer – order yours *com pouco açúcar* (with a small amount of sugar) or even *sem açúcar* (without sugar). *Batidas* – fruit juice with *cachaça* – are mixed in a blender or shaken and come in as many varieties as there are types of fruit in the tropics. Don't forget that the *cachaça* makes them quite potent, even though they taste just like fruit juice.

WINES

Restaurants offer a selection of the best Brazilian wines, produced in the cooler southern states. In the Italian areas of Rio Grande do Sul you should try the small farmers' own wines.

Santa Catarina and Paraná produce some reasonable wines, while those from Espírito Santo, Minas Gerais and São Paulo are not to be recommended. Excellent wines imported from Argentina and Chile are not expensive in Brazil, so you may want to take advantage of this fact.

SPIRITS

The usual variety of spirits are available, both *importado* (imported) and *nacional* (domestic). Imports are very expensive, but some of the brands you may be familiar with are produced locally.

SOFT DRINKS

Among the non-alcoholic beverages, a real treat are the fresh fruit juices. Any hotel or restaurant will have three or four types but the snack bars specializing in *suco de fruta* have an amazing variety. The fruit is on display – guavas, mangoes, pineapples, passion fruit, persimmons, tamarind, as well as more familiar apples, melons, bananas and strawberries.

Delicious fruit milkshakes called *vitaminas* make a nutritious snack. Most common are the *mista* or mixed fruit – usually papaya and banana with a touch of beetroot to give it a pretty color; *banana com aveia*, which is banana and raw oatmeal; and *abacate*, made of avocado, are great for breakfast.

Street vendors sell coconut milk (the colorless liquid in the shell), often from a trailer near the beach. Restaurants or bars that serve *água de coco* will usually hang the cocos near the door. The top is lopped off and you drink the liquid juice through a straw. After drinking your fill, ask to have the coco split open to sample the soft, gelatin-like flesh beginning to form inside the shell.

Another tropical treat is sugar cane juice, served at snack bars that advertise *caldo de cana*. Street vendors use a crank-handle wringer to squeeze the juice.

Alongside the familiar Coca-Cola and Pepsi drinks, there is the Brazilian *guaraná*, flavored with a small Amazon fruit. Quite sweet, but good, it is a favorite with children, and is flavored with the fruits of the *guaraná* bush, which are used unrefined in a drink that has medicinal and tonic properties often compared to those of ginseng. This is mainly found in the Amazon region.

TEA

Those who can't do without their morning brew can try tea grown in Brazil, and many of the fancier hotels and restaurants offer English brands too. Try the indigenous South American *mate* (pronounced matchee) tea. The black tea is usually drunk as a refreshing iced drink; in Brazil's far south the green tea, called *chimarrão*, is sipped through a silver straw with a strainer at the lower end. This is a gaucho tradition.

COFFEE

Finally, there is wonderful Brazilian coffee. *Café* is prepared strong and liberally sweetened.

At breakfast time, coffee with hot milk *(café com leite)* is drunk. At other times, coffee is served between meals, black, in tiny cups. These *cafezinhos* or "little coffees," can be ordered at any *botequin*. There are even little stand-up bars that serve only *cafezinho*.

Cappucinos, lattes, etc. are hard to come by.

Decaffeinated coffee is not popular and not usually offered in restaurants, but it is now available in most supermarkets.

Culture

Museums

Brazil's historical museums are unlikely to be at the top of most visitors' list of attractions. With rare exceptions, there are just not enough resources available for proper upkeep and acquisitions. Those worth visiting are described in the Places section of this book. Temporary exhibitions are announced in the major Brazilian newspapers under the heading of *Exposições*.

Art Galleries

Those showing the work of contemporary artists abound in the larger cities, especially Rio de Janeiro and São Paulo. The art museums also organize periodic exhibits. Shows are listed in the papers under *Exposições*.

The Bienal or Biennial Art Exposition held in São Paulo every two years (2004, 2006, etc.) lasts from March–June and is Latin America's largest contemporary art show.

Music and Dance

Music is Brazil's forte. A variety of musical forms have developed in different parts of the country, many with accompanying forms of dance. While the Brazilian influence (especially in jazz) is heard around the world, what is known of Brazilian music outside the country is just the tip of an iceberg.

Take in a concert by a popular singer or ask your hotel to recommend a nightclub with live Brazilian music: *bossa nova*, *samba*, *choro* and *serenata* are popular in Rio and São Paulo – each region has something different to offer. If you are visiting at Carnival, you'll hear and see plenty of music and dancing in the streets, mostly *samba* in Rio and *frevo* in the northeast. There are also shows all year long that are designed to give tourists a taste of Brazilian folk music and dance.

Many visitors to Brazil are surprised to find a very lively and active Brazilian rock-music industry, even though few Brazilian rock musicians have made an impact on the world music scene.

A rock concert in Brazil is something not to be missed if that is your taste in music. The atmosphere is unimaginable, as the audience almost becomes part of the show, a seething, vibrant, ever-moving mass of enjoyment. The music is a magical blend; undeniably rock, yet at the same time Brazilian, with Latin rhythms pumped out by swollen percussion sections seamlessly and effortlessly merging with the power of electronic amplification.

The classical music and dance season runs from Carnival through mid-December. Besides presentations by local talents, major Brazilian cities (mainly Rio, São Paulo and Brasília) are included in world concert tours by international performers. One of the most important classical music festivals in South America takes place in July each year in Campos do Jordão in the state of São Paulo.

If you want to go to a live music performance, check in the weekend section of the local paper, under the heading *Lazer* (leisure), which will give listings of clubs, theaters, bars and dance halls holding concerts.

Theater

In order to enjoy the theater, you really do have to understand the language. Rio de Janeiro and São Paulo, especially, have busy seasons starting after Carnival and running through to November.

Movies

Some Brazilian cinema is very good – the country had three Academy Award nominations for best foreign language film in a period of four years. *Central Station* was very successful around the world. More recently, *City of God* – a Tarantino-style take on Rio's *favelas* – was acclaimed by critics as the best movie of 2003. Without a knowledge of Portuguese, however, you may as well watch the exported films back home with subtitles in your language. But the majority of movies shown in Brazil are foreign-made, mostly American, all in the original language with Portuguese subtitles. Check out what's playing under the cinema heading in the local papers. An international film festival, Festival do Rio, the largest in Latin America, is held annually in September in Rio de Janeiro, and another takes place in São Paulo every October.

Nightclubs

For information on clubs in the main cities, see the relevant chapters in the Places section of this book. But beware, what is hot and happening one week can be deserted the following week.

In many establishments ID is required, which has nothing to do with age restrictions. Carry a photocopy of your passport rather than the real thing. Many nightclubs will not allow you to enter if wearing shorts. Prostitutes frequent many establishments – particularly those popular with tourists.

Outdoor Activities

Participant Sports

AQUATIC SPORTS

As is to be expected in a land that has such an extensive coastline and major inland waterways, as well as a mild climate, a variety of aquatic sports can be enjoyed in Brazil. Almost any coastal town has boat rental facilities and many resort hotels rent sailboats, fishing tackle, jet-skis, diving gear and surf and windsurf boards. Sailboats, speed boats or schooner-like Brazilian *saveiros*, can all be rented complete with equipment and crew. In Rio go to Marina da Gloria.

Excursion clubs arrange white-water canoeing, kayaking and sailing outings. Rapids-shooting rafting excursions can be arranged through hotels in Rio.

Diving

Diving equipment and tuition are available. Some of the more spectacular places to dive include Fernando de Noronha island, off Brazil's most northeastern point, and the coral Abrolhos archipelago off the coast of southern Bahia. More accessible are the Sun Coast, east of Rio de Janeiro (Cabo Frio, Búzios), and the Green Coast between Rio and São Paulo (Angra dos Reis, Parati).

Surfing

Brazil's seemingly endless coastline offers good opportunities for surfing. Saquarema, in the state of Rio de Janeiro, is the site of international championships.

Swimming

Ocean swimming is a delight, especially in the north and northeast, where the water is warm all year round. Many hotels have swimming pools, as do the private clubs. Be aware that many city beaches, especially in Rio, are badly polluted.

Fishing

There is a large variety of fish, both ocean and freshwater varieties, all along the coast as well as in the rivers and the flooded Pantanal marshlands. Fishing equipment can be rented along with a boat and guide, and special fishing excursions are organized. The website www.brasilfishing.com.br is a useful resource.

Professional fishermen in the northeast will sometimes take an extra passenger or two on their *jangada* rafts.

CAMPING

If you want to go hiking and camping, contact the Camping Clube do Brasil, Rua Senador Dantas 75, 29° Andar, Rio de Janeiro, tel: 021-2210 3171 or 0800-227 050. www.campingclube.com.br. They have camping sites throughout the country and they organize treks in out-of-the-way parts of Brazil. If you prefer to backpack on your own, check the maps available from the IBGE – Brazilian Institute of Geography and Statistics – tel: 0800-218181; www.ibge.gov.br.

CLIMBING AND CAVING

There are plenty of peaks to climb in Brazil, if you enjoy rock climbing or mountaineering. In Rio, you can even climb the city's landmarks, Sugarloaf mountain and Corcovado. There are excursion clubs that arrange outings to nearby mountainous regions and areas where you can go spelunking (caving). Contact one of the following organizations:

Centro Excursionista Brasileiro, Avenida Almirante Barroso 2–8 Andar, Centro, Rio de Janeiro CEP230031, tel: 021-2252 9844 or 2262 6360; www.ceb.org.br;
Sociedade Brasileira de Espeleologia Rua Francisca Resende Merciai 113, Campinas CEP13085480 Tel: 19-3289 1611; www.sbe.com.br

CYCLING

Since the 1992 environment conference in Rio, good cycling facilities have been developed, including a cycle lane running the length of the Copacabana, Ipanema, Leblon, São Conrado and Barra beaches, and on into the city center.

ECO-TOURISM

This term is frequently used to describe any kind of nature or adventure tourism and does not mean that any consideration has been given to the environment. It may involve anything from catching caiman in the Amazon to fishing for piranha in the Pantanal, neither of which are sustainable activities.

GOLF

Golf is not a big sport in Brazil and is played mostly in Rio and São Paulo. There are only a couple of public golf courses in Brazil and although country clubs are quite exclusive, you can arrange (through your hotel) to play as a visitor.

HANG GLIDING

Hang gliding is popular, especially in Rio, where modern Daedaluses leap off the mountains and soar on air currents before landing on the beach below. Inexperienced flyers can go tandem with an instructor. In some places paragliding is available.

HORSEBACK RIDING

The Pantanal, home of Brazilian cowboys, is a popular place for horseback riding, and a good way to see local wildlife. The old gold trails in the mountains in the southern states offer scenic rides. The country's long, open beaches are ideal for galloping along the surf.

HUNTING

Hunting is illegal in Brazil. The only shooting of wildlife permitted is with a camera.

JOGGING

Joggers have a beautiful place to keep in shape while in Rio: the in-town beaches have wide sidewalks, with the distance marked in kilometers along the way. In São Paulo, Ibirapuera Park is a favorite spot for runners.

The biggest races are the Rio Marathon and the São Silvestre race, held in São Paulo on December 31, with the starting line in one year and the finishing line in the next.

MOTOR RACING

Brazil is a rarity in that it is on both the Formula One and ChampCar racing circuits. The Formula One Grand Prix takes place in March at São Paulo's Interlagos circuit while Rio plays host to the ChampCar race and also the motorbike Grand Prix. Brazilian drivers are prominent in all categories.

TENNIS

Some of the larger hotels have tennis courts. There are a few public courts, but the game is played mostly at clubs. Since the charismatic "Guga," Gustavo Kuerten, won the French Open and became a top player, interest in tennis in Brazil has definitely been on the increase.

TREKKING

There are lots of places to trek in the country, whether hiking through lush forest trails, exploring scenic national parks, or climbing through mountainous regions. A guide is normally advisable.º

VOLLEYBALL

On the beaches, especially in Rio, you can spend many hours being entertained by the skill of volleyball players (Brazil has won both world and Olympic titles). The atmosphere is relaxed, although the games are often skilful, and you may be able to join in.

Spectator Sport

SOCCER (FUTEBOL)

This is Brazil's national sport and a passion that unites all ages and classes. During World Cup season, the country grinds to a halt as everyone tunes in to watch the matches on television.

If you're a soccer fan, arrange through your hotel to see a professional game – there are organized tours. The boisterous fans are often as interesting to watch as the actual game itself.

Especially exciting are the games between top rival teams in Rio's giant Maracanã Stadium, which squeezes in crowds of up to 160,000; or in São Paulo's Pacaembu Stadium. There is rarely any violence, but it is recommended that you get a reserved seat rather than sit in the packed bleachers (uncovered stadium seating). Many hotels can book tickets and transport – a worthwhile extra to avoid the crush.

Most weekend afternoons, or in the early evening, you can see a fast and furious "sand lot" match taking place between neighborhood teams on the beaches or in the parks of Brazil.

CAPOEIRA

A uniquely Brazilian sport, *capoeira* is a relic from slavery days, when fighting, and especially training for fighting, by the slaves had to be hidden. *Capoeira* is a stylized fight-dance, with its own accompanying rhythms and music, using the feet a great deal to strike out and requiring a graceful agility. This tradition has been kept alive chiefly in Salvador and Rio, where there are academies teaching *capoeira* (you can watch the classes free of charge). You can arrange to see a presentation or you may catch a street group performing on a beach or in a busy square.

HORSE RACING

Horse racing is popular and several cities have tracks. The top prize event, called the Grande Premio do Brasil, is held at the Rio de Janeiro track in the first half of August.

Shopping

What to Buy

GEMSTONES

One of the major attractions of shopping for gemstones in Brazil, besides the price, is the tremendous variety. Brazil produces amethysts, aquamarines, opals, topazes, and many colors of tourmalines, as well as the more precious diamonds, emeralds, rubies and sapphires.

Some 65 percent of the world's colored gemstones are produced in Brazil, which is also one of the world's major gold producers. Brazil today is one of the top jewelry centers in the world and costs are attractive because the operation is 100 percent domestic, from the mining of the gems to the cutting, crafting and designing of jewelry.

The value of a gemstone is determined largely by its color and quality, not necessarily by size. When choosing a gem look for color, cut, clarity and cost. The stronger the color, the more valuable the stone. Unless you are an expert gemologist, it's highly advisable to buy from a reliable jeweler, where you will get what you pay for and can trust their advice. The two leading jewelers operating nationwide are H Stern and Amsterdam Sauer, but there are other reliable smaller chains. The top jewelers have shops in the airports and shopping centers, and in many hotels.

LEATHER GOODS

Shoes, sandals, bags, wallets and belts are all good buys. Although found everywhere, some of the finest leather comes from Brazil's south. Shoes are plentiful and handmade leather items can be found at street fairs or in covered markets, sometimes run by the local tourism board.

WOODEN OBJECTS

Brazil has beautiful wood. Gift shops sell items such as salad bowls and trays, and wood carvings can be found at the craft fairs. The grotesque *carranca* figureheads are difficult to fit into your suitcase but very unusual. They are unique to São Francisco riverboats. Many wooden items may be made from endangered tropical hardwoods. Although it is not illegal to export these products, the industry is contributing to the mass deforestation of the Amazon.

MUSICAL INSTRUMENTS AND CDS

A fun thing to take home are the peculiar percussion instruments that you hear the samba bands playing, usually on sale at street fairs. From Bahia comes the *berimbau*, a simple instrument consisting of a wire-strung bow and a gourd sound-box. It has a characteristic sound, but is surprisingly difficult to master. If you enjoy Brazilian music, buy some CDs or tapes, too.

FASHION

Boutiques in most cities are clustered in certain districts, and shopping malls enable you to visit many shops in less time.

If you want something uniquely Brazilian, buy lace or embroidery from the northeast, or a tiny bikini or a beach cover-up which can be wrapped around in various ways.

T-shirts are everywhere in Brazil. From beautifully designed and expensive ones for the evening to humble but colorful screen-printed day-wear, they are excellent value and usually of good quality.

Regional Crafts

Ceramics are a particularly good purchase in the northeast, where clay bowls, water jugs, and other items are commonly used in the home. Also from the northeast come primitive clay figurines depicting folk heroes, customs and celebrations. *Marajoara* ceramic pieces, decorated with geometric patterns, come from the island of Marajó at the mouth of the Amazon River.

Beautiful handmade lace and embroidered clothing are produced mostly in the northeast, especially in the state of Ceará, while Minas Gerais is a traditional producer of handmade weavings and tapestries.

Also in Minas Gerais, soapstone items are on sale everywhere. Both decorative and utilitarian objects – cooking pots, toiletry sets, quartz and agate bookends and ashtrays – can be found in many souvenir stores.

Straw and natural fibers (banana leaves, palm bark) are fashioned into baskets, hats, bags, mats, etc. especially in the northeast.

Indian handicrafts are mainly made in the northern Amazon region and include adornments (necklaces, earrings), utensils (sieves, baskets), weapons (bows, arrows, spears) and percussion instruments (like the "rain sticks" that imitate the sound of falling rain) made out of wood, fibers, thorns, teeth, claws, colorful feathers, shells and seeds.

Cotton hammocks are popular all over Brazil, but the best place to buy them is in the north and northeast, where they are used extensively instead of beds. They are sometimes finished with lacy crocheted edgings.

PAINTINGS

These can be bought at galleries as well as crafts fairs and markets. Brazilian primitive or "naïve" paintings are popular. *(See pages 118–24 for more on Brazilian art and artists.)*

RELIGIOUS ARTICLES

Popular amulets include the *figa* (a carved clenched fist with the thumb between the index and middle fingers) and the *Senhor do Bonfim* ribbons (to be wrapped around a wrist or ankle and fastened with three knots) from Salvador.

Also from Salvador come bunches of silver fruits, which Brazilians hang in their homes to ensure there is always plenty of food on the table.

COFFEE

Ground and roasted Brazilian coffee can be found at any supermarket or bakery. The vacuum-packed variety will stay fresh longer. You can also get coffee packaged in a handy carton at the airport.

Where to Buy Crafts

Handicrafts shops and markets are plentiful throughout Brazil. In most of the larger towns in the northeast and in the Amazon there is a central craft market or a craft center. A few of them are listed below.

RIO DE JANEIRO

Pé de Boi
Rua Ipiranga 55, Botafogo
Tel/fax: 021-2255 5833.
Eskada, Avenida Gen. San Martín 1219, Leblon.
Gaia Jóias
Rua Fernando Mendes 28c
Copacabana
Tel: 021-2255 9646.
The Hippy Fair
Praça General Osório, Ipanema.
Lively, touristy handicrafts market that attracts artisans from across Brazil. Sunday.

SÃO PAULO

Amoa Konoya Arte Indígena
Rua João Moura 1002
Tel: 011-3061 0639.
Fabulous collection of Indian handicrafts from the Amazon and other parts of Brazil. Baskets, bows and arrows, feather, wood and clay objects and CDs of Indian music.
Casa do Amazonas
Alameda dos Jurupis 460, Moema
Tel: 011-5051 3098.
Large variety of Indian art and crafts.
Cariri
Rua Francisco Leitão 277, Pinheiros
Tel: 011-3064 6586.
A wide range of Brazilian crafts – basketware, painted clay folkloric figures, wooden sculptures, and hammocks.
Arte Nativa Aplicada
Rua Dr Melo Alves 184
Tel: 011-3088 1811.
Textiles, table mats and lamps in interesting tribal patterns.
Jacques Ardies Gallery
Rua do Livramento 221
Tel: 011-3051 3625.
Primitive, "naive" art.

Language

Although Portuguese, not Spanish, is the language of Brazil, a knowledge of Spanish will go a long way. You will recognize many similar words, and most Brazilians will understand you if you speak in Spanish. You will, however, find it difficult to understand them. Although many upper-class Brazilians know at least some English or French and are eager to practice on foreign visitors, don't expect people on the street to speak your language. An effort by a foreigner to learn the local language is always appreciated. Pronounciation can be confusing. For example, "R" is pronounced "H," so that "Rio" sounds like "Hee-o."

At most large hotels and top restaurants you can get by with few problems in English. But if you like to wander around on your own, you might want to invest in a good pocket dictionary.

Addressing People

First names are used a great deal in Brazil. In many situations in which English-speakers would use a title and surname, Brazilians often use a first name with the title of respect: *Senhor* for men (written *Sr* and usually shortened to *Seu* in spoken Portuguese) and *Senhora* (written *Sra*) or *Dona* (used only with first name) for women.

There are three second-person pronoun forms in Portuguese. Stick to *você*, equivalent to "you," and you will be all right. *O senhor* (for men) or *a senhora* (for women) is used to show respect for someone of a different age group or social class or to be polite to a stranger. As a foreigner, you won't offend anyone if you use the wrong form of address. But if you want to learn when to use the more formal or informal style, observe and go by how others address you. In some parts of Brazil, mainly the northeast and the south, *tu* is used a great deal. Originally, in Portugal, *tu* was used among intimate friends and close relatives, but in Brazil, it's equivalent to *você*.

If you are staying for some time and are serious about learning the language, there are Portuguese courses for non-native speakers. Meanwhile, here are some of the most essential words and phrases.

Greetings

Tudo Bem, literally meaning "all's well," is one of the most common forms of greeting: one person asks, "*Tudo bem?*" (or "*Tudo bom?*") and the other replies, "*Tudo bem*" (or "*Tudo bom*"). This is also used to mean "OK," "all right," "will do," or as a response when someone apologizes, as if to say, "that's all right, it doesn't matter." "Ta legal" is a formal slang expression commonly heard. It means "OK" or "That's cool". Other forms of greetings are:

Good morning (good afternoon) *Bom dia (boa tarde)*
Good evening (good night) *Boa noite*
How are you? *Como vai você?*
Well, thank you *Bem, obrigado*
Hello (to answer the telephone) *Alô*
Hello (common forms of greeting) *Bom dia, boa tarde*, etc.
Hi, hey! (informal greeting also used to get someone's attention) *Oi*
Goodbye (very informal and most used) *Tchau*

Emergencies

I need... *Eu preciso de...*
- **a doctor** *um médico*
- **a mechanic** *um mecânico*
- **transportation** *condução*
- **help** *ajuda*

Goodbye (literally "until soon") *Até logo*
Goodbye (similar to "farewell") *Adeus*
My name is (I am) *Meu nome é (Eu sou)*
What is your name? *Como é seu nome?*
It's a pleasure *É um prazer*
Pleasure (used in introductions as "Pleased to meet you") *Prazer*
Good! Great! *Que bom!*
Health! (the most common toast) *Saúde*
Do you speak English? *Você fala inglês?*
I don't understand (I didn't understand) *Não entendo (Não entendi)*
Do you understand? *Você entende?*
Please repeat more slowly *Por favor repete, mais devagar*
What do you call this (that)? *Como se chama isto (aquilo)?*
How do you say...? *Como se diz...?*
Please *Por favor*
Thank you (very much) *(Muito) Obrigado* (or *Obrigada*, if a woman is speaking)
You're welcome (literally "it's nothing") *De nada*
Excuse me (to apologize) *Desculpe*
Excuse me (taking leave or to get past someone) *Com licença*

Pronouns

Who? *Quem?*
I (We) *Eu (Nós)*
You (singular) *Você*
You (plural) *Vocês*
He (she) *Ele (ela)*
They *Eles (Elas)*
My (mine) *Meu (minha)* depending on gender of object
Our (ours) *Nosso (nossa)*
Your (yours) *Seu (sua)*
His (her or hers) *Dele (dela* or *deles)*
Their, theirs *Delas*

Getting Around

Where is the...? *Onde é...?*
- **beach** *a praia*
- **bathroom** *o banheiro*
- **bus station** *a rodoviária*
- **airport** *o aeroporto*
- **train station** *a estação de trem*
- **post office** *o correio*
- **police station** *a delegacia de polícia*
- **ticket office** *a bilheteria*
- **marketplace** *o mercado*
- **street market** *feira*
- **embassy (consulate)** *a embaixada (o consulado)*

Where is there a...? *Onde é que tem... ?*
- **currency exchange** *uma casa de câmbio*
- **bank** *um banco*
- **pharmacy** *uma farmácia*
- **(good) hotel** *um (bom) hotel*
- **(good) restaurant** *um (bom) restaurante*
- **snack bar** *uma lanchonete*
- **bus stop** *um ponto de ônibus*
- **taxi stand** *um ponto de taxi*
- **subway station** *uma estação de metrô*
- **service station** *um posto de gasolina*
- **newsstand** *um jornaleiro*
- **public telephone** *um telefone público*
- **supermarket** *um supermercado*
- **department store** *uma loja de departamentos*
- **boutique** *uma boutique*
- **jeweler** *um joalheiro*
- **hairdresser (barber)** *um cabeleireiro (um barbeiro)*
- **laundry** *uma lavanderia*
- **hospital** *um hospital*

A ticket to... *Uma passagem para...*
I want to go to... *Quero ir para...*
How can I get to...? *Como posso ir para...?*
Please take me to... *Por favor, me leve para...*
Please call a taxi for me *Por favor, chame um taxi para mim*
I want to rent a car *Quero alugar um carro*
What is this place called? *Como se chama este lugar?*
Where are we? *Onde estamos?*
How long will it take to get there? *Leva quanto tempo para chegar lá?*
Please stop here (Stop!) *Por favor, pare aqui (Pare!)*
Please wait *Por favor, espere*

What time does the bus (plane, boat) leave? *A que horas sai o ônibus (avião, barco)?*
Where does this bus go? *Este ônibus vai para onde?*
Does it go by way of...? *Passa em...?*
Airport (bus station) tax *Taxa de embarque*
I want to check my luggage (on a bus, etc.) *Quero despachar minha bagagem*
I want to store my luggage (at a station) *Quero guardar minha bagagem*

Shopping

Do you have...? *Você tem...?*
I want... please *Eu quero... por favor*
I don't want... *Eu não quero...*
I want to buy... *Eu quero comprar...*
Where can I buy... *Onde posso comprar...?*
- **cigarettes** *cigarros*
- **film** *filme*
- **a ticket for...** *uma entrada para...*
- **a reserved seat** *um lugar marcado*
- **another the same** *um outro igual*
- **another different** *um outro diferente*
- **this (that)** *isto (aqui)*
- **something less expensive** *algo mais barato*
- **postcards** *cartões postais*
- **paper (envelopes)** *papel (envelopes)*
- **a pen (a pencil)** *uma caneta (um lápis)*
- **soap (shampoo)** *sabonete (xampu or shampoo)*
- **toothpaste** *pasta de dente*
- **sunscreen** *filtro solar*
- **aspirin** *aspirina*

Forms of Transport

Taxi – *Taxi*
Bus – *Onibus*
Car – *Carro*
Plane – *Avião*
Train – *Trem*
Boat – *Barco*

How much? *Quanto?*
How many? *Quantos?*
How much does it cost? *Quanto custa? Quanto é?*
That's very expensive *É muito caro*
A lot, very (many) *Muito (muitos)*
A little (few) *Um pouco (poucos)*

At the Hotel

I have a reservation *Tenho uma reserva*
I want to make a reservation *Quero fazer uma reserva*
A single room (A double room) *Um quarto de solteiro (Um quarto de casal)*
With air conditioning *com ar condicionado*
I want to see the room *Quero ver o quarto*
Suitcase (Bag or purse) *Mala (Bolsa)*
Room service *Serviço de quarto*
Key *Chave*
The manager *O gerente*

At the Restaurant

Waiter *Garçon*
Maitre d' *Maitre*
I didn't order this *Eu não pedi isto*
The menu (The wine list) *O cardápio (A carta de vinhos)*
Breakfast *Café da manhã*
Lunch *Almoço*
Supper *Jantar*
The house specialty *A especialidade da casa*
Carbonated mineral water *Água mineral com gás*
Uncarbonated mineral water *Água mineral sem gás*
Coffee *Café*
Tea *Chá*
Beer (bottled) *Cerveja*
Beer (draft) *Chope*
White wine (red wine) *Vinho branco (Vinho tinto)*
A soft drink (Juice) *Um refrigerante (Suco)*
An alcoholic drink *Um drink*
Ice *Gelo*
Salt *Sal*
Pepper *Pimenta*
Sugar *Açúcar*
A plate *Um prato*
A glass *Um copo*
A cup *Uma xícara*
A napkin *Um guardanapo*
Well done *Bem passado*
Medium rare *Ao ponto*
Rare *Mal passado*
I'm a vegetarian *Eu sou vegetariano/a*
I don't eat meat/fish *Eu não como carne/peixe*
The bill, please *A conta, por favor*
Is service included? *Está incluído o serviço?*
I want my change, please *Eu quero meu troco, por favor*
I want a receipt *Eu quero um recibo*

Money

Cash *Dinheiro*
Do you accept credit cards? *Aceita cartão de crédito?*
Can you cash a travelers' check? *Pode trocar um travelers' check? (cheque de viagem)*
I want to exchange money *Quero trocar dinheiro*
What is the exchange rate? *Qual é o câmbio?*

Time

When? *Quando?*
What time is it? *Que horas são?*
Just a moment please *Um momento, por favor*
What is the schedule? (bus, tour, show, etc.) *Qual é o horário?*
How long does it take? *Leva quanto tempo?*
Hour *Hora*
Day *Dia*
Week *Semana*
Month *Mês*
At what time...? *A que horas...?*
At one o' clock (two, three) *A uma hora (duas, três)*
An hour from now *Daqui a uma hora*
Which day? *Que dia?*
Yesterday *Ontem*
Today *Hoje*
Tomorrow *Amanhã*
This week *Esta semana*
Last week *A semana passada/*
Next week *A semana que vem*
The weekend *O fim de semana*
Monday *segunda-feira* (often *2a*)
Tuesday *terca-feira* (often *3a*)

Wednesday *quarta-feira* (often *4a)*
Thursday *quinta-feira* (often *5a)*
Friday *sexta-feira* (often *6a)*
Saturday *sábado*
Sunday *domingo*

Numbers

Ordinal numbers are written with ° i.e. a degree sign after the numeral, so that *3° andar* means 3rd floor. BR followed by a number refers to one of the federal interstate highways, for example BR-101, which follows the Atlantic coast.

1	*um*
2	*dois*
3	*três*
4	*quatro*
5	*cinco*
6	*seis*
7	*sete*
8	*oito*
9	*nove*
10	*dez*
11	*onze*
12	*doze*
13	*treze*
14	*quatorze*
15	*quinze*
16	*dezesseis*
17	*dezessete*
18	*dezoito*
19	*dezenove*
20	*vinte*
21	*vinte um*
30	*trinta*
40	*quarenta*
50	*cinqüenta*
60	*sessenta*
70	*setenta*
80	*oitenta*
90	*noventa*
100	*cem*
101	*cento e um*
200	*duzentos*
300	*trezentos*
400	*quatrocentos*
500	*quinhentos*
600	*seiscentos*
700	*setecentos*
800	*oitocentos*
900	*novecentos*
1,000	*mil*
2,000	*dois mil*
10,000	*dez mil*
100,000	*cem mil*
1,000,000	*um milhão*
half a dozen	*meia*

Commas and periods in numbers take an inverted form in Portuguese: 1,000 is written 1.000 and one and a half (1.5) is written 1,5.

Place Names and Abbreviations

The following will help you understand Brazilian addresses and place names:

Al. or *Alameda* = lane
Andar = floor, story
Av. or *Avenida* = avenue
Casa = house
Centro = the central downtown business district, also frequently referred to as *a cidade* (the city)
Cj. or *Conjunto* = a suite of rooms or sometimes a group of buildings
Estr. or *Estrada* = road or highway
Fazenda = ranch, also a lodge
Lgo. or *Largo* = square or plaza
Lote = lot
Pça. or *Praça* = square or plaza
Praia = beach
Rio = river
Rod. or *Rodovia* = highway
R. or *Rua* = street
Sala = room

Further Reading

General Reading

The Brazilians, by Joseph A. Page. Perseus, 1996.
The Brazil Reader, by Robert M. Levine and John J Crocitti (eds). Latin American Bureau, 1999.
The Cloud Forest, by Peter Matthiessen. New York, 1987.
Ninety-Two Days: A Journey in Guiana and Brazil, by Evelyn Waugh. Penguin, 1995.

History & Travel

A Concise History of Brazil, by Boris Fausto. Cambridge University Press, 1999.
Brazilian Adventure, by Peter Fleming. Putman, 1983. Account of a 1925 expedition.

Fiction

Brazil, by John Updike. Penguin, 1995.
Dom Casmurro, by Machado de Assis. New York, 1999.
Dona Flor and Her Two Husbands, by Jorge Amado. Serpent's Tail, 1999.
The Emperor of the Amazon, by M. Souza. Hypermass, 1983.
Soulstorm, by Clarice Lispector. New Directions, 1989. Short stories by writer, noted for her blend of suspense and romance.
The War of the Saints, by Jorge Amado. Serpent's Tail, 1994.
The Brothers by Milton Hatoum. Bloomsbury, 2000. Set in Manaus during the Rubber Boom, a fictional story of twin brothers.
Turbulence, by Chico Buarque. Bloomsbury. A nostalgic account of Rio de Janeiro.

Civilization & Society

Amazon Frontier: The Defeat of the Brazilian Indians, by J. Hemming. London, 1995. Chronicles the first

150 years from the time the Europeans first explored Amazonia.

At the End of the Rainbow? Gold, Land and People in the Brazilian Amazon, by G. Macmillan. Earthscan, 1995.

The Fate of the Forest, by S. Hecht and A. Cockburn. Penguin, 1990.

Fazendas: The Great Houses and Plantations of Brazil, by Fernando Tasso Fragosa Pires and Nicholas Sapieha. A picture book that traces the development of Brazil's sugar and coffee plantations and cattle ranches.

Futebol: The Brazilian Way of Life, by Alex Bellos. Bloomsbury, 2002. A wonderful, entertaining combination of history and anecdote that will fascinate even those who have no interest in foorball.

Bookshops

Rio de Janeiro

FNAC
Barra Shopping,
Avenida das Americas 4666,
Loja B, 101–116.
General bookstore.

Livraria Argumento,
Rua Dias Ferreira 417, Leblon.
Art and travel; also literature and children's books.

Nova Livraria Leonardo da Vinci
Avenida Rio Branco 185, Loja 2.
Wide selection of books about Brazil, also art and photography.

Jamer Books and Things
Rua Marques Sao Vicente 124,
Loja 101.
Specializes in children's books.

São Paulo

Livraria Cultura Editora
Avenida Paulista 2073, Conjunto Nacional.
Wide selection of books on all topics, including many about Brazil; the best in Latin America.

Livraria e Papelaria
5a Avenida Paulista 2239.
Wide selection of books.

Recife

Livro 7
Rua Sete de Setembro 329.
Foreign language books.

Disinherited Indians in Brazil, Survival International, 2001.

Murder in the Rainforest, by Jan Rocha. LAB, 1999

Tropical Truth, by Caetano Velosa, Bloomsbury. The John Lennon of Brazil tells how tropicalismo revolutionized Brazilian culture as well it politics.

Travelers' Tales Brazil by Annette Haddad and Scott Doggett. Travelers' Tales Inc., 1997. Fifty travel essays, varying in quality, on the country's commingling of cultures.

Race & Black Culture

Benedita da Silva, an Afro-Brazilian woman's story of politics and love. Benjamin and Mendança. LAB, 1998.

Other Insight Guides

Apa Publications has more guidebook titles than any other guidebook publisher. There are over 200 *Insight Guides* covering the countries, regions and cities of the world, all using Apa's well-known formula of expert writing and beautiful photography.

There are also more than 100 *Insight Pocket Guides*, which have recommended itineraries designed for the short-stay visitor.

A third series comprising 120 titles, Compact Guides are concise mini encyclopedias to use on the spot.

Major *Insight Guides* are available to *Latin America, Rio de Janeiro, Chile, Ecuador, Peru, Venezuela, Argentina, Buenos Aires, Guatemala, Belize & Yucatán,* and *Amazon Wildlife.*

Insight Guide: Rio de Janeiro takes a closer look at what many people have called the most beautiful city in the world, focusing on the culture of Rio's unique people – the *cariocas*.

Insight Guide: South America is the perfect companion for those taking a tour af the whole South American continent. From the lost cities of the Incas to the nightclubs of Rio, it's all here.

ART & PHOTO CREDITS

APA Photo Agency 130/131
Daniel Augusto Jr. 46, 190
Aristides Alves 95
Ricardo Azoury 120, 208, 239, 310
Nair Benedicto 6/7, 66
Jan Butchofsky-Houser front flap top, 100, 255
Camera Tres Fotographic 282
Campos-Davis/Apa 83, 125, 148, 153, 155, 157, 160, 161, 165, 256
Campos-Davis/SCP 16, 60, 87R, 192, 206, 211, 300, 304, 317, 325
Corbis 319
Country of New York Library 328
Sue Cunningham spine, 38, 41, 57, 59, 62, 67, 78, 88, 116, 117, 140, 158, 163T, 170T, 176, 177, 178,179T, 182, 183, 185, 186, 187T, 188, 189, 192, 193, 193T, 195, 199, 206, 211, 220, 223, 227, 235, 238T, 240, 245, 248, 251, 273R, 275L,276T, 277L, 277R, 278, 283, 292, 302, 304, 309T, 317, 325
Patrick Cunningham/SCP 305
Salomon Cytrynowicz 69
Mark Downey/Lucid Images 81
Ary Diesendruck/Corbis 187
Jane Egginton 167
Empics 27, 104, 105
Douglas Engle/Latinphoto.org 39, 40, 94
Robert Fried back cover bottom 1, 17, 19, 22, 51, 90, 101, 103, 147T, 151T, 157T, 155T, 165T, 226, 261, 270, 274T, 281, 283T, 294, 301
Galeria Jacques Ardies 118, 123, 124
Andreas Gross 108/109, 322T
Richard House 70, 275R, 297, 298L, 299
Houserstock 237
Huw Hennessy 158T, 281T
Volkmar Janicke back cover right, back flap bottom, 18, 159, 176T, 190T, 249T, 254R, 271, 323
Jornal do Brasil 34, 36, 37
Wolfgang Kaehler/Corbis 238
Vautier de Nanxe 10/11, 14, 20/21, 42, 43, 44, 47, 48, 54/55, 56, 63, 75, 77, 84, 106, 111, 126/127, 180/181, 202, 205, 207, 209, 221, 224, 225, 228, 229, 230, 234, 270, 241, 242, 243, 247, 259, 260, 264, 265, 284, 286, 303, 311, 326
John H. Maier Jr. 8/9, 12/13, 52/53, 58, 61, 79, 85, 86L, 87L, 92/93, 96, 97, 98L, 98R, 99, 110, 112, 113 ,114, 115, 132, 136, 138/139, 141, 144/145, 147, 149, 151, 152, 154L, 156, 162, 163, 164, 166, 168, 169, 171, 172, 173L, 173R, 174, 175, 179, 216/217, 244, 253, 262, 285, 287, 290/291, 307, 308, 309, 322
Ricardo Malta 102, 191
Luiz C. Marigo/Bruce Coleman 23
Delfim Martins 49
Juca Martins 196, 316, 321, 324,
Vanja Milliet 28, 30, 31, 33, 35, 72/73, 74, 76, 121, 122, 197,
Courtesy of Museu Paulista USP 29, **Courtesy of Museu Nacional de Belas Artes** 150
Andrea Pistolesi/Getty Images 320
Carol Quintanilla 200, 201
Carlos Reyes-Manzo/Andes Press Agency 298T
Brian Rogers/Biofotos 257
Mauricio Simonetti 45, 86R, 298R
Michael Small 71
Cardinale Stephane/Corbis Sygma 82
Topham Picturepoint 32, 107
Tony Stone 314/315
Mireille Vautier front flap bottom, back cover left, 2/3, 4/5, 24/25, 50, 89, 91, 119, 203, 205T, 210, 210T, 211T, 212, 213, 223T, 225T, 226T, 236T, 241T, 246T, 250, 252, 254L, 260T, 262T, 265T, 266, 267, 279, 310T, 312, 313
Luis Veiga 327
Uwe Waltz GDT/Bruce Coleman Ltd. 295
Martin Wendler/NHPA 268/269, 300T
Paulo Whitaker/Reuters 80
Staffan Widstrand/Bruce Coleman Ltd. 273L
Konrad Wothe/Bruce Coleman Ltd. 274

Picture Spreads

Page 64/65: *All* Sue Cunningham except *top centre left, below centre right*: Dave Houser and *top centre right*: Robert Fried.
Page 215/215: *Top row from left to right*: Mireille Vautier, Jan Butchofsky-Houser, Mireille Vautier, Sue Cunningham; *bottom row*: Mireille Vautier, Sue Cunningham, Volkmar Janicke, Dave Houser, Mireille Vautier.
Page 232/233: *Top row from left to right*: Sue Cunningham, Sue Cunningham, Sue Cunningham, Dave Houser/Jan Butchofsky; *bottom row*: Sue Cunningham, Sue Cunningham, Mireille Vautier, Sue Cunningham, Sue Cunningham.
Page 288/289: *Top row from left to right*: Sue Cunningham, Sue Cunningham, NHPA/Martin Wendler; *centre row*: NHPA/Haroldo Palo, Patrick Cunningham/SCP, Sue Cunningham, Sue Cunningham; *bottom row*: NHPA/James Carmichael Jr, Volkmar Janicke, Sue Cunningham, Campos-Davis/SCP.

INSIGHT GUIDE BRAZIL

Cartographic Editor **Zoë Goodwin**
Design Consultants **Carlotta Junger, Graham Mitchener**
Picture Research **Hilary Genin**

Map Production Berndtson & Berndtson Productions

Index

Numbers in italics refer to photographs

d

e

f

g

n

o

p

q–r

t

u–w

x–z